Breaking the Ties That Bound

Breaking the Ties That Bound

THE POLITICS OF MARITAL STRIFE

IN LATE IMPERIAL RUSSIA

BARBARA ALPERN ENGEL

CORNELL UNIVERSITY PRESS *Ithaca and London*

First published 2011 by Cornell University Press
Printed in the United States of America

Library of Congress Cataloging-in-Publication Data
Engel, Barbara Alpern.
    Breaking the ties that bound : the politics of marital strife in late imperial Russia / Barbara Alpern Engel.
        p. cm.
    Includes bibliographical references and index.
    ISBN 978-0-8014-7909-0
    1. Marriage—Russia—History—19th century.
2. Marriage—Russia—History—20thcentury.   3. Divorce—
Russia—History—19th century.   4. Divorce—Russia—
History—19th century.   5. Women—Family relationships—
Russia—History—19th century.   6. Women—Family
relationships—Russia—History—20th century.   7. Family
policy—Russia—History—19th century.   8. Family policy—
Russia—History—20th century.   I. Title.
    HQ637.E54 2011
    306.890947'09034—dc22   2010032432

Cornell University Press strives to use environmentally responsible suppliers and materials to the fullest extent possible in the publishing of its books. Such materials include vegetable-based, low-VOC inks and acid-free papers that are recycled, totally chlorine-free, or partly composed of nonwood fibers. For further information, visit our website at www. cornellpress.cornell.edu.

Cloth printing   10 9 8 7 6 5 4 3 2 1

Contents

Acknowledgments

During the twelve years that this book has been in progress, I have benefited from the friendship, support, and scholarly assistance of many institutions and individuals. I am very pleased to acknowledge and thank them here. Grants from the International Research and Exchanges Board, with funds provided by the U. S. Department of State (Title VIII program) and the National Endowment for the Humanities; and the Council on Research and Creative Work of the University of Colorado made possible the initial phases of research for the book. A Faculty Fellowship from the University of Colorado, a Research Fellowship from the National Endowment for the Humanities, and a Fellowship from the John Simon Guggenheim Foundation enabled me to complete the research and to write. In addition to delightful company, a residency at the Study and Conference Center of the Rockefeller Foundation in Bellagio provided a supportive and stimulating environment in which to think through some of the knottier issues of the book. I am very grateful to all these organizations. None of them is responsible for the views expressed.

I also owe thanks to the staff of the Central Russian Historical Archive (RGIA) for facilitating my research over the years with characteristic graciousness and professionalism, often under very trying conditions; and to the staffs of the Central Historical Archive of the City of St. Petersburg; the Central Historical Archive of Moscow; the State Archive of the Russian Federation; the M. E. Saltykov-Shchedrin Public Library and its newspaper and manuscript divisions; the V. I. Lenin State Library in Moscow; the Helsinki University Slavonic Library in Finland; the Law Library of Columbia University, and the Slavic and Baltic Collection of the New York Public Library, now regrettably closed. I am also very grateful to the staff of the Interlibrary Loan Division of Norlin Library (University of Colorado) for their assistance in locating and obtaining needed materials.

In the course of the years I have spent researching and writing this book I have benefited from the encouragement and assistance of many friends and colleagues, whom I welcome this opportunity to thank. The book owes its very existence to Gita M. Lipson, who introduced me to the rich archival repository at RGIA that became its inspiration and key source. For sharing research and ideas, I thank Dan Kaiser, William Wagner, and Louis Menashe; for stimulating conversations here in Boulder, intellectual support and bibliographic suggestions, I am grateful to Lee Chambers, Linda Cordell, Laura Osterman, and Rimgaila Salys. I also thank Abby Schrader for ensuring the copying of crucial archival files, Kate Pickering-Antonova for retrieving the copies, and Amelia Glaser for delivering them to me in Colorado; and Elena Nikolaeva for research on child custody issues and for providing the images of chancellery officials.

For their thoughtful reading and invaluable critiques of earlier drafts of this book, I express my deepest appreciation to Rachel Fuchs, Martha Hanna, Diane Koenker, Christine Worobec, Richard Wortman, and the late Marlene Stein Wortman. I owe a special thanks to Laura Engelstein, whose critical insights have stimulated me to think and rethink this book, and whose meticulous commentary greatly enriched its penultimate and final versions. Her scholarly generosity is exemplary. Finally, I thank John Ackerman for his supportive and helpful advice on final revisions and other manuscript-related matters. I have always wondered what it would be like to have an editor who actually *edited*, in addition to acquiring a book. I'm very glad to know at last.

I am deeply grateful to my St. Petersburg friends, Inna Ratner and Sergei and Anya Bobashev, whom I think of as my Russian family; Liuda Timofeeva; Masha Koreneva, Olga Lipovskaia, and the late Sarra M. Leikina, whose warmth and generosity I, like all who knew her, will always miss. All of them made my research visits less lonely and provided warm companionship and excellent food, despite the daunting obstacle of my vegetarianism. Far closer to home, LeRoy Moore endured the emotional as well as physical absences that my absorption in this book entailed with characteristic grace and good will. For this, and more, my love and gratitude.

Sections of both chapter 1 and the conclusion were first published in *Journal of Modern History* 77, no. 1 (March): 70–96, copyright 2005 University of Chicago. Earlier versions of chapter 2 were presented at the 2005 Conference of the American Association for the Advancement of Slavic Studies and at the Russkii Kruzhok of the Harriman Institute in 2007. Chapter 3 originated in a paper presented at the Interdisciplinary Conference on Russian Women and Gender, held at the Harriman Institute of Columbia University in May 2003. Portions of chapters 5 appeared in *A Dream Deferred: New Studies in Russian and Soviet Labour History,* ed. Donald Filtzer et al. (Bern: Peter Lang, 2009), 293–314, and were originally presented at the Conference on Labor History of Russia and the Soviet Union, held in Amsterdam in April 2005. I presented an earlier version of chapter 8 at the 2004 Conference of the American Association for the Advancement of Slavic Studies. My thanks to editors, audiences, and commentators for their comments and critiques.

Note on Dates and Names

All dates in this book are given according to the Julian calendar, unless otherwise indicated. The Julian calendar was twelve days behind the Gregorian in the nineteenth century, and thirteen days behind in the twentieth. I have transliterated the Russian according to the Library of Congress system, with a few modifications. When giving the first names of individuals, I have omitted diacritical signs and the additional i (Avdotia instead of Avdot'iia). I have also used anglicized versions of well-known names and places.

Abbreviations

ARCHIVES

RGIA   Rossiiskii gosudarstvennyi istoricheskii
                arkhiv
TsGIA SPb   Tsentral'nyi gosudarstvennyi
                istoricheskii arkhiv gorod Sankt-Peterburga
GARF   Gosudarstvennyi arkhiv Rossiiskoi Federatsii
TsIAM   Tsentral'nyi istoricheskii arkhiv Moskvy

ARCHIVAL CITATIONS

op.   *opis':* archival inventory
d.   *delo:* file
ob.   *obratno:* reverse side of page

Breaking the Ties That Bound

Introduction

MARRIAGE AND ITS DISCONTENTS

"All happy families resemble one another, but each unhappy family is unhappy in its own way." Thus begins *Anna Karenina*, Leo Tolstoy's great novel of contemporary life, which appeared in installments from 1875 to 1877. It concludes with the death of its beautiful high-society heroine, who flings herself beneath the wheels of an onrushing train. Anna's flight from an arranged and loveless marriage and into the arms of the dashing Count Vronsky had brought only short-lived happiness. Ostracized by members of her former social circle, deprived of her beloved son, and dependent for her position on the passionate attachment of Vronsky, Anna finds herself picking quarrels with him over trifles and risking the alienation of the one person on whom her life depends. Like other nineteenth-century authors whose heroines defied social and sexual morality for the sake of love, Tolstoy can imagine no fate for Anna other than death. But this was rarely the fate of the real-life women, most of them from backgrounds far more humble than Anna's, who left their husbands in the decades after the publication of Tolstoy's novel. This book is about those women and the forces that encouraged them to imagine a different life for themselves, the institutions that helped and/or hindered them, and the responses of a wide variety of other people, including an ascending hierarchy of officials, up to and including men who spoke in the name of the tsar, to the challenge to Russia's patriarchal family order.

In the final decades of the nineteenth century, Russia experienced a widely perceived "marriage crisis." The crisis was a product of, and inseparable from, the profound social, economic, and cultural changes that occurred in the aftermath of the emancipation of the serfs in 1861 and the accompanying "Great Reforms." Even as Tsars Alexander II (1855–1881), Alexander III (1881–1894), and Nicholas II (1894–1917) preserved their monopoly on political power and, until 1905, denied their subjects fundamental civil rights, their policies generated new opportunities for social mobility that shook to its foundations Russia's hierarchical social order. That social order rested on estates (*soslovie*, pl. *sosloviia*), legally

1

constituted categories that were in most cases hereditary and established an individual's rights and responsibilities in relation to the state. Consisting of four main estates— nobility, clergy, townspeople, and peasantry—the *soslovie* order was complicated by new social categories, created as the need arose, and further divided into those who enjoyed important exemptions (or privileges) and those who did not. Peasants and lower townspeople (*meshchane*) endured the burden of recruitment and poll-tax paying until the military and poll tax reforms of 1874–87, and bore other disabilities thereafter, while the merchantry, who constituted the privileged portion of townspeople, were free of them, as were nobles, clergy, and professionals.[1]

Beginning in the 1880s and accelerating in the 1890s, a state-sponsored policy of economic modernization and rapid industrialization intensified the pressure on this system by vastly expanding the number of people whose legal status no longer corresponded to their occupation or way of life. To meet a growing need for professional expertise, institutions of higher education proliferated, offering specialized training in medicine, law, engineering, and other professions to an increasingly diverse student body, thereby adding to the ranks of individuals for whom *soslovie* ascription had lost its significance. A similar disparity between legal identity and occupation characterized the hundreds of thousands of peasants, a substantial minority of them female, who flocked to Russia's towns and cities to work as laborers, servants, and in other nonagricultural capacities. Groups emerged outside the *soslovie* system, such as educated professionals, who tended to share social and cultural values despite their diverse origins, and factory workers, primarily peasant in origin. The resulting "disparity between social origin and social status," as Gregory Freeze has put it, affected Russia's long-standing gender order, too, creating new possibilities for self-definition at home as well as at work.[2]

---

1. See Gregory Freeze, "The *Soslovie* (Estate) Paradigm and Russian Social History," *American Historical Review* 91, no. 1 (1986): 11–36. Even after 1887, the law restricted personal mobility and treated *meshchane* as well as peasants as "workhorses," burdening them with mutual responsibility for fulfilling a variety of government needs. See A. Zorin et al., *Ocherki gorodskogo byta srednego Povolzh'ia* (Ulianovsk: Izdatel'stvo Srednevolzhskogo nauchnogo tsentra, 2000), 312. On townspeople, see also V. M. Bukharev, "Provintsial'nyi obyvatel' v kontse XIX–nachale XX veka: mezhdu starym i novym," *Sotsial'naia istoriia: Ezhegodnik* (2000): 19–34; B. N. Mironov, *Sotsial'naia istoriia Rossii (XVIII–nachalo XX v.): Genezis lichnosti, demokraticheskoi sem'i, grazhdanskogo obshchestva i pravovogo gosudarstva*, 3d ed., 2 vols. (St. Petersburg: Dmitrii Bulanin, 2003), 1: 110–22, 232–36, 250–57; Iu. M. Goncharov, *Gorodskaia sem'ia Sibiri vtoroi poloviny XIX–nachala XX v.* (Barnaul: Izdatel'stvo Altaiskogo gosudarstvennogo universiteta, 2002); Iu. M. Goncharov and V. S. Chutkov, *Meshchanskoe soslovie zapadnoi Sibiri vtoroi poloviny XIX–nachala XX v.* (Barnaul: Az Buka, 2004).

2. Introduction to *Russia's Missing Middle Class: The Professions in Russian History*, ed. Harley Balzer (Armonk, NY: M. E. Sharpe, 1996), 11–12; Barbara Alpern Engel, *Between the Fields and the*

These upheavals placed new strains on, and generated far-reaching critiques of, Russia's patriarchal gender and family order. Like family law elsewhere in Europe and the United States in this period, Russia's family law reinforced the authority of husbands and fathers.[3] Requiring a husband to "love his wife as his own body, live in accord with her, respect and defend her, and forgive her weaknesses and ease her infirmities" and to support her according to his station, the law enjoined a wife to "submit to [*povinovat'sia*] her husband as head of the household and to love, respect, and render him unlimited obedience [*neogranichennoe poslushanie*]." The law obliged spouses to cohabit at a residence of the husband's choosing, except when he was exiled by decision of a court or banished by his community.[4] Wives also had to obtain their husband's permission to take a job, enroll in school, or gain the internal passport that Russians required in order to live more than roughly twenty miles from their official place of residence. Russia's patriarchal family order was mitigated—how much is a question addressed in chapter 3—by married women's legal right to own and manage their own property in all its forms, including dowry, which distinguished their status from that of their counterparts in most of Western Europe and the United States. Articles 109 and 110 of family law put the matter straightforwardly: "Marriage does not create the common property [*imushchestvo*] of spouses; each can own and acquire property [*sobstvennost'*] of their own."[5]

In the period after the Great Reforms, members of Russia's educated elite, legal professionals especially, grew critical of a patriarchal family order that, in their view, constituted a key pillar of the country's authoritarian political regime. Aiming to reform the social order by enhancing individual rights in the family and society, they aspired to limit, although not to abolish altogether, the near-absolute authority of husband over wife. But above all, reformers sought to extend the rule of law by increasing the ability of the courts (and by extension themselves) to adjudicate family affairs.[6] They focused on aspects of family law that seemed to them most backward by comparison with Western practices. They thus sought to make marriage and divorce civil rather than religious matters, adjudicated before civil rather than religious courts. Reformers also aimed to legalize marital separation, which Russian law forbade, in contrast to

---

City: Women, Work, and Family in Russia, 1861–1914 (New York: Cambridge University Press, 1994); Freeze, "The *Soslovie* (Estate) Paradigm," 30.

3. See Roderick Phillips, *Putting Asunder: A History of Divorce in Western Society* (New York: Cambridge University Press, 1988).

4. *Svod zakonov Rossiiskoi imperii* (St. Petersburg, 1887), vol. 10, pt. 1, articles 103–7.

5. Ibid., articles 109–10. For the history of women's unusual legal status, see Michelle Lamarche Marrese, *A Woman's Kingdom: Noblewomen and the Control of Property in Russia, 1700–1861* (Ithaca, NY: Cornell University Press, 2002).

6. See the discussion in William G. Wagner, *Marriage, Property, and Law in Late Imperial Russia* (Oxford: Clarendon, 1994), 62–69.

Catholic countries such as France and Italy, where the law restricted divorce but held separation to be legal.[7]

This put reformers into conflict with the Russian Orthodox Church. Until December 1917, the regulation of marriage and divorce in Russia remained the monopoly of religious rather than civil institutions. Of these, the Russian Orthodox Church was unquestionably the most important and powerful, and it resisted reform to the end. Regarding marriage as a holy sacrament, to be dissolved only under exceptional circumstances, the church permitted divorce only very reluctantly and only on the grounds of adultery, abandonment, sexual incapacity, and penal exile—never cruelty. Although divorce rates increased in the early twentieth century as clerical obstructionism eased, divorce remained exceedingly difficult for those of the Orthodox faith, the majority of ethnic Russians, until the end of autocracy itself.[8]

The church retained this monopoly in the face of unprecedented challenges to Russia's hierarchal familial and social order. By the close of the nineteenth century, industrialization and economic modernization were transforming the public sphere and calling into question older ways of life in both public and private, particularly in the empire's rapidly growing cities. The expansion of the marketplace and proliferation of consumer goods permitted the crafting of new social identities and encouraged more individualistic values, undermining older and more family-centered ways of being in the world. Advertising enticed women to consume the items displayed in department-store windows and on the pages of popular magazines and to employ beauty aides to decorate the self. Books and magazines dispensed advice on appropriate dress and deportment for people who aspired to a higher status than the one into which they had been born. Prescriptive literature also propounded new roles for wives that mirrored the cult of domesticity circulating in Western Europe and the United States and raised expectations for marital felicity.[9] Romantic love and personal choice were celebrated in fiction, on stage, in song. Whether or not such changes increased the number of discontented wives—impossible to ascertain on the basis of existing records—there can be no doubt that they provided a language with which wives might speak of their

7. On France, see William M. Reddy, "Marriage, Honor, and the Public Sphere in Postrevolutionary France: *Séparations de Corps, 1815–1848," Journal of Modern History* 65 (September 1993): 437–72; and on Italy, see Mark Seymour, *Debating Divorce in Italy: Marriage and the Making of Modern Italians, 1860–1974* (New York: Palgrave Macmillan, 2006).

8. For the different policies affecting Jews, see ChaeRan Y. Freeze, *Jewish Marriage and Divorce in Imperial Russia* (Hanover, NH: University Press of New England, 2002).

9. Sally West, "The Material Promised Land: Advertising's Modern Agenda in Late Imperial Russia," *Russian Review* 57, no. 3 (1998): 345–63; Catriona Kelly, *Refining Russia: Advice Literature, Polite Culture, and Gender from Catherine to Yeltsin* (New York: Oxford University Press, 2001).

— Зина, твои расходы не соотвѣтствуютъ моему бюджету.

— Такъ увеличьте вашъ бюджетъ.

— Напротивъ, сократи ты свои расходы.

— Сократить я не могу. Все, что я готова для васъ сдѣлать — это часть своихъ расходовъ перенести на кошелекъ другаго.

FIGURE 1.

"Zina, your expenses exceed my budget."

"Then increase your budget."

"To the contrary, reduce your expenses."

"I can't reduce them. All I'm ready to do

for you is to transfer some of my expenses to

someone else's pocketbook."

Strekoza, *no. 40 (1895), M. E. Saltykov-Shchedrin Public Library*

discontent and emboldened some to seek more from their lives, including their intimate lives, than had their mothers or grandmothers.

Given the threats to the patriarchal family that urbanization and modernization posed, it is perhaps ironic that the institution best able to respond represented the more anachronistic rather than the more modern aspects of Russia's polity. We know about discontented wives because, between 1884 and 1914, thirty to forty thousand of them sought relief by petitioning an administrative body, the Imperial Chancellery for Receipt of Petitions (henceforward, the chancellery). The chancellery, which spoke in the name of the tsar, provided a kind of extralegal loophole, a way around the rigid law that forbade separation. Charged with "reconciling the contradictions between the strictness of the law [*surovyi zakon*] and the demands of higher justice," the Imperial Chancellery as agent of the imperial will was empowered to supercede the law forbidding marital separation by granting a wife the right to live on her own.[10] In the course of this thirty-year period, its officials became increasingly inclined to do so—indeed in key respects, more inclined than the judicial reformers who endeavored to supplant them. As I will argue, their very anachronism accounts for this apparent contradiction. Conservative not only in their politics but also in their attention to the particularities of the cases before them and paternalistic in their desire to protect the powerless, chancellery officials offered a surprisingly flexible response to the growing tensions between the conservative marital order and the pressures of modernity. Even so, their responsiveness was always constrained by the very administrative system that empowered them to act.

The women to whose appeals they responded tended to represent the more "modern" sectors of the population, broadly speaking. Deriving from all walks of life, they were nevertheless more likely than the overall population to live in cities and to know how to read and write, if sometimes only in the most rudimentary fashion. At the time of petitioning, the majority, perhaps two-thirds, resided in one of Russia's two major cities, Moscow and St. Petersburg, but others dwelt in cities, towns, and villages spread across the vast stretch of the Russian Empire. Although from 1890 to 1902 the majority of petitioners, almost 58 percent, were ascribed to the peasantry, that proportion was nevertheless smaller than their proportion of the general population of European Russia at that time—roughly 84 percent. Townswomen (*meshchanki*), the second largest group, were over-represented: 27.1 percent of petitioners, although only approximately 10 percent of the general population.[11] Members of the various privileged strata, also over-represented, constituted the remainder. Chancellery records do not distinguish petitioners by religion and often do not even mention it, but my impressionistic sense is that most petitioners belonged to the Russian Orthodox Church while a significant

10. S. N. Pisarev, *Uchrezhdenie po priniatiiu i napravleniiu proshenii i zhalob, prinosimykh na Vysochaishee imia, 1810–1910 gg. Istoricheskii ocherk* (St. Petersburg: R. Golike i A. Vil'borg, 1909), 138.

11. Wagner, *Marriage, Property, and Law,* 91.

minority were Jewish or Catholic or adhered to the Old Belief, a branch of Orthodoxy that split from the mainstream church in the seventeenth century. The dossiers of petitioners provide the primary source for this book.

If, as Michelle Perrot and Ann Martin-Fugier have contended, appeals for separation (and divorce) can be seen as a sign of modernity, then these petitions, the tip of a far larger iceberg, suggest its growing impact in Russia, and not only in the capital cities of Moscow and St. Petersburg, where information and assistance was relatively accessible, but in comparatively remote corners of the empire as well.[12] But if taken as a whole these appeals provide evidence of a new sense of individual rights and possibilities that in some respects transcended social divides, considered individually they are profoundly inflected by social status. That status was not necessarily the status conferred by *soslovie*. Access to wealth as well as inherited privilege shaped the resources available to women who sought to escape unhappy marriages, the terms with which the women articulated their grievances and imagined a different future, the responses of their husbands, and the ways that others, tsarist officials foremost among them, interpreted their appeals. Providing unique access to the self-definitions of ordinary Russians, petitions and related testimony promise insight into the vexed question of the nature of social class in late imperial Russia, particularly that of the highly contested "middle."

A controversy continues to divide historians of Russia over whether professionals, businessmen, elements of the tsarist bureaucracy, and others who might be construed as belonging to the "middle" remained fragmented, forming a "sedimentary society" of accumulated layers and diverse social identities, or constituted a genuine "middle class," whose members held shared values and ideals and a sense of identity.[13] While historians have long recognized that the formation of separate and gendered spheres and an ideology of domesticity played a key role in the constitution of a middle class else-

---

12. Michelle Perrot, "The Family Triumphant," in *A History of Private Life*, ed. Michelle Perrot, 5 vols. (Cambridge, MA: Harvard University Press, 1990), 4: 162.

13. The literature is huge, and the following citations by no means exhaust the subject. For the fragmented perspective, see Edith W. Clowes, Samuel D. Kassow, and James L. West, ed. *Between Tsar and People: Educated Society and the Quest for Public Identity in Late Imperial Russia* (Princeton, NJ: Princeton University Press, 1991), especially the introduction and articles by Abbott Gleason and Alfred J. Rieber; Mironov, *Sotsial'naia istoriia*, 1: 142–43; and Goncharov, *Gorodskaia sem'ia*. Among the first to espouse the existence of a Russian middle with unified values was Elise Kimerling Wirtschafter, in *Social Identity in Imperial Russia* (DeKalb: Northern Illinois University Press, 1997), chap. 3. For a recent example drawing on class, gender, and domesticity as a basis for the argument, see Catherine Evtukhov, "A. O. Karelin and Provincial Bourgeois Photography," in *Picturing Russia: Explorations in Visual Culture*, ed. Valerie Kivelson and Joan Neuberger (New Haven: Yale University Press, 2008), 113–17.

where in Europe, few historians who engage the question of a Russian "middle class" have systematically addressed it from that angle.[14]

The question of social status has influenced my selection of cases for this book. While people from a wide variety of social backgrounds comment on, adjudicate, and bear witness to the marital conflicts that are the subject of this book, the full-length cases I read are drawn from the laboring classes (most peasants and townspeople) and people who in other national contexts are considered part of the "middle." My selection thus broadly reflects the profile of modern Russian society as it emerged in the last decades of the nineteenth century and early years of the twentieth. I have included in the category of "middle" teachers, engineers, physicians, lawyers, and agronomists, whom Russian historians often refer to as the "educated classes," and businessmen and white-collar workers, but omitted members of the hereditary nobility—unless they earned their living in one of these capacities or were married to someone who did.[15] Because in this book social identity is a question rather than a given (townspeople who traded, for example, might enjoy considerable wealth), I have adopted an open-ended approach whenever possible. Thus I follow the chancellery's lead by providing ascribed status and occupation when I refer to people individually; referring to groups, I use the term "middling classes" and "laboring classes" as, indeed, did many contemporary Russians.

Within this "middle" the merchantry occupies a special place as a group whose social identity was highly fluid and whose family relations, deservedly or not, by mid-century had become synonymous with patriarchal excess. Merchant status, uniquely within Russia's *soslovie* order, was based exclusively on wealth: merchants required a minimum of fifteen thousand rubles capital to belong to the first merchant guild, between five and seven thousand rubles to belong to the second. Without the capital, merchants lost their privileged status, although not necessarily the right to trade,

---

14. The literature on domesticity and class formation is even more enormous. Among the works that have most influenced my thinking are Mary Ryan, *Cradle of the Middle Class: The Family in Oneida Country, New York, 1790–1865* (New York: Cambridge University Press, 1981); Bonnie Smith, *Ladies of Leisure: The Bourgeoises of Northern France in the Nineteenth Century* (Princeton, NJ: Princeton University Press, 1984); Leonore Davidoff and Catherine Hall, *Family Fortunes: Men and Women of the English Middle Class, 1780–1950* (Chicago: University of Chicago Press, 1987); Marion Kaplan, *The Making of the Jewish Middle Class: Women, Family, and Identity in Imperial Germany* (New York: Oxford University Press, 1991); and Nancy Reagin, "The Imagined Hausfrau: National Identity, Domesticity, and Colonialism in Imperial Germany," *Journal of Modern History* 73, no. 1 (2001): 54–86.

15. Jurgen Kocka, "The Middle Classes in Europe," *Journal of Modern History* 67, no. 4 (1995): 783–806. For an account of noble marital conflicts, see V. A. Veremenko, *Dvorianskaia sem'ia i gosudarstvennaia politika Rossii (vtoraia polovina XIX–nachalo XX v.)* (St. Petersburg: Evropeiskii dom, 2007).

and reverted to the peasant or townsperson status from which they or their forebears usually derived.[16] Customarily insular and conservative, historians agree, members of Russia's merchant estate experienced substantial social and cultural change in the second half of the nineteenth century. Abandoning their traditional caftans for West European styles of dress and shaving their beards, they gave vast sums to secular as well as religious charities and became increasingly receptive to the need to educate not only sons but daughters. The upper strata, in Moscow and elsewhere, began to favor the leisure activities of the educated elites: they played tennis, painted, composed, and enjoyed intellectual pursuits.[17] They nevertheless remained the most anomalous element in Russia's hypothetical "middle" and thus constitute a kind of test case for the existence of a new domesticity.

This book thus aims to fill a large gap in our understanding of social life in the last decades of imperial Russia. Russian historians have only recently begun to explore in depth the development, self-definition, social expectations, and occupational and public profiles of Russia's laboring and middling classes. With few exceptions, published works touch only in passing, or not at all, on the constitution of private life. We still know virtually nothing about what husbands and wives expected of each other in marriage, how they viewed domesticity and the family sphere, how they regarded the care and raising of their children, or how such attitudes might have varied according to social status and evolved in response to broader social and cultural changes. Historians of Western Europe have produced a substantial body of scholarship treating both the family and its breakdown, but there is no comparable scholarship on imperial Russia, aside from parts of my own work, V. A. Veremenko's important study of the noble family, ChaeRan Y. Freeze's pioneering book on the Jewish family, and several articles by Gregory Freeze that treat divorce.[18]

---

16. Alfred J. Rieber, *Merchants and Entrepreneurs in Imperial Russia* (Chapel Hill: University of North Carolina Press, 1982), 86–90; Mironov, *Sotsial'naia istoriia Rossii*, 1: 114–21.

17. Jo Ann Ruckman, *The Moscow Business Elite: A Social and Cultural Portrait of Two Generations* (DeKalb: Northern Illinois University Press, 1984), 154; David L. Ransel, "Neither Nobles nor Peasants: Plain Painting and the Emergence of the Merchant Estate," in *Picturing Russia*, ed. Kivelson and Neuberger, 76–80. See also I. G. Kuskova, *Riazanskoe kupechestvo: Ocherki istorii XVI–nachala XX veka* (Riazan: Mart, 1996), 120; and M. V. Briantsev, *Kul'tura russkogo kupechestva. Vospitanie i obrazovanie* (Briansk: Izdatel'stvo Kursiv, 1999). "The merchant became a literary [and I would add, real-life] hero by stepping directly into the shoes of the affluent intelligentsia" (Beth Holmgren, *Rewriting Capitalism: Literature and the Market in Late Tsarist Russia and the Kingdom of Poland* [Pittsburgh: University of Pittsburgh Press, 1998], 32–33).

18. Boris Mironov's magisterial study of Russia's social history represents something of an exception to this generalization about the neglect of private life. But its teleological approach, expressed in such chapter headings as "From the Authoritarian to the Democratic Family," obscure as much as they illuminate about Russia's complex and contradictory passage to "modernity," however defined.

About these matters and more, the material held in the archives of the Imperial Chancellery for the Receipt of Petitions has much to tell us. But it requires careful treatment. Dossiers were generated under conditions of highly unequal power, which affected their content. The proceedings began with a wife's petition, often composed by someone else and invariably claiming her victimization at her husband's hands. Then both spouses either wrote in their own hand or, if illiterate or semi-literate, narrated their version of their personal and marital history to a police officer charged with recording oral testimony verbatim. Spouses' narratives were constructed for a purpose: to find a common language with officials and to convince the chancellery of the rectitude of their side of the story. They thus share the "fictional" quality identified by Natalie Zemon Davis in her exploration of sixteenth-century French pardon tales. That is, their authors "shape[d] the events" of their marriage into a story, embellishing in the process.[19] To the extent these narratives were successful—as the narratives of wives in particular increasingly became—it was because they drew on broader cultural presuppositions that coincided with those held by officials.

And held not only by officials. The chancellery also generated other and more varied documentation as its officials endeavored to ascertain the "real reason" for the breakdown of a marriage. Witnesses named by both parties were summoned and questioned, and local authorities were invited to report on the outcome of inquiries and to share what they already knew. If the "real reason" proved especially elusive, undercover (*neglasnyi*) investigations were launched, in which a policeman or gendarme would query neighbors and others in a position to shed light on the source of the couple's disputes; sometimes, these investigators even subjected a husband or wife suspected of sexual misconduct to secret surveillance. While chancellery officials might receive petitioners and their husbands during the hours each week designated for that purpose, their deliberations occurred behind closed doors and in the absence of the contending parties or their representatives and were based on written statements and reports rather than oral testimony. These materials, many labeled "secret" or "strictly secret," were retained in chancellery dossiers, or at least the fully documented dossiers that have been preserved

---

See Mironov, *Sotsial'naia istoriia*. For studies that attend to personal life more closely, see Engel, *Between the Fields and the City*; Veremenko, *Dvorianskaia sem'ia*; ChaeRan Y. Freeze, *Jewish Marriage and Divorce*; and Gregory L. Freeze, "*Krylova vs. Krylova*: 'Sexual Incapacity' and Divorce in Tsarist Russia," in *The Human Tradition in Modern Russia*, ed. William B. Husband (Wilmington: Scholarly Resources, 2000), 5–17; and Freeze, "Profane Narratives about a Holy Sacrament: Marriage and Divorce in Late Imperial Russia," in *Sacred Stories: Religion and Spirituality in Modern Russia*, ed. Mark D. Steinberg and Heather J. Coleman (Bloomington: Indiana University Press, 2007), 146–78.

19. Natalie Zemon Davis, *Fiction in the Archives: Pardon Tales and Their Tellers in Sixteenth-Century France.* (Stanford, CA: Stanford University Press, 1987), 3–4.

(a fraction of the total). Dossiers also offer a wealth of other documentation that was originally generated for purposes quite unrelated to a particular case.[20]

The multi-vocal character of dossiers enables me to explore the ways that a broad range of individuals, not only petitioners and spouses but also witnesses, investigators, and agents of the tsarist state in an ascending hierarchy of authority spoke about marriage and its discontents, and what their words can tell us about changing gender definitions and expectations of intimate life during the thirty years preceding the outbreak of World War I. Even the narrative "fictions" of contending couples are revealing. Expressing their authors' perceptions of acceptable and unacceptable marital and sexual conduct, they can be taken to reflect those of the milieu from which the authors derived. The couples that figure in the pages to follow are not "typical," to be sure. In addition to disproportionately reflecting the views of more "modern" sectors of the population, they represent cases in which differences between husband and wife were irreconcilable, and husbands, rather than saying goodbye and good riddance, clung to their authority when wives took the unusual step of appealing to the chancellery. Women who took that step were likely to have been more resourceful and self-assertive than other women of their milieu. Nevertheless, the marital conflicts described fit larger patterns and highlight the limits of acceptable conduct in this period of Russia's history, and not only in the minds of contending parties. The testimonies of spouses, witnesses, and representatives of the state, from police and gendarmes up to and including chancellery officials, provide access, however indirectly, to values and expectations for harmonious marriage that are usually left unarticulated, and that underwent real change in this period.[21] Certain allegations remained virtually ubiquitous (the drunken, feckless, and abusive husband; the sexually errant wife) and tell us what wives in unhappy marriages and/or their advisers thought was most likely to persuade officials of the rectitude of their case. However, as subsequent chapters show, the cases had "scripts," tropes and narratives that otherwise varied considerably, and that evolved over time, reflecting not only individual experience but also different social backgrounds and the flux in cultural values.

My exploration of the meanings of narratives and testimonies, and of the gender constructs that they reflect, is based on a close and careful reading of 260 of the 1,987 fully documented cases that have been preserved in the chancellery archives, about

---

20. I use the word "dossier" in the sense that Michel Foucault has defined it. Many of the dossiers I draw on for this book consisted of documents of very different provenance, composed for different purposes, all of which "speak, or appear to speak, of one and the same thing" (Michel Foucault, ed., *I, Pierre Riviere, Having Slaughtered My Mother, My Sister and My Brother...*, trans. Frank Jellinek [Lincoln: University of Nebraska Press, 1982], x).

21. Phillips, *Putting Asunder*, 321.

half of which I draw on directly in this book.[22] These fully documented cases are supplemented by a sampling of 565 of the brief reports that are the only remains of cases that were expunged from the archive for reasons I have been unable to ascertain.[23] I draw on these to test the representativeness of the fully documented cases and to ascertain broader patterns in the character of allegations as well as the evolution of chancellery decision making. To place these cases in their wider context, I have examined published memoirs, diaries, and other personal documents deriving from the social groups under study as well as advice literature, fiction, and other evidence drawn from the contemporary popular and specialized (especially legal) press. Cartoons from the St. Petersburg satirical weekly *Strekoza,* which began publication in 1875 and was sold on the streets to an audience of unknown composition and size, illustrate many key points. Most of the cartoons feature members of a generic "middle class," virtually indistinguishable in home furnishings and dress from their counterparts in the United States and Western Europe. I also draw on the work of other historians and literary scholars, without whose pioneering studies of the cultural flux of these years this book would have been much the poorer.

In writing this book, I have tried to respect the multi-vocal and multi-layered character of the dossiers, which reflect what people said to themselves, to one another, and to an ascending hierarchy of imperial authorities about a vast number of subjects, most but not all involving marital and gender relations, over the course of three turbulent decades. The themes I have chosen as my focus are the result of the interaction among the issues that engaged the people in my sources, the current concerns of historians of Russia, and my long-standing feminist predispositions, which prompt me to seek the sources of female agency in historically specific institutions, practices, and ways of regarding the world. By agency, I mean most minimally the capacity to act, to do something, intentionally or not, but also and more expansively, to "adopt and adapt" culture in order to act on the world.[24] If I privilege some voices, and inevitably I do, those voices tend to be voices that represent change rather than stasis, as is often the way of the historian.

Nevertheless, change there was, as the following chapters demonstrate. It took place within a remarkably brief period of time, and in quick jumps rather than gradually or in

22. The number is provided by V. A. Veremenko, "'Litso s vidom na zhitel'stvo' (gendernyi aspekt pasportnoi sistemy Rossii kontsa XIX–nachala XX vv.)," *Adam i Eva,* no. 7 (2004): 233.

23. The sample is drawn from RGIA, fond 1412, op. 250, d. 80–86, 100–4.

24. Introduction to Gabrielle M. Spiegel, ed., *Practicing History: New Directions in Historical Writing after the Linguistic Turn* (New York: Routledge, 2005), 15–17. My thinking has also been influenced by William Sewell, "The Concept[s] of Culture," in ibid., 76–95; and Sherry B. Ortner, *Anthropology and Social Theory: Culture, Power, and the Acting Subject* (Durham, NC: Duke University Press, 2006).

linear fashion. Change was reflected in the ways that people used language and framed their cases and in the practices of administrative institutions. People began to imagine their lives and options differently and to act accordingly, while legal and administrative systems increasingly came to grips with the consequences of marital breakdown. Perhaps most striking of all was the evolution in the attitudes of chancellery officials, whose arbitrary authority allowed the flexibility to cope with the unpredictable consequences of marital breakdown. And as I will argue, women petitioners contributed to bringing about this change. Partly as a result of their actions and compelling narratives, chancellery officials became more tolerant of female aspirations, more respectful of the female person, and less wedded to administrative constraints on female mobility and the authoritarian family structure still upheld by imperial law.

The Ties That Bound

On September 16, 1887, I married at the insistence of the townsman Nikolai N. Pantiugin. He assured me that he was only fifty years old and, having three small children from another marriage and wanting to establish them, I agreed. He also told me he was well off. Once I married him, however, I learned that he wasn't fifty but sixty-seven and utterly incapable of conjugal life. He also had no financial means at all and was only trying to get his hands on my and my children's property. And when I refused to transfer my property to him, he demanded two hundred rubles from me in exchange for approving my passport. Constantly insulting and oppressing me, he made life impossible after seven days of cohabitation.

That September day, Olga Pantiugina took a step she would regret for many years. Thirty-two years old and already twice widowed, she agreed to marry for the third time a virtual stranger, whom she had met in the railroad town of Bologoe, Novgorod. Why she took such an incautious step remains unclear. Her second marriage to a merchant had left her economically independent, if barely, the recipient of three hundred rubles a year in dividends from investments, an amount roughly equal to the annual wages of a textile worker. Olga Pantiugina also owned a house in Kolpino, a suburb of the city of St. Petersburg, and enjoyed access to a sum of money, the amount of which she refused to divulge, which her late husband had bequeathed to their three small children. Whatever prompted her third marriage, it was certainly not unfulfilled sexual longings. Soon after becoming a widow for the second time, she rented a room in her house to an agent for the railroad, a man considerably younger than she, one Vladimir Iakovlev. In time, the two became sexually intimate. Over the next few years she accompanied Iakovlev as he was transferred from one railway station to another, and eventually to Bologoe, renting an apartment and claiming him as her "boarder" all the while. It was for the sake of the children that she agreed to marry Nikolai Pantiugin very shortly after their initial meeting, Olga maintained. Nikolai had presented himself as a man of substantial means. Owner of two small shops and two houses in the town of Bologoe, a supplier of wood for the railroad, he appeared to have resources sufficient to ensure her and the children's economic well-being. Nikolai Pantiugin claimed to have been attracted by Olga's maturity and ability to read and write, enabling her to be useful to his business. As it eventually became clear, however, Nikolai's financial affairs were in serious trouble: his shops were losing money and one of his houses, used as collateral for a loan of eleven thousand rubles, was about to be sold at auction.[1]

Their cohabitation lasted for a mere week after their wedding. Olga stole away late one night while Nikolai was asleep, and into the waiting arms of her "boarder," Iakovlev, her husband claimed. Soon after, she began to seek a way to sever ties with her husband and end his ability to extort money in exchange for her freedom. Her efforts, lasting nine frustrating years, have much to tell us not only about the structures that reinforced the marital bond and upheld husbands' authority over wives during the reigns of Russia's last two tsars but also about the social, economic, and cultural processes that challenged those very structures during the same period.

STRUCTURES

Although people's ability to free themselves from the bonds of matrimony is always constrained by law, the nature and degree of those constraints have varied enormously over time and across cultures.[2] In Russia, those constraints were unusually severe because of the influence of the Russian Orthodox Church, which, regarding marriage as a sacrament, fiercely protected its control of the regulation of marriage and divorce among its faithful. Limiting the grounds for divorce to adultery, sexual incapacity, abandonment, and penal exile, even then the church granted divorce only reluctantly, and only after a cumbersome and expensive process. Several eyewitnesses of the act itself were required to demonstrate adultery, while sexual incapacity had to antedate the marriage, have lasted at least three years, and be verified by a state-approved physician. Abandoned spouses could sue successfully only after five years had elapsed and a lengthy investigation had failed to locate the missing spouse. Until 1904, the "guilty" party in a divorce suit was forbidden to remarry. In 1890, the Russian Orthodox Church granted a total of 879 divorces (only 190 based on adultery). Although the rate increased significantly in the early twentieth century as the church eased its obstructive stance, rates in Russia remained far lower than those in most of Western Europe, not to mention the United States.[3] The limited grounds for divorce in Russia never included cruel treatment.

---

1. RGIA, fond 1412, op. 226, d. 8 (Pantiugina, O., 1887), l.

2. See Giacomo Francini, "Divorce and Separations in Eighteenth-Century France: An Outline for a Social History of Law," *History of the Family* 2, no. 1 (1997): 100.

3. On the laws governing divorce, see *Svod zakonov Rossiiskoi imperii* (St. Petersburg, 1957), vol. 10, pt. 1, articles 45–60; Sergei P. Grigorovskii, ed., *Sbornik tserkovnykh i grazhdanskikh zakonov o*

Finally, and most saliently for women whose unsuccessful marriages offered none of the grounds for divorce, in Russia both legal and administrative structures severely limited the ability of women simply to leave an unhappy marriage. Separation was illegal according to article 103 of family law, which in gender-neutral language strictly forbade any action that "might lead to the separation of spouses." Although the legal requirement of spousal cohabitation was commonplace in Europe in this period, two characteristics of the Russian system distinguished it from its European counterparts: the absence of legal remedies, to be treated in the next section, and the internal passport system. Passport regulations gave the law forbidding separation patriarchal teeth. In Russia, everyone who wished to travel more than roughly twenty miles (thirty *versta*) from their ascribed place of residence, take a job, enroll in school, or rent an apartment required an internal passport. Those who lacked the requisite document or held a document that had expired were subject to fines or even forcible return to their home or place of ascription under police escort (*po etapu*). Married women, who were inscribed on their husband's passport, could obtain a passport of their own only with his permission.

Russia's passport regime secured the state's monopoly over the "legitimate means of movement," in John Torpey's resonant phrase; it also reflected and helped sustain Russia's social and gender order.[4] Internal passports contained information on the bearer's legal estate (*soslovie*), permanent place of residence, date of birth or age, religion and ethnicity, and marital status. Peter the Great (1689–1725) initiated the system to ensure that peasants and townspeople paid the poll tax and fulfilled their military obligations. Although by the time that the serfs were emancipated in 1861 the laws regulating individual mobility had been extended to everyone, including the nobility and service elite, passport law continued to discriminate among Russia's subjects in terms of their rights and privileges.[5] Until 1906, the source and duration of the passport varied according

---

brake i razvode, uzakonenii, usynovlenii i vnebrachnyia deti: s polozheniiami i raziasneniiami po tsirkuliarnym i separatnym ukazam Sviatleishego Synoda, 6th ed. (St. Petersburg: Trud, 1904), 154–209. For a discussion of their operation, see William G. Wagner, *Marriage, Property, and Law in Late Imperial Russia* (Oxford: Clarendon, 1994), 67–68, 70; on the history, see Gregory Freeze, "Bringing Order to the Russian Family: Marriage and Divorce in Imperial Russia, 1760–1860," *Journal of Modern History* 62 (December 1990): 709–46. Comparative rates are in Roderick Phillips, *Putting Asunder: A History of Divorce in Western Society* (New York: Cambridge University Press, 1988).

4. John Torpey, *The Invention of the Passport: Surveillance, Citizenship and the State* (Cambridge: Cambridge University Press, 2000), 6; V. A. Veremenko, "'Litso s vidom na zhitel'stvo' (gendernyi aspekt pasportnoi sistemy Rossii kontsa XIX–nachala XX vv.)" *Adam i Eva*, no. 7 (2004): 201–42.

5. Brief overviews of Russia's passport legislation are provided by Mervyn Matthews, *The Passport Society: Controlling Movement in Russia and the USSR* (Boulder, CO: Westview, 1993), 1–8; and Charles Steinwedel, "Making Social Groups, One Person at a Time: The Identification of Individuals by Estate, Religious Confession, and Ethnicity in Late Imperial Russia," in *Documenting Individual*

to the bearer's social status. To obtain the document, townsmen, artisans, and peasants required the permission of the estate administration of the village, county, or city to which they were ascribed; and until 1897, they were eligible only for short-term (one year or less) passports, for which they paid a fee. That year, the fee was abolished and passports extended to at least a year. By contrast, members of the privileged orders, among them nobles, civil servants, honored citizens, merchants, and professionals, had the right to a permanent passport booklet that left them free to choose their official place of residence.[6] These social distinctions were eliminated only in 1906, when in an effort to encourage mobility and foster economic development, passport law was revised to remove the disabilities of peasants, townspeople, and artisans and place them on an "equal footing," as the law put it, with persons of other estates.[7]

Gender distinctions transcended these social divides, and persisted even after social distinctions had been eliminated from passport law. Whatever their social status, wives required their husband's permission to obtain a passport. The law made no distinction even for someone like the well-born, wealthy, and privileged princess Maria Tenisheva. Having left her husband, Tenisheva, like other wives lacking the necessary document, would have "wound up somewhere, together with fugitives and people without a passport," had she not lived with a friend at the friend's estate after her husband refused to grant permission for the passport.[8] If women had held a passport before the wedding, they surrendered it at the church, where it was preserved together with other documents relating to the marriage. To be sure, decisions of the State Senate, Russia's highest judicial body, made exceptions to these rules for peasants and townswomen under extreme circumstances; peasant courts sometimes made exceptions in extreme cases as well. In this respect, peasant women were almost a privileged group by the early twentieth century. Nevertheless, the rules remained in force until March 12, 1914, when pass-

Identity: The Development of State Practices in the Modern World, ed. Jane Caplan and John Torpey (Princeton, NJ: Princeton University Press, 2001), 73–78. For a detailed discussion of the development of passport law to the mid-nineteenth century, see V. G. Chernykha, "Pasport v Rossiiskoi imperii: Nabliudeniia nad zakonodatel'stvom," *Istoricheskie zapiski* 122 (2001): 91–131; Chernukha, "Pasport v Rossii v vtoroi chetverti XIX v.," *Angliiskaia naberezhnaia 4*, no. 4 (St. Petersburg, 2004): 163–90. My thanks to Boris Anan'ich for his assistance in obtaining these articles.

6. Clergy required the permission of ecclesiastical authorities. For passport law at the end of the nineteenth century, see *Svod zakonov Rossiiskoi imperii*, vol. 14 (St. Petersburg, 1890); Aristarkh L. Shestoperov, ed., *Polnyi sbornik uzakonenii i rasporiazhenii pravitel'stva, otnosiashchikhsia do vidov na zhitel'stvo, so vkliucheniem deistvuiushchikh pasportnykh pravil i polozheniia o vidakh na zhitel'stvo* (Samara: N. A. Zhdanova, 1903).

7. Quoted in Veremenko, "Litso," 204.

8. Kniaginia Maria Tenisheva, *Vpechatleniia moei zhizni. Vospominaniia* (Moscow: Zakharov, 2002), 71.

port law was revised to permit wives to obtain their own passport simply by requesting it, after a long campaign by feminists, among others, to reform family law.[9]

INSTITUTIONS

The other distinctive feature of the Russian legal system was the absence of judicial separation, which elsewhere in Europe might free a woman from a broken relationship in cases where divorce was difficult or impossible.[10] Russia's civil courts lacked the authority to intervene on women's behalf, despite the appeals of innumerable unhappily married women.[11] Introduced in 1864, Russia's reformed court system was modeled on West European institutions. It created a professionally trained, independent judiciary to preside over Russia's regular courts. To make justice accessible even to the most humble, the regular court system was supplemented by Justice of the Peace courts, which were rather like small-claims courts, in which litigants pled their own case.[12] Even when they were prone to find in a woman's favor, as judges became increasingly likely to do as the nineteenth century drew to a close, all they could do was to refuse husbands' requests to restore their wife to their household, because judges lacked the authority to approve the all-important passport, which was vested in administrative, rather than legal institutions.

Many jurists found the resulting situation a source of enormous frustration. In the second half of the nineteenth century, marriage, the family, and women's social roles and status became contested issues, part of a more general assault on Russia's authoritarian social and political order that will be discussed in more detail below. Members of Russia's educated elite, professionals in particular, grew critical of the patriarchal

9. On peasant courts, see Beatrice Farnsworth, "The Litigious Daughter-in-Law: Family Relations in Rural Russia in the Second Half of the Nineteenth Century," *Slavic Review* 45, no. 1 (1986): 49–64. On the feminist campaign, see Linda Harriet Edmondson, *Feminism in Russia, 1900–1917* (Stanford, CA: Stanford University Press, 1984), 139–41.

10. See Phillips, *Putting Asunder,* for a general discussion of judicial separation. On England, see Olive Anderson, "State, Civil Society, and Separation in Victorian England," *Past and Present* 163 (May 1999): 162–201; on France, see William M. Reddy, "Marriage, Honor, and the Public Sphere in Postrevolutionary France: *Séparations de Corps,* 1815–1848," *Journal of Modern History* 65 (September 1993): 437–72; and for Italy, see Mark Seymour, *Debating Divorce in Italy: Marriage and the Making of Modern Italians* (New York: Palgrave Macmillan, 2006).

11. On women's appeals to Justice of the Peace and other courts and the helplessness of judges, see Joan Neuberger, "Popular Legal Cultures: The St. Petersburg *Mirovoi Sud,*" in *Russia's Great Reforms, 1855–1881,* ed. Ben Eklof, John Bushnell, and Larissa Zakharova (Bloomington: Indiana University Press, 1994), 239; and Iakob Ludmer, "Bab'i stony (Iz zametok mirovogo suda)," *Iuridicheskii vestnik,* nos. 11–12 (1884): 446–67; 658–79.

12. W. Bruce Lincoln, *The Great Reforms: Autocracy, Bureaucracy, and the Politics of Change in Imperial Russia* (DeKalb: Northern Illinois University Press, 1990), 114–15; see also Samuel Kucherov, *Courts, Lawyers, and Trials under the Last Three Tsars* (New York: F. A. Praeger, 1953).

family and the church-governed marital regime. Embracing a companionate and affective ideal of marriage, they believed that for a union to be truly "moral," the relations of husband and wife must be based on mutual respect and affection, rather than coercion. To this end, but also to enhance the rights of women, they advocated limiting, although not abolishing altogether, the near-absolute authority of husband over wife through reform of family law. Legal reform offered a primary means not only to expand individual rights in the family and society but also to extend the rule of law into a domain where the church reigned supreme. Beginning in the 1860s, progressive jurists worked to revise marital law so as to facilitate divorce and legal separation and to bring such matters before civil rather than religious courts. In this, reforming jurists pursued a more far-reaching agenda, as William Wagner has argued. Drawing their authority from the legal system that they administered and the specialized training in the law that such administration required, legal professionals employed the issue of women's rights in marriage as a means to political ends. By extending the rule of law, jurists aimed to limit the arbitrary authority of the tsar as well as to expand the realms in which their own professional expertise would prove authoritative.[13]

They proved unable to revise statutory law to this end, however. Reformers encountered the staunch resistance of conservatives and of the Russian Orthodox Church. Russia's rulers sided with conservatives, not least because they depended on the existing marital regime to uphold social stability and hold back the forces of change and thus to help preserve autocracy itself. Although reformers did succeed in expanding married women's legal rights in a number of realms—among them access to child custody, child support, alimony, and, in the case of peasant women, the right to receive a passport under exceptional circumstances—until well into the twentieth century, women who sought relief from the strictures barring marital separation could obtain it only by personal petition to administrative bodies. At their summit reigned the tsar, whose absolute authority enabled him or, more accurately, those who spoke in his name to circumvent the law forbidding marital separation by approving a separate passport.

The history of what I call extralegal separation really begins in 1826, with the notorious Third Section of His Majesty's Secret Chancellery. Better known to the public and to students of Russian history as a political police whose charge was censorship and the ferreting out of sedition wherever it might rear its head, the Third Section was also tasked with "moral surveillance" over the empire, a responsibility that included

13. William Wagner, *Marriage, Property, and Law,* 61–137; Wagner, "The Trojan Mare: Women's Rights and Civil Rights in Late Imperial Russia," in *Civil Rights in Imperial Russia,* ed. Olga Crisp and Linda Edmondson (Oxford: Oxford University Press, 1989), 65–84; Laura Engelstein, *The Keys to Happiness: Sex and the Search for Modernity in Fin-de-Siècle Russia* (Ithaca, NY: Cornell University Press, 1992), 17–95. On the development of a judicial ethos, see Richard Wortman, *Development of a Russian Legal Consciousness* (Chicago: University of Chicago Press, 1976), 268–89.

serving as guardian of "family morality and peace.[14] From its inception in 1826 to its elimination in August 1880, the Third Section responded to petitions from unhappily married women and, less often, men. Initially few and deriving almost exclusively from nobles, the quantity of these appeals grew quickly after the emancipation of the serfs in 1861, and the social background of petitioners diversified; petitions numbered well over a thousand a year by the end of the 1870s.[15] After several years of shuttling from one administrative institution to another after the abolition of the Third Section, separation petitions became the purview of the newly reformed Petitions Commission in 1884; in 1895, the commission was reorganized and renamed the Imperial Chancellery for Receipt of Petitions.[16] Because their functions remained essentially the same, for the sake of simplicity, I hereafter refer to the Petitions Commission and the Imperial Chancellery as "the chancellery." In addition to resolving marital conflicts, the chancellery entertained petitions concerning a range of other issues. Of the more than approximately 65,000 petitions received in 1908, only 1,508 involved marital disputes.[17] Nevertheless, marital disputes were sufficiently numerous and time-consuming to investigate that a particular division of the chancellery (the Fourth) was devoted to them. From 1884 to 1914, its officials, who numbered 9 in 1887, 10 in 1895, and 13 in

14. I. M. Trotskii, *Tret'e otdelenie pri Nikolae I* (Moscow: Izdatel'stvo vsesoiuznogo obshchestva politkatorzhan i ss-poselentsev, 1930), 56; V. Bogucharskii, "Tret'e otdelenie Sobstvennoi ego imperatorskogo velichestva kantseliarii o sebe samom," *Vestnik Evropy* 3 (1917): 117; Veremenko, "Litso," 221–25. See also Sidney Monas, *The Third Section: Police and Society in Russia under Nicholas I* (Cambridge, MA: Harvard University Press, 1961); and Peter Stansfield Squires, *The Third Department: The Establishment and Practices of the Political Police in the Russia of Nicholas I* (London: Cambridge University Press, 1968).

15. The Holy Synod, the ruling body of the Orthodox Church, also received complaints about family discord, as did local authorities. See V. A. Veremenko, "Semeinye nesoglasiia i razdel'noe zhitel'stvo suprugov: problema zakonodatel'nogo regulirovaniia v Rossii vo vtoroi polovine XIX–nachala XX veka," *Dialog so vremenem* 18 (2007): 328; and N. V. Zanegina, "Osobennosti otnoshenii muzha i zheny v dvorianskikh sem'iakh Rossii kontsa XVIII–pervoi poloviny XIX v. (na materialakh Tverskoi gubernii)," in *Rod i sem'ia v kontekste tverskoi istorii* (Tver: Tverskoi gosudarstvennogo universitet, 2007), 64–77.

16. When the Third Section was eliminated, its higher police functions and the Gendarme Corps was integrated into the Ministry of the Interior (MVD). For a brief period, the newly created Department of the State Police of the MVD, in which were concentrated all police activities, accepted women's petitions. However, the arrangement quickly proved administratively untenable because the subordination of the Department of State Police to the State Senate meant that the Senate held the authority to overturn decisions made in the name of the tsar.

17. S. N. Pisarev, *Uchrezhdenie po priniatiiu i napravleniiu proshenii i zhalob, prinosimykh na Vysochaishee imia, 1810–1910 gg. Istoricheskii ocherk* (St. Petersburg: R. Golike i A. Vil'borg, 1909), 178–89.

1900, served as the highest court of appeals for women seeking to escape an unhappy marriage but ineligible for divorce, Olga Pantiugina among them.

Treatments thus far have underscored the chancellery's connection with the most retrograde aspects of late absolutism. Andrew Verner finds in the chancellery the quintessence of the arbitrary, personalistic mode of rule that doomed Russia's Old Regime. This was government by "grantsmanship—the bestowal of privileges and favors by the tsar" on subjects who solicited them personally and had the good fortune to have their requests forwarded to the tsar by a bureaucrat. Likewise, for Dominic Lieven, the chancellery serves as an embodiment of pre-reform values. The Petitions Chancellery, he writes, was a "cross between, on the one hand, the most ancient conception of monarchy in which the king sat under a tree and dispensed justice personally to his subjects and, on the other, a modern ombudsman." True to this character, it became a key player in efforts to preserve the "personal, patriarchal, and unbureaucratic aspects of the monarchy."[18]

Without challenging these readings, a recent article by A. V. Remnev has emphasized the chancellery's public relations dimension as well as its symbolic significance in the autocratic political order. By providing Russia's subjects with direct access to the tsar, the chancellery helped to "maintain the illusion of an autocracy resting directly on the people [*narodnosti samoderzhaviia*]," and to sustain in the common people their faith in monarchical justice.[19] The chancellery thus served as the embodiment of the "custodial *Polizeistaat*" in which the government exercises its authority administratively, and as Laura Engelstein puts it, "in the spirit (optimally) of benevolent paternalism."[20]

Its first three directors—Otto Rikhter, Dmitrii Sipiagin, and Baron Aleksandr A. Budberg—were staunch proponents of autocracy who enjoyed unusually close relations with the tsar. Born in 1830 to a Baltic noble family and a graduate of the Imperial Corps of Pages, Otto Rikhter had served as companion to Alexander III, with whom he remained very close. Widely if unevenly read, of "limited intelligence and administrative ability," Rikhter was a man of "unquestioning loyalty," on whom Tsar Alexander III became increasingly dependent toward the end of his reign.[21] Rikhter's successor, Dmitrii Sipiagin, was another paragon of loyalty, a steadfast believer in the need to

18. Andrew Verner, *The Crisis of Russian Autocracy* (Princeton, NJ: Princeton University Press, 1990), 50–52; Dominic Lieven, *Nicholas II: Emperor of All Russias* (London: John Murray, 1993), 113, 114.

19. A. V. Remnev, "Kantseliariia proshenii v samoderzhavnoi sisteme pravleniia kontsa XIX stoletiia," *Istoricheskii ezhegodnik* (1997): 17, 19.

20. Engelstein, *The Keys to Happiness*, 19.

21. Sergei Witte, *The Memoirs of Count Witte*, ed. and trans. Sidney Harcave (Armonk, NY: M. E. Sharpe, 1990), 154, 485. See also *Dnevnik gosudarstvennogo sekretaria A. A. Polovtsova, 1883–1886*, ed. P. A. Zaionchkovskii, 2 vols. (Moscow: Nauka, 1966), 1: 298; and N. A. Epanchin, *Na sluzhbe trekh imperatov* (Moscow: Izdatel'stvo zhurnala Nashe Nasledie, 1996), 165–66. On dependence, see

FIGURE 2. *Otto Rikhter. From S. N. Pisarev,* Uchrezhdenie
po priniatiiu i napravleniiu proshenii i zhalob, prinosimykh
na Vysochaishee imia, 1810–1910 gg. Istoricheskii ocherk.

FIGURE 3. *Dmitrii Sipiagin. From S. N. Pisarev,*
Uchrezhdenie po priniatiiu i napravleniiu proshenii
i zhalob, prinosimykh na Vysochaishee imia, 1810–1910 gg.
Istoricheskii ocherk.

FIGURE 4. *Baron Aleksandr A. Budberg. From S. N. Pisarev,*
Uchrezhdenie po priniatiiu i napravleniiu proshenii i zhalob,
prinosimykh na Vysochaishee imia, 1810–1910 gg. Istoricheskii ocherk.

restore the monarch's unmediated relationship to his people. Born in 1854 to a wealthy landowning family and educated in law at St. Petersburg University, Sipiagin had occupied a number of governorship posts before becoming head of the chancellery in 1895. During his leadership, Sipiagin sought in vain to transform the chancellery into a supragovernmental organ through which would filter all important measures and legislative proposals before they reached the tsar.[22] His successor, Baron Aleksandr A. Budberg, a scion of the landed Baltic nobility, was born in 1851 and graduated from the law faculty of St. Petersburg University in 1875. Having served briefly in the Ministry of Justice and fought in the Russo-Turkish War of 1877–78, Budberg returned to civil service and joined the chancellery in 1891, becoming its head in 1899, when Sipiagin was appointed to head the Ministry of the Interior. A trusted confidant of Tsar Nicholas II, he was one of three men with whom the tsar consulted concerning the language of the October Manifesto.[23]

Chancellery officials shared a sense of exalted mission and of personal connection to the tsar. In their own eyes, their mission was more noble than that of ordinary government bureaucrats. "We had a lot of work, but because we knew that we served a worthy and vital [*zhivoi*] cause, we did not find it burdensome," remembered Vasilii I. Mamantov. Mamantov served as assistant to Baron Budberg, director of the chancellery after Sipiagin; after Budberg's retirement in 1913, he became director in his own right. "To the extent we were able, we helped render mercy and justice to those whom fate had made unfortunate, and who had placed their hopes in the emperor's protection."[24] Long after most civil servants had shifted their loyalties from the Romanov dynasty to the state and the nation, chancellery officials retained a sense of personal service to the autocrat in whose name they acted.

Richard Wortman, *Scenarios of Power: Myth and Ceremony in Russian Monarchy*, 2 vols. (Princeton, NJ: Princeton University Press, 1995–2000), 2: 298.

22. See A. M. Lebov, "Odin iz ubitykh ministrov," *Istoricheskii vestnik* 107 (February 1907): 485; N. A. Veliaminov, "Vospominiia o D. S. Sipiagine," *Rossiiskii arkhiv: Istoriia otechestva v svidetel'stvakh i dokumentakh XVIII–XX vv.* 6 (1995): 377–92. "According to Sipiagin, any desire of the monarch merits unquestioning execution as the expression of divine beneficence, deriving from God's anointed," wrote State Senator A. A. Polovtsov in 1901, "Dnevnik A. A. Polovtsova," *Krasnyi arkhiv* 3 (1923): 94.

23. Pisarev, *Uchrezhdenie po priniatiiu*, 172; *Gosudarstvennye deiateli Rossii XIX–nachala XX v. Biograficheskii spravochnik* (Moscow: Izdatel'stvo Moskovskogo universiteta, 1995); D. N. Shilov and Iu. A. Kuz'min, *Chleny gosudarstvennogo soveta Rossiiskoi imperii, 1801–1906. Bio-bibliograficheskii spravochnik* (St. Petersburg: Dmitrii Bulanin, 2007), 88–90. On 1905, see Verner, *Crisis of Russian Autocracy*, 236, 238.

24. Vasilii I. Mamantov, *Na gosudarevoi sluzhbe. Vospominaniia* (Tallinn: Tallina Eesti Kirjastus, 1926), 168.

TABLE 1. Educational Background of Chancellery Officials, 1887–1906

Year and number	School of Pages/Cadets	University	Imperial School of Jurisprudence	Home	Alexander Lycée	Other
1887 (9)	5	2	1	1		
1891 (9)	2	4	1	1	1	
1895 (10)		9 (6 law)				1
1900 (13)		11 (6 law)	1			1
1906 (11)		8 (6 law)	2			1

Source: Spisok chinam kantseliarii ego imperatorskogo velichestva po priniatiiu proshenii na 1887, 1891, 1895, 1900, 1906.

Note: These numbers include the head of the chancellery, his assistant, and the director and his assistant, as well as officials who served in the division of the chancellery that dealt with marital disputes. I have excluded the sizable number of officials who served in other sectors of the chancellery.

At the same time, the profile of chancellery officials, like that of other members of the imperial administration, became increasingly professional over time. In the division of the chancellery that dealt with marital disputes, the proportion of chancellery officials with higher education, and education in the law in particular, increased steadily, mirroring the growing professionalization of the imperial administration as whole. (See table 1.) Although higher education, even education in the law, by no means transformed its recipient into a proponent of the rule of law, it did heighten respect for the law and awareness of its possibilities and limitations, as we shall see.[25]

Adherents of a patriarchal and paternalistic view of politics, chancellery officials were nevertheless prepared to curtail patriarchal authority within the family in cases where, in officials' eyes, a husband abused it. In the absence of legal guidelines by which to evaluate a woman's complaint of mistreatment, several factors shaped their response. One was their own paternalism, which encouraged officials to view women as the weaker and more vulnerable sex and be receptive to women's self-presentation as victims, and especially in the case of privileged women a tendency toward chivalry, too. ("What's the point of this?? [K chemy eto??]," an official wrote, underlining it twice, in the margin of the letter composed by an aggrieved townsman husband,

25. On the reactionary views of some bureaucrats with a background in the law, see Daniel Orlovsky, "High Officials in the Ministry of Internal Affairs, 1855–1881," in *Russian Officialdom: The Bureaucratization of Russian Society from the Seventeenth to the Nineteenth Century,* ed. Walter McKenzie Pintner and Don Karl Rowney (Chapel Hill: University of North Carolina Press, 1980), 265, 279–80.

declaring that he and his well-born wife had become sexually intimate after a relatively brief acquaintance).[26] Another was officials' understanding of the meaning of marriage. As Nancy Shields Kollmann has noted, Peter the Great, in his second marriage in 1712, became the first public figure to affirm affective love as a marital ideal. Sentimental and romantic literature furthered this development by emphasizing the significance of individual emotions and self-fulfillment.[27] Nineteenth-century tsars themselves modeled new marital ideals. In the scenarios of power of Tsars Nicholas I and Alexander III, conjugal love and the affective family became key elements. Tsar Alexander III regarded his family as a "sacred personal sphere," a sanctuary from the outside world where he was free to express his tender and humane feelings. His son, Tsar Nicholas II, so different from his father in other respects, shared this love for family life: for Nicholas, home and children formed the "sacred center" of life.[28] Such views of marriage were shared by leading chancellery officials. Dmitrii Sipiagin, married at the age of fifty to a woman who herself was no longer young, enjoyed a warm and companionable relationship with her. According to his physician, Sipiagin displayed toward his wife a "love-friendship" (*druzhba-liubov'*) that touched the heart.[29] The Baltic German culture of both Budberg and Rikhter idealized marriages based on friendship, companionship, and lifelong mutual affection.[30] Their views also resonated with elements of the discourse on the "woman question" that engaged educated society in the second half of the nineteenth century.

26. RGIA, fond 1412, op. 212, d. 74 (Alad'ina, T., 1894), 7.

27. Nancy Shields Kollmann, "'What's Love Got to Do with It?': Changing Models of Masculinity in Muscovite and Petrine Russia," in *Russian Masculinities in History and Culture*, ed. Barbara Evans Clements, Rebecca Friedman, and Dan Healey (New York: Palgrave, 2002), 24–29. On the impact of sentimentalism, see Olga Glagoleva, "Dream and Reality of Russian Provincial Young Ladies, 1700–1850," *Carl Beck Papers*, no. 1405; N. L. Pushkareva, *Chastnaia zhizn' russkoi zhenshchiny: nevesta, zhena, liubovnitsa (X–nachalo XIX v.)* (Moscow: Ladomir, 1997), 174–76; Wagner, *Marriage, Property, and Law*, 85.

28. Wortman, *Scenarios of Power*, 2: 176, 333.

29. N. A. Vel'iaminov, "Vospominaniia," 384.

30. Heidi W. Whelan, *Adapting to Modernity: Family, Caste, and Capitalism in the World of the Nineteenth-Century Baltic German Nobility* (Cologne: Bohlau, 1999), 104, 111–12; 115–20. Whelan also notes that divorce was easier for Baltic Germans, as Lutherans, and that grounds included incompatibility of temperament and mutually avowed dislike, 122–23. As of 1900, at least three of the chancellery's eight senior officials dealing with marital disputes were Lutherans (Barons Budberg, von Freiman, and Shteiger). If, as I suspect, Baron Akkurti von Kenigsfeld was likewise a Lutheran, then the proportion of Lutherans rises to half. It is surely ironic that in their eagerness to retain control of marriage and the family, the Russian Orthodox Church left marital affairs at least partly in the hands of those who did not share the faith. Information on religion is derived from RGIA, fond 1412, op. 251, d. 365, *Obshchii spisok*, 1901–3, 79–88; and Shilov and Kuz'min, *Chleny*, 88.

Nevertheless, from the first, progressive intellectuals who looked to the law as a medium for social change questioned officials' competency to resolve marital disputes. They singled out, in particular, the extralegal nature of the chancellery's proceedings and its administrative character. Commenting in 1883 on the Petition Commission's new authority over marital disputes, the liberal *Vestnik Evropy* observed that the commission was bound to retain all the shortcomings of the Third Section. "In their long years of practice, the Third Section and gendarme field officers never established guiding principles for the resolution of marital disputes and could not by the very nature of things. The Petitions Commission in all probability will not establish them either; its activity will likewise remain unregulated by positive law." Writing in 1884, the reform-minded jurist K. K. Arsen'ev was more critical still. "Administrative, secret proceedings in the hands of individuals unaccustomed to being guided by the law and vested with discretionary authority are hardly likely to eventuate in precise and well-defined rules for resolving marital disputes," he declared. The chancellery's reach was bound to be limited, too: "It is also most likely that only a small number of individuals will resort to the central organs of administrative authority."[31]

In fact, the chancellery's functions in resolving marital disputes were neither as arbitrary nor as incompatible with a modern legal system as such critics held, and its practices bear an uncanny resemblance to those of courts of equity in England and Scotland. A court of equity, like the chancellery, acted to mitigate the harshness "which would otherwise fall on individuals from the strict observance of a general rule." A court of equity, too, ruled according to the particular circumstances of a case and its own precedents rather than established rules, by contrast with a court of law, which "rigidly adhere[d] to its own established Rules, be the Injustice arising from thence ever so apparent." Both the chancellery and courts of equity functioned alongside of, rather than in opposition to, courts of law, their jurisdiction beginning where that of the law either ended or was deficient, that is, "where a remedy is not otherwise provided by common or statute law."[32] Lacking the power to make law or dispense with established law, both operated in a distinct jurisdiction. Ironically, perhaps, even the hostility to the chancellery's authority, which proponents of a law-governed order never ceased to demonstrate, greatly resembled the antagonism which some British legal thinkers displayed toward equity courts, especially in the period before and during the English

---

31. "Delo o supruzheskikh nesoglasiiakh…," *Vestnik Evropy*, no. 11 (1883): 355; K. I. Arsen'ev, "Razluchenie suprugov kak neobkhodimyi institut brachnogo prava," *Vestnik Evropy*, no. 3 (1884): 297.

32. In the words of Blackstone, equity depended "essentially, upon the particular circumstances of each individual case." See David Lieberman, *The Province of Legislation Determined: Legal Theory in Eighteenth-Century Britain* (Cambridge: Cambridge University Press, 1989), 74–75; 166–67. My thanks to Mithi Mukherjee for this reference.

Civil War, when such courts became subject to political attack because of their links with the monarchy.[33]

The features that distinguished the chancellery from equity courts are nevertheless important to bear in mind. The chancellery was always something other than a court. Functioning within a strictly administrative framework, it was part of the imperial bureaucracy and relied on administrative personnel (mainly the police) to gather, report on and interpret evidence, and on administrative structures to provide relief. For women of the laboring classes, especially, relief often took the form of a one-year passport that required renewal (and a new investigation) for as long as five years. Moreover, the chancellery's decisions, like its procedures and evidence, remained "strictly secret," known only to the plaintiff and defendant and the person who informed them of the outcome of a case. These features continued even as chancellery officials became increasingly likely to be trained in, and show respect for, the law and to articulate attitudes toward women, childrearing, and sexuality, among other matters, that differed little from the values of those who criticized their venue and their work. Over the decades of its operation, as the courts extended their competency to rule on issues related to marital breakdown, and the purview of the chancellery and the courts came increasingly to overlap, these characteristics left the chancellery vulnerable to criticism not only from advocates of a law-governed state but also from the men and women whose marital conflicts officials sought to remedy.

IDEAS AND OPPORTUNITIES

The far-reaching institutional changes launched by Tsar Alexander II, known collectively as the Great Reforms, stimulated ideological as well as economic challenges to Russia's traditional gender order. The emancipation of the serfs in 1861 was central to the process. Releasing from servitude to noble landowners almost half of the peasant population of Russia, the emancipation of the serfs deprived many nobles of their livelihood and forced their daughters to earn a living. Equally important, the emancipation prompted many educated members of society to reject the entire way of life associated with serfdom, which allowed some (nobles) to exercise near-absolute authority over others (peasant serfs) and to live off their labor. Critically minded individuals denounced the authoritarian, patriarchal family on similar grounds, although in this case they regarded women, not serfs, as the primary victims. Writing in 1859, for example, the radical critic Nikolai Dobroliubov called the family a "Realm of Dark-

---

33. Peter Charles Hoffer, *The Law's Conscience: Equitable Constitutionalism in America* (Chapel Hill: University of North Carolina Press, 1990), pp. 17–19; 26–28; 32–36.

ness," where "despotism" reigned, constraining and distorting the dignity and will (*lichnost'*) of everyone subject to it, women especially.[34]

Informing Dobroliubov's critique was an enhanced concern with the individual person conveyed by the word *lichnost'*. Once signifying a single individual, by the nineteenth century, for liberals at least, the term *lichnost'* had come to mean the individual's struggle for autonomy and the right to express himself freely, unconstrained by the arbitrary authority of others. This is the sense of the term evoked by Elizaveta Vodovozova in her richly descriptive memoir of the 1860s. "The emancipation of the person [*lichnost'*] was the watchword, the foundation stone of the era of the 1860s," Vodovozova writes. In this era, women might lay claim to the prerogatives of *lichnost'*, too. Their labor might be an important precondition. Stressing the necessity of personal autonomy and individual development, the ethos of the era promoted women's economic independence for its own sake. Even married women should earn their own living according to this view, so as to emancipate themselves and avoid "hanging on the neck of a man."[35] These views shaped a new sexual ethos. For men of the 1860s, shared ideals, complete equality, and love freely chosen became essential ingredients in sexual unions, sanctified by marriage or not. Discussions of women's status in the family and society and of sexual relations became known as the "woman question."[36] These ideas constituted a significant "cultural movement," reshaping the ways that individuals lived their lives and experienced themselves for decades thereafter.[37]

The expansion of women's access to education during this period promoted the circulation of new ideas. Fostering the growth of a female reading public and offering some women a means to earn their livelihood, *gymnasia*, six-year secondary schools for girls modeled on those for boys, were approved in 1858; in 1876, a supplementary year of pedagogical training became available to *gymnasia* students, qualifying graduates for employment as a domestic teacher or tutor, and as teachers in elementary schools and

34. N. A. Dobroliubov, *Izbrannye sochineniia*, ed. A. Lavretskii (Moscow: Khudozhestvennaia literatura, 1947), 126–27.

35. E. N. Vodovozova, *Na zare zhizni. Memuarnye ocherki i portrety*, 2 vols. (n.p.: Khudozhestvennaia literatura, 1964), 2: 194–95, 196.

36. Irina Iukhina, *Russkii feminizm kak vyzov sovremennosti* (St. Petersburg: Aleteiia, 2007), 123–28; Barbara Alpern Engel, *Mothers and Daughters: Women of the Intelligentsia in Nineteenth-Century Russia* (New York: Cambridge University Press, 1983); and Richard Stites, *The Women's Liberation Movement in Russia: Feminism, Nihilism, and Bolshevism, 1860–1930* (Princeton, NJ: Princeton University Press, 1978).

37. I draw my definition of a cultural movement from Sherry Ortner, *Anthropology and Social Theory: Culture, Power, and the Acting Subject* (Durham, NC: Duke University Press, 2006), 11. Iukhina, *Russkii feminizm*, is particularly illuminating on the long-term consequences of the radical discourse of the 1860s. See also Bianka Pietrow-Ennker, *Russlands "neue Menschen": Die Entwicklung der Frauenbewegung von den Anfängen bis zur Oktoberrevolution* (Frankfurt am Main: Campus, 1999).

the first four classes of girls' secondary schools. In 1872, four-year "Courses for Learned Midwives" opened in St. Petersburg, and in 1876, with one year of training added, were renamed "Women's Medical Courses." That same year, largely due to the efforts of Russia's fledgling women's movement, the government sanctioned the opening of "higher courses" for women, essentially women's universities that awarded no degree. Kazan University became the first to take advantage of the opportunity; in 1878, Kiev and St. Petersburg followed. The St. Petersburg courses, known as the Bestuzhev courses, became the most well-known and long-lasting.[38]

Even during the more repressive era that followed the assassination of Tsar Alexander II on March 1, 1881, some of the ideas of the 1860s, the woman question in particular, continued to reverberate, and indeed more widely than before. In the reign of Tsar Alexander III (1881–1894), women's access to higher education was restricted, liberal journals closed, and censorship tightened, while the government sought to undo many of the liberal initiatives of the previous reign. Nevertheless, it was in this period that individuals who had reached adulthood after the initial ferment of ideas had subsided, and who remained outside the circles of the educated and privileged, expressed ideas associated with the woman question. Stringent censorship did not prevent popular magazines from celebrating women's abilities and attainments. Aiming mainly to entertain literate urban women of moderate means, the widely read *Vestnik mody* offered its readers a popularized version of the woman question, challenging notions of women's inferiority and extolling women's achievements in fields such as medicine.[39]

The appearance of Leo Tolstoy's novella, "The Kreutzer Sonata," which set off heated discussions of the "sexual question," also made the "crisis of marriage" and the subject of private life the center of wide-ranging debates.[40] The novella began to circulate in manuscript in 1889, read aloud in drawing rooms and other semiprivate spaces; it was finally published in 1891. Its male narrator, who acknowledges that he murdered his wife in a fit of sexual jealousy, relates the story of his unhappy marriage to a stranger on a train. Violating long-standing cultural taboos with its explicit references to sexuality, the novella at the same time adopted a negative view of sexuality itself. Sexual

---

38. Christine Johanson, *Women's Struggles for Higher Education in Russia, 1855–1900* (Kingston: McGill University Press, 1987).

39. Carolyn Marks, " 'Providing Amusement for the Ladies': The Rise of the Russian Women's Magazine in the 1880s," in *An Improper Profession: Women, Gender, and Journalism in Late Imperial Russia,* ed. Barbara T. Norton and Jehanne Gheith (Chapel Hill: University of North Carolina Press, 2001), 110–12. See also V. D. Orlova, "Otrazhenie povsednevnykh zabot zhenshchiny v massovykh pechatnykh izdaniiakh nachala XX v.," in *Zhenskaia povsednevnost' v Rossii v XVIII–XX vv. Materialy mezhdunarodnoi nauchnoi konferentsii 15 sentiabria 2003 goda* (Tambov: Tambovskii gosudarstvennyi universitet, 2003), 43.

40. Peter Ulf Møller, *Postlude to "The Kreutzer Sonata": Tolstoj and the Debate on Sexuality in Russian Literature in the 1890s,* trans. John Kendal (Leiden: Brill, 1988), 216.

FIGURE 5. *Family life according to the Domostroi*
First frame: He marries her
Second frame: And he begins at once to beat her
Third frame: And she beats him
Fourth frame: And relatives stick their noses in
Fifth frame: And a bird flies in the window
Sixth frame: And these are their children
Seventh frame: And there's an automatic spanking machine to punish them
Eighth frame: And a mechanical teacher of arithmetic
Ninth frame: And she falls in love with the mechanical teacher
Tenth frame: And they separate and go to different countries and live there with others, and their descendants scatter across the ocean.
Strekoza, no. 41 (1905), M. E. Saltykov-Shchedrin Public Library.

По нынѣшнимъ временамъ.

— Какъ, Мари, ты недавно вышла замужъ и уже· разводишься со своимъ· мужемъ? Что это значитъ?

— А то, что мы совершенно не подходимъ .другъ къ ·другу... Представь себѣ, онъ лѣтомъ хочетъ жить на дачѣ въ Озеркахъ, а я—въ Павловскѣ.. Ясно, что мы не созданы одинъ для другого.

FIGURE 6. *"In our times"*
"So, Marie, you just got married and you've already separated from your husband? What does that mean?
"It means we're completely incompatible. . . . Imagine, in the summer he wants to live at a dacha in Ozerki, and I, at Pavlovsk. It's clear we're not made for each other."
Semeinye iliuzii *(1908),* M. E. Saltykov-Shchedrin Public Library.

relations, the novella suggested, degrade men and women even within marriage: sexual desire, elicited by the wife herself, was to blame for the murderous outcome of the narrator's marriage. The novella was explicitly antifeminist: apart from the murdered wife, Tolstoy's sole female character is a lady "plain and no longer young," a caricature of the woman intellectual, who smoked and appeared harassed, and in whose mouth Tolstoy placed hollow-sounding speeches on behalf of love-marriage, women's dignity, and women's education. In the furor that ensued, writers and philosophers, virtually all of them male, attacked Tolstoy's views from all sides on the pages of contemporary newspapers and thick journals. Some criticized him for denying the possibility of sexual equality, others for disparaging the Christian sacrament of marriage. Still others, among them Elizaveta D'iakonova and her classmates at the Bestuzhev courses, belonged to the "moralist camp," as Laura Engelstein has dubbed it, interpreting the novella as calling for a single sexual standard, but only privately.[41]

Whatever the response, the novella clearly had a "consciousness-raising" impact, either by itself or as a result of its interplay with the discourse on the woman question, with which Tolstoy himself so clearly took issue.[42] This is evident in the works of the few women authors, feminist in orientation, who addressed Tolstoy's ideas in print. Offering a view of the problems of conventional marriage very different from Tolstoy's, such writers placed female subjectivity at the center of their narrative. Thus Olga Runova ("How I Fell in Love," [1899], published in one of Russia's largest daily newspapers, the conservative *Novoe vremia*) and Maria Krestovskaia ("The Howl," [1900]) played variations on the theme of the loveless and stifling marriage.[43] Feeling "buried alive" in a marriage arranged at her grandmother's behest and revolted by her husband, the heroine of Runova's tale, a provincial schoolteacher, falls deeply in love with a zemstvo veterinarian and dreams of eloping with him and abandoning her "hateful and repellent life." But in the end, she remains with her husband, her life changed only by the recognition that personal happiness is beyond her grasp.[44] Likewise, Maria Krestovskaia graphically depicted her heroine's distaste for sexual contact with her husband but provided no alternative. "Sometimes he would still turn up, with his caresses long gone cold, and take me, as one might take a glass of tea from the

---

41. Engelstein, *Keys to Happiness*, 220. Elizaveta D'iakonova, *Dnevnik russkoi zhenshchiny* (1912; repr., Moscow: Zakharov, 2004), 206–7. For the full range of views, see Møller, *Postlude*.

42. Møller, *Postlude*, 117.

43. O. Runova, "Kak ia byla vliublena," *Novoe vremia*, no. 8301 (1899); on Krestovskaia, see Catriona Kelly, *A History of Russian Women's Writing, 1820–1992* (New York: Oxford University Press, 1994), 137–39; and Rosalind Marsh, *Women and Russian Culture: Projections and Self-Perceptions* (New York: Berghahn Books, 1998), 192–94.

44. Runova, "Kak ia byla vliublena."

hand of a housemaid, not looking at her face and scarcely noticing that she was there at all."[45]

Anastasia Verbitskaia's novel *She Was Liberated!* (*Osvobodilas!* [1899]) appears to have had the greatest appeal to readers. Verbitskaia's educated and cultivated heroine, Lizaveta Melgunova, can be seen as a rejoinder to Tolstoy's unflattering portrait of the modern woman. Like Tolstoy's nameless female passenger, Melgunova is plain and no longer young, "with the face of a governess, thin and faded." Miserable in her marriage to a philandering physician, she is helpless to leave him, bound by her love for her only child and fear of losing custody and by her inability to support the two of them on her own. The "passport question," although never identified as such, plays a role in the novel and sets the stage for its tragic ending. Insisting on his marital rights, the physician refuses to release his unhappy wife. "I'd find you even in the depths of the ocean," he says when she informs him that she plans to leave, and he threatens to exercise the powers that men enjoyed by law to hold her prisoner. "I'll have you brought back under police escort [*po etapu*].... You're going nowhere!"[46]

A brief but rapturous affair makes it still harder for Lizaveta to endure her marriage. She has long since ceased to have sexual relations with her husband, having spurned his overtures after discovering his repeated infidelities. But she yearns for the intimacy and comfort of sexual contact, if not for sex itself. She yearns even more for the shared ideas and ideals that constituted a key element in the 1860s vision of marriage and that she had once enjoyed with her husband. These longings prompt her to fall in love and share one night of sexual bliss with a younger man, a student radical subsequently exiled to far-off Siberia and unlikely ever to return. In a final reconfiguring of the Tolstoyan plot, Verbitskaia's adulterous heroine takes her own life after a forced sexual encounter with her husband, suicide being the only means to escape from him. The novel found an eager readership. First published in 1899 in *Mir bozhii*, it then appeared as a book that by 1912 was in its fourth edition.

Circulating in "thick" journals and the popular press, popularized versions of the "woman question" and discussions of the "marriage question" both reflected and helped normalize female marital discontent. They legitimated the restlessness of some married women and offered them a vocabulary with which to speak of their unhappiness, while encouraging others to respond with sympathy to their appeals.

---

45. Quoted in Kelly, *History of Russian Women's Writing*, 138. Compare with Leo Tolstoy's Anna Karenina, likewise cold to her husband's embraces, whose revulsion we can guess at only by the light that leaves her eyes in his presence.

46. Anastasia Verbitskaia, *Osvobodilas!* 4th ed. (Moscow: Pechatnoe delo, 1912), 4, 99, 137–38.

How in the world did such petitioners scattered across the vast expanses of Russia learn about the chancellery? When the chancellery was instituted in 1884, a decision had been made to avoid publicizing its role in resolving marital discord, since to publicize it would be to acknowledge the fact that an administrative body was formally empowered to act in violation of the law forbidding spousal separation.[47] In consequence, neither the laws governing the Imperial Chancellery for Receipt of Petitions nor official publications regarding its functions and procedures made any mention of that role. Instead, they described its competency in the most general terms: The chancellery accepted petitions that involved the "granting of a grace [*milost'*] under special circumstances that are not subject to the operation of the general laws, when this will not infringe on civil rights and interests that the law protects."[48] Articles 11 and 12 of the rules governing the petitioning process barred lawyers from representing individual petitioners.

Still, the evidence suggests that its functions soon became fairly widely known. "Tomorrow I will send in a petition and they will give me a passport and I will go away," declares the fictional heroine of Anton Chekhov's short story "The Wife" (1892). It features a noble couple resident in the countryside.[49] Petitioning authorities for redress of grievances was a process with which peasants had long been familiar; illiterate or semiliterate villagers simply turned to a literate neighbor.[50] The street lawyers who plied their trade in taverns, marketplaces, and in the vicinity of the courts made it their business to learn what their clients needed to know and were prepared to compose such petitions for a small fee.[51] Educated women or women with the economic wherewithal might consult licensed attorneys, who were certainly aware of the chancellery's mission. Although, as noted above, attorneys were barred from representing their clients, their hand is sometimes evident in petitions and subsequent correspondence, in

47. See RGIA, fond 1412, op. 241, d. 21, 8; *Otchet po Gosudarstvennomu sovetu za 1884* (St. Petersburg, 1886), 47–48.

48. On the regulations establishing the chancellery, see *Svod zakonov Rossiiskoi imperii* (St. Petersburg, 1895), vol. 1, pt. 2, 167–70.

49. Anton Chekhov, "The Wife," in *The Tales of Chekhov*, trans. Constance Garnett, 13 vols. (New York: Ecco, 1985), 5: 32.

50. Corinne Gaudin, *Ruling Peasants: Village and State in Late Imperial Russia* (DeKalb: Northern Illinois University Press, 2007), 92.

51. Vladimir Berenshtam, *Za pravo* (St. Petersburg: Biblioteka dlia vsekh, 1905), 73; Joan Neuberger, "'Shysters' or Public Servants? Uncertified Lawyers and Legal Aid for the Poor in Late Imperial Russia," *Russian History* 23, nos. 1–4 (1996): 295–310; and William E. Pomeranz, "Justice from Underground: The History of the Underground *Advokatura*," *Russian Review* 52, no. 3 (1993): 321–40. Rules for petitioning the chancellery required the person who composed the petition to sign his/her name, a rule that was usually observed.

references to the laws governing marriage or in the involvement of experts, medical experts especially, to certify, for example, that a petitioner was in no physical or psychological state to resume cohabitation. Women might also be directed to the chancellery by others to whom they appealed for relief, such as the police, the governor's office, the courts, or, by the early twentieth century, feminist organizations, the Russian Society to Protect Women in particular, which claimed to handle hundreds of such appeals every year. In 1902, for example, the Baku Society to Protect Women sheltered the townswoman Anastasia Obraztsova, a former brothel prostitute, and paid for her consultation with a lawyer after her husband began to treat her cruelly and threatened her with a knife but refused to approve her passport.[52]

In 1895, a guide to the rules of the chancellery, published unofficially, began to include a model letter that potential petitioners might copy, which Praskovia Ariian then reproduced in her feminist *First Women's Calendar,* first published in 1899. The tone and detail of the model petition echoed that of countless real ones, many submitted before as well as after the publication of the model. It described a husband drunk and unemployed and a wife whose efforts to support herself and three small children were continually thwarted by the husband, and it concluded with an appeal to the emperor's mercy: "In this hopeless position, wishing to preserve my right to honest labor and ability to feed my children and raise them in the spirit of religion and morality, which is impossible because of the bad example my husband sets, I resolved to fall at the feet of His Majesty, so that, after verifying the truth of the above, you will give me and the children a separate passport to live anywhere in the Russian Empire."[53]

Thus, while the chancellery was neither as well known nor as accessible as the courts, the Justice of the Peace courts especially, those who made use of it were not limited mainly to "members of the higher and middling estates who have the possibility of spending time in the capital and personally seeing to their case," as some of its critics charged.[54] Although, at the time of petitioning, the majority, perhaps two-thirds, resided in one of Russia's two major cities, Moscow and St. Petersburg, others dwelt in Riga, Novgorod, Saratov, Samara, Irkutsk, and other urban centers, small and large. Provincial women's appeals offer evidence of the "cultural integration" that, according

---

52. RGIA, fond 1412, op. 225, d. 2 (Obraztsova, A., 1902), 1. The Russian Society to Protect Women played a role in another separation appeal as well. See ibid., op. 228, d. 83 (Sokolova, T., 1909).

53. *Pravila o poriadke priniatiia i napravleniia prosheniia i zhalob, na Vysochaishee imia prinosimykh (Svod Zakonov t. 1 i ch. II po prodolzheniiu 1895 g.) s privedeniiem pozdneishikh uzakonenii i so prilozheniem obraztsov form proshenii i zhalob* (St. Petersburg: Iuridicheskii knizhnii magazin, 1895), 14–15. A different letter appears in the 1902 version of this same publication. Instructions for petitioning the chancellery can be found in Praskov'ia Ariian, ed., *Pervyi zhenskii kalendar* (St. Petersburg: Trud, 1901), 95, and on 96, the model letter.

54. Arsen'ev, "Razluchenie suprugov," 297.

to Richard Stites, began in the pre-Reform era.[55] Still other petitioners, albeit less than 10 percent, remained in or near the peasant villages where they or their husbands first saw the light of day. Some of those villages were so remote that it took chancellery investigators a day or more just to get there, traveling by train and then by peasant cart. Even for such women, the system over which the chancellery presided had certain advantages. Once a woman petitioned, the chancellery assumed the entire cost of investigation, even when it required travel to a remote village. Dossiers of appeals from the provinces often contain the itemized expenses of the investigating officer.[56] Suing for divorce in ecclesiastic court or bringing a suit in the regular courts, by contrast, could be a very expensive process.

To bring a suit in the regular courts (although not the Justice of the Peace courts or the township courts, the latter presided over by peasant judges), plaintiffs had to pay fees for registering documents, retaining lawyers, and compensating witnesses. These represented a substantial burden if the plaintiffs failed to apply or qualify for the special exemptions granted the poor. In one chancellery case I have read, which went to court in 1912, the woman's inability to produce the five rubles required to cover the expenses of her witnesses led a Kostroma circuit court to decide in her husband's favor and order her to resume cohabitation.[57] Petitioners to the chancellery were even exempt from the usual fee for registering official documents involving legal matters (article 10 of its regulations). The chancellery's economic accessibility is evident in the large proportion of laboring and poor women among the appellants.

Petitioning operated by rather different rules than did the courts. As Thomas Kuehn, among others, has noted, in ascertaining the "truth" of past experience, court cases are both revealing and problematic as sources. Legal rules and terms operate as a kind of filter, transfixing social realities and subtly restructuring them.[58] Those rules were less salient for petitioners. The process of petitioning had its own conventions, to be sure. Petitions were addressed to an all-powerful monarch whose authority and mercy the

55. From the late 1830s and the early 1840s, Russia's provinces "were on a slow but continuous trek toward cultural integration with the rest of the country" (Richard Stites, *Serfdom, Society, and the Arts: The Pleasure and the Power* [New Haven: Yale University Press, 2006], 49).

56. See, for example, RGIA, fond 1412, op. 223, d. 43 (Matrosova, M., 1886).

57. The Moscow district court upheld the decision in 1913 and refused her request for child support on the basis of her husband's willingness to resume cohabitation. See ibid, op. 221, d. 195 (Kuz'mina, A., 1906), 41, 44, 51–52.

58. Thomas Kuehn, "Reading Microhistory: The Example of *Giovanni* and *Lusanna*," *Journal of Modern History* 61, no. 3 (1989): 515. Legal rules were also of little moment in appeals for divorce deriving from the laboring classes, who could not afford to consult a lawyer. See Gregory Freeze, "Profane Narratives about a Holy Sacrament: Marriage and Divorce in Late Imperial Russia," in *Sacred Stories: Religion and Spirituality in Modern Russia*, ed. Mark D. Steinberg and Heather J. Coleman (Bloomington: Indiana University Press, 2007), 155–57.

process was intended to uphold, a political reality that played a role in shaping appeals. Most petitions referred to the writer's helplessness as well as victimization at her husband's hands and her worthiness for the tsar's special favor; many appealed for justice without reference to law, thus reaffirming the absolute authority of the ruler.[59] Still, the formulaic character of petitions should not be overstated. For one thing, by no means all petitioners employed the humble terms of supplicant that offered the "archetypal expression of the relation between subject and ruler in a paternalistic state," as Sheila Fitzpatrick has put it.[60] Even when they did, the language of supplication often served as a kind of "envelope" which held a much more complex message. Olga Pantiugina's petition, and in some respects even the model petition cited above, alert us to the existence of other modes of self-presentation and address. The fact of the matter is that on the subject of marital conflict, the state never provided a "clear script" for petitioners.[61] The absence of a clear script is even more evident in the detailed narratives of marital breakdown that followed the petition, in which husbands and wives drew on the cultural expectations of their milieu to structure their stories, with richly varied results.

Nevertheless, for the petitioner the process might be fraught with difficulties. If John Comaroff is correct in his assertion that power rests "in the relative capacity to construct reality," then in trying to make a compelling case the power of most petitioners was quite modest.[62] Although they might craft petitions, submit extended counternarratives, name witnesses, submit evidentiary documents, even bombard the chancellery with letters updating a case or questioning a decision, they exercised only limited control over their own story. Investigations proceeded according to a template that the chancellery devised for the purpose of ascertaining the "truth" of a case. It began with efforts to reconcile the quarreling couple and, failing that, to convince the husband voluntarily to agree to a separate passport for the wife. A substantial minority of husbands, roughly 20 percent, did agree, sometimes in return for their wives' written promises never again to ask for financial or child support, and at least once in return for the transfer of a sizable sum of money from wife to husband.[63] If the husband agreed to

---

59. On the role of the state in shaping the content of petitions, see Madhavan K. Palat, "Regulating Conflict through the Petition," in *Social Identities in Revolutionary Russia*, ed. Madhavan K. Palat (New York: Palgrave, 2001), 86–112.

60. Sheila Fitzpatrick, "Editor's Introduction: Petitions and Denunciations in Russian and Soviet History," *Russian History* 24, nos. 1–2 (1997): 4, 6.

61. Gaudin, *Ruling Peasants*, 127.

62. John L. Comaroff, "Foreword," in *Contested States: Law, Hegemony, and Resistance*, ed. Mindie Lazarus-Black and Susan F. Hirsch (New York: Routledge, 1994), xii.

63. Reconciliation efforts succeeded in around 20 percent of cases by the chancellery's reckoning but in a far smaller proportion(1–2 percent) of those cases about which the chancellery submitted reports that have been preserved. On the chancellery's figures, see Wagner, *Marriage, Property, and Law*, 91. For a case that involved the transfer of a substantial sum of money, see Barbara Alpern Engel,

the passport in the presence of a representative of the chancellery, his wife was ensured it in perpetuity unless the husband appealed for reconsideration.

If the husband refused, officials began their investigation by enumerating the "questions to be addressed," which determined the evidence to be gathered and the shape of the final report. In addition to queries concerning the couple's economic and social status, age at marriage, and so on, in the first years of the chancellery's operations the questions included: "What is the petitioner's behavior, character, life style, and morality? Has she been observed in any reprehensible behavior? Is she involved in an illicit relationship with another man? Has she ever been under suspicion or in court, and for what in particular, and how did the case end?" Identical questions followed concerning the husband. By the mid-1890s, the form had become more gender neutral, referring to the age, conduct, character, and so on of the "spouses."[64]

Set within this framework, the evidence in a case arrived at the chancellery both raw and in a form thoroughly digested by others. Investigative reports were usually generated at succeeding levels of the administrative hierarchy, officials at each level deciding which words to trust and flattening contradictions in the narratives. Police officers usually conducted investigations on the spot if the plaintiff was a townswoman, peasant, or wife of an artisan, or if the district lacked a gendarme. Underpaid, overworked, poorly trained and educated, police officers brought the values of their humble backgrounds to their interpretation of a case.[65] Gendarme officers either supervised such investigations or, if the parties derived from privileged backgrounds, usually conducted the investigations themselves. Although gendarmes sometimes simply rewrote the reports of policemen and transmitted them upward, more often their reports expressed their own values, which, unlike those of policemen, were inflected by a paternalism rooted in gendarmes' role as protector of the oppressed. Gendarmes derived from the bottommost layer of the nobility–privileged but mostly landless—and were a highly select group—a "gentleman's club," in the words of Dominic Lieven. To qualify as a gendarme, a man had to meet strict criteria—to have graduated in the top third of a military or cadet school, completed a minimum of six years of military service, and performed well in oral interviews that subjected his conduct, knowledge, and views to

"Freedom and Its Limitations: A Peasant Wife Seeks to Escape an Abusive Husband," in *The Human Tradition in Imperial Russia*, ed. Christine D. Worobec (Lanham, MD: Rowman and Littlefield, 2009), 115–28.

64. TsGIA SPb, fond 569, op. 20, d. 103, 15. The updated questions are set forth in V. A. Veremenko, *Dvorianskaia sem'ia i gosudarstvennaia politika Rossii (vtoraia polovina XIX–nachalo XX v.)* (St. Petersburg: Evropeiskii dom, 2007), 243.

65. Neil Weissman, "Regular Police in Tsarist Russia, 1900–1914," *Russian Review* 44 (January 1985): 45–68; and Weissman, *Reform in Tsarist Russia: The State Bureaucracy and Local Government, 1900–1914* (New Brunswick, NJ: Rutgers University Press, 1981), 24–25. The low level of education of some police rendered their reports almost completely illegible to this reader.

intensive scrutiny. By the close of the nineteenth century, gendarmes, like chancellery officials, were often schooled in the law.[66] In addition, the governors-general of a city or governors of a province often added their interpretations of a case. These men, the "tsar's viceroys," as Richard Robbins has called them, were well born and increasingly well educated and prepared for their position; like chancellery officials, they owed primary loyalty to the tsar with whom they were directly linked.[67] Speaking to chancellery officials as elite to elite as well as "man to man," the voices of gendarmes and governors carried special weight.

To show how the process might unfold in practice, I now return to the Pantiugin case with which this chapter begins. The case is by no means "typical," but then no case really is. At seventy-six pages, the Pantiugin dossier is lengthier than some but much shorter than others; most cases were resolved within one year, whereas this case dragged on for nine. I have chosen it mainly because it conveys with unusual vividness the difficulty of adjusting the messy details of everyday life to fit the format of chancellery procedures, the bureaucratic red tape in which women's pleas might become enmeshed, and the range of authorities whose voices repeated, amplified, or distorted the words of those whose actions they judged. As the contradictory portraits of Olga Pantiugina emerge in her dossier, they demonstrate the difficulties a woman might experience in controlling her own story and the still greater difficulties a reader might experience in establishing the "truth" of a case. In the chapters to follow, I sometimes summarize, thereby flattening out, the story of a marriage, suppressing contradictions and discordances, much as did those who reported on their investigations to the chancellery. This more detailed look at a dossier is intended to alert the reader to such elisions. As the reader follows the unfolding of this case, it might be useful to bear in mind that the couple in question cohabited for precisely *eight days*.

OLGA PANTIUGINA'S CASE

From the beginning, Olga Pantiugina had difficulty making a successful case. A woman who had run away with her lover only a short time after her marriage, she

---

66. A. P. Martynov, "Moia sluzhba v otdel'nom korpuse zhandarmov," in *"Okhranka": Vospominaniia rukovoditelei politicheskogo syska*, ed. Z. I. Peregudova, 2 vols. (Moscow: Novoe literaturnoe obozrenie, 2004), 1: 50–51; Dominic Lieven, "The Security Police, Civil Rights, and the Fate of the Russian Empire, 1855–1917," in *Civil Rights in Imperial Russia*, ed. Crisp and Edmondson, 252; Jonathan Daly, *Autocracy under Siege: Security Police and Opposition in Russia, 1866–1905* (DeKalb: Northern Illinois University Press, 1998), 54–56. For gendarmes' "high personal morality," see George Yaney, *The Systematization of Russian Government* (Urbana-Champaign: University of Illinois Press, 1973), 224. On legal and other training, see Z. I. Peregudova, *Politicheskii sysk Rossii 1880–1917* (Moscow: ROSSPEN, 2000), 337–41.

67. Richard G. Robbins, Jr., *The Tsar's Viceroys: Russian Provincial Governors in the Last Years of the Empire* (Ithaca, NY: Cornell University Press, 1987), 1–43.

was ill suited to play the role of a victim who deserved the sympathy of investigators and merited the "mercy" of a separate passport, although she did the best she could. Between 1887 and 1893, Olga Pantiugina petitioned the chancellery three times. Each time, the investigation yielded a different picture. The first was decidedly negative, drawn by a police investigator openly sympathetic to her husband and repelled by Olga's self-confidence and forthright speech. Reporting to the chancellery on his fruitless efforts to reconcile the Pantiugins, the investigator described how Nikolai Pantiugin, "in tears," accused his wife of conduct that brought him shame and sought to persuade her to "abandon her vicious life," as the officer put it, and return to his home. Rather than acceding to this appeal to her better moral self, the officer reported, Olga swore at [*rugala*] Nikolai with expressions the officer found "most impermissible." Refusing to be intimidated by the officer's presence, Olga proved equally unyielding about sexual matters. Because her petition had alleged that Nikolai was incapable of fulfilling his conjugal obligations, the officer posed the question to Nikolai directly: "Did you have sexual congress with your wife?" "Yes," Nikolai replied. Having led an "abstemious life," he had preserved his sexual capacities to that very day. He felt "perfectly capable of fulfilling his conjugal duties," Nikolai asserted. Not fulfilling for her, his wife retorted, according to the officer's report: "In the course of their week-long marriage, although there was a kind of sexual congress, it was very far from what a young woman required."[68]

The officer's report doomed Olga's case. It suggested that she was, at the very least, no one's victim. Moreover, because Olga had declined to name witnesses, no one spoke favorably on her behalf. Her husband's children from a previous marriage were the only witnesses to the couple's marital difficulties, she declared, and she certainly did not expect them to speak the truth. The one witness named by Nikolai proclaimed him to be a "moderate fellow" who, when he drank at all, never drank to excess. This was sufficient for the chancellery. Having considered this written evidence behind closed doors, in February 1888, five months after Olga petitioned, officials concluded that the investigation had failed to uphold her claims. "Since her allegations of his incapacity for sexual relations were refuted by her own words during the questioning [presumably a reference to 'a kind of sexual congress'], and since she herself is guilty of infidelity, her petition is rejected," their report concluded. Intended for the eyes of the tsar, such a summary brought an end to the case.[69]

A second report offered a more nuanced but also a more contradictory picture of Olga and her marriage. Chancellery rules forbid petitioners to reopen an appeal once it had been rejected unless they could present compelling new evidence. In 1890, Olga claimed she could. With this petition, she produced two bills of exchange dated August

68. RGIA, fond 1412, op. 226, d. 8 (Pantiugina), 6–7.
69. Ibid., 12.

1888, each worth one hundred rubles, which she claimed her husband had required from her in exchange for a separate passport. He approved the passport for a year, she asserted, and after that revoked it.[70] This time, Olga named witnesses to corroborate her story, among them neighbors and police in the town of Kolpino, where she owned a house. This second investigation, far more thorough than the first, produced a welter of conflicting testimony in a variety of voices. In addition to the testimony of witnesses that Olga herself had named, at the request of officials the police in the Aleksandr-Nevskii quarter of St. Petersburg, where she was then in residence, submitted their own reports. So did the governors of St. Petersburg and Novgorod provinces. Each of these reports summarized the outcome of an investigation. That from Kolpino was brief, noting only that Olga owned a house in Kolpino, did not work for a living, and "according to rumor, had lived with Iakovlev, from whom she is now separated." The police officer of the Aleksandr-Nevskii quarter reported that Olga lived a "modest" life, had no occupation other than housework, and, "based on the testimony of her cook, a peasant woman from Vyshnii Volochek, is having an affair with her boarder, Vladimir Iakovlev, twenty-four years of age, by whom she is pregnant." By contrast, the St. Petersburg governor's report made no mention of the servant's testimony, noting only that Olga lived a "reputable" life and was known to have done nothing wrong.[71]

The most extensive report, and the most damning for Olga, derived from the governor of Novgorod province, where Nikolai was still living. According to this version of the story, in which the testimony of numerous local witnesses was summarized in the governor's words, Nikolai was "calm, well-behaved, and morally upright." He had married ignorant of the "moral qualities" of his wife, who brought no dowry to the wedding, just her clothing and three children. She was so poor that Nikolai had had to give her two hundred rubles for clothing and other items needed for the wedding ceremony. Nikolai learned of Olga's relationship to Iakovlev only after the marriage, when Iakovlev showed up at his house, purportedly shouting, "She's not your wife, she's mine; today she's with you but tomorrow she'll be with me. I'll take her away from you." Iakovlev agreed to leave only after Nikolai gave him a gold bracelet. Eight days after the wedding, Olga fled her husband for her lover, "openly continuing her sexual connection [*sviaz*]," then asked her husband for a separate passport. The governor rejected Olga's contention that Nikolai extorted money from her, explaining the two hundred rubles in bills of exchange as compensation for the money spent on the wedding: "The husband has no need to extort money from his wife because he is a man of means. He is willing to reconcile with her but not to approve a passport." In the

70. In the file is a note from the townspeople's administration (*meshchanskoe upravlenie*) of Vyshnii Volochek, Tver, stating that Pantiugin had appeared in their office on June 17, 1889, forbidding them to issue her a passport without his permission.

71. RGIA, fond 1412, op. 226, d. 8, 21–29.

governor's opinion, the breakdown of the marriage was exclusively the result of Olga's immoral conduct. The governor's report determined the outcome of the case, which Olga again lost.[72]

Only in her third and final effort did Olga Pantiugina manage to present herself in a positive light, and even then this more positive self-presentation was not sufficient to incline the authorities in her favor. On October 26, 1893, the persistent Pantiugina petitioned again, having managed to live on passports approved by her husband since 1889. She was petitioning now, Olga wrote, because her husband had recently appeared at her house and after staying for several days, beat her and demanded that a police officer return her under police escort to his own place of residence. "But my husband has no permanent place of residence and lives a nomadic life," she explained in her petition.[73] This time, she managed to adduce evidence to confirm her allegations of Nikolai's acquisitive aims and coarse and violent conduct and to produce a witness who spoke unequivocally in her favor.

A friend from Kolpino, a hereditary honored citizen with whom she and her second husband had shared an apartment, testified to Olga's exemplary qualities.[74] She was "entirely moral, a thrifty housewife, an exemplary wife to her husband, and a solicitous mother to her children." Nikolai Pantiugin, by contrast, had made a bad impression on this witness. Without a job or permanent place of residence, he "never declined an offer of vodka." Nikolai married for money, he asserted, upholding Olga's original claim, and adding that when Olga refused to allow Nikolai access to her property, he behaved so badly that the police had to be summoned. A second document, a report from a Kolpino police officer elaborated on these circumstances, reporting that Nikolai had counted on the marriage to improve his declining trade and material circumstances: his house was mortgaged for eleven thousand rubles and was about to be sold at auction. "The financial situation became clear not long after the wedding; and he, having been refused money by his wife, abruptly altered his lifestyle: he began to drink, to find fault with her, and to threaten her with beatings." She then returned to Kolpino with a separate passport; they had lived separately ever since. But every so often he paid a visit, and the visits invariably eventuated in fights. "He is always drunk and demands money from his wife.... He has no property at all, gets drunk, and wanders from monastery to monastery as a pilgrim." Absent from this report are any references to Iakovlev, the lover.[75]

---

72. Ibid., 31, 33.

73. Ibid., 38.

74. Hereditary honored citizen was an honorific category that conferred privileged status, which the bearer, or his or her forebears, had earned by some exemplary activity.

75. RGIA, fond 1412, op. 226, d. 8 (Pantiugina), 38, 41, 45–46.

Unfortunately for Olga, bureaucratic red tape intervened between her and her passport, a not uncommon occurrence. A third document noted that Nikolai had disappeared. This third document brought what might have been a favorable case to a close. "In light of the husband's disappearance," the chancellery refused her request. Instead, they sent her a printed form, explaining that according to the procedures for appealing to His Majesty, newly revised in 1892, petitioners in matters involving disappearance (*bezvestnaia otluchka*) must present to the local authorities a preliminary request for assistance in locating the missing party.[76] That Olga wanted to separate from, rather than to locate the missing party, was of no import.

And there the file might have closed, had not Pantiugin himself contacted the chancellery in November 1894. He had approved a one-year passport for his wife in 1892, Nikolai complained, with the understanding that when the year ended, she would live with him again. But Olga failed to fulfill their agreement. And the Kolpino police refused to restore her to him under police escort as he requested. Olga's most recent petition to the chancellery, the police had explained to him, gave her the right to a temporary (usually six-month) passport while the case was under investigation. Nikolai asked the chancellery to reject his wife's appeal. "My wife's allegations...cannot have any compelling basis. She lives a life in conflict with the rules of honor, that is, a debauched and exceedingly extravagant lifestyle, from which I've tried to save her and return her to a moral and more religious and dignified way of life," he wrote. As evidence of her unseemly conduct, he quoted part of a letter she had sent to the local police, seeking to enlist their authority to buttress her own, more vulnerable position. "Police surveillance could well be set over the person who calls himself Pantiugin...," her denunciation read, "since that subject, despite his advanced years, is capable of everything reprehensible and shrinks from no vulgarity, and all his foul deeds he tries to conceal beneath a hypocritical, God-fearing, and supposedly, God-loving man, when in fact he is what people call a wolf in sheep's clothing." Her claims that he was difficult to live with he dismissed entirely. The blame was entirely hers, he insisted, referring again to her adulterous and disorderly conduct: "She has no desire for family life with her husband, because she has grown accustomed to living with her lover, with whom she conceived an illegitimate daughter. She married me exclusively from financial considerations."[77]

Pantiugin emphasized the contrast between himself and his wife. As a woman who carried on openly with a lover, Olga, in his rendition, had violated the most fundamental requirement of female honor, thereby threatening public order. Nikolai's conduct,

---

76. Ibid., 52, 53–54.

77. Ibid., 57–58, 61, 66, 67, 68. For similar efforts to use denunciation for a person's own advantage, see Jeffrey Burds, *Peasant Dreams and Market Politics: Labor Migration and the Russian Village, 1861–1905* (Pittsburgh: University of Pittsburgh Press, 1998), 186–218.

in contrast, was exemplary as both husband and tsarist subject according to his own self-presentation: "As concerns myself, I have the honor to inform Your Majesty that my lifestyle is God-fearing and seemly [*bogopristoinyi*], hardworking, and very sober, and that in my position as a townsman, I have through my labor obtained sufficient means to feed a wife, which everyone who knows me in my town will confirm, as will the local police." Thus the chancellery should reject "the petition with which my wife has burdened it, which is based on lies, and ask the appropriate party to bring my wife back to my home and then let me know what His Imperial Majesty has granted an honorable, God-fearing toiler [*truzhennik*], faithful to the throne."[78] This time, the reports upheld this positive picture: Nikolai was sober and quiet, and together with his daughter kept a shop in the town of Bologoe, which earned around one thousand rubles a year. Before the chancellery could arrive at a final decision, however, Nikolai agreed to approve Olga's passport. He did so most probably and as in former years, in exchange for money. A chancellery report closed the case on September 12, 1895, noting that her behavior was "good" and that the husband had agreed to the passport.[79]

. . .

In the Pantiugin case, as in many others on which this book relies, the "truth" of the marriage is never quite clear, differing according to the accounts of husband, wife, witnesses, policemen, governors, and so on, although officials almost invariably claimed to have discovered the "truth" nonetheless. Was Nikolai Pantiugin a drunken, brutal, money-grubbing sponger or a hard-working, God-fearing businessman and family man—or even some combination of the two? How much did his character and behavior even matter, given that Olga, too, had very likely married for money and had certainly been involved in a protracted liaison with her boarder, flagrantly violating the norms of female chastity?

The answers to such questions depended to a significant degree on the testimony and reporting of others, which almost invariably reflected the gendered expectations of the time and milieu in addition to other factors. These expectations, which required modesty, chastity, and assiduous housewifery (*domovitost'*) from an honorable married townswoman, rendered it exceedingly difficult for Olga to make an effective case. Frank, outspoken, and subject to no man's authority, as well as sexually self-assertive, at least as she emerges from the dossier, in fact Olga displayed none of the characteristics of chaste and helpless victim of male despotism that usually persuaded officials of the merits of a woman's case in the early years of the chancellery's practice. These rigorous expectations would gradually ease, in part due to broader cultural shifts and the turnover in chancellery personnel, in part because of the impact of women's

78. RGIA, fond 1412, op. 226, d. 8 (Pantiugina), 57–58.
79. Ibid., 68–72, 76.

own self-presentations. But in Pantiugina's case as in others, the "real cause" of marital breakdown as officials came to interpret it depended not only on the petitioner or her husband's skill in crafting a story that contained sufficient "truth" to withstand considerable scrutiny, but also on whether that story included narrative elements that evoked a sympathetic response in others—initially in witnesses, but ultimately, in the men who interpreted other people's words for their superiors—that is, gendarmes, governors and governor generals, and finally, chancellery officials, at the top.

Making Marriage
ROMANTIC IDEALS AND FEMALE RHETORIC

"When I finished my studies at the pension in 1888, at the age of seventeen,...I became aware that my father wanted to marry me off as soon as possible," began the 1890 petition of Olimpiada Sergunina, daughter of the Moscow merchant Ivan Kozlov. "Completely subject to my father's will and inexperienced, I married according to his wishes the Moscow merchant Petr Sergunin, having seen him exactly twice before the marriage. Feeling neither love nor sympathy for him, I hoped that both would develop as we lived together." In her detailed follow-up narrative, Sergunina related how her father and two male cousins pressured her into going to the theater to meet the prospective husband and afterwards, attend a dinner at the Slavianskii Bazaar, the restaurant favored by the Moscow merchantry, where her future in-laws and other friends of the family were also present. There, in the company of these witnesses and without any forewarning, her father announced the couple's engagement. As had the initial petition, this follow-up account stressed Sergunina's lack of volition: only after Kozlov had made the announcement did he ask if the young people assented. The future groom agreed, "and, completely taken aback, so did I," Olimpiada Sergunina wrote. The wedding date was set.[1]

Unusually detailed in its description of how a marriage was made—and, it must be said, in the lack of volition of husband as well as wife—in its substance Sergunina's claim of marriage made at others' behest differed little from those of other female petitioners, many but by no means all deriving from the merchantry, who incorporated this theme into their stories of marital breakdown. Such claims of involuntary marriage took me by surprise: I had rarely seen anything comparable in my reading about marital breakdown in other European settings, including France, where

---

1. RGIA, fond 1412, op. 228, d. 42 (Sergunina, O., 1890), 1, 4. A year after the wedding, Sergunina remained a virgin.

arranged marriages remained the norm.[2] Why, I wondered, was involuntary marriage mentioned so often in Russia, where it provided an important theme not only in separation cases but also in suits for divorce?[3] In the 260 complete separation dossiers that I have read, 13 petitioners claimed to have married at the will of others; in 14 more, witnesses and/or investigators refer to the woman's marriage without attraction and/or at others' volition as one of the reasons for marital breakdown.[4] Together, these twenty-seven cases constitute over 10 percent of the full dossiers.

If such claims were intended to serve a rhetorical function—that is, to convince officials of the merits of a woman's case—they did so only ambiguously. To be sure, by stressing the woman's passivity at the hands of powerful others, claims of involuntary or unwilling marriage augmented a portrait of female helplessness designed to elicit the sympathy of paternalistic officials. At the same time, however, such claims invoked the claimant's right to emotional satisfaction and/or mutuality, and in so doing, implicitly (and sometimes explicitly) challenged Russia's patriarchal marital order. Although the law forbade marriage by coercion, declaring it illegal to "perform a marriage by force, without the consent of the betrothed couple [*zhenikh i nevesta*]," arranged marriages remained the norm for just about everyone except nobles and educated elites. The boundary between arrangement and coercion might sometimes be less than clear. Law endowed parents or guardians with enormous authority over their children, especially over daughters, who ordinarily remained at home until marriage, while sons might go off to school or work. Requiring children to render submission (*pokornost'*) and obedience (*poslushanie*) to their parents, the law also gave parents the right to employ "domestic corrective measures"—that is, physical chastisement—should children prove recalcitrant or disobedient and, chastisement failing, to imprison a child if circumstances warranted. Parental authority extended to children of "both sexes and any age." Although circumscribed when a son left home for school or work and a daughter

2. For one French example, couched unlike this one in highly sentimental rhetoric, see William Reddy, *The Invisible Code: Honor and Sentiment in Postrevolutionary France, 1814–1848* (Berkeley: University of California Press, 1997), 79. Reddy's analysis does not address the claim of involuntary marriage.

3. See Gregory Freeze, "Profane Narratives about a Holy Sacrament: Marriage and Divorce in Late Imperial Russia," in *Sacred Stories: Religion and Spirituality in Modern Russia*, ed. Mark D. Steinberg and Heather J. Coleman (Bloomington: Indiana University Press, 2007), 160–61; T. B. Kotlova, *Rossiiskaia zhenshchina v provintsial'nom gorode na rubezhe XIX–XX vekov* (Ivanovo: Izdatel'stvo Ivanovskogo gosudarstvennogo universiteta, 2003), 40–41, 55.

4. The proportion is likely to be higher. I began to realize that this was a prominent theme only after having read dozens of dossiers, and it is probable that I overlooked other examples in the initial phase of my research. How a marriage came about was not among the questions officials asked investigators to explore.

married, parental authority ceased only with the parents' death. Holding parents and guardians responsible for their children's future, the law obliged them to find employment for sons when they came of age and "to give their daughter in marriage." Finally, parents enjoyed a kind of veto power over spousal choice. Their permission (or in the case of men in state service, the consent of their superior) was required for marriage, irrespective of the couple's age.[5]

The potential challenge to patriarchal authority of women's claims of involuntary marriage may be why the claims failed utterly to move officials of the chancellery, who were agents, after all, of a patriarchal state. Even in those cases where investigation fully upheld them, women's claims of involuntary marriage had no discernible impact on chancellery decision making and make almost no appearance in the final reports summarizing the reasons that officials had arrived at a particular decision. What mattered to them was not how a marriage came about, but what happened after the wedding. Only in four summary reports did officials even reiterate a claim of unwanted marriage, and in only two of these did they include the claim of forced marriage among the reasons for marital breakdown. In both cases, the unwilling party was male, not female.

But if officials remained unresponsive to claims of involuntary marriage, the question of women's volition evidently mattered a lot, not only to petitioning women but to others as well. This chapter explores why this was so. It argues that ideas concerning marriage and marital choice that came to Russia from abroad starting in the eighteenth century took on particular meaning in the Russian context. Declaring sentimental attachment the only proper foundation for marriage, Enlightenment ideas fostered and privileged an emotional style that offered at least an implicit challenge to hierarchical family relations, at first among elites exclusively. To privilege one's own emotional inclinations over the needs and expectations of one's elders or superiors was to claim the right to individual self-expression of a most fundamental sort. In that sense, romantic love is linked to modern subjectivity, as Dipesh Chakrabarty, among others, has sug-

5. *Svod zakonov Rossiiskoi imperii* (St. Petersburg, 1857), vol. 10, pt. 1, articles 61, 62, 164, 174, 177–79. See also Iu. M. Goncharov, *Gorodskaia sem'ia Sibiri vtoroi poloviny XIX–nachala XX v.* (Barnaul: Izdatel'stvo Altaiskogo gosudarstvennogo universiteta, 2002), 48. Laws empowering parents to imprison children might rarely be exercised, however. See V. A. Veremenko, *Dvorianskaia sem'ia i gosudarstvennaia politika Rossii (vtoraia polovina XIX–nachalo XX v.)* (St. Petersburg: Evropeiskii dom, 2007), 82–83. In France, both parties were freed from the requirement of parental permission when they reached the age of twenty-five years. See Michelle Perrot, "Roles and Characters," in *A History of Private Life: From the Fires of Revolution to the Great War,* ed. Michelle Perrot, trans. Arthur Goldhammer (Cambridge, MA: Harvard University Press, 1990), 168–72. The U.S. law requiring parental consent to marriage was steadily eroded in the course of the nineteenth century. See Ellen Rothman, *Hands and Hearts: A History of Courtship in America* (New York: Basic Books, 1984), 119–22.

gested.[6] But in Russia, where patriarchal family relations both reflected and reinforced the patriarchal political order, romantic love might take on broader associations. Its significance as an assertion of selfhood against the superordinate authority of others acquired particular salience, especially in the second half of the nineteenth century, as ideals of romantic choice resonated ever more broadly. Important for some as well—although this is harder to measure—was probably the association of the love marriage with an imagined "West" and the modernity that it signified.

To be sure, unlike men, women rarely expressed themselves in terms such as these. As Sergunina did in her petition, women invariably framed their references to the absence of love or attraction in the making of marriage in terms of their injured rather than assertive self. Nevertheless, for petitioners and others to interpret the absence of love or attraction as an injury, and the decisive role of parents or guardians as an injustice, they first had to believe in the importance of love or attraction as the essential basis for marriage. The significance of that belief can be understood only in the context of long-standing marital practices that privileged parental choice.

CHANGING MARITAL NORMS?

For most late nineteenth-century Russians, historians tell us, marriage was first and foremost an economic and social rather than a personal matter. This was particularly the case for peasants and townspeople. Much of the extant scholarship on this subject emphasizes the primacy of family and community in the making of marriage and the relative unimportance of individual inclination, not to mention passionate attraction, and for good reason. Members of the laboring classes regarded marriage as holy and necessary for every respectable man and woman; peasants, at least, rejected marriage based on passionate "love" as sinful according to Orthodox canons.[7] For peasants and most townspeople, the married couple still served as the basic unit of production. As a result, household and family needs customarily took precedence in marital decisions. By linking two family networks as well as two individuals, the marriage bar-

6. Dipesh Chakrabarty, *Provincializing Europe: Postcolonial Thought and Historical Difference* (Princeton, NJ: Princeton University Press, 2000), 3, 27–30; Jeffrey R. Watt, *The Making of Modern Marriage: Matrimonial Control and the Rise of Sentiment in Neuchatel, 1550–1800* (Ithaca, NY: Cornell University Press, 1992). On emotional styles, see Barbara H. Rosenwein, *Emotional Communities in the Early Middle Ages* (Ithaca, NY: Cornell University Press, 2006), esp. 15, 23.

7. B. N. Mironov, *Sotsial'naia istoriia Rossii (XVIII–nachalo XX v.): Genezis lichnosti, demokraticheskoi sem'i, grazhdanskogo obshchestva i pravovogo gosudarstva*, 3d ed., 2 vols. (St. Petersburg: Dmitrii Bulanin, 2003), 1: 162–63; "Passion is not what justified and ennobled marriage in the eyes of peasants, and the goal of marriage was not carnal pleasure but family life, children, and maintaining a household" (T. G. Leont'eva, "Sel'skie zatvornitsy: zhenshchiny i baby v dorevoliutsionnoi derevne," in *Iz arkhiva Tverskikh istorikov: sbornik nauchnykh trudov*, 3 [2002]: 116).

gain provided access to economic resources and business and patronage connections, as well as social standing and prestige, what Pierre Bourdieu would call symbolic capital.[8] Matchmakers or go-betweens were often essential to the process.

The role of elders in the arrangement of marriage was facilitated by the relatively early age of marriage in Russia, especially for girls. In the second half of the nineteenth century, Russians continued to marry earlier than did Western Europeans. The average age at marriage for women was 21.4 years, lower in villages and higher in cities, whereas in Western Europe, women married at 24 or 25.[9] "It was time. I was twenty-three," declared Natalia Bychkova, a townswoman, who had earned her living with her needle since the age of sixteen. Of her employer and patroness's proposal to find her a match she remembered: "I was healthy at that time, my cheeks were all rosy and although my braids weren't long, they were curly. My body was ready—in a word, I was ready to be married off."[10] Townspeople were particularly eager to settle daughters, who often made no contribution to the family economy. By the time she turned twenty-five, an unmarried woman risked becoming an old maid.[11] Sons married later, at age 24.2 on the average, which was also earlier than their European counterparts. But especially for men, these averages conceal significant differences. The age of marriage was lowest for peasants and somewhat higher for townsmen. For both, parental will carried substantial weight. Young men in towns along the lower Volga did not "get married [*zhenilis'*]" but were instead "married off [*zhenili*]" by their parents as soon as they returned from military service, and before some woman turned their heads.[12]

Among groups for whom marriage was first and foremost an economic matter, historians also include merchants, who depended on marriage to obtain the capital necessary to establish or diversify a business, or the personal connections needed to borrow or expand. Ordinarily, merchants approached marriage as a kind of "business transaction," and in a spirit of "strict calculation."[13] In this group, sons might enjoy

8. Pierre Bourdieu, *Outline of a Theory of Practice*, trans. Richard Nice (New York: Cambridge University Press, 1999), 171–83.

9. Mironov, *Sotsial'naia istoriia*, 1: 169. For Europe, see J. Hajnal, "European Marriage Patterns in Perspective," in *Population in History: Essays in Historical Demography*, ed. D. V. Glass and D. E. C. Eversley (London: E. Arnold, 1965), 102.

10. N. A. Bychkova, "Kak zhili vashi babushki i prababushki," *Rossiiskii arkhiv* 11 (2001): 437–38.

11. N. M. Shchapov, *Ia veril v Rossiiu* (Moscow: Mosgorarkhiv, 1998), 130; G. B. Zhirnova, *Brak i sem'ia russkikh gorozhan v proshlom i nastoiashchem (po materialam gorodov srednei polosy Rossii)* (Moscow: Nauka, 1980), 25.

12. A. N. Zorin et al., *Ocherki gorodskogo byta dorevoliutsionnogo Povolzh'ia* (Ulianovsk: Izdatel'stvo Srednevolzhskogo nauchnogo tsentra, 2000), 93, 108.

13. Iu. M. Goncharov, "Soslovnaia spetsifika gendernogo semeinogo poriadka v russkom provintsial'nom gorode vtoroi poloviny XIX v." in *Sem'ia v rakurse sotsial'nogo znaniia*, ed.

some freedom of choice, but only if they had established themselves economically, and independently of their father or mother. Merchant status was vested solely in the head of the household, who enjoyed absolute control over family property. Whatever his age, a merchant son remained categorized as a merchant son, until he himself acquired the capital necessary to register for merchant status in his own right. For this reason, merchant men often preferred to wait to build up a business before they wed, and so tended to marry later, between twenty-eight and thirty, to women younger than themselves by six to eight years. The older and more economically independent the son, the more difficult it might be for his parents to determine his choice.[14] Although no one has studied the subject, to my knowledge, anecdotal evidence suggests that in arranged marriages especially, engagements tended to be brief, lasting less than a few months. They consequently offered fewer opportunities for couples to become more closely acquainted than did the lengthy engagements of their British and U.S. counterparts. They also offered less time for engagements to fail.[15]

Historians also tell us that this pattern had begun to change toward the end of the nineteenth century. Although the age of marriage remained largely unaltered, parental control began to ease and new courtship practices to emerge, mirroring practices that had already become commonplace among nobles and professionals. Propertied parents—that is, merchants and the more well-to-do townspeople—who could no longer arrange marriages "arranged situations," permitting urban youth to associate more freely at working bees or for those further up the social ladder at evening parties, dances, and the like. Such parents usually monitored and tried to limit the circle of potential suitors. Most historians attribute these changes to parents' growing respect for the personal rights and dignity of their children, even as they emphasize the continuing importance of parental priorities.[16]

Iu. M. Goncharov (Barnaul: Izdatel'stvo NP Azbuka, 2001), 238. See also Ivan Belousov, *Ushedshaia Moskva* (Moscow: Russkaia kniga, 2002), 82–87; and N. A. Varentsov, *Slyshannoe. Vidennoe. Peredumannoe. Perezhitoe.* (Moscow: Novoe literaturnoe obozrenie, 1999), 626.

14. Iu. M. Goncharov, *Gorodskaia sem'ia Sibiri vtoroi poloviny XIX–nachala XX v.* (Barnaul: Izdatel'stvo Altaiskogo gosudarstvennogo universiteta, 2002), 130–31, 181, 377. For two examples of arranged marriages of merchant sons, see V. N. Kulik, "Zhenshchiny dinastii Riabushinskikh," in *Rod i sem'ia v kontekste Tverskoi istorii: sbornik nauchnykh trudov* (Tver: Tverskoi gosudarstvennyi universitet, 2005), 180, 183.

15. On the dangers of lengthy engagements, see Ginger Frost, *Promises Broken: Courtship, Class, and Gender in Victorian England* (Charlottesville: University Press of Virginia: 1995).

16. Quoted from Marion A. Kaplan, *The Making of the Jewish Middle Class: Women, Family, and Identity in Imperial Germany* (New York: Oxford University Press, 1991), 86. See also Olga A. Kuznetsova, *Kul'turnyi oblik rossiiskoi provintsial'noi burzhuazii v XIX–nachale XX v. (na materialakh Verkhnego Povolzh'ia* (Ivanovo: Ivanovskaia gosudarstvennaia tekstil'naia akademiia, 2006), 34, 245–46; Zorin et al., *Ocherki gorodskogo byta*, 233–38; Iu. M. Goncharov, *Semeinyi byt gorozhan Sibiri*

THE "LOVE MARRIAGE"

In the relative unimportance of romantic love in the making of marriage and in the significance of pragmatic concerns, Russia was hardly distinctive. "From a broad historical perspective," writes Marion Kaplan, "love has had a rather weak association with—and has very rarely preceded—a marriage. At least until the age of the automobile, financial and social considerations were at the heart of the decision to marry." According to Mary Jo Maynes, "Despite the argument for ties of affection and companionate marriage, actual practice would suggest that in many regions of Europe, middle-class families continued to arrange marriages with an eye towards family honor even where the sentiments of sons and daughters were allowed fuller sway."[17] Where Russians may have differed is not in the extent to which individuals controlled their own marital choices—impossible to determine in any case—but in the ways that individual volition as expressed in the making of a marriage came to be linked to broader conceptions of selfhood, at least in the minds of some.[18]

The idea that marriage should be based on a couple's mutual attraction or romantic love first entered Russia in the second half of the eighteenth century, under the influence of the European Enlightenment. Propounding the possibility of individual happiness on earth, the Enlightenment "rehabilitated the passions," among them romantic love and sexual desire, as elements essential to such felicity. Marriage became the means to happiness, and romantic and sexual love, the sole justification for a union.[19] Belles-lettres introduced these ideas to Russia's reading and theatergoing public. In literary texts, "the force and extremity" of feeling served as the most compelling evidence of love, while on the stage, "enlightened" people agreed that a romantic union was the only basis for marital happiness. The challenges such ideas raised to family interests and the patriarchal order were played out on the Enlightenment stage, where romantic love and its defiance of patriarchal authority served as a major theme.[20] During the

vtoroi poloviny XIX–nachala XX v.: monografiia (Barnaul: Izdatel'stvo Altaiskogo gosudarstvennogo universiteta, 2004), 234–36; and Kotlova, *Rossiiskaia zhenshchina*, 23–27.

17. "Introduction," in *The Marriage Bargain: Women and Dowries in European History*, ed. Marion Kaplan (New York: Harrington Park Press, 1985), 1; Mary Jo Maynes, "Class Cultures and Images of Family Life," in *The History of the European Family*, ed. David Kertzer and Marzio Barbagli, 3 vols. (New Haven: Yale University Press, 2002), 2: 216.

18. I write "may" because, in fact, to my knowledge no one has explored the subject from this perspective, making comparisons with "the West" impossible.

19. Cissie Fairchilds, "Women and the Family," in *French Women and the Age of Enlightenment*, ed. Samia I. Spencer (Bloomington: Indiana University Press, 1984), 98–99. See also James Traer, *Marriage and the Family in Eighteenth-Century France* (Ithaca, NY: Cornell University Press, 1980), 49, 70–72.

20. Liubov' S. Artem'eva, "'Videnie vliublennogo: liubov' i brak v kul'ture russkogo sentimentalizma," *Adam i Eva* 2 (2001): 268; Elise Kimerling Wirtschafter, *The Play of Ideas in Russian*

1830s and the 1840s, the immensely popular writings of George Sand contributed to the spread of romantic ideals, especially among the nobility and service elites, by emphasizing their heroines' quest for emotional self-realization.

The plays of Aleksandr Ostrovskii, accessible to a broader audience, are likely to have had a still greater impact. Featuring characters deriving from a diverse milieu, the merchantry in particular, Ostrovskii's early plays, especially, highlight the conflict between individual feeling and the patriarchal order. They often portray tyrannical merchant fathers who force their will on those subject to them and deny other people's feelings so as to pursue their own economic interests. In *A Family Affair, We'll Settle It Ourselves* (1849), Samson Silich, merchant father, declares of his young daughter: "She'll marry the man I'll tell her to. She's my child; if I want, I can eat her with my mush, or churn her into butter!" In *Poverty Is No Vice* (1853), one of the works most frequently performed in late nineteenth-century popular theaters, the plot turns on the plans of a wealthy merchant to marry his daughter Liuba to a rich industrialist, despite her love for one of his clerks. "These are my orders," the father asserts. Liuba responds: "I don't dare disobey your command.... Make me do whatever you like, only don't compel me to marry a man I don't love!"[21] Although love wins out in the end, it triumphs only because the wealthy suitor disqualifies himself. The merchant father in *Don't Get into Another's Sleigh* (1852) articulates most explicitly this fatherly effacement of daughterly will: "Can a girl be trusted to know whom she likes or dislikes? No, that's wrong. The man must please *me*. I shall not give her to the man she loves, but to the man I love."[22] These comedies, which employed the spoken language of ordinary people and were based on Ostrovskii's own experiences in the merchant quarter of Moscow in the 1840s, poked fun at abuses of patriarchal authority even as they critiqued it. They continued to be widely staged in capital cities and provincial towns long after the practices of the merchants who inspired them had begun to change.[23]

Enlightenment Theatre (DeKalb: Northern Illinois University Press, 2003), 56, 156.

21. Alexander Ostrovsky, *Plays*, ed. and trans. George Rapall Noyes (New York: Scribners, 1917), 110, 266.

22. Quoted from N. A. Dobroliubov's essay, "Realm of Darkness," where Dobroliubov used it to highlight the oppressive practices of the Russian merchantry. See N. A. Dobroliubov, *Selected Philosophical Essays*, trans J. Fineberg (Moscow: Foreign Languages Publishing House, 1956), 297.

23. For the continuing popularity of Ostrovskii's plays among provincial audiences, see I. F. Petrovskaia, *Teatr i zritel' provintsial'noi Rossii, vtoraia polovina XIX v.* (Leningrad: Iskusstvo, 1995), 42–43 and 151–53; and E. Anthony Swift, *Popular Theater and Society in Tsarist Russia* (Berkeley: University of California Press, 2002). Marital volition was a theme in Hebrew and Yiddish literature in Russia as well, but in that case, the unwilling subject was male, not female. See Michael Stanislawski, *Autobiographical Jews: Essays in Jewish Self-Fashioning* (Seattle: University of Washington Press, 2004), 58.

The problematic relationship between romantic love and patriarchal authority assumed new meaning during the reform era. Part of the assault on Russia's traditional social and gender order, the question of marital choice became in this period associated with other burning issues of the day, in particular the emancipation of the person (*lichnost'*) and the rejection of arbitrary authority. "The theme of a young woman sacrificed in marriage based on economic interest was a classic theme of the 1860s," writes Peter Møller.[24] Ostrovskii's early plays provided grist for the radical mill. Radical journalists elaborated the connection between the question of marital volition and more wide-ranging critiques of arbitrary authority and its suppression of individual selfhood. Women's inability to act on their feelings was a key consequence of family despotism, Nikolai Dobroliubov contended in his critical essay "Realm of Darkness" (1859), which focused on Ostrovskii's plays. Tyranny "warped" the human natures of daughters who submitted to their father's will in marriage, "crushed every independent feeling, deprived them of all ability to stand up for their sacred rights, their right to the inviolability of their feelings, to responding independently to the promptings of their heart, to enjoy mutual love!"[25]

Other critical thinkers also linked women's affective choice with the right to their own person. A conflict over marriage introduces Nikolai Chernyshevskii's enormously influential novel, *What Is to Be Done?* (1863). The story opens with the heroine, Vera Pavlova, defying her ferocious mother's efforts to force the daughter to assent to a materially advantageous, but loveless union. "If you so much as touch me, I will leave the house," the defiant Vera informs her mother. "If you shut me up, I will throw myself out of the window....I will not be his wife...and without my consent the marriage cannot take place."[26] For the progressive critic Aleksandr M. Skabichevskii, writing at the end of the 1870s, the right to choose a husband represented the "most elemental understanding of female freedom." Reviewing the works of the minor novelist Iulia Zhadovskaia, a noblewoman whose despotic father had forbidden her to marry the seminarian she loved during the days of serfdom, the critic equated Zhadovskaia's position with that of a serf. "The young lady shares [with her serf housemaids, Masha and Dasha,] one and the same bitter cup of servile dependence," he wrote. Just like Masha and Dasha, who are married off by the master's orders to those whom the master chooses, so parents proceed with young ladies, disposing of their fate according

24. Peter Møller, *Postlude to the "Kreutzer Sonata": Tolstoj and the Debate on Sexual Morality in Russian Literature in the 1890s*, trans. John Kendal (Leiden: Brill, 1988), 218. See also Irina Iukhina, *Russkii feminizm kak vyzov sovremennosti* (St. Petersburg: Aleteiia, 2007), 123–28.

25. Dobroliubov, *Selected Philosophical Essays*, 316. See also 261, 293–94, 306, 318.

26. Nikolai G. Chernyshevsky, *What Is to Be Done? Tales about New People*, trans. Benjamin Tucker, revised by Liudmilla B. Turkevich (New York: Vintage, 1961), 43–44.

to their own practical considerations, without taking into consideration their attachments of the heart (*serdechnye vlecheniia*).[27]

There is evidence that even in this early period, the idea that affective choice was essential to conjugal felicity resonated beyond the relatively narrow circles of the nobility, intellectuals, and writers. To jurors in one trial adjudicated in this period, involuntary marriage offered a compelling explanation for marital breakdown and the crimes to which it led. "Yes, I wanted to murder Matvei, so that such a man should disappear from the earth. They forced me to marry him," declared the twenty-three-year-old peasant woman Natalia Sergeeva in 1869, confessing her crime before the circuit court in Kashin, Tver. The lawyer who defended Sergeeva explained her actions with reference to the injury forced marriage inflicted on her inner life: there are two kinds of crime, he declared, one due to a spoiled, criminal nature, the other the result of grief. Sergeeva's case belonged in the latter category: "She was married against her will by her stepmother and then had to devote her entire life to the man who would always be an obstacle to her happiness." The jury was deeply affected by the speech, finding her guilty but worthy of indulgence, and letting her go free inasmuch as her husband had escaped with light wounds.[28] In another case, it was the presiding judge in a Riazan circuit court who raised the issue. Endeavoring to learn what had led the peasant defendant to murder his bride in a fit of jealousy, he inquired: "Did your wife marry according to her own inclination [*po oxote*]?"[29] In yet another case, the peasant defendant herself mentioned love. Having remained silent each time the presiding judge in the Rzhev circuit court asked why she tried to poison her husband, she finally declared: "I didn't love him. I didn't want to marry him; everyone laughed at me. I married him against my will, not by agreement."[30]

Another legacy of the radical 1860s had broader resonance as well: the rhetorical link between forced, or even arranged, marriage and abuses of patriarchal authority. It gave to complaints about lack of volition in marital choice a political tinge that was likely absent in other national contexts. By the latter part of the century, family despotism had become a "stock narrative," writes Susan Morrissey, shaping the ways that suicide was explained and understood.[31] The trope of family despotism was particularly evident in the reception of the suicide of a young bride, forced to marry a man of her father's choice in 1885. Taking her own life on her wedding night, the bride left

27. "Pesni o zhenskoi nevol'e," in A. M. Skabichevskii, *Sochineniia A. Skabichevskogo. Kriticheskie etiudy...*, 2 vols. (St. Petersburg: Obshchestvennaia pol'za, 1895), 544, 547.

28. *Sudebnyi vestnik*, no. 33 (February 9, 1869), 1–2.

29. Ibid., no. 105 (April 22, 1870), 1.

30. Ibid., no. 338 (December 15, 1870), 1–2. Whether these claims of forced marriage originated with the woman or her lawyer is impossible to know.

31. Susan Morrissey, *Suicide and the Body Politic in Imperial Russia* (Cambridge: Cambridge University Press, 2006), 248, 251.

behind two suicide notes, as reported in *Novosti i birzhevaia gazeta*. One asked for the forgiveness of her father, a Kazan merchant, and requested that her sister beg forgiveness from the man she loved; the other, intended for the groom, explained the suicide as her only means of escape. Her father had repeatedly turned a deaf ear to the young woman's pleas to end a match with a man whom she did not love, the paper reported: "Whether you love or not, you'll do as I say," the father would insist, affirming the "legitimacy and firmness of his fatherly will," or so the story went. Her death agitated all of Kazan. The public wondered: Was the suicide a "heroic" act of protest against her circumstances? Or was the death at her own hands more mundane, an effort by the bride to hide a sexual "lapse" before the groom discovered it in a culture in which bridal virginity still carried great significance? These questions were on the minds of people in the enormous crowd, reflecting "all classes and stations of life," that accompanied her funeral cortege. After an autopsy that demonstrated the bride was "a virgin" had cleansed of private shame her act of protest against her father's coercive authority, the bride received a solemn (*torzhestvennyi*) public funeral.[32]

LOVE OR MONEY?

In the second half of the nineteenth century, the necessity of *disinterested* marital choice also became a matter for public discussion, joining romantic love and personal choice as ingredients for a happy marriage. This was despite—or perhaps because of—the leading role that dowry played in marital arrangements across much of the social spectrum, betokening the economic significance of marriage and the husband's future role as primary breadwinner. The landed nobility was generally an exception to this pattern: by the mid-nineteenth century, the dowry had largely disappeared among this group, replaced by a gift from parents to bride.[33] But the dowry provided couples from other social groups with the most important infusion of capital they would ever receive, the means to establish a household and the economic wherewithal for many a financial endeavor. It was absolutely essential for those who engaged in commerce. "Even if it amounted only to fifty rubles, it had to be there!" asserted Sergei Dmitriev, son of a shop clerk and a shop clerk himself, writing of turn-of-the-century Iaroslavl.[34]

---

32. *Novosti i birzhevaia gazeta*, no. 31 (1885). Extracts from the article can be found in Anna I. Volkova, *Vospominaniia, dnevnik i stat'i* (Nizhnii Novgorod: A. S. Vishniakova, 1913), 44–45. This attention to the "natural" text of the body, rather than to the "deliberately constructed text of the suicide note," was typical of this positivist era. See Irina Paperno, *Suicide as a Cultural Institution in Dostoevsky's Russia* (Ithaca, NY: Cornell University Press, 1997), 108–9.

33. Michelle Lamarche Marrese, *A Woman's Kingdom: Noblewomen and the Control of Property in Russia, 1700–1861* (Ithaca, NY: Cornell University Press, 2002), 62.

34. S. V. Dmitriev, *Vospominaniia* (Iaroslavl: Aleksandr Rutman, 1999), 199. For a discussion of the economic importance of the dowry, see Margaret Hunt, *The Middling Sort: Commerce, Gender, and the Family in England 1680–1780* (Berkeley: University of California Press, 1996), 151–52.

FIGURE 7.

"Ah, Pierre, how sad I am . . ."

"Why?"

"When I think that every bird, every butterfly is now
married . . . while I . . ."

"But my dear, you're not a bird or a butterfly. No one will marry you
without a dowry. And where is it? You don't have one!"

Strekoza, *no. 27 (1900)*, M. E. Saltykov-Shchedrin Public Library.

In the late nineteenth century, a period of unprecedented economic and social mobility, such transfers of cash may have become particularly significant because Russia remained capital-poor. They could involve substantial amounts of money, for the merchantry, especially: Ivan Kozlov, for example, transferred ten thousand rubles in cash to the Sergunins and supplied Olimpiada with five thousand rubles worth of items in her trousseau.[35]

Among people much further down the social and economic ladder, the cash value of the dowry was considerably less. Nevertheless, having a dowry was often just as essential to women's ability to find a suitable mate. The significance of the dowry is evident in the role that others sometimes played in providing it. If parents were unable to supply the dowry, brothers, uncles, or other relatives might step in. Her employer/patroness supplied the townswoman Natalia Bychkova, a needlewoman, with a dowry of two hundred rubles, "good money for those times."[36] The townswoman Aleksandra Boiarina, whose widowed and impoverished mother had given her as a child to another family, acquired a dowry worth one thousand rubles from her guardian.[37] To be sure, for many impoverished women, such "dowries" amounted only to a trousseau, providing the bedding, pillows, sheets, towels, and other household items essential to housekeeping, plus clothing that might last the bride for the remainder of her life.[38] Moreover, judging by separation cases, some members of the laboring poor dispensed altogether with such capital transfers, either from poverty or the expectation that the wife would continue to earn her own wage; so did some members of the educated elite. Still, the necessity of even a modest outlay to ensure a woman's ability to find a husband is indicated by the widespread urban charitable practice of dowering a marriageable young maiden (*nevesta,* in the sources). One wealthy merchant, for example, bequeathed to the textile town of Shuia the sum of twenty thousand rubles in 1885, intended to dower five impoverished townswomen a year with one hundred rubles each. Other towns and cities received bequests earmarked for the same purpose; and in 1901 a mutual aid society was formed, with government approval, for the specific purpose of dowering prospective brides.[39]

35. RGIA, fond 1412, op. 228, d. 42, 36.

36. Bychkova, "Kak zhili," 438.

37. RGIA, fond 1412, op. 213, d. 95 (Boiarina, A., 1893), 1, 16.

38. For the distinction between dowry and trousseau, see David Ransel, *Village Mothers: Three Generations of Change in Russia and Tataria* (Bloomington: Indiana University Press, 2000), 86–87.

39. Kotlova, *Rossiiskaia zhenshchina,* 33–38; G. L. Ul'ianova, *Blagotvoritel'nost' moskovskikh predprinimatelei, 1860–1914* (Moscow: Mosgorarkhiv, 1999). See the entries for Maksim Azovtsev, Varvara Alekseeva, Aleksei Ashukin, and Ivan Baev, for example. The role of the dowry in late nineteenth-century Russia differed little from the role it played in other European cultures. On the mutual aid society, see *Moskovskaia kassa nevest. Ustav* (Moscow: n.p., 1901). Comparable associations of

FIGURE 8.

"Tell me, Paul, honestly: you didn't marry me for my money, did you?
"Of course, I didn't. After all, it was my creditors who got your money, not
me."

Strekoza, *no. 6 (1895), M. E. Saltykov-Shchedrin Public Library.*

The persistence of the dowry notwithstanding, the emphasis on disinterested choice in marriage became increasingly commonplace in discussions of men's motivations for marriage, men who sought to present themselves as autonomous individuals in particular. Through the early twentieth century, criticism of those who married primarily or exclusively for mercenary reasons appeared in a variety of venues. Criticism was aimed, in part, at the commercialization of marriage, a matter of concern elsewhere in Europe, too.[40] In Russia, however, the primary point was not the rising cost of marriage, but rather that material considerations might outweigh, even replace, love as a basis for union, despite the fact that material considerations were nothing new. Marrying exclusively for financial advantage degraded the dignity of the man (and more rarely, at least in these critiques, the woman) who deigned to sell himself. Such critiques reflected the enhanced importance attached to the idea of the Western-style, self-made autonomous individual, for whom romantic love necessarily served as the primary basis for entering marriage. This individual was male, not female.

Merchant suitors, unlike avaricious merchant fathers, were rarely the target of such critiques, perhaps because of the belief that fathers, not sons, continued to play the key role in making marriages. Thus, for example, in *Don't Get into Another's Sleigh*, the first play of Aleksandr Ostrovskii to be staged, the fortune-seeker is an aristocrat, not a merchant. He elopes with a wealthy shopkeeper's daughter, only to abandon her when he learns of her father's intention to disinherit her if she marries him. Fortune-seeking men from a variety of backgrounds, none of them commercial, continued to figure in Ostrovskii's later plays as well.[41] In the early works of Anton Chekhov, it was students or writers who sought fortunes in their bride.[42]

Advice literature on courtship and marriage also reflected the conviction that love should be the primary or sole basis for conjugal union. To be sure, the author of *Good Manners*, first published in 1881, and in its fifth edition by 1910, tried to balance love and money. He asserted that while most men married "for love," they also anticipated a dowry and he advised prospective suitors to assure themselves of the precise amount before tendering a marriage proposal. But for the most part, the emphasis was on love and love alone. "Marriages must be only for love, and marriages concluded for reasons

<hr>

a charitable nature existed in Russia's Jewish community. See ChaeRan Y. Freeze, *Jewish Marriage and Divorce in Imperial Russia* (Hanover, NH: University Press of New England, 2002), 30–31.

40. See Kaplan, *Making of the Jewish Middle Class*, 86–87; 99–103.

41. See *Diary of a Scoundrel* (1868), *The Final Victim* (1878) and the Balzaminov trilogy. The plight of women and role of money in Ostrovskii's plays is discussed in Marjorie L. Hoover, *Alexander Ostrovsky* (Boston: Twayne Publishers, 1981).

42. See, for example, "Before the Wedding" and "Wedding American Style," in *The Complete Early Short Stories of Anton Chekhov. "He and She" and Other Stories: Volume* 1 (1880–1882), trans. Peter Sekirin (Toronto: Megapolis, 2001), 26–28, 29–30.

other than love are to the highest degree immoral," asserted the author of the advice book *Marital Satisfactions*. "A marriage can only be happy if founded on love, on the mutual attraction of hearts that feel connected to one another by mutual respect and attachment, and who find it impossible to exist without one another." A husband choosing a wife should "care least of all about her material status," advised the *Handbook for Young Spouses* (1900). "Marriage for love is the only basis for a happy, moral marriage," intoned *How to Marry and Be Happy* (1909).[43]

Disapproval of marriage for mercenary reasons could be found in other venues, too. Cartoons published in the satirical journal *Strekoza* lampooned suitors for whom money was more important than the woman. In 1907, the editor of *Novobrachnaia gazeta*, published with the goal of facilitating "marriages for love" by expanding the circle of potential contacts, condemned outright those who sought economic advantage in marriage. The papers' advertisements frequently mentioned financial needs or status in addition to describing the personal or physical qualities desired or on offer, establishing a harmonious relationship between "affect and filthy lucre," to quote Stephen Lovell. Thus, for example, a middle-aged lady with a nice figure boasted a capital of forty thousand rubles; a nobleman who owned a pharmacy in the provinces sought not only a plump and kindly brunette but also capital of ten to fifteen thousand rubles, and the like.[44] The editor, however, professed outrage at this continuation of a "custom that belongs to earlier times," and that had nothing in common with love: "It is impossible to understand what he seeks," he wrote of one such advertisement, "a wife with a dowry, or a dowry with a wife. What astonishes is the shamelessness of a person openly expressing that of which a person should be ashamed....A man who seeks a dowry cannot be a good husband; he is a kept man."[45] While some writers spoke in favor of material considerations in marriage, such critiques of mercenary marriage seem to have

43. *Khoroshii ton: Sbornik pravil i sovetov na vse sluchai zhizni obshchestvennoi i semeinoi* (St. Petersburg: German Goppe, 1881), 128–31; *Brachnye udovol'stviia. Prakticheskie vrachebnye i ne vrachebnye nastavleniia vstupivshim v brak* (Moscow: F. Ioganson, 1882), 1, 2; *Nastol'naia kniga dlia molodykh suprugov s polnym izlozheniem pravil supruzheskoi zhizni* (Moscow: S. A. Zhivareva, 1900), 8; A. Debe et al., *Kak vyiti zamuzh i byt' schastlivoi v supruzheskoi zhizni...* (Moscow: A. A. Levinson, 1909), 18. See also *Polnyi pismovik: samouchitel' sostavliat' bez pomoshch' postoronnikh: pis'ma, dogovory, akty, prosheniia i drugie delovye bumagi, soderzhashchii obraztsy i formy pisem vsekh rodov* (Moscow: Vil'de, 1894), 17. Compilers of these letter-writing guides plagiarized freely from one another, offering identical letters as well as variations on the theme of passionate love.

44. See *Novobrachnaia gazeta*, no. 21 (1907). For the goals, see *Novobrachnaia gazeta*, no. 20 (1907), 1. More than half of the ads placed by men in *Brachnaia gazeta* in 1908 raised financial demands of some kind. See Stephen Lovell, "Finding a Mate in Late Tsarist Russia: The Evidence from Marital Advertisements," *Cultural and Social History* 4, no. 1 (2007): 64–65, 68.

45. *Novobrachnaia gazeta*, no. 2, 40.

been the more compelling: it was the critiques of mercenary marriage that most influenced the self-presentation of husbands in discordant unions.[46]

ROMANCE AND MARRIAGE

The language of affective choice also influenced the self-presentation of a substantial minority of wives. The influence was felt more broadly, too. It is evident in many of the personal documents examined for this study, in addition to those associated with separation cases. These writings suggest that the women who composed them, most but not all deriving from the propertied and privileged, approached the prospect of marriage with the idea that love should precede rather than follow marriage, and that a woman should exercise a degree of control over her marital fate. How typical the women were is impossible to determine on the basis of the kind of sources used for this book. But whether or not the "love marriage" had become a kind of normative ideal or "new cultural reality" in the provinces as well as in cities by the late nineteenth century, as the historian N. B. Kotlova has proposed, these writings indicate that the ideal of affective choice might serve as a vehicle for female self-affirmation and even self-assertion.[47]

This was certainly the case for Vera Tret'iakova and Elizaveta Andreeva. Their memoirs are among a relatively small number of such personal narratives that have appeared in print.[48] Exceptional by their very nature in a milieu not ordinarily given to memoir writing or, so far as we know, diary keeping, they are less typical still as their authors derived from the most elite of merchant households. This was a milieu distinguished by its aspirations to culture and cultivation, where the new ideals of marriage are most likely to have exerted an impact. Still, atypical although the authors surely are, their narratives highlight the connection that some might make between marital choice and female selfhood.[49]

The accounts of both Vera Tret'iakova and Elizaveta Andreeva detail their authors' struggle on behalf of emotional self-realization and against the weight of patriarchal

---

46. For a book favoring marriage by calculation, see *Kak smotrit obshchestvo na tserkovnyi ili grazhdanskii brak? Otvety na anketu, postavlennuiu knigoizdatel'stvom, so stat'eiu Tertychnogo "Otchego ne prochny nashi braki?"* (Kiev: Trud i zhizn', 1908).

47. Kotlova, *Rossiiskaia zhenshchina*, 41.

48. Other memoirs include Aleksandra Kobiakova, "An Autobiography," in *Russia through Women's Eyes*, ed. Toby Clyman and Judith Vowles (New Haven: Yale University Press, 1996), 60–74; V. N. Kharuzina, *Proshloe: Vospominaniia detskikh i otrocheskikh let* (Moscow: Novoe literaturnoe obozrenie, 1999); M. V. Voloshina-Sabashnikova, *Zelenaia zmeia: istoriia odnoi zhizni* (St. Petersburg: Enigma, 1993); Volkova, *Vospominaniia;* and Elizaveta D'iakonova, *Dnevnik Russkoi zhenshchiny* (1912; repr., Moscow: Zakharova, 2004).

49. On the elites, see Joanne Ruckman, *The Moscow Business Elite: A Social and Cultural Portrait of Two Generations, 1840–1905* (DeKalb: Northern Illinois University Press, 1984).

authority. In Tret'iakova's rendering, especially, the struggle for the right to love assumes quasi-heroic form, involving debilitating suffering and the overcoming of obstacles for the sake of marriage to her beloved. The twenty-year-old Tret'iakova fell in love with Aleksandr Ziloti—pianist, conductor, and composer—virtually at first sight in 1886, dreaming of him nightly long before she got to know him. No sooner did their romance begin to ripen than her father forbade their marriage: "No one is more unsuited for family life than an artist," she quotes him saying to her. "If one of my girls should think of marrying an artist, then she should know that I'll never give my consent." Intense suffering followed this blow to her most cherished feelings. She fell into a state of nervous collapse, which involved a spell of hysterical paralysis of her hands and legs, blindness, and inability to speak. Then she resolved to assert herself. As her health improved, Tret'iakova made up her mind to elope with Ziloti, which dispelled her grief and rage at her father. Her father's unexpected agreement to the marriage then made elopement unnecessary.[50] Self-assertion was equally necessary before Elizaveta Andreeva succeeded in marrying the poet Konstantin Balmont, whose divorced status rendered him unacceptable to her parents.[51] The attention of these writers to the drama of marital choice suggests its saliency to a more "modern" and individualized merchant sense of self on the part of women as well as men.

Two letters from women that I have found in separation dossiers indicate a comparable effort to exert control over their marital fates, albeit by different means. The two actually initiated courtship, rather than passively waiting for another to take the initiative. Their behavior reflects, to say the least, an unusual freedom from the norms of female propriety. That these two women conducted themselves as they did is indicative of women's increasing physical mobility, which made it possible for some not only to hope for a union with a man of their own choosing but also to act directly on that hope. One letter is from a young woman of unknown age and origin resident in the industrial town of Ivanovo. The woman was encouraged to believe that she had found her mate by a lengthy conversation on a train, where to chat with a stranger was no longer

50. V. P. Ziloti, *V dome Tret'iakova* (Moscow: Vysshaia shkola, 1992), 261, 293–94, 299, 301, 304, 312–13. Tret'iakova had a consultation with the famous expert on hysteria, Doctor Jean Martin Charcot, who told her that if she arranged her life according to her own desires, her nerves would recover of themselves (307). The Charcot she depicts bears little resemblance to the manipulator of female patients that recent accounts of hysteria have offered. Perhaps Tret'iakova put the words she wanted into his mouth. She was not the only Russian merchant woman to consult Charcot: so did Ekaterina Sabashnikova-Baranovskaia.

51. E. A. Andreeva-Balmont, *Vospominaniia* (Moscow: Izdatel'stvo Sabashnikovykh, 1997), 235–37. We learn from another memoirist that Andreeva's mother was the more adamant and cursed the daughter when she left home (Voloshina-Sabashnikova, *Zelenaia zmeia*, 84).

considered a "crime against good manners" even by an arbiter of propriety.[52] Her letter, undated but probably composed in the early 1890s, essentially proposed marriage to its recipient, a man already married to another woman. It is worth quoting in some detail, revealing as it does the constraints on women's lives as well as the heightened expectations of men and life that rendered such constraints less tolerable.

"Most respected Sergei Andreevich," the letter begins. "Very likely you remember that I had the opportunity to travel with you in early May from Ivanovo to Kineshma. And now, against the rules, I want to make you a proposal, forgive me for my immodesty." Although the circumstances of her family life were very difficult, she declared, she had rejected her many local suitors, who all lacked the requisite "spiritual qualities." "All of them, these *Ivanovtsy*, are soulless materialists and dandies in public, and in private life coarse and savage." That was why she was writing to her new acquaintance. "I like you very much, although I know you very little, but for heaven's sake, don't think that this is a confession of love," she wrote. "Of course, you know me too little, but you can spend time at our house and know me better. It won't obligate you to anything. I'd know how to share with you the difficult moments of your life and try to ease them. I know that you and I would get on in everything very quickly." Fiscal assurances complemented sentiment: "I am a poor girl, but I'll have a dowry and a very good one, thanks to my father and a female relative."[53]

A similar initiative from Sofia Seslavina, a noblewoman, eventuated in marriage to Ivan Stepanov, a merchant's son who earned his living selling property in the vicinity of the city of Odessa. Aged thirty-six when she encountered her future husband, likewise on a train, Seslavina was well past the usual age of marriage, which may help explain her bold and perhaps desperate initiative as well as her relative freedom of action. Three weeks after they met in 1898, she sent him a letter requesting a meeting:

> You surely will be very surprised to receive a letter from a person with whom you've conversed twice, and perhaps you'll find it strange that I write after such a short acquaintance.... But I feel as if I've known you all my life. I cannot remember when I have had such a serious and interesting conversation with a man as I had with you...during our trip from Kineshma to Kobylnia. Since we parted I haven't

52. A woman should, however, exercise proper caution: "Tact will tell you with whom to speak and with whom to remain silent" (*Khoroshii ton,* 197). Compare with the warnings of sexual danger for women to be found in advice literature in the United States, albeit dating from a somewhat earlier period. See Patricia Cline Cohen, "Safety and Public Transport, 1750–1850," in *Gendered Domains: Rethinking Public and Private in Women's History: Essays from the Seventh Berkshire conference,* ed. Dorothy O. Helly and Susan M. Reverby (Ithaca, NY: Cornell University Press, 1992), 119, 121.

53. Her letter ended up in the file of his wife's appeal for legal separation, which contains several letters from other women, manifestly his lovers (RGIA, fond 1412, op. 226, d. 120 [Postnikova, E., 1897], 32–34).

stopped thinking about what we spoke of, and with pleasure noted that your views on life are exactly the same as mine. I would be happy to converse with you again, and all the more because I would like to speak with you on a very serious subject. I don't want to put on paper what I would like to tell you personally.

Suggesting a place where they might meet in early June, the letter continued: "I leave for Odessa tomorrow morning on a train and how happy I would be to meet you again in a 'railway car' [quotation marks in the original]." The author was unwilling to sign her own name to the letter but was certain that its recipient would guess who she was. Recognizing that she violated social norms, in a subsequent letter, Seslavina urgently requested that Stepanov say not a word to others about her letters. "I would find it extremely unpleasant if people learned that I write to you." Nevertheless, she continued to take the initiative in their relationship and was first to broach the topic of marriage.[54]

Such self-assertion was surely out of the question for most women of the propertied classes, merchant women in particular, who were economically dependent, married young, lived at home until they wed, and in provincial towns, in particular, were largely confined to the domestic sphere.[55] Still, some tried to fulfill the ideal of the love marriage by falling in love with the man others had chosen for them. Thus Evlampia Koginova, daughter of a well-to-do Kharkov merchant, adopted the language of romance when writing to the man her father selected. "My dear Vasia," she wrote in 1875 to Vasilii Parmanin, her intended; referring to herself as "your Dunina," she signed the letter, "yours forever." "It's sad, very sad, that two loving hearts have to greet the New Year so far from one another," she wrote in another letter. "I want only one thing: never to greet another New Year's in this way." Elizaveta Ignatenko and her father, a merchant in Rostov on the Don, had fought bitterly over her desire to marry a merchant's son. In the heat of such fights, "the father even permitted himself to insult his daughter physically [i.e., beat her]," reported the gendarme investigating the case, causing Elizaveta to flee her father's house and seek temporary shelter with her aunt but also to abandon hope of the longed-for union. The letters Elizaveta addressed to Mikhail Avetchin, the man she subsequently married, betray her efforts to rouse in herself the requisite romantic feelings. "Misha, my dear Misha, and if I have not invented my feelings, if they are not false, but sincere? If only that were so! But they must be: I want it and you, Misha, right? Then that [their marriage] would be a different matter. Despite everything, we would be happy," she wrote in 1886, as if she could somehow marshal the "love" she knew she was supposed to feel. Such expectations might render more burdensome a marriage based on another's will. "How difficult life is with a husband I don't love," wrote Varvara Zvereva to a friend in 1909, shortly after she married an office

54. Ibid., op. 228, d. 103 (Stepanova, S., 1900), 50, 54.
55. See V. S. Levandovskaia, "Vospominaniia," *Neva*, no. 9 (1993): 318.

clerk at the insistence of her widowed mother, a townswoman who kept horses for the Arzamas zemstvo.[56]

The account that Iurii Bakhrushin provides of his parents' marriage, which draws on letters from the family archive, depicts vividly the kind of pressures to which women of this milieu remained subject. Presented with the proposal of the merchant Aleksei Bakhrushin, who according to his own account had fallen in love with her at first sight, his future wife Vera, a merchant daughter, was torn. "I can't say no; I have nothing against him," she wrote to a close friend. "Can I say yes? No, again I can't, because I feel absolutely nothing for him. He's a tall young man, thirty years old, horribly ugly." Perhaps someday she would grow to like him, she supposed, but her feelings were given no opportunity to ripen: everyone she knew was pressing her to consent, which would secure the alliance of two prominent Moscow merchant households. "Everyone praises him a lot, and all ours want me to marry him. Imagine what will happen if I reject such a suitor!" To accept the proposal under such circumstances, she wrote the friend, would be to violate her conscience, indicating the importance of attraction for her as well.[57] Within a month, however, she had acceded to the match.

The story of one merchant marriage, as narrated in the diary of Serafima Rakhmanova, provides an unusually sustained look at the ways that two young people in late nineteenth-century merchant Moscow negotiated the tensions between the new romantic ideals and the parental authority and pragmatic considerations that continued to shape their marital choices. The diary is part of the family archive of the Rakhmanovs, adherents of the schismatic Old Belief, which broke with official Orthodoxy at the end of the seventeenth century and is often viewed as more conservative in its family practices than was the case in the surrounding culture.[58] Excerpts from the diary were published in *Moskovskii zhurnal* in 1992–93, together with photographs of the author, her husband, and other members of the family. In the next section, I summarize the story the diary tells at some length, because it demonstrates so vividly the ways that the language of "romance" might affect a woman's self-perception, even if that particular woman was eventually prepared to sacrifice romance on the altar of duty. In her diary, Serafima Rakhmanova recorded how she experienced and then renounced "love" at the behest of her parents, and thereafter, how she picked and chose among her suitors, finally settling for the best that she could get.

---

56. RGIA fond 1412, op. 226, d. 16 (Parmanina, E., 1885), 92–99; op. 212, d. 21 (Avetchina, E., 1887), 31 ob.; and op. 219, d. 37 (Zvereva, V., 1911), 32–33.

57. Iu. A. Bakhrushin, *Vospominaniia* (Moscow: Khudozhestvennaia literatura, 1994), 213–14.

58. Goncharov, *Gorodskaia sem'ia*, 153–54.

"A LOVE STORY"

When the diary begins, sometime in the 1890s (the year is not provided), Serafima—daughter of the merchant Fedor Semenovich Rakhmanov, a trader in grain and an Old Believer—was a thoroughly unexceptional young woman who nourished neither aspirations for an independent life nor intellectual ambitions. Encouraged by her mother to read *War and Peace,* she confided to her diary that she skipped the war and read only about "Peace" and even then, looked ahead to see how many pages were left. Serafima expressed little interest even in marriage, the goal of every merchant maiden's life. "I unwillingly distribute provisions and make jam. I don't like small children, and the figures of women in that condition [i.e., pregnant] displease me so much that I never want to be like them." What she wanted was expensive, elegant clothing, rosy cheeks, and the well-padded figure that was considered most desirable in merchant women; she devoured flour in the hopes of gaining weight.[59]

Embracing a romantic ideal, Serafima lacked the will to act on it. Soon after she began keeping her diary, Lev Ovsiannikov, the son of a merchant family that had fallen on hard times, declared his romantic attachment to Serafima, and she responded in kind. Their exchange took place during one of the dances that merchants and more well-to-do townspeople had begun to arrange for their offspring in an effort to accommodate the new expectations by enabling the young to court within a carefully selected milieu. Permitted to spend time alone together, the two discussed their expectations of marriage—his, to "live with one's beloved"; hers, "to bring the beloved happiness." The one apparent obstacle, his previous affair with a chambermaid about which Serafima somehow learned, he easily overcame, declaring, "I'm no monk," and seizing and kissing her hand. Even so, Serafima was prepared to take no risks on behalf of her feelings. When Lev left on a trip, the young couple agreed to refrain from corresponding, "from the fear that a letter would fall into the hands of the authorities [*vlast' imushchikh*]," that is, her parents. And at the first real obstacle, Serafima abandoned the field. Learning that her beloved's father was trying to arrange his marriage to a daughter of the enormously wealthy Riabushinskii family, she resolved to renounce him and encouraged him to redirect his attentions where his parents wished. "I looked at the matter from the practical point of view," she confided to her diary, recognizing the realities of merchant marriage. For the sake of the love that she had bestowed on Lev, she asked only that he keep their romance secret. As for herself, while continuing to love Lev, she was prepared to "await a fiancé with substantial means."[60]

---

59. "Iz istorii odnoi liubvi," *Moskovskii zhurnal,* no. 11–12 (1992), 26, 28. Fedor Rakhmanov was a member of the Directorate of the Society of Trading Rows.

60. Ibid., 24–26, 30. She planned to write all this in a letter to him but failed to send it after her aunt forbid her to correspond.

Yet when a suitor finally appeared, she had herself begun to change, thanks to the influence of Vladimir Ivanovich Ostrovskii, toward whom she also developed tender feelings. Ostrovskii was a man of advanced opinions, a bearer of the ideas of the 1860s into this conservative merchant milieu. "What are you planning to do with your life, peel potatoes?" he once asked her, deriding her narrow interests. For Vladimir's sake, Serafima attempted to recast her life along more "useful" lines. This involved rising early, teaching one of her brothers to read, reading *Russkie Vedomosti* aloud to her mother, and playing games with her younger siblings to draw closer to them. At Vladimir's instigation, Serafima even tried to read the essays of the radical literary critic Nikolai Dobroliubov. Her interest was piqued by Dobroliubov's discussion of merchant "tyrants," but by little else. In any event, to her "they remain articles, written in a book, whereas life has set me other goals."[61]

The goal life set was marriage. Yet now that Serafima had begun to develop herself, to "strive for intellectual development and moral self-perfection" in her words, marriage seemed premature: "I have just left school and have not even looked about me, I have no idea what my calling [*prizvanie*] is, I lack goals, I am unprepared for the struggle." Nevertheless, when a suitor appeared, a man whom she had never met, she "passively fulfilled Papa's will" and agreed to meet him. This was to be no old-fashioned "showing" (*smotrenie*) of the bride, during which the potential groom and his parents evaluated the merits of the proposed bride, a practice still widespread among the peasantry from which most merchants derived. The first, and last, encounter between the two took place at the Tretiakov Gallery. The suitor, awkward and shy, proved unable to conduct a conversation about art or any other subject about which his potential bride tried to engage him. "He's no match for me," Serafima boldly informed her father, who reluctantly acceded. Even a proposal from Lev, her former suitor, evoked mixed feelings. Initially ecstatic and eager to say yes, Serafima accepted her parents' objections with suspicious ease: "He has no job," her mother said; "I also think I shouldn't marry him," Serafima responded. "I'm in no hurry to give up the single life [*devich'ia zhizn'*]," she explained to her diary. [62]

Another suitor appeared, Ivan Vasil'evich Shibaev, the son of a second guild merchant from an Old Believer background similar to her own; another first encounter was arranged at an appropriately elevated setting, this time at the Rumiantsev Museum. Far more socially adept than the first had been, the second suitor passed muster: he was tall, well built, and self-confident, dressed in a black suit that suited him well. His face "breathed satisfaction with life, while his gray eyes gazed affectionately" on her, Serafima confided to her diary, although it is difficult for this reader to imagine how he could feel genuine affection for a young woman he was meeting for the first time. "I decided there

61. "Iz istorii odnoi liubvi," *Moskovskii zhurnal*, no. 4 (1993): 35, 37.
62. Ibid., 36–39.

would be no reason to be ashamed of such a husband: he knows how to conduct himself in society, he's traveled abroad," and held the rank of honored citizen.[63]

And what alternative did she have, in the end? While informing her mother that she liked Ivan, she also assured herself that she would have to marry somebody one day, such was "the force of circumstances." The bargaining began. She would bring a dowry of thirty thousand rubles and a trousseau, including furs, clothing, linens, furniture, and jewelry worth another twenty thousand. Only after the agreement had been finalized did Ivan actually propose, again at the Rumiantsev Museum amid discussions of art and theater, "Allow me to ask for your hand," he said. "Perhaps you're marrying because your parents want you to?" Serafima inquired. "I assure you, Serafima Fedorovna, that in our time such things never happen," he responded. She accepted his proposal; he kissed her hand. Feeling "more happy than sad," she made her preparations for the wedding, which took place within a matter of weeks.[64]

Serafima's marriage to Ivan was not a love match, but nor was it forced on her. An arranged marriage, it was very much a product of its time. The Rakhmanovs, among the more generous of the Moscow merchantry, were enlightened people.[65] Her father, Fedor Semenovich, was no tyrant; and her mother, Olga Viktorovna, emerges from her daughter's diary as intelligent, well read, and thoughtful. The parents permitted their daughter to finish school and even encouraged her to continue her studies. They did not live a self-contained life as some merchant families continued to do: Serafima attended parties and dances and was permitted to spend unchaperoned time with young men. The family visited the theater and art galleries—even the traditional "viewing" took place in that untraditional setting. Clearly very fond of their daughter, her parents respected her feelings, if sometimes reluctantly. Although by no means a rebel, Serafima herself was also no fool. Having nibbled the fruit of knowledge and acquired the aspirations to self-development that she conscientiously recorded in her diary, she remained perfectly aware of her limited choices and made her peace with them. Accepting the fate of marriage, the only available future if she wished to avoid painful family conflict and the goal of most merchant girls, her only real choice was among her suitors.

The diary breaks off at the wedding, but photographs that accompany its publication suggest that the marriage was not an unhappy one. This should not be surprising: arranged marriages often succeed, especially when, as in Serafima's case, the partners had some say in the matter. As Marion Kaplan reminds us in her study of imperial Germany's Jewish minority, romantic expectations could find satisfaction even in an

---

63. Ibid., no. 6: 52. Vasilii Shibaev was at that time a trustee of the Rogozh Cemetery, at the center of Moscow Old Belief, as were members of the Rakhmanov family.

64. Ibid.

65. On their philanthropy, see Ul'ianova, *Blagotvoritel'nost'*, 262–63.

arranged marriage. She writes: "Many partners grew to care deeply for each other. It would be inaccurate to assume that their feelings were stunted simply because they acted on their economic interests."[66] Russians' belief that affection would grow *after* marriage is reflected in the expression, "you will come to love him when you grow used to him [*sterpetsia-sliubitsa*]." And countless couples whose marriages were arranged by others no doubt came to care for one another deeply, if not to love romantically, united by their shared labors, their children, and the years they spent together.

INVOLUNTARY MARRIAGE

When such marriages failed, however, a woman's lack of volition might provide part of the explanation. Imagine, for a moment, a different outcome for Serafima's marriage. Let us suppose that Ivan turned out to be a drunkard or that he married Serafima only for her money or that he soon became involved with another woman—or, not uncommonly, all three, and that she appealed to the chancellery for relief. Or, as happened more rarely and required far more female self-assertion, that she became dissatisfied with the marriage for other reasons or fell in love with another man and appealed for relief. At that point, she might draw on her reading, her reading of Dobroliubov perhaps, to recast the story her diary tells. The revised version might emphasize her father's insistence that she marry a man of his choosing (those merchant "tyrants") and her own passivity and lack of choice and/or romantic attraction, referring as well to her superficial acquaintance with her intended before the wedding. Unhappily married women who petitioned the chancellery might have revised their marital history in precisely this fashion; it is often impossible to know for certain. What matters here is not whether their allegations of involuntary marriage were "true" in some absolute sense, but that the women chose to incorporate those allegations into their marital history. Functioning as a kind of portent of doom, although never as the sole explanation for marital breakdown, the absence of romantic or affective choice in the making of marriage was intended to detract from its legitimacy and to herald its failure, while also asserting the importance of women's emotional gratification.

Petitioners who referred to involuntary unions invariably presented themselves as passive pawns in the marital maneuvers of others, although at least in some cases, evidence in the dossier complicates the story. That some derived from the merchantry is not surprising: women's subjection to patriarchal authority and role as passive pawns in the commercial transaction of their elders, long a literary trope, surely encouraged them to conceive of and tell the story of their marriage in the terms offered by that framework. Evlampia Parmanina, merchant daughter, is one example. "Submitting to the wishes of my father, I married a man whom I did not know and did not love, and who did not love me," she wrote to the chancellery in 1885. Her straightforward account

---

66. Kaplan, *Making of the Jewish Middle Class*, 87. See also Kuznetsova, *Kul'turnyi oblik*, 41–42.

is cast into question by the affectionate letters she sent during the couple's engagement ("Your Dunina"), cited above, which her estranged husband had preserved.[67]

But others whose narratives were at odds with the evidence were of more humble backgrounds. Writing in 1891, three years after her wedding, the townswoman Anna Kuz'minskaia claimed that "Because fate deprived me of my parents at a very early age, fifteen and a half, I married a young man, the son of an official, without taking into consideration my own feelings or hopes, in obedience to my grandmother's demand." The investigation revealed that she was twenty at the time of her marriage. "I had not yet reached the age of sixteen [the legal age of marriage] or become a woman [probably, began menstruating] when my parents, having overcome my resistance, married me off to the nineteen-year-old peasant Dmitrii Kulikov," began the petition of Evdokia Kulikova, a peasant woman, composed for her by a lawyer in 1896. While supporting their daughter's petition for separation, Kulikova's parents took issue with the role in which she had cast them, refusing to endorse her account of victimization at their hands. The girl had married at age seventeen or eighteen, and not at fifteen, as she claimed, her mother testified; moreover, Evdokia herself desired the marriage. Her father, too, denied applying any pressure, while a former employer recalled Evdokia eagerly awaiting her husband's return from the army.[68]

The trope of familial despotism might come into explanatory play even in cases where the woman had in fact chosen her mate. Invoking the idea of marriage as a source of "freedom," the appeal of Valentina Avvakumova implied that genuine volition required the complete self-command of the actor: "I was born in the city of Tomsk to a merchant family, where reigned the strictest imaginable regime, completely suppressing any independence," Valentina Avvakumova wrote in 1904. "Having reached the age of twenty, I naturally could no longer endure such constraint, such absence of the most elemental liberty [svoboda], and all my dreams were devoted to escaping to freedom, whatever the cost, even if it meant marriage." Thus she married a man whom she hoped she would "learn to love with time."[69] However a marriage had actually come about, lack of volition had come to play a significant rhetorical role in some women's accounts of marital failure.[70]

67. RGIA, fond 1412, op. 226, d. 16 (Parmanina), 1.

68. Ibid., op. 221, d. 192 (Kuz'minskaia, A., 1891), 1; op. 221, d. 204 (Kulikova, E., 1897), 1, 24, 25.

69. RGIA, fond 1412, op. 212, d. 4 (Avvakumova, 1904), 1 ob. Because she does not claim forced marriage, I do not include her in the thirteen cases. For a similarly worded appeal in 1913, also penned by a merchant daughter, see "Po chastnoi zhaloby kuptsy Aleksandry Emel'ianovy." TsGIA SPb, fond 356, op. 1, d. 20014, 5.

70. For other examples of narratives that incorporate the theme of marriage made at the behest of others, see RGIA, fond 1412, op. 212, d. 33 (Agafonova, Z., 1894), 53; op. 221, d. 63 (Kokovina, Z., 1899), 55; op. 226, d. 98 (Ponomareva, A., 1891); op. 213, d. 7 (Bakusheva, V., 1901); and op. 220, d. 25 (Il'ina, M., 1893).

Complaints of women's lack of volition, if verified, often elicited a sympathetic response from others. Expressing concern about the emotional suffering that women endured as a consequence of loveless marriages, investigators and witnesses alike referred to marriages made at the behest of others as explanatory factors in marital breakdown. Well-born men such as gendarmes and governors, applying the norms of their own milieu, were particularly likely to express such views. The gendarme reporting on the Sergunin case, for example, wrote: "In my opinion, the cause of their quarrels is her lack of attraction to him. She married at an early age, by her father's will." In 1891, a Kostroma gendarme officer provided a ringing condemnation of another marriage of convenience, that of Zinaida Razorenova and Mikhail Kokovin, whose match was made entirely to address his family's financial needs. The officer called the arrangement "one of the most shameful of human actions—the buying and selling of a woman as a thing." The result was a union "without sympathy, love, or trust in each other—in a word, those human feelings which ordinarily unite those who enter marriage." Such a union, in his opinion, could never have led to happiness.[71]

But concern with women's volition in marriage, and the conviction that a woman should feel attraction to her partner, was not limited to the well-born and privileged. Although the concern was by no means shared by everyone, the frequency with which investigators and witnesses from even the laboring classes referred to these matters suggests a heightened sensitivity to individual emotion in this period, certainly in towns but to some extent in peasant villages, too. New trends in popular culture may well have contributed. The love marriage provided a frequent theme for *chastushki*—spontaneous, rhymed couplets that became immensely popular in towns and villages toward the end of the nineteenth century. *Chastushki* were attentive to individual feeling and impatient of constraints imposed by others. Rather than unhappily married people bemoaning their fate, the new songs depicted unmarried young people who insisted on their right to choose. Robert Rothstein compares their impact to that of sentimentalism and romanticism.[72]

Whatever the reason, humbly born respondents sometimes manifested considerable awareness of and responsiveness to the feelings of petitioners. Anna Ponomareva had tried to resist her arranged match with a peasant from Arkhangel province, reported a policeman in 1892, elaborating the claim she made in her petition. "She didn't take to him because of his unprepossessing and unattractive appearance and unwillingly

---

71. Ibid., op. 228, d. 42 (Sergunina), 3; op. 221, d. 63 (Kokovina), 28.

72. Robert Rothstein, "Death of the Folk Song," in *Cultures in Flux: Lower-Class Values, Practices, and Resistance in Late Imperial Russia,* ed. Stephen P. Frank and Mark D. Steinberg (Princeton, NJ: Princeton University Press, 1994), 118–20. Such songs had become part of courtship rituals in the provincial towns of Central Russia by the late nineteenth century. See Zhirnova, *Brak i svad'ba,* 28–29, 30.

acceded to the wedding. She cried a lot before she agreed." Discussing the unsuccessful Boiarin union in 1893, a semiliterate seamstress in Moscow observed that the match had been the mother's idea, pressed on an unwilling daughter. The seamstress had noticed that Aleksandra Boiarina showed little feeling for her intended, Petr. Aleksandra declared she didn't like him and avoided him as much as possible before the marriage, the seamstress had observed. The police officer who reported on Aleksandra Boiarina's suicide attempt repeated her statement to him that it was in part to escape the marriage arranged by her mother. The mother, "completely indifferent to her daughter's grief and inclined at all times to take the husband's side," made the most "depressing" impression on the policeman. Maria Krasovskaia, second wife of a boilermaker, had barely known her husband and was "talked into marriage by a relative," a St. Petersburg policeman reported in 1892. The mother of Varvara Dobychina, a forty-eight-year-old peasant woman from a village outside Kharkov, virtually apologized for her role in the unsuccessful marriage of her daughter Varvara, who had run off with another man. Varvara hadn't wanted to marry the townsman Mikhail Dobychin, a stove maker, the mother acknowledged. "Although I knew that then, I talked my daughter into marrying him. Dobychin was alone and an orphan, and I considered him a good man; and by taking him into my family, I thought that with our combined efforts, we'd be able to work and live." The peasant neighbors of Evrosinia Kosterina testified in 1901 that according to rumor, she had married her husband, Dmitrii, only at the urging of her parents, who lived more poorly than his. On the very day of the wedding she had been heard to say that he "didn't please her." One neighbor also noted the incompatibility of their characters. The illiterate Evrosinia was "more developed" and of a more "imposing [predstavitel'nee]" appearance than Dmitrii, a peasant employed as a weaver. "She's bold and gay, whereas he is modest and even quiet, which she might not like." Another neighbor also found that Dmitrii's character was unsuitable for Evrosinia in every way (i po kharakteru k nei vo vse ne podkhodit). "The young couple felt neither sympathy nor love before the marriage," he concluded.[73] While such expressions of sympathy for women pressed into loveless unions were very far from universal, the testimony discussed above indicates the considerable resonance of the affective ideal, although certainly not its triumph over other considerations.

LOVE AND MARRIAGE: THE MEN'S SIDE

If the absence of love or affective choice in the making of a marriage represents a prominent theme in women's narratives, its opposite, the centrality of romantic

73. RGIA, fond 1412, op. 226, d. 98 (Ponomareva), 50–51; op. 213, d. 95 (Boiarina), 12; op. 221, d. 160 (Krasovskaia, A., 1889), 46; op. 216, d. 36 (Dobychina, V., 1898), 21; op. 221, d. 126 (Kosterina, E., 1901), 7, 8. See also RGIA, fond 1412, op. 223, d. 42 (Matrosova, M., 1882), 28; op. 221, d. 97 (Kuzmicheva, A., 1887), 8.

choice in the decision to wed, plays at least as great a role in the counternarratives of husbands, or more precisely, of husbands who derived from the propertied or privileged classes. Men of the laboring classes made no such claims. That men emphasized their disinterested love for their wives indicates the greater freedom from familial constraints that men everywhere enjoy, and which men enjoyed in Russia, too. Such gendered differences are vividly reflected in the advice books and letter-writing guides that proliferated in this period, which portray men as free to declare their love while women, more cautious, are also more constrained and must often first consult with parents, guardians, and the like before responding to a declaration. But men's declarations of disinterested love also show clearly the impact of critiques of material considerations in the making of marriages. Not only for professionals and those who engaged in mental rather than manual labor, but even for some of those who engaged in commerce, disinterested romantic love had become normative, at least as an ideal. A component of modern manhood, its invocation appeared necessary for earning the sympathy of the officials on whom the men's continued cohabitation with their wives depended.

Declarations of disinterested choice are not unexpected from professional men, whose self-presentation was often modeled on Western-style liberal individualism. Sergei Stefanovskii, a teacher at a zemstvo primary school in Viatka, for example, "fell in love" with his future wife's attractive appearance and "her gay and open character." He chose her despite her family's poverty and the absence of a dowry, preferring her to another woman with a dowry of one thousand rubles, or so Stefanovskii claimed. Ivan Pakhitonov was an artist when he met and fell in love with his future wife, a medical student. "Believing that genuine love is most possible when both partners are materially independent," he informed an investigating officer, he did everything in his power to facilitate her studies. The physician Petr Zakharov also declared that he selected his wife solely on the basis of attraction. "She married without a dowry and was so poor that she was wed in a dress that I gave her." Even in cases where there is considerable evidence that money or material advantage played a leading role in a man's marital choice, the man might vehemently deny the role of calculation, sensitive to the opprobrium that now attached to it. "I don't sell myself," the Vilno *gimnazia* teacher Sergei Kotov claimed to have told a friend who recommended a match with a wealthy women, although in 1906 Kotov requested two thousand rubles from the father of his future bride.[74]

More indicative of the impact of affective ideals was the propensity of men from other backgrounds to insist they were similarly motivated. In 1889, the arranged mar-

74. Ibid., op. 228, d. 106 (Stefanovskaia, S., 1895), 10; op. 226, d. 19 (Pakhitonova, M., 1892), 23; op. 219, d. 33 (Zakharova, S., 1898), 13; op. 221, d. 34 (Kotova, L., 1907), 14–17. See also op. 226, d. 67 (Plotnikova, A., 1912). In an alternative version of this rhetoric, the physician Stepan Stsepurzhenskii refused to reunite with or share child custody with his wife, whom he married without love, and "only to legitimize my daughter" (ibid., op. 228, d. 26 [Stsepurzhenskaia, S., 1890], 56–57).

riage of Mikhail Agafonov, a Moscow townsman and Old Believer, brought a sizable dowry and the promise of greater wealth in the future, resources that Mikhail subsequently used to repair his own family's failing fortunes. The semiliterate Mikhail insisted nevertheless that the dowry was "unpretentious" (*nemudriashchaia*) and provided only "so I wouldn't take offense." What had attracted him to the marriage, he insisted, was the "beauty" of his wife, Zinaida. Ivan Skachkov, an accountant in a state bank in Tiumen, Siberia, declared in 1901, "I married for love, not calculation." The Moscow merchant Ilia Petrov asserted that he chose his "beloved wife," the illegitimate daughter of an actress, from a poor household; his father, not her family, provided her trousseau. By his own account, the hereditary honored citizen Nikolai Kupriianov did much the same: "Our marriage was a love match; I received not a kopeck in dowry for my wife."[75] As Diana O'Hara observes in a different context, these antimaterialist statements in fact point to an underlying pragmatic attitude toward marriage, despite the emphasis on love. "The very self-professed negation of economic motives uses property as a yardstick by which to measure love," she contends.[76] But such statements are also evidence that disinterested "love" also mattered for some, at least rhetorically.

THE CHANCELLERY RESPONDS

Although by the latter part of the nineteenth century, the idea that persons should choose their own partners on the basis of romantic love or attraction had become broadly familiar, there is little evidence that the absence of such choice in the making of a marriage elicited the sympathies of chancellery officials. For them, women and men pressured or forced into marriage were praiseworthy primarily when they made their peace with their fate. A woman being forced into marriage is mentioned in only two chancellery reports, which is under 1 percent of those that I have sampled. The first such mention, and the one in which officials appear most critical, occurred in 1887 in the case of Aleksandra Gashunina, who had married a civil servant twenty-seven years her senior some thirteen years earlier "at her mother's insistence," at the age of sixteen, "barely having completed her studies at the local women's monastery." There the reference ends. The second reference concerned the nineteen-year-old townswoman Aleksandra Grigor'eva, who petitioned the chancellery in 1903, after three years of marriage to a silversmith eleven years her senior. In the report on her case, the reference to lack of volition served merely to underscore the virtuous self-denial that rendered Grigor'eva worthy of the emperor's mercy, rather than to explain the breakdown of her marriage. She had been married to her husband, Nikolai, a St. Petersburg

---

75. Ibid., op. 212, d. 33 (Agafonova, Z., 1894), 60; op. 228, d. 59 (Skachkova, S., 1901), 8; op. 226, d. 49 (Petrova, Iu., 1898), 10; op. 221, d. 213 (Kupriianova, V., 1901), 21, 22.

76. Diana O'Hara, *Courtship and Constraint: Rethinking the Making of Marriage in Tudor England* (Manchester, UK: Manchester University Press, 2000), 215.

townsman, "against her will, and from the first days of her marriage he had treated her coarsely and spent his entire earnings exclusively on himself," the report reads. Officials praised Grigor'eva for remaining steadfast in her abusive marriage and doing everything in her power to convince her husband to mend his ways. For two years, "she had endured his coarse treatment, trying by means of admonitions and requests to incline him to change his reprehensible way of life," but to no avail.[77] On this basis, officials recommended that her passport be approved.

Men's lack of volition in the making of a marriage was accorded far more significance in explaining marital breakdown, but it earned the men no more sympathy from officials. Thus the 1896 report on the marriage of Mikhail and Maria Gunazova, both peasants from Kharkov province, stated that Gunazov "married the petitioner against his will, and according to the will of his father." This was the reason for his antipathy toward his wife and severe mistreatment of her. "Declaring to his father, 'you married me off to her, so you go live with her, I don't want to,'" the report continued, "He began to treat her brutally, verbally insulting her practically every day and beating her so cruelly that she sometimes lost consciousness." Ioakim Golovanov, a peasant from Tula province, mistreated his wife for similar reasons, the chancellery reported in 1903. "He married the petitioner without any inclination [*raspolozhenie*] whatsoever...and even tried to conceal himself and avoid the wedding."[78] The witnesses "explain all the ensuing conflicts with his wife by this feeling of disinclination." While attending more closely to the denial of men's selfhood in the making of marriage, officials nevertheless expected husbands, like wives, to come to terms with their lot. In both of the above cases, officials approved a passport for the wife over the husband's objections.

• • •

In the late nineteenth century, ideals of romantic choice circulated ever more widely in Russia. Disseminated by belles-lettres, prescriptive literature, and periodicals, played out on the stages of provincial towns as well as capital cities, they raised challenges to long-standing marital practices according to which the needs of household and family took precedence over individual desires. One result, the evidence suggests, is an easing of parental control over marriage or, more commonly, parental efforts to exercise control in more subtle ways, such as stage-managing meetings with suitable eligible partners. But the key point of this chapter lies elsewhere, in the significance of affective choice to the tenor of women's appeals and what references to it reveal about attitudes toward women's subjectivity. To a significant minority of female petitioners, romantic ideals offered a way to speak of themselves that not only underscored their victimization and passivity at the hands of powerful others but also, and at the same time,

---

77. RGIA, fond 1412, op. 250, d. 100, 1; d. 103, 48–49.
78. Ibid., d. 104, 31; d. 100, 119–119 ob.

invoked the fundamental rights that involuntary marriages violated—the freedom to act on their feelings, the right to dispose of themselves as they chose. That women incorporated involuntary marriage in their petitions or follow-up narratives is all the more telling because, unlike other explanations of marital breakdown to be discussed in subsequent chapters, it elicited no sympathy from officials, although it certainly elicited it from witnesses and investigators. Respondents who identified the absence of women's affective choice as a source of marital breakdown implicitly recognized women's right to emotional self-expression and a role in the making of their marriage, the demands of ascriptive authority notwithstanding.[79] And while it is always difficult to know the extent to which cultural ideals mold individual expectations, the evidence in this chapter also suggests that ideals of affective union, associated as they had become in Russia with condemnations of familial despotism, encouraged some women (and men) to be attentive to, perhaps even to chafe at, circumstances that in an earlier period might have passed without mention.

79. See the discussion in Charles Taylor, *Sources of the Self: The Making of Modern Identity* (Cambridge, MA: Harvard University Press, 1989), 290–91. See also Watt, *The Making of Modern Marriage,* 5.

Money Matters

In April 1906, the Civil Cassation Department of the State Senate, Russia's highest court of appeals, denied a suit brought by Marfa N. with the goal of evicting her disreputable husband and his children from her home. Mrs. N. had based her claim on the law that guaranteed the right of a married woman to own, manage, and dispose of property separately from her husband. Her right to manage her own property, her suit contended, included the right to remove occupants of her property who disturbed the peace, among them her husband and his offspring from a previous marriage. The Senate demurred. Forced to choose between a married woman's inalienable right to manage and dispose of her property and the law requiring spousal cohabitation, which eviction of the husband would violate, the Senate gave precedence to marital law. The Senate ruled that her husband's disreputable behavior, the basis of her claim, did not grant Mrs. N. the right to demand from the court a decision that would effectively separate the residences of husband and wife. In this case, the law forbidding marital separation trumped the law guaranteeing married women's separate right to property.[1]

In Russia, married women's subordinate status in life and law coexisted, sometimes uneasily, with a right to own, manage, and dispose of property that was distinctive in much of contemporary Europe. These rights originated with the nobility. Russian noblewomen's rights to property, having declined in the seventeenth century, in the course of the eighteenth century grew progressively more secure. A law of 1731, which abolished the policy of single inheritance instituted by Tsar Peter the Great in 1714, not only permitted nobles to bestow land on marriageable daughters but also

1. M. I. Pen'kovskii, ed., *Kassatsionnaia praktika. Ne voshedshiia v ofitsial'nyi sbornik resheniia Grazhdanskago Kassatsionnago Departamenta Pravitel'stvuiushchago Senata s 1897 g. po 1914 g., s postateinym i predmetnym ukazateliami* (Petrograd: Pravo, 1915), 374–75. See also William G. Wagner, *Marriage, Property, and Law in Late Imperial Russia* (Oxford: Clarendon, 1994), 220.

invested the women with full rights of ownership of their estates; a decree of 1753 formalized married women's separate control of property and granted them the freedom to dispose of assets without their husband's consent. Thereafter, many noble families acted to secure their daughters' right to property in land and chattel in the form of the dowry. In such cases, the women bore responsibility for collecting taxes, supplying serf recruits, and fulfilling other public obligations connected with the ownership of land, rights that women defended and that were recognized by the courts. The historian Michelle Lamarche Marrese has demonstrated convincingly that at least until the emancipation of the serfs, noblewomen continued to exercise their property rights actively, even as prescriptive literature came increasingly to emphasize women's exclusively domestic calling.[2]

Over time, married women's independent right to own and control property came to be enjoyed by women of other social groups as well and was mirrored in the customary practices of Russia's peasantry, which recognized married women's inalienable right to dowry and income earned by their own labor.[3] After 1864, the Senate consistently ruled in favor of women in disputes with husbands or others who encroached on women's right to control their property. In the case of Murashkovskaia v. Murashkovskii, for example, the Senate affirmed: "not only does the property of a wife not become the property of her husband, but he does not even acquire through marriage the right to use or manage it.... [T]he dowry of a wife, just as any property acquired by her during marriage, through purchase, gift, inheritance, or any other legal means, therefore is considered her separate property." In this 1870 decision, as in others, the Senate opposed the efforts of "husbands, in-laws, or the creditors of husbands to erode the control of a wife over her own property."[4] The ability of married women to buy, sell, and enter contracts rendered their status unusual in Europe through the early twentieth century.[5]

Even as Russia's property law secured a married woman's rights as a propertied individual, however, other factors served to undercut those rights and render their exercise

2. Michelle Lamarche Marrese, *A Woman's Kingdom: Noblewomen and the Control of Property in Russia, 1700–1864* (Ithaca, NY: Cornell University Press, 2002).

3. It remains unclear whether peasant practices were a reflection of imperial law or derived from their own customary practices. Property rights did not extend, however, to women in regions that had been incorporated into the Russian Empire and that were permitted to retain their own laws, which were generally less favorable to women. See V. A. Veremenko, *Dvorianskaia sem'ia i gosudarstvennaia politika vtoraia polovina XIX–nachala XX v.* (St. Petersburg: Evropeiskii dom, 2007), 147–50.

4. Quoted in Wagner, *Marriage, Property, and Law,* 207.

5. Ursula Vogel, "Property Rights and the Status of Women in Germany and England," in *Bourgeois Society in Nineteenth-Century Europe,* ed. Jurgen Kocka and Allan Mitchell (Oxford: Berg, 1993), 241–69; and Mary Lyndon Shanley, *Feminism, Marriage, and the Law in Victorian England* (Princeton, NJ: Princeton University Press, 1989).

and/or defense more difficult and less likely. One key factor was family law. By enjoining women to unlimited obedience, placing divorce out of reach for the vast majority of people, and requiring spouses to cohabit, a requirement reinforced by passport law, family law endowed a husband with enormous authority over a wife's behavior and spheres of activity. The law also assumed a male breadwinner and an economically dependent wife, enjoining husbands to support their wives according to their means and social station.[6] In some ways, Russia's growing economic and cultural modernization reinforced wifely dependence as well. Although the ideology of separate spheres that circulated ever more widely in Russia in the second half of the nineteenth century did not explicitly bar women from participating in activities outside the home, the new emphasis on women's domestic roles undoubtedly encouraged a more critical attitude on the part of others toward such activities, even as it enhanced the value of the work that women did at home. It also encouraged women to make that work the exclusive center of their lives. As will be seen, such ideas never gained complete ascendancy. Nevertheless, they clearly influenced many women, in particular those deriving from the merchantry and the wealthier strata of townspeople, since such ideas were especially well suited to older, estate-based beliefs about women's proper place. A final factor complemented these others: the expansion of the marketplace and the growing importance of capital, rather than or in addition to land, as a source and measure of wealth.[7] In consequence, by the second half of the nineteenth century, if not earlier, the law securing married women's separate ownership and management of property and actual practice were often quite at odds. This chapter explores how women negotiated the resulting tensions. Although disputatious marriages can tell us little directly about the ways that married women might have exercised their independent right to property in harmonious or at least, nonconflictual unions, they provide abundant and compelling evidence of the cultural, economic, and legal factors that might easily override the authority of the law securing women's right to their own property.

LAW AND LIFE COLLIDE: THE DOWRY

Perhaps nowhere was the tension between married women's legal right to own and manage property and popular practice more evident than in relation to the dowry—the cash, goods, or immovable property that the bride brought to her marriage. In its treatment of the dowry, even more than in its treatment of married women's property rights in general, Russian law was distinctive. Other European legal and customary systems regarded the dowry exclusively as a "means of contributing to the

---

6. *Svod zakonov Rossiiskoi imperii* (St. Petersburg, 1857), vol. 10, articles 106–8.

7. Marrese observes a "vital difference" in the relation between noble and merchant women to property, based on a survey of purchase and sale of urban property (*A Woman's Kingdom*, 128–31). On more critical attitudes, see ibid., 200–201.

new household"; in Russia, by contrast, the law gave married women full ownership and control.[8] As Michelle Marrese has shown, Russian law's unusual treatment of the dowry evolved in response to the needs of the landed nobility, which sought to preserve its right to property in land. She has also demonstrated that in the pre-emancipation period, nobles took abundant advantage of the right to bestow land or the means to purchase land in the form of dowry for their daughters. Whether other social groups were similarly inclined to transfer the dowry to a daughter remains a question.

There is strong evidence to suggest that, at least for Russia's urban population, the answer is no. By the second half of the nineteenth century, if not before, the requirements of trade and commercial activity and a more rigid division between gendered spheres combined to produce attitudes and practices concerning dowry in the form of capital and movable goods that differed little from that found elsewhere in Europe. Russia's property law notwithstanding, when they married off their daughters, merchants, artisans, and tradespeople transferred dowry capital and goods either to the husband himself or to the head of his household, to whose disposition it became subject. Only personal items such as clothing and underwear—the trousseau, strictly speaking—remained the exclusive property of the bride.[9]

Initially, these differences between the practices of nobles and peasants and those ascribed to towns (merchants, artisans, and townspeople) were probably linked to their different forms of wealth. People engaged in commerce, petty trade, or even artisanal activities required capital; and marriage in Russia as elsewhere was a primary means to obtain it. Protestations to the contrary notwithstanding, money mattered a lot in the making of a marriage, especially to those engaged in commerce but also to others, even professionals.[10] Historians of people who engaged in commerce agree on the overriding importance of the "marriage bargain" in late nineteenth-century Russia. It was necessitated by the highly competitive and uncertain economic climate and the relative difficulty of obtaining liquid capital, despite the expansion of banking in the second half of the nineteenth century, and by the fact that most enterprises were owned and run

---

8. "Introduction," in *The Marriage Bargain: Women and Dowries in European History*, ed. Marion Kaplan (New York: Harrington Park Press, 1985), 1. Elsewhere, the dowry might revert to the wife on the husband's death or desertion.

9. The status of immovable property was more ambiguous. For both kinds of property, see Veremenko, *Dvorianskaia sem'ia*, 160–61. Such practices prompted the liberal jurist Aleksandr Zagorovskii to argue that the "legal consciousness" of Russian society regarded the dowry as at the husband's disposal (A. I. Zagorovskii, "Lichnye i imushchestvennye otnosheniia mezhdu suprugami," *Russkaia mysl'*, bk. 4 [1897], 67).

10. T. I. Liubina, "Brak i razvody v provintsial'noi chinovnich'ei srede vtoroi polovine XIX–nachala XX v.," in *Rod i sem'ia v kontekste tverskoi istorii: sbornik nauchnykh materialov*, no. 1 (Tver: Tverskoi gosudarstvennyi universitet, 2005), 233.

by kin.[11] Marriages among people who lived in towns along the lower Volga were based on "strict calculation," write A. N. Zorin and N. V. Zorin. When they selected a bride, parents of eligible young men used the opportunity to enhance the family's fortunes; after marriage, the bride's dowry became part of the household's property.[12] Whether merchants chose their brides themselves, or entered marriages arranged by others, they regarded the dowry in much the same fashion—as "inert matter, which only the masculine principle of the merchant could activate."[13] The gendered culture of entrepreneurship reinforced such attitudes.[14] By contrast with the culture of landed property, it remained on the whole inhospitable to married women's active participation (energetic and strong-minded widows being a prominent and noteworthy exception), while the cult of domesticity reinforced the belief that the world of commerce was men's sphere and married women belonged at home.[15] As capital increasingly displaced land as a source of wealth, if not prestige, in the years after the emancipation of the serfs, such attitudes toward the dowry became increasingly widespread, adopted even by people who did not earn their income through trade—professionals, for example—and civil servants.

The result was that dowry in cash and movable property was almost invariably given to the husband to manage. Prescriptive literature, for example, while casting aspersions on men who married for money, took the practice for granted, even in cases where the prospective husband was not himself a businessman. "Capital taken for the wife as a dowry must be put to good use," counseled an advice book that appeared in 1897 with a male audience in mind. The author acknowledged that proper disposition of

11. V. N. Kulik, "Zhenshchiny dinastii Riabushinskikh," in *Rod i sem'ia,* 179; Iu. M. Goncharov, "Soslovnaia spetsifika gendernogo semeinogo poriadka v russkom provintsial'nom gorode vtoroi poloviny XIX v.," in *Sem'ia v rakurse sotsial'nogo znaniia: Sbornik nauchnykh statei,* ed. Iu. M. Goncharov (Barnaul: Izdatel'stvo NP Azbuka, 2001), 238; N. A. Varentsov, *Slyshannoe. Vidennoe. Peredumannoe. Perezhitoe* (Moscow: Novoe literaturnoe obozrenie, 1999), 626. On the family character of businesses, see P. A. Buryshkin, *Moskva kupecheskaia* (New York: Izdatel'stvo imeni Chekhova, 1954), 58; Iu. A. Petrov, *Moskovskaia burzhuaziia v nachale XX veka: predprinimatel'stvo i politika* (Moscow: Mosgorarkhiv, 2002), 162.

12. A. N. Zorin et al., *Ocherki gorodskogo byta dorevoliutsionnogo Povolzh'ia* (Ulianovsk: Izdatel'stvo srednevolzhskogo nauchnogo tsentra, 2000), 93–94.

13. Goncharov, "Soslovnaia spetsifika," 238.

14. Muriel Joffe and Adele Lindenmeyr, "Daughters, Wives, and Partners: Women of the Moscow Merchant Elite," in *Merchant Moscow: Images of Russia's Vanished Bourgeoisie,* ed. James L. West and Iurii A. Petrov (Princeton, NJ: Princeton University Press, 1998), 104; Catriona Kelly, "Teacups and Coffins: The Culture of Russian Merchant Women," in *Women in Russia and Ukraine,* ed. Rosalind Marsh (New York: Cambridge University Press, 1996), 64–65.

15. Iurii Goncharov, *Gorodskaia sem'ia Sibiri vtoroi poloviny XIX–nachale XX v.* (Barnaul: Izdatel'stvo Altaiskogo gosudarstvennogo universiteta, 2002), 274.

— Знаешь, Соничка, отецъ твой не хочетъ дать за тобою приданаго.
— А знаешь что? Не будь дуракомъ, Мишенька, и если тебѣ не дадутъ
приданаго, то и не женись на мнѣ!

FIGURE 9.

"You know, Sonia, your father doesn't want to give a dowry for you."

"Then you know what? Don't be a fool, Misha. If you don't get a dowry,

don't marry me."

Strekoza, *no. 2 (1885), M. E. Saltykov-Shchedrin Public Library.*

СВАХА.

Господинъ.—Да, милая... но у вашей невѣсты огромная бородавка подъ носомъ!
Сваха.—За эфту самую бородавку за то ейный тятенька лишнихъ пять тысячъ тебѣ жертвуетъ.

FIGURE 10. *The matchmaker*
Gentleman: *"My dear, the bride you've offered me has an enormous wart beneath her nose!"*
Matchmaker: *"That wart would cost another man 5,000 rubles more."*
Strekoza, *no. 42 (1900), M. E. Saltykov-Shchedrin Public Library.*

capital might be tricky for the inexperienced. "You must seek out a business that will offer good returns on the capital you use. Any mistake in that regard will bring the loss of someone else's money," the author warned, acknowledging women's legal right to the dowry even as he assumed men's authority to manage it. To entrust capital to the bride rather than the groom could poison a couple's life. Not only might it disturb the appropriate conjugal balance of power but, seeing his wife's capital "inactive," or expended without any control or accounting, the husband might well suffer and become bitter, leading him to drink and carouse with his comrades. *Good Manners* counseled men who hoped to obtain a dowry to make sure of the amount beforehand, lest their disappointed hopes for a "good position" sow the seeds of discord.[16] Cartoons that appeared in the satirical journal *Strekoza* in the final decades of the nineteenth century reflect these predispositions as well. The liberal jurist Aleksandr Zagorovskii echoed them, attributing them to long-standing Russian practices. He concluded that "the legal consciousness of our society" regarded dowry property as being at the disposal of the husband, irrespective of women's rights in law.[17]

In disputatious marriages, too, propertied parents usually assumed that the husbands would manage dowry capital. Plaintiffs, defendants, witnesses, and investigators refer explicitly to such transfers. At his marriage in 1888, the Moscow merchant Petr Sergunin received ten thousand rubles in cash that the Sergunins invested in their troubled business, Sergunin and Sons, which traded in gold, silver, and diamonds in the Passazh in Moscow. When Maria Tikhomirova, the daughter of a merchant from the town of Egoriev married in 1892, her dowry of ten thousand rubles, "according to custom" was put at the disposal of her husband and in-laws. Tatiana Popova was the daughter of Mikhail Popov, the well-to-do St. Petersburg bookseller, whose shop sat on the corner of Nevskii Prospekt and the Fontanka. When she married Nikolai Sokolov in 1895, he "received" her dowry of twenty-five thousand rubles and in addition, her father provided money for the groom to open a tobacco warehouse in the Vyborg section. Likewise, when Aleksandra Razaeva, daughter of a merchant from Kurgan, Tomsk province, married a shop clerk in 1895, her father opened a well-stocked store for him on the ground floor of the father's house. When the eighteen-year-old Elena Loseva married the hereditary honored citizen Aleksandr Sinitsyn in 1906, her mer-

---

16. I. K-v, *Polnyi pismovik i sovety molodym liudiam, kak derzhat' sebia v obshchestve, bezoshibochno delat' vybor zhenikha i nevesty i byt' schastlivym v supruzheskoi zhizni* (Moscow: Gerbek, 1896), 191–93; *Khoroshii ton: sbornik pravil i sovetov na vse sluchai zhizni obshchestvennoi i semeinoi*, 2d ed. (St. Petersburg: German Goppe, 1885), 130–31.

17. Zagorovskii, "Lichnye i imushchestvennye otnosheniia," 67.

chant father Sergei Losev "handed over" to Sinitsyn her dowry portion in the amount of fifty thousand rubles.[18]

When dowry givers endeavored to protect a daughter's interests by limiting the ability of the future son-in-law (or the head of his household) freely to dispose of the dowry, it often indicated the giver's distrust. Thus, disapproving of their new son-in-law, whom the daughter had wed despite the parents' objections, Sergei Losev bestowed a far larger sum, 150,000 rubles, directly on his daughter. The wealthy Siberian merchant Ivan Molchanov likewise distrusted the intentions of his future son-in-law, the lawyer Vladimir Ptitsyn, perhaps because of the liberal speeches Ptitsyn was in the habit of making before the city duma (council). Instead of giving Vladimir his daughter Alevtina's fifty thousand ruble dowry, Molchanov registered it in her name and permitted her only to receive the interest. Having promised his daughter Sofia 125 rubles a month or 1,500 rubles a year after her marriage, Eduard Karpant'e, hereditary honored citizen, notarized this financial commitment at the insistent request of his noble future son-in-law. But Karpant'e apparently knew of the young man's potentially mercenary aims, for the document strictly forbade Sofia to transfer the notarized commitment to anyone during the father's lifetime or even to promise to do so at his death. And at least one dowry giver appears to have treated the dowry explicitly as an agreement between himself and his daughter, just as nobles had once done. In 1891, on her marriage to Nikolai Nrodov, the wealthy Moscow merchant Dmitrii Vorob'ev gave his daughter Natalia a landed estate in Rostov, Iaroslavl province, and fifty thousand rubles in cash. It remains unclear whether the father did so because he distrusted his future son-in-law, the son of a well-to-do peasant who owned weaving factories in his village, or because dowry practice concerning land, by contrast with capital, was more ambiguous.[19]

The Kokovin-Razorenov match, which features yet another distrustful dowry giver, illustrates why some fathers might marry their daughters to men they did not trust. It also provides an extreme but not unique example of the ways in which money might figure in the making and breaking of a marriage. This was a union forged, like others in the merchant milieu, at the initiative of the couple's parents and with the needs of the family uppermost: "not according to the attraction of love but by my father's will," as Zinaida Kokovina subsequently put it. Although the father, Fedor Razorenov, a well-to-do Old Believer merchant, owner of textile mills in Kostroma province, barely knew Ivan Kokovin when Kokovin asked for his daughter's hand, he accepted the suit

18. RGIA, fond 1412, op. 228, d. 42 (Sergunina, O., 1890), 36; op. 228, d. 55 (Sinitsyna, E., 1907), 20; op. 229, d. 47 (Tikhomirova, M., 1894) 1; op. 228, d. 83 (Sokolova, T., 1909), 30; op. 227, d. 9 (Razaeva, A., 1909), 56.

19. Ibid., 20; op. 226, d. 149 (Ptitsyna, A., 1892), 101; op. 212, d. 51 (Azancheeva, S., 1900), 65 ob.; op. 224, d. 53 (Nrodova, N., 1901), 1. On the ambiguous status of immovable property, see Veremenko, *Dvorianskaia sem'ia*, 161.

with alacrity. Zinaida was twenty-eight at the time, well beyond the usual age of marriage, and her parents were desperate to settle the older sister so that, strictly following birth order, their more comely younger daughter could finally wed. The initiative for the marriage came from Ivan's formidable mother, the merchant widow Aleksandra Kokovina, who served as head of the family firm, Aleksandra Kokovina and Sons of Kineshma, which traded in metal products and cement. For the Kokovins, the goal was to obtain a portion of the Razorenov family fortune in the form of the dowry and improved access to liquid capital through bank loans, which the Razorenovs' greater commercial visibility and success was presumed to offer. But Razorenov, distrustful of his future in-laws' intent and business acumen, sought to protect his daughter's assets. Although he eventually agreed to the Kokovins' demand that he invest his daughter's twenty-five thousand ruble dowry in the family's trading house, he also insisted in the teeth of their resistance that they issue a signed bill of exchange for that amount, made out in his daughter's name. Until the very eve of his wedding, Ivan Kokovin sought to change this arrangement. The day before, he wrote his future father-in-law to ask in the name of "conjugal solidarity" that the bill of exchange registering the dowry investment be issued in his name instead of his bride's. "A husband loses prestige in his wife's eyes," Ivan asserted, "when she has the right to manage her own means without the agreement of the husband."[20]

The marriage was a failure from the first. Having arranged it primarily if not exclusively with the dowry in mind, the Kokovins, including the husband, had no interest in the bride and may have tried to punish her for her father's refusal. They certainly made her feel unwelcome and unloved. At marriage, Zinaida joined their household, which was headed by her husband's widowed mother and included several adult married brothers and their wives. This was not an uncommon arrangement in late nineteenth-century Russia, especially among those engaged in commerce. Complex households, consisting of at least two married couples, enabled business people to make the most of their assets by concentrating the capital requisite for success in commercial affairs. Complex households were especially common among Old Believers such as the Kokovins.[21]

Such households were notorious for the difficulties they posed to an in-marrying daughter-in-law, but by Zinaida's description the Kokovin household was more inhospitable than most. "From the first days of my stay in the [Kokovin] household, everyone in the family treated me coldly and in an unfriendly way and made my life unpleasant; their

20. RGIA, fond 1412, op. 221, d. 64 (Kokovina, Z., 1899), 29, 30, 55.

21. See B. N. Mironov, *Sotsial'naia istoriia Rossii (XVIII–nachalo XX v.): Genezis lichnosti, demokraticheskoi sem'i, grazhdanskogo obshchestva i pravovogo gosudarstva*, 3d ed., 2 vols. (St. Petersburg: Dmitrii Bulanin, 2003), 1: 235. See also Goncharov, *Gorodskaia sem'ia*, 370–71; and Zorin, et al., *Ocherki gorodskogo byta*, 92–93.

contempt deeply offended my pride," Zinaida asserted in her petition to the chancellery. "I couldn't go out to take a walk when I wanted, I couldn't eat when I wanted, I couldn't visit my friends," she complained. Before she could take a step she required the permission of her husband's mother; she was also required to obey the orders of every family member "without a murmur." Even this, she could have endured. What made the situation intolerable was the husband's behavior. He treated her "not only coldly but coarsely, as if trying to underscore the fact that I am alien." Failing to behave as a husband should even in the first days of their marriage, Ivan "never caressed me or welcomed me; he avoided my company and spent his free time with his mother and brothers." Indeed, the couple never had sex at all; when she petitioned seven years after the wedding, Zinaida remained a virgin, having returned to her parents' home after several months of marriage, when she realized she had simply been "a victim of financial calculations."[22]

USING/ABUSING WOMEN'S ASSETS

The power of cultural norms is especially evident in cases where dowry or inherited property was given explicitly to the wife. Even in these cases, women rarely managed or disposed of their property themselves. The assumption that the world of business was men's sphere and the home women's, that it was a husband's responsibility to support his wife—a responsibility inscribed in law—influenced how wives treated their own assets. Women's youth and inexperience at marriage may have reinforced these factors.[23] As a result, even when the assets were in the women's own name, wives usually ceded to their husband the right to manage them. Thus, at her marriage in 1891, Natalia Nrodova granted to her husband, Nikolai, a power of attorney to manage her landed estate in the countryside. "I trusted him to manage my property," she remembered. Until he ceased to support her and their children, she never even requested that

22. RGIA, fond 1412, op. 221, d. 64 (Kokovina), 1–2, 8. These strict rules probably differed little from those of countless other Old Believer households, where the daughter-in-law was required to show the utmost respect for all her husband's relatives irrespective of their age and was strictly punished for any violation of the family order. See N. A. Aralovets, *Gorodskaia sem'ia v Rossii 1897–1926: Istoriko-demograficheskii aspekt* (Moscow: Institut rossiiskoi istorii RAN, 2003), 100. The Kokovin alliance was not the only one in which the family's financial considerations loomed so large that the husband proved unwilling or unable to consummate his marriage. See ibid., op. 228, d. 42 (Sergunina).

23. Merchant women and townswomen married young, usually before they reached the age of twenty; merchant husbands were generally seven or eight years older, having already acquired business experience. See Iu. M. Goncharov, *Kupecheskaia sem'ia vtoroi poloviny XIX–nachala XX vv.: po materialam komp'iuternoi bazy dannykh kupecheskikh sem'ei Zapadnoi Sibiri* (Moscow: Institut etnologii i antropologii RAN, 1999), 233–34; and Zorin et al., *Ocherki gorodskogo byta*, 96–97. Zinaida Kokovina was very much an old maid, at least to the merchant way of thinking, when she married at twenty-seven.

Nikolai show her the accounts. To explain why she transferred her own dowry property to her merchant husband, Vera Molodtsova referred explicitly to the ideology of separate spheres. After her marriage, Molodtsova asserted, she had done "everything possible to help my husband Nikolai, occupying myself with the household and transferring to him my entire property, a dowry of twenty thousand rubles and other items I brought to the marriage worth five thousand more." The townswoman Tatiana Alekseeva, eighteen years old when she wed, had apprenticed in her own mother's shoemaking shop, which became part of her dowry. At Tatiana's marriage, she transferred the shop to her husband, Petr, along with one thousand rubles in cash. The same assumptions might even be at work for women who were nobly born. When she married at the age of eighteen, Evgenia Pykhanova owned a dairy farm that she had inherited from an aunt. She entrusted it to her husband, Andrei, a professional agronomist, to manage. A graduate of the Moscow Agricultural Institute, Andrei boasted the expertise that his young wife lacked.[24]

Inscribed in the law, the unconditional obedience and submission that wives owed their husbands reinforced women's tendency to defer to their husband in matters of property; it also encouraged husbands to expect their wives to defer. If a husband sought access to his wife's assets, she might find it difficult to refuse him. Olga Kozyreva, the daughter of a noble, almost twenty-five years old when she wed, had initially given her dowry of forty-eight thousand rubles to her brother to manage. Although the brother regularly paid her interest from the capital, her engineer husband, Dmitrii Kozyrev, wanted to control the money himself. "To calm him" when he became angry at her initial refusal, Olga acceded to his demand, letting him receive the interest, from which he allotted her money for household expenses; she also gave him a power of attorney to run her affairs. Zinaida Agafonova likewise acceded to the request of her husband, Mikhail, to be appointed guardian of the 177,500 rubles in capital, yielding 7,000 yearly in interest that she inherited from her grandmother in 1892, although she quickly came to regret it, since her preference for a lavish lifestyle conflicted with her husband's abstemious ways.[25]

Some men responded not only with anger but also with violence when their wives refused to acquiesce to financial demands. One example is Nikolai Andreev, a merchant's son. Andreev had already squandered the dowry of his wife, Olga, and pawned even the children's crosses to spend on drunken binges. When he asked Olga to borrow more money from her uncle to cover his debts, she refused. Although she was eight months pregnant with their fifth child at the time, the enraged Nikolai struck her so hard that she fell to the floor and beat her about the head with his fists. Still, Olga con-

24. RGIA, fond 1412, op. 224, d. 53 (Nrodova), 1; op. 223, d. 102 (Molodtsova, V., 1905), 1; op. 212, d. 126 (Alekseeva, T., 1900), 30, 48; op. 226, d. 163 (Pykhanova, E., 1910), 7.

25. Ibid., op. 221, d. 61 (Kozyreva, O., 1900), 2; op. 212, d. 45 (Agafonova, Z., 1894), 11.

tinued to defer to him in other matters. "She was always tender to her husband," even when he hit her, the investigator reported of her exemplary conduct. "She bore everything patiently and never complained to anyone of his cruel treatment." She finally petitioned, he asserted, "only at her parents' insistence." The merchant Vasilii Nosin likewise lost his temper under similar circumstances, or so the investigator concluded. Having spent the entire seven thousand ruble dowry he had obtained for his wife, Tatiana, in 1872, he beat and abused her when, nine years later, she refused to give him any of her substantial inheritance for use in his trade.[26]

Women's willingness to defer to their husbands is especially noteworthy in the marriages of Maria Gladysheva and Aleksandra Noskova, because both of them were already experienced businesswomen when they wed. Before her marriage to a shop clerk in 1884, the townswoman Maria Gladysheva had owned and managed a workshop employing fifteen seamstresses in Moscow. After the wedding, the husband began drinking heavily and ceased showing up for his job, squandering not only his own assets but his wife's property as well. Eventually she was forced to close the shop. Even then, ties of obligation, loyalty, and perhaps affection remained: from her wages as a seamstress in someone else's shop, Gladysheva continued to pay for her unemployed husband's apartment and food.[27] Deference to her husband's wishes made it even more difficult for Aleksandra Noskova to preserve her assets. Born to a merchant household, Olga first began selling groceries at the Bologoe station of the Nikolaevskii railroad in 1878 after her husband, Dmitrii, a peasant and former manservant, forced her from his house not long after their marriage. But when he reappeared, she took him back, while continuing to trade. The two cohabited until Dmitrii abandoned her once more, after having used up her entire property and capital. Then he found a job and demanded his wife join him, and she acceded. He did not keep the position for long, however, on account of his drinking; so the two moved back to Bologoe and settled together in her mother's house until the mother, fed up with Dmitrii's drunken and unruly conduct, threw him out of her house. Mother and daughter began trading together. Again Dmitrii turned up, urging his wife to separate her business from her mother's and resume cohabitation. Despite her husband's past behavior, Olga agreed. Only when he proved more a hindrance than a help in her business did her forbearance finally come to an end: she told him to "stop making scandals and find himself some work," whereupon he disappeared.[28]

26. Ibid., op. 212, d. 148 (Andreeva, O., 1891), 1, 34–35; 61–64; op. 224, d. 45 (Nosina, T., 1882), 22, 27. See also op. 226, d. 6 (Palenova, O., 1882), 1.

27. It is difficult to know what motivated her, because we learn about the marriage from the chancellery's summary report of the investigation, rather than the words of the parties involved (ibid., op. 250, d. 102, 27–28).

28. Ibid., op. 224, d. 46 (Noskova, 1882), 1–2, 15–16.

The well-documented case of Ekaterina Sabashnikova-Baranovskaia illustrates even more vividly how normative expectations of female behavior might complicate a woman's relationship to her property, but also how a husband's legal authority might make it difficult for a woman to defend her rights. Born to a wealthy and cultivated merchant household, Ekaterina Sabashnikova was an unusually energetic young woman with a practical turn of mind, who as the eldest child in the family took responsibility for the fate of the family fortunes. Although she was only twenty years old when her widowed father died in 1879, she did her best to take his place in addition to managing the household and raising her younger siblings, responsibilities more typical for an eldest daughter. "Valuing her remarkable intellect, persistence, and businesslike approach [*delovitost'*]," the guardian of the family's financial affairs consulted her on all major decisions, her younger brother Mikhail remembered. Ekaterina took over her father's study, where she was often seen hard at work. But after her marriage at the age of twenty to Aleksandr Baranovskii, a lawyer, in 1880, at his request she gave up her role as co-manager of the family's assets and allowed her husband to take her place, although he had never managed a business. Thereafter, his role in the family's business affairs only grew. A year later, after the death of the guardian of the Sabashnikov family's property, at Aleksandr's behest Ekaterina appointed his older brother Egor guardian and installed Aleksandr as manager of a sugar-refining factory in which the family held controlling shares.[29] The Baranovskii brothers' management of the Sabashnikov family's assets was disastrous, resulting in the loss of thousands of rubles and leaving their financial affairs in a muddle. Eventually, the other partners forced the brothers to leave their positions.

It was at this point, when his wife's compliance no longer sufficed, that Aleksandr Baranovskii began to draw on his legal authority, in particular his authority to determine his children's place of residence and circumstances, in pursuit of his own mercenary ends. Having lost the right to manage the Sabashnikov assets, he (and his brother) sought to gain ownership of them instead. But here Ekaterina drew the line. After she refused to sign over her property, her husband removed their five children to his brother's estate in Mogilev province and then to an estate of his own. When Ekaterina followed to be with the children, he forbade her friends or family to visit or her own servants to attend her. Having isolated her from all sources of emotional and personal support, he subjected Ekaterina to psychological pressures, including tirades

29. M. V. Sabashnikov, *Zapiski Mikhaila Vasil'evicha Sabashnikova* (Moscow: Izdatel'stvo im. Sabashnikovykh, 1995), 53, 57, 58. Information on Baranovskii is drawn from that account, as well as from the words of Baranovskii himself. On the financial arrangements, see RGIA, fond 1412, op. 213, d. 18 (Suprugi Baranovskikh, 1890), 3.

in the presence of their ailing child, over her refusal to transfer her property, or so the chancellery concluded having examined the evidence.[30]

Other men, too, used their legal right to command a wife and children's presence and/or superior access to social resources and knowledge of the ways of the world to obtain access to their wives' assets. Employing the power of the passport, for example, a husband might seek to force his wife to purchase her own freedom. Take the townsman Aleksei Korolev, a conductor on the railroad. Determined to force his wife, Natalia, to transfer to him control of the house in Samara, worth eight thousand rubles, that she had purchased with her inheritance and on whose proceeds she lived, he demanded that, in exchange for approving her passport, she allow him to manage and receive the proceeds from her house over a fifteen-year period while paying a minuscule rent. Sergei Lebedev, a townsman, would approve a passport for his wife, Elena, a well-to-do woman who in 1907 owned her own home and directed a joint-stock company in Moscow, only if she paid him thirty thousand rubles. The townsman Feodor Bol'shikh, bookkeeper for a private trading house, offered to approve a passport for his wife if she promised not to pursue her claims in court. He had retained his wife's dowry of twenty-two hundred rubles in cash and five thousand rubles worth of goods when she fled his home. In a variation on this theme, Vasilii Nosin offered his wife, Tatiana, a one-year passport if she agreed to abandon the suit she had brought in a St. Petersburg court to recover her misappropriated inheritance. Likewise, in exchange for approving her passport, Petr Alekseev asked his wife, Tatiana, to surrender a court decision requiring him to pay her six hundred rubles plus court costs.[31] Such maneuvers were so commonplace and, apparently, well known that in some cases—although not the above—petitioners claimed falsely to have been subject to them.[32]

A husband's authority, wifely deference, and more were operative in the case of Tatiana Sokolova, who appears to have been helpless to resist her own exploitation, notwithstanding her father's considerable wealth and support. Nikolai Sokolov, it will be recalled, was provided with a substantial dowry and tobacco storehouse at his wedding in 1895 by his father-in-law, Mikhail Popov. Five years later, he had finally exhausted his father-in-law's good will. Sokolov had failed to make a profit on the

---

30. Ibid., 149–51. One entire, very thick dossier is devoted entirely to letters Ekaterina wrote to others during this period. Mikhail Sabashnikov gives a brief and largely accurate version of the marital breakdown in *Zapiski*, 133–39.

31. Ibid., op. 221, d. 108 (Koroleva, N., 1900), 1, 29; op. 222, d. 41 (Lebedeva, E., 1907), 1; op. 213, d. 84 (Bol'shikh, M., 1886), 16; op. 224, d. 45 (Nosina), 22; op. 212, d. 126 (Alekseeva), 39. In exchange for the passport, the nobleman L. Grabbe insisted that his wife sign over to him her entire estate. See Veremenko, *Dvorianskaia sem'ia*, 240.

32. For false claims, see RGIA, fond 1412, op. 212, d. 33 (Agafonova), 1; and op. 212, d. 4 (Avvakumova, V., 1904), 1.

tobacco storehouse that the father-in-law bought for him and had run up a mass of debts, which his father-in-law paid to protect him from bankruptcy. Given to drink and physically abusive, Nikolai had also become sexually involved with the family's chambermaid. At this, "seeing my intolerable position," as Tatiana wrote, her father gave her and the three children thirty-five hundred rubles and encouraged her to establish a life of her own. But she proved unable to do so. She explained this failure in terms of her husband's use of force to get his way, but while Nikolai certainly abused his authority, his wife, constrained by habits of deference and submission, also appears to have done nothing to resist him. Nikolai, she wrote, "took the money from me by force," and set up housekeeping with his lover (their former chambermaid) in an apartment he rented. "We moved there," her account continues, "my husband, the children, and the chambermaid, now as mistress." After husband and mistress drove her from the apartment, Tatiana rented an apartment with the help of her father. But her husband and his lover retained custody of the children and received 150 rubles a month in child support from Mikhail Popov, the children's grandfather. "I tried hard to gain custody of the children," the children's mother wrote, "but my husband would not permit it." Ignorant of the possibility or unwilling to reveal her private affairs in public, she did not seek child custody through the courts, as she certainly could have done. When Popov died in 1907, bequeathing Tatiana eighty thousand rubles in capital with the right to use the interest, she continued the child support payments, although according to her own allegations the husband and his lover spent the money on themselves: "the children receive no moral training; they aren't even sent to school."[33]

Once she became an heiress, Nikolai initiated even more aggressive efforts to gain command of her property. To this end, he employed methods both institutional and illegal (he apparently tried to have her murdered). When her passport ran out, he refused to renew it. More seriously, he endeavored to have her declared insane, taking advantage of a husband's authority to challenge his wife's sanity as many times as he pleased. At his request, she was twice summoned to the St. Petersburg Medical Board for an examination by psychiatrists; he also dispatched a psychiatrist to examine her in her apartment. These efforts having failed, Nikolai had the police bring her to the Special Bureau of the Provincial Administration, where she was examined yet again and finally declared insane.[34]

She was saved from incarceration in a madhouse only because, like a feminist fairy godmother, the Society to Protect Women came to her rescue. A philanthropic organization that formed at the turn of the century primarily for the purpose of reforming prostitutes, the society also assisted hundreds of unhappily married women

33. Ibid., op. 228, d. 83 (Sokolova), 30–31.
34. Ibid., 31–32.

to escape abusive marriages.[35] Sokolova contacted the organization (it is unclear how she learned of it) and its head sent her for consultation to three psychiatrists, among them the well-known Vladimir Bekhterev, himself a member of the organization. The psychiatrists found her to be sane:

> She answers all questions properly, explains her situation in a lucid and logical way, laughs in the appropriate places, and conducts herself appropriately under the circumstances. She seems normal....Although she received a very meager education and her intellectual perspective is rather limited, she is well aware of things and her intellectual abilities show no noticeable defects. She explains coherently her social position and financial interests, and I see no reason to dispute her ability to fulfill her legal obligations [*pravosposobnost'*].

When the Medical Board dismissed these findings and at her husband's insistence summoned her again, claiming that the board was required to examine a woman's sanity as often as her husband requested, the society again came to her rescue. With its assistance, in 1911 Sokolova petitioned the State Senate, which eventually ruled in her favor. On the basis of the psychiatrists' report, the Senate annulled the Medical Boards' finding of madness in March 1911.[36]

Occasionally, the shoe was on the other foot. Husbands had a monopoly neither on mercenary motives nor on extravagant habits. Satirical cartoons published in contemporary mass media certainly made much of avaricious, although not necessarily immoral, wives, who succumbed to the blandishments of the new consumer economy and whose desire to spend money exceeded their husband's willingness to provide it. Spendthrift wives occasionally figure in chancellery dossiers as well.[37] Thus, for example, the townswoman Zinaida Agafonova's desire to entertain guests lavishly, drink champagne and fine wines, and spend evenings in pleasure gardens in the company of a male acquaintance and summers at a rented dacha after she inherited a fortune from her grandmother in 1892 served as the source of constant conflict with her husband, Mikhail. An Old Believer loyal to the tenets of his faith, abstemious and antisocial, Mikhail sternly disapproved of his wife's openhanded ways. He preferred to invest the interest from her capital in repairing his and his parents' house and in business.

35. Wagner, *Marriage, Property, and Law*, 89–90. On the organization's patronizing efforts to redeem prostitutes, see Laurie Bernstein, *Sonia's Daughters: Prostitutes and Their Regulation in Imperial Russia* (Berkeley: University of California Press, 1995).

36. Ibid., 32–35. Ilia Popov, a physician, likewise attempted to have his wife declared insane in order to obtain access to her inheritance. See ibid., op. 226, d. 111 (Popova, S., 1901).

37. On the consumer economy, see Sally West, "The Material Promised Land: Advertising's Modern Agenda in Late Imperial Russia," *Russian Review* 57, no. 3 (1998): 345–63.

Although Zinaida's request for a passport rested not only on her husband's unjust appropriation of her resources—his "demand that I turn over to him the capital that belongs to me," as she put it, and abuse when she refused—but also on his alleged refusal to allow her to convert from Old Belief to Russian Orthodoxy, officials found in her husband's favor. They did so in terms that underscore the degree to which officials, like others, regarded inherited wealth, like property in land, as belonging to the family rather than the individual and the owner as primarily its steward.[38] Mikhail had, they noted, done everything in his power to restrain his wife's "thoughtless [*neumelyi*] and extravagant expenditures," scolding her for them, unfortunately in "very coarse terms" and strictly limiting the funds she had at her disposal. At the same time, "using her money," he had little by little improved both his parents' and his own family's material situation." Officials concluded that whatever Mikhail Agafonov's "coarseness and harshness, the result of his lack of upbringing," he was better able than his wife "to oversee the interests and material well-being of the children."[39] By denying Zinaida a passport, officials sought to ensure Mikhail's continued control over her person and her expenditures.

THE POWER OF THE LAW

Property law, by contrast, stood firmly on women's side. When women took their husbands to court for misappropriating their assets, judges almost invariably found in women's favor. However, if these contentious marriages are any guide, such findings did them little good. Most of the women whose husbands had appropriated their assets lacked the knowledge, will, or resources necessary to pursue their interests in court, and women who did pursue them acted only after relations between themselves and their husbands had long passed the critical juncture when assets remained to be preserved. Couples who still lived together were understandably reluctant to sue one another in court, even when their disputes involved property: "I didn't want to make things public and take my husband to court, and so forgave him everything," as Zinaida Agafonova put it.[40] Going to court only exacerbated tensions, as the jurist Aleksandr Borovikovskii noted.[41] As a result, women's assets were often, quite simply, gone.

An exception to this rule is Natasha Nrodova, one of the few women who appealed to the chancellery and sued successfully in court. Owner of a landed estate, she finally took action when she realized that her husband had mortgaged her estate to his own father for a mere pittance and spent every kopeck of the income on himself. In 1893, she brought suit before the Moscow circuit court to discontinue the power of attorney

38. Marrese, *A Woman's Kingdom*, 222–27.
39. RGIA, fond 1412, op. 212, d. 33 (Agafonova), 186–87.
40. Ibid., 1, 9.
41. A. L. Borovikovskii, *Otchet sud'i*, 3 vols. (St. Petersburg: Pravda, 1909), 2: 214.

she had granted her husband and to recover her financial losses. The court ruled in her favor. Recognizing her inalienable right to her own property, the court also agreed to evict the husband from the house that she owned in Moscow. Confronting precisely the same conflict between property and marital law with which this chapter begins, the Moscow circuit court arrived at a different conclusion than would the Senate over a decade later. Nrodov had no right to use property that belonged to his wife if she disapproved, the Moscow circuit court found. If Nrodov wanted to require her to co-habit with him, he could exercise his legal right to cohabitation *only* in a dwelling that he himself rented or owned. Emphasizing the husband's obligations to his wife rather than his authority over her person, the court noted that it was the husband who was supposed to provide a home for his wife, and not the wife to provide a roof for her husband.[42] This decision was apparently not unique. Among the "undesirable conse-quences" of women's separate property rights the liberal jurist Aleksandr Zagorovskii included "the wife removing husband from her house as an objectionable lodger."[43] Nrodova also brought suit to the Moscow orphan's court, again successfully, to have the guardianship of their children's property transferred from her husband to herself.

Other cases provide evidence of favorable court decisions, too, although in most of these, the rulings came too late to preserve a woman's assets. In 1893, the townswoman Aleksandra Boiarina's older sister, a shop clerk in a store on the Arbat, took steps to protect her more passive sibling's interests. In Aleksandra's name, she brought suit in the Moscow circuit court to regain Aleksandra's dowry of one thousand rubles, which the husband had expended, and the trousseau items that he had pawned. Although the court ruled in Aleksandra's favor, in this case as in others, the assets were simply gone. Aleksandra gained only the pawn ticket, plus a court order for the one thousand rubles the court recognized as hers, less the costs of litigation. Much the same happened to Tatiana Alekseeva. When her mother-in-law sold her shoemaking shop and husband drove her from the house, Alekseeva successfully sued them in the Moscow circuit court. In its favorable ruling, the court awarded her 600 rubles plus court costs of 210 rubles, 34 kopecks. But the shop was gone. The chancellery's investigation of 1902 found her working as a shop clerk in a bakery, earning twelve rubles a month plus room and board and owning no property save her clothes. Likewise, Vera Molodtsova, hav-ing left her husband on account of his exceedingly abusive and brutal behavior, brought suit to regain her dowry of twenty thousand rubles plus five thousand in household

42. RGIA, fond 1412, op. 224, d. 53 (Nrodova), 58.

43. Zagorovskii, "Lichnye i imushchestvennye otnosheniia," 66. Another undesirable conse-quence, according to him, was men registering immovable property in their wives' name to avoid losing it when they went bankrupt. This practice, apparently widespread among the commercial classes, may make ownership of urban property an unreliable guide to women's commercial activity in Russia.

items, which her husband refused to return. Although the chancellery's documents do not record the outcome, it seems likely that she failed to obtain the money: the close of her separation case found her without any means of her own, giving lessons to support herself and her children and taking midwifery courses to qualify for a professional career.[44] So far as can be ascertained from the chancellery's records, most of the women whose husbands appropriated their dowries never sought to pursue their interests in court. This may be because to do so would have subjected their personal problems to public scrutiny, or because courts lacked the authority in any case to grant the all-important passport. The chancellery, by contrast, enjoyed passport authority; and its deliberations were strictly secret. For these reasons, it may have proved a more attractive option for the women who figure in this chapter.[45]

• • •

Having described the myriad economic activities of eighteenth- and early nineteenth-century noblewomen, Michelle Marrese has concluded that married women's right to property offered them a kind of autonomy, "the chance to circumvent the absolute obedience prescribed for them in family law."[46] The evidence in this chapter suggests strongly that this was far less likely to be the case in the later period. This may have been partially due to the nature of the dowry—land and money for purchase of land for nobles in the period Marrese surveys, liquid assets in addition to household items and clothing for the commercial classes in the postreform era. But the difference is surely also related to fundamental economic and cultural changes that suggest the ambiguous impact of modernization on women. The expansion of the marketplace increased the propensity to regard dowry funds as liquid capital—that is, as a source of investment and potentially of greater wealth, rather than as a fixed sum to be drawn on for household expenses and to provide for the future of children. Recognizing this reality, and the importance of "the masculine principle" in activating dowry assets, most dowry givers handed them over to the husband, despite the widespread recognition that the dowry was, by law, women's inalienable property.

But even when assets were placed in women's hands, the women were often unwilling or unable to manage them. The cult of domesticity discouraged women's activity in public and commercial life, while the culture of commerce and entrepreneurship, by contrast with the culture of landed property, remained on the whole inhospitable

---

44. RGIA, fond 1412, op. 213, d. 35 (Boiarina, A., 1893), 20; op. 212, d. 126 (Alekseeva), 39, 46, 55; op. 223, d. 102 (Molodtsova), 1–2.

45. Maria Tikhomirova declared: "I don't demand the dowry back. I just want to preserve the other things that I brought with me to marriage, and that my father gave me" (ibid., op. 229, d. 47 [Tikhomirova], 1).

46. Marrese, *A Woman's Kingdom*, 100.

to married women's active participation. To manage liquid assets required freedom of movement as well as knowledge or expertise that had largely become the monopoly of men. The submission expected of wives reinforced the tendency to depend on their husbands or defer to their wishes. The result was that women simply entrusted their assets to their husbands.

When women did seek to maintain control of their assets, their legal rights were often of surprisingly little use. A husband's ability to control the residence of his wife and children, as reflected in and reinforced by his authority over the passport, put him in a position to hold his wife and her assets hostage and circumscribed her ability to go about her business. Thus, having set up her own shop on rented property, Aleksandra Noskova, still inscribed in her husband's passport, was unable freely to conduct her own affairs. A passport in her own name was essential, she pleaded in 1887, for her to travel to Moscow and Petersburg to purchase the goods she sold in her shop. "I'm terrified [*strashno*] to travel anywhere without a passport," she wrote, "so please separate me from my husband in everything."[47] Indeed, the women who appealed to the chancellery because their husbands abused or sought access to their property, while extreme cases, may not have been the most extreme of all. These women, at least, had the knowledge and resources to petition for redress. What, for example, might have become of Tatiana Sokolova had the Society to Protect Women not entered the picture and saved her from incarceration in a madhouse? Her experience, like Noskova's, demonstrates the extent to which a married woman's separate right to manage and dispose of property might be circumscribed by her inability to dispose of herself.

47. RGIA, fond 1412, op. 224, d. 46 (Noskova), 18.

Disciplining Laboring Husbands

"I've been married for six years and my husband treats me very cruelly." Thus began the 1891 petition of the townswoman Evdokia Eremeeva, wife of a St. Petersburg metalworker. "Returning home every night to our apartment, he finds fault with me for trifles and beats me cruelly, for which the two attached medical certificates serve as evidence. I've turned to the local police several times to get him to stop, and each time he swore he'd stop beating me, but within two or three days he'd break his vow and begin again and more recently, he's threatened to kill me."[1]

In appeals to the chancellery deriving from women of Russia's nonprivileged orders, primarily peasants and townspeople, allegations concerning the husband's domestic violence were virtually ubiquitous, while also figuring, albeit less frequently, in the petitions of their more privileged counterparts. An effective rhetorical device that drew on the familiar stereotype of the coarse and violent laboring class male (see, for example, the illustrations in this chapter) and on ritual laments that were sung in a female voice, allegations of wife beating in most cases also reflected the experience of the petitioner as perceived by others as well as herself.[2] In well over half of the cases involving peasant women and townswomen, chancellery officials found that the husband had engaged in abusive, insulting, crude, cruel, and/or violent treatment in addition to a wide range of other marital misdemeanors.

There can be no question that domestic violence was widespread among Russia's laboring classes. Since the late 1960s and the rediscovery of women's history, historians have commented on the frequency of such violence in both village and town and sought to explain it in terms of popular gender norms and the culture of everyday life. Peasants believed women were prone to

1. RGIA, fond 1412, op. 217, d. 13 (Eremeeva, E., 1891), 1.
2. See Y. M. Sokolov, *Russian Folklore,* trans. Catherine Ruth Smith (Hatboro, PA: Folklore Associates, 1966), 230. On the ritual lament as a model for appeals, see Golfo Alexopoulos, "The Ritual Lament: A Narrative of Appeal in the 1920s and 1930s," *Russian History* 24, nos. 1–2 (1997): 117–31.

excessive behavior, writes Christine D. Worobec, and thus force was necessary to control them. Steve A. Smith proposes that the prevalence of wife beating in the village was due to the anxieties aroused in men by their responsibilities for asserting authority in the household and controlling female sexuality, essential for upholding masculine honor. Explaining the ubiquity of violence in the towns of the mid-Volga region, A. N. Zorin emphasizes the pleasure that men derived from tormenting wives who were even more powerless than they.[3] Whether domestic violence in Russia differed from practices elsewhere in causality or intensity, as these explanations imply, is a question that lies outside the scope of this book.[4]

What this chapter can shed light on is attitudes toward domestic violence, as articulated by the men and women whose voices have been preserved in the chancellery's files. Their views are important. As many historians of wife beating concur, men's physical chastisement of wives is subject to often unarticulated but nevertheless real cultural norms that are historically specific and that (ideally) render such treatment appropriate under some circumstances and inappropriate under others, and that (again ideally) define and constrain excesses and, when excesses occur, grant the abused the right to some sort of redress, if only escape from her abuser. By the second half of the nineteenth century in Russia, the norms governing the behavior of the laboring classes had come to differ markedly from those of their privileged fellow countrymen. Although privileged men might also physically abuse their wives, such treatment of women had become unacceptable for men of their status, as evidenced by their unwillingness to acknowledge it.

This chapter explores how the concerns of an influential sector of educated society, mainly men trained in the law, intersected with the actions of women of the laboring classes to affect the interpretation of Russian law. In the postreform period, such men came to regard domestic violence as a problem that merited public intervention. They were affected, as we shall see, not only by concerns particular to the Russian context but

3. Christine D. Worobec, *Peasant Russia: Family and Community in the Post-Emancipation Period* (Princeton, NJ: Princeton University Press, 1991), 188; S. A. Smith, "Masculinity in Transition," in *Masculinity in Russian History and Culture,* ed. Barbara Clements, Rebecca Friedman, and Dan Healey (New York: Palgrave, 2002), 94; and A. N. Zorin et al., *Ocherki gorodskogo byta dorevoliutsionnogo Povol'zhia* (Ulianovsk: Izdatel'stvo Srednevolzhskogo gosudarstvennogo universiteta, 2000), 291. See also Barbara Alpern Engel, *Between the Fields and the City: Women, Work, and Family in Russia, 1861–1914* (New York: Cambridge University Press, 1994), 23–28.

4. The literature on domestic violence in various times and places is immense, and far too extensive to cite here. Books that I have found helpful in thinking through my own analysis include Dipesh Chakrabarty, "Domestic Cruelty and the Birth of the Subject," in *Provincializing Europe: Postcolonial Thought and Historical Difference* (Princeton, NJ: Princeton University Press, 2000), 117–48; Elizabeth Foyster, *Marital Violence: An English Family History, 1660–1857* (New York: Cambridge University Press, 2005); and Elizabeth Pleck, *Domestic Tyranny: The Making of Social Policy against Family Violence from Colonial Times to the Present* (New York: Oxford University Press, 1987).

also by the efforts of women in villages and towns to put an end to domestic abuse. The actions of both eventuated in an expansion of the venues to which women might appeal for relief; a gradual reinterpretation of Russian law in women's favor; and by the early twentieth century, an evolution in the attitudes of chancellery officials themselves.

EDUCATED ELITES AND DOMESTIC VIOLENCE

Like ideas concerning the importance of affective choice in marriage, critiques of domestic violence in Russia originated in the late eighteenth century, the consequence of Enlightenment ideas that redefined the relations both of men and women and of ruler and ruled.[5] Enlightenment and sentimental literature redefined the relations of men and women in marriage, fostering greater marital equality and mutuality between husbands and wives, thereby rendering physical violence less acceptable to noble elites, their primary audience. The nobles' propensity to regard such abuse critically was also encouraged by a new attentiveness to the distinction between legitimate political authority, which subjected the ruler to the restraints of law and tradition, and "despotism," in which the ruler exercised authority arbitrarily. Although concerned primarily with the nature of rulership, these ideas might carry over to private as well as public life, the domestic sphere having come to figure as a realm of virtue, although not yet of domesticity.[6] These ideas had consequences for the ways in which Russians evaluated themselves and others. By the close of the eighteenth century, some Russian writers, like others affected by the European Enlightenment, had begun to employ the "condition of women" as a criteria for evaluating the development of a civilization.[7]

The Charter of the Nobility of 1785 also fostered a critical attitude toward domestic violence, at least among the nobility. Recognizing the dignity of the well-born and their capacity to govern the self, the charter distinguished the nobility from the remainder of Russia's subjects by exempting its members from corporal punishment, thereby marking nobles as superior. The implications for noblewomen were clear: if violence brought "dishonor" to noble men, did it not insult women, too? Subsequently,

5. Work on the Russian early modern period suggests an intense reluctance to circumscribe the authority of husbands over wives and a high degree of tolerance for physically abusive treatment of women. See Daniel Kaiser, "Invading the 'Private': Spousal Violence and the State in Early Modern Russia," *Forschungen zur osteuropäischen Geschichte* 58 (2001): 135–42; and Nancy Shields Kollmann, "The Extremes of Patriarchy: Spousal Abuse and Murder in Early Modern Russia," *Russian History* 25, nos. 1–2 (1998): 133–40.

6. For critiques of political despotism, see Cynthia Whittaker, *Russian Monarchy: Eighteenth-Century Rulers and Writers in Dialogue* (DeKalb: Northern Illinois University Press, 2003); on virtue and the domestic sphere, see Elise Kimerling Wirtschafter, *The Play of Ideas in Russian Enlightenment Theater* (DeKalb: Northern Illinois University Press, 2003).

7. Chakrabarty, "Domestic Cruelty," 118. For a Russian example, see Yuri Slezkine, *Arctic Mirrors: Russia and the Small Peoples of the North* (Ithaca, NY: Cornell University Press, 1994), 57, 58–59.

challenges to the legitimacy of punishment and the notion of illegitimate cruelty, while aimed primarily at the master-serf relationship, also carried over to family relations and likewise undermined the legitimacy of marital violence among noble elites.[8] The heightened expectations for masculine self-command were surely one reason for the upsurge of appeals to local authorities, and in the second quarter of the nineteenth century, to the Synod and the Third Section from noble wives endeavoring to curtail their husband's abusive behavior. Complaining to the Third Section of her husband's mistreatment in 1835, the noblewoman Nadezhda Stakhovicheva, for one, explicitly linked marital violence with behaviors associated with the lower orders. Her husband, she asserted, was guilty of the "kind of cruel treatment that would be reprehensible even in someone of the lower orders [*i vo nizkom soslovii liudei*].[9]

By the mid-nineteenth century, restrained and respectful treatment of women had become an important marker of men's gentility. Such restraint was to be exercised under all circumstances: however provocative a wife's behavior, a husband with pretensions to genteel status should never "permit himself" to strike her. By contrast, men of the laboring classes were condemned only for striking their wives "without cause." This terminology, which emphasized male self-command and the inviolability of the female body in the case of elites, while treating laboring men's physical chastisement of their wives as acceptable under certain circumstances, was far from unique to Russia. But in the Russian case these attitudes were linked to efforts to overcome Russia's purported "backwardness" in relation to an imagined West.

According to the historian Abby Schrader, prominent officials believed that gentlemanly treatment of women raised the moral tone of Russian society and distinguished elites from their uncultivated and/or lower-class countrymen, whose brutal behavior toward their wives offered a strong indicator of their "backward" domestic relations and contributed to Russian society's moral depravity. "It is well known that among the lower and, in part, among the middle estates women do not enjoy the respect that they deserve," declared the statesman Petr Valuev, presumably including merchant couples

---

8. Susan Morrissey, *Suicide and the Body Politic in Imperial Russia* (New York: Cambridge University Press, 2006), 134–35.

9. N. V. Zanegina, "Osobennosti otnoshenii muzha i zheny v dvorianskikh sem'iakh Rossii kontsa XVIII–pervoi poloviny XIX v. (na materialakh Tverskoi gubernii)," in *Rod i sem'ia v kontekste Tverskoi istorii: sbornik nauchnykh trudov* (Tver: Tverskoi gosudarstvennyi universitet, 2005), 64–77; V. A. Veremenko, "Semeinye nesoglasiia i razdel'noe zhitel'stvo suprugov: problema zakonodatel'nogo regulirovaniia v Rossii vo vtoroi polovine XIX–nachale XX veka," *Dialog so vremenem* 18 (2007): 328. Quoted from GARF, fond 109, 2-aia ekspeditsiia, op. 1835, d. 504, 16. On violence and dishonor, see Irina Reyfman, *Ritualized Violence Russian Style: The Duel in Russian Culture and Literature* (Stanford, CA: Stanford University Press, 1999), 123.

in this category. "Even husbands do not perceive their wives as equals but frequently consider them slaves and treat them cruelly."[10]

Curtailing marital violence thus became part of a domestic civilizing mission by reform-minded officials. Schrader contends that during the reform era, improving the domestic relations of the laboring classes constituted one element of official efforts to overcome Russia's backwardness. Reformers actually considered revising penal law to empower police and judges to punish wife beaters in the same way as they punished assailants who battered a stranger. In the end, however, reformers backed away from changing the law, which would have applied equally to all social orders, hesitant to involve the state in domestic disputes and expose elite spousal relations to the public gaze. Thereafter, penal law continued to leave men's domestic authority largely unregulated. Although a wife and her parents might press charges against a violent husband, the wording of the penal codes made it clear that only in extreme cases were they likely to obtain redress, as several historians have noted.[11]

But this by no means brought an end to efforts to curtail domestic violence. Appeals from battered women provided the stimulus, and jurists rather than feminists took the lead.[12] In 1871, less than a decade after the Justice of the Peace courts began to function, appeals from battered women who sought relief from those courts prompted the State Senate, Russia's highest judicial instance, to provide a remedy that made wife battering a punishable offense. Introduced in 1864 as part of the thoroughgoing reform of Russia's legal order, Justice of the Peace courts held jurisdiction over the most petty and common criminal cases and over minor civil suits that involved amounts less than five hundred rubles in value and concerned damages, insults, and offenses to human dignity. Designed to be accessible to the most humble citizens, especially at first, Justice of the Peace courts allowed plaintiff and defendant to present their cases in their own

---

10. On conduct as a marker of social status, see Andreas Schönle, "The Scare of the Self: Sentimentalism, Privacy, and Private Life in Russian Culture, 1780–1820," *Slavic Review* 57, no. 4 (1998): 729. On domestic violence, see Abby Schrader, *Languages of the Lash: Corporal Punishment and Identity in Imperial Russia* (DeKalb: Northern Illinois University Press, 2002), 30, 164.

11. Schrader, *Languages of the Lash*, 164–67. "Virtually the only legal remedy available for mistreatment by a husband or a parent was criminal action for severe injury" (William G. Wagner, *Marriage, Property, and Law in Late Imperial Russia* [Oxford: Clarendon, 1994], 65).

12. On the role of feminists in the United States, see Linda Gordon, "A Right Not to Be Beaten: The Agency of Battered Women, 1880–1960," in *Gendered Domains: Rethinking Public and Private in Women's History: Essays from the Seventh Berkshire Conference*, ed. Dorothy O. Helly and Susan M. Reverby (Ithaca, NY: Cornell University Press, 1992), 232–34; for Great Britain, see Maeve Doggett, *Marriage, Wife-Beating, and the Law in Victorian England* (Columbia: University of South Carolina Press, 1993), 103, 105–6, 111.

words. Almost from the first, the courts were presented with a substantial number of cases that involved domestic violence.[13]

O. Sokolovskaia, wife of a collegiate assessor, brought the decisive suit. An Orel Justice of the Peace court had found her husband guilty of "disturbing the peace and insulting his wife in word and deed in a public place and making threats," and sentenced him to three months of confinement. He appealed that decision all the way to the Senate. In its 1871 decision upholding earlier findings, the Senate drew a distinction between spousal behavior in private and public, according to which only the latter was subject to the law. "In domestic life, amid the quotidian clashes between spousal rights and duties, it is difficult to avoid quarrels and outbursts of anger [*vspyshki*], and therefore the law cannot admit insult suits by one spouse against the other," the Senate reasoned. But in the given instance, the issue was not domestic conflict but public disorder, which was a criminal offense. More significantly, the Senate opened the door to "insults" that had occurred even in the home. If the "insult" had occurred in private, and if the plaintiff or her lawyer could convince the court that the perpetrator had been guilty of "arbitrariness [*samoupravstvo*]," and that his behavior had the "character of violent actions [*nasil'stvennye postupki*]," even "without the infliction of terrible blows," he might be subject to arrest for up to three months.[14] These decisions greatly expanded the ability of Justice of the Peace courts to respond to complaints about domestic violence even in cases where the plaintiff did not suffer serious injury.

Thereafter, peasant women became the primary although not the sole focus of efforts to reform the law so as to curtail men's abuse of their absolute authority and expand the realms where jurists' professional expertise would prove authoritative. Their image in public life rendered peasant women particularly suitable for this purpose. The liberal press depicted peasant women as "defenseless in the face of difficult economic conditions, the rule of men in the village, the structure of the patriarchal household and, most of all, the drunkenness of the *muzhik* himself," as Cathy Frierson has put it. In consequence, for some the harsh treatment of peasant women became emblem-

---

13. Joan Neuberger, "Popular Legal Cultures: The St. Petersburg *Mirovoi Sud*," in *Russia's Great Reforms, 1855–1881*, ed. Ben Eklof, John Bushnell, and Larissa Zakharova (Bloomington: Indiana University Press, 1994), 232, 239; for early appeals on the grounds of marital cruelty, see *Sudebnyi vestnik*, no. 31 (February 7, 1869): 1–2.

14. Veremenko, "'Semeinye nesoglasiia,'" 334–36. On the decisions, see N. S. Tagantsev, ed., *Ustav o nakazaniiakh, nalagaemykh mirovymi sud'iami. Izdanie 1885 goda. S dopolneniiami po svodnomu prodolzheniiu 1912 goda s prilozheniiam motivov i izvlechenii iz reshenii kassatsionnykh departamentov Pravitel'stvuiushchego Senata*, 21st ed. rev. (St. Petersburg, 1913), articles 130, 142. The relevant Senate decisions are cited in section 45 of article 142. See also article 133, section 18.

atic of all that was wrong with peasant life.[15] Jurists who sought reform of marital law made much of peasant women's lack of legal recourse, basing their accounts on such women's appeals to the courts on their own behalf. Like peasant men, peasant women were barred by law from bringing suit in Justice of the Peace courts, over which well-educated men presided as judges, and were consigned instead to their own, peasant cantonal (*volost'*) courts, another product of the reform era, in which cases were adjudicated by peasants. As described by rural Justices of the Peace—and, it must be said, judging by published decisions of the *volost'* courts—peasant judges in this early period treated women's complaints far less sympathetically than did their educated counterparts.[16]

The bind in which this placed high-minded justices became grist for the mill of marital reform. In articles that appeared in the liberal *Iuridicheskii vestnik,* which circulated primarily among readers involved in implementing law, Justices of the Peace practicing in rural areas emphasized their powerlessness to provide relief for victimized peasant women. Scorned by their own peasant courts, driven "beyond endurance" by their ignorant and brutish husbands, such women turned to the civil courts only to discover that judges had no remedies to offer them. One after another, wrote Justice of the Peace Valerian Nazar'ev, "peasant women appeared before me with bloody stains instead of faces, sobbing violently, describing with swollen, shaking lips their husbands' beastly treatment."[17] Beaten to a pulp, clutching in their hands the braid that their husband had torn from their head, these women sought relief from justices helpless to provide it. "The facts," wrote Justice of the Peace Iakob Ludmer in conclusion to the first of two articles, "unembellished" and "taken directly from life" were more than sufficient to prove that "women's moans"(the title of his article) had a claim on the most serious attention of Russia's lawmakers. The only cure, as he saw it, was to permit divorce on the grounds of cruelty.[18] Nazar'ev's and Ludmer's accounts were followed by

---

15. Cathy A. Frierson, *Peasant Icons: Representations of Rural People in Late Nineteenth-Century Russia* (New York: Oxford University Press, 1993), 171. Townswomen were largely absent from this discourse.

16. On *volost'* court practices, see *Trudy Kommisii po preobrazovaniiu volostnykh sudov: Slovesnye oprosy krest'ian, pis'mennye otzyvy razlichnykh mest i lits i resheniia: Volostnykh sudov, S"ezdov mirovykh posrednikov i gubernskikh po krest'ianskim delam prisutsvii,* 7 vols. (St. Petersburg: Tip. Vtorogo otd. Sobstvennoi E. I. V. kantseliarii, 1873–74).

17. Quoted in Laura Engelstein, *The Keys to Happiness: Sex and the Search for Modernity in Fin-de-Siècle Russia* (Ithaca, NY: Cornell University Press, 1992), 121. See also Neuberger, "Popular Justice," 239.

18. Iakob Ludmer, "Bab'i stony," pts. 1–2, *Iuridicheskii vestnik,* nos. 11–12 (1884): 447, 678–89. His examples of abusive relationships are, with one exception, drawn from the peasantry, but his influence can be perceived in depictions of spousal abuse in urban areas, too. See V. A. Volzhin, *Kartinki iz*

others in a similar vein, similarly highlighting the helpless suffering of peasant women at the hands of violent husbands.[19]

Portraits of peasant women's suffering, which appeared in the mid-1880s, contributed to the first of many decisions by the State Senate that aimed to ameliorate peasant women's lot. In 1888, the Senate issued the first of what would become a series of decisions that limited a husband's authority to govern his wife's mobility. "A husband has the right to demand his wife cohabit with him," the decision of 1888 in the case of the peasant woman Natalia Vorontsova declared, "but it does not give him the right to demand that she be sent off to the village where he does not live and has no household." Subsequent decisions went further, requiring state authorities overseeing the peasantry to provide relief for peasant women whose husbands treated them cruelly or failed to support them. They also mandated that police officials and others with administrative authority over the peasantry investigate the substance of a peasant wife's allegations concerning her husband's cruelty and neglect. If those allegations proved true, the authorities were to override the husband's authority to govern the wife's movements by approving her passport. Thus institutions overseeing the peasantry—and only such institutions—were required to issue a wife a passport without her husband's permission if they found that the husband had in fact neglected or abused her.[20] In that sense, at least, peasant women enjoyed a privilege denied women of other social estates, including townswomen.

The existence of venues to which abused women might appeal for relief surely encouraged some women to redefine the parameters of acceptable marital behavior, to alter if not to abandon fatalistic ways of regarding their lot in life, and to resist a level or frequency of violence that once they might have endured. To the extent that the views that prompted such reforms filtered down the social ladder to the women whose plight so preoccupied reformers—a matter virtually impossible to ascertain—they are

---

sudebnoi zhizni (St. Petersburg: A. Muchnik, 1891); M. Ratov, *Zhenshchina pered sudom prisiazhnykh (mysli i fakty) (po povodu stat'i g. Dzhanzhieva)* (Moscow: A. I. Mamontov, 1899).

19. See N. Lazovskii, "Lichnye otnosheniia suprugov po russkomu obychnomu pravu," *Iuridicheskii vestnik*, nos. 6–7 (1883): 358–414; Vereshchagin, "O bab'ikh stonakh," *Iuridicheskii vestnik*, no. 4 (1885): 750–61; and Mikhail I. Kulisher, *Razvod i polozhenie zhenshchiny* (St. Petersburg, 1896) The articles in *Iuridicheskii vestnik* were marshaled by members of the Editorial Commission of the Civil Cassation Department of the Senate as evidence of the necessity of revising family law. See RGIA, fond 797, op. 91, d. 53, 34–39.

20. Quoted in V. A. Veremenko, "'Litso s vidom na zhitel'stvo' (gendernyi aspekt pasportnoi sistemy Rossii kontsa XIX–nachala XX vv.)," *Adam i Eva*, no. 7 (2004): 215–16. See also Wagner, *Marriage, Property, and the Law*, 221–22. For all the relevant Senate decisions concerning peasant women's access to the passport, see I. M. Tiutriumov, *Obshchee polozhenie o krest'ianakh, i prod. 1912 i 1913 gody (s raz"iasneniami Pravitel'stvuiushchego Senata)* izd. 3-e, ispravlennoe i znachitel'no dopolnennoe (Petrograd: Zakonovedenie, 1915).

likely to have had the same effect. Still, it required courage and resourcefulness as well as desperation for women to take advantage of new opportunities for redress, and to "wash their dirty linen in public." From that perspective, the women who took their cases to the courts or the chancellery were doubtlessly atypical, even of abused women. How much relief the courts could actually provide remains a question, however. As the historian V. A. Veremenko points out, even if convicted of "insult" and sentenced to prison, once a husband had completed his term of arrest, he returned to his family, his "conjugal rights" completely intact.[21]

WOMEN APPEAL

Under some circumstances, legal change that favors the powerless has the potential to enhance their social status and bargaining position, as the historian Elizabeth Clark has noted. "To the extent that weaker parties in status relationships could invoke the protection of the state—what legal scholars label 'calling in the giant'—the new norms...redistributed power to benefit the more vulnerable at the expense of their aggressors."[22] The legal remedies must be sufficient, however. Even when they are, to the extent that laws remain at odds with prevalent popular attitudes, the ability of legal norms to benefit the vulnerable may be modest indeed. Laws penalizing domestic violence offer a vivid example of the limits of the law. Chancellery files suggest not only that in many instances the legal remedies offered by Justice of the Peace courts were insufficient to curtail domestic violence, in cases involving members of the laboring classes at least, but also that the attitudes toward gender relations that were reflected in those remedies were at odds with popular beliefs about gender relations and gender roles.

To be sure, my sample is highly skewed: examples of the failure of judicial remedies derive from the chancellery's archive, not the archival records of the Justices of the Peace. They thus represent incorrigible cases and not those in which a chastened husband ceased to beat his wife; had he ceased to beat her, presumably, she would have needed to appeal no further. But while they may not be representative, the examples certainly demonstrate the limits of the legal remedies available to Justices of the Peace. The examples also suggest that those remedies might not only fail to curtail domestic violence but even, in some cases, exacerbate it instead. The cases involving favorable Justice of the Peace decisions also show that many justices, while lacking the specialized legal education required of judges in regular courts, shared the propensity of liberal Russian jurists to be concerned with ensuring a woman's personal security against

---

21. Veremenko, "Semeinye nesoglasiia," 336.

22. Elizabeth Clark, "'The Sacred Rights of the Weak': Pain, Sympathy, and the Culture of Individual Rights in Antebellum America," *Journal of American History* 82, no. 2 (1995): 392.

abuses of marital power. They suggest as well that such justices sometimes ignored the law that required peasants to appeal only to their own cantonal courts.

Women who brought suit before the Justice of the Peace courts sought one thing and one thing only: an end to marital violence. Some endeavored to use an appeal to the courts as leverage in renegotiating a relationship, coming to terms with their husband before a decision could be reached; others evidently hoped that a decision in their favor would convince husbands to mend their ways. Although in almost all of these cases, justices exercised their authority to punish abusive men by sentencing them to confinement, such punishment rarely protected their wives from further abuse. Indeed, in many of the cases that came to the chancellery's attention, appeals to Justice of the Peace courts had an effect precisely opposite to the one that the woman intended. Instead of preserving the woman from future abuse, it further enraged the husband by shaming him before the community as well as depriving him temporarily of freedom. The reaction of husbands, too, is typical. As historians of domestic violence have noted, punishing a husband for exercising what he believed to be his marital rights could damage the woman's interests at least as much as the man's. For women, imprisonment of a husband was often the least favorable outcome of an appeal, "not only because it might lead to destitution or his revenge, but also because [the women] desired neither imprisonment nor punishment, but less violence," writes Jennifer Davis of domestic violence cases in Victorian England.[23]

Revenge was indeed the response of several of these husbands to their wives' attempt to curtail their marital authority. Punished by a Justice of the Peace court in 1870 for beating his wife, Avdotia, in the presence of witnesses, the peasant Fedor Ivanov threatened to kill her after his release.[24] When punished by a Justice of the Peace in 1871 for his cruelty toward his wife, Avdotia, and their three children, the townsman Nikolai Voronin swore revenge as well.[25] The townsman Nikolai Gerasimov responded with fury when his wife, Lidia, took him to the Justice of the Peace court of the Prechistinskaia quarter of Moscow, accusing him of cruelty. During the hearing, Nikolai pulled out a knife and attacked Lidia, stabbing her in the shoulder before he could be restrained. Punishment for domestic violence prompted other men, humiliated and outraged by this reversal of the proper gender order, to abandon their marriages alto-

23. Jennifer Davis, "Prosecutions and Their Context: The Use of Criminal Law in Later Nineteenth-Century London," in *Policing and Prosecution in Britain, 1750–1850*, ed. Douglas Hay and Francis Snyder (Oxford: Clarendon, 1989), 412. Contemporary studies of domestic violence also suggest that some offenders become more likely to engage in violence after being prosecuted for their behavior and that such punishment works best when the abuser is well integrated into a community. See Rosemary Chalk and Patricia A. King, eds., *Violence in Families: Assessing Prevention and Treatment Programs* (Washington, DC: National Academy Press, 1998), 175, 181.

24. GARF, fond 109, 2-aia ekspeditsiia, op. 1870, d. 383.

25. Ibid., op. 1871, d. 500, 1.

gether. In 1883, a Justice of the Peace court sentenced the townsman Ivan Glagolevskii to a month and a half in detention for beating his wife and her parents; after he was released, his wife never saw him again. She appealed to the chancellery because she still lacked the passport she needed to earn her own living.[26] Fedor Grigor'ev disappeared after serving a one-month sentence for abusing his wife, Aleksandra, who found herself in a position identical to Glagolevskaia's. Aleksandra Grigor'eva, incidentally, was one of several peasant women who successfully brought suit before a Justice of the Peace, notwithstanding the law requiring peasants to restrict themselves to their own courts. A peasant from Luzhskii district of St. Petersburg province, Aleksandra had requested that her local peasant cantonal administration appoint a guardian to protect her property from her husband's avariciousness; to protect herself from his violence, however, she turned to the Justice of the Peace, and the justice ruled in her favor.[27]

Some townswomen sought to avoid such a vengeful outcome by using a favorable court decision as leverage, the intervention of a more powerful party buttressing the women's weaker bargaining position. A successful suit enabled the townswoman Anastasia Mertsalova to extract a promise from her husband that he would change his ways. When a Justice of the Peace court in Bogorodsk district, Moscow, found him guilty of wife beating, Anastasia forgave him at his request after he swore an oath to stop "tormenting" her. Two weeks passed in peace, but then he hit her so hard she required hospitalization and drove her from the house.[28] Other women tried to use a favorable court decision to negotiate for their freedom. After a Justice of the Peace in Riazan sentenced Ivan Bokarev, a shoemaker, to prison for abusing his wife, Evdokia, in 1886, the couple struck a deal. In return for her forgiveness and request that his sentence be abrogated, Ivan agreed to issue her a separate passport. He was duly freed but then refused to honor his commitment.[29] Asked by a Moscow Justice of the Peace what she wanted from her domestic violence suit against her worker husband, another wife answered with a single word: "passport." The newspaper *Novosti* quoted a peasant woman, married to a blacksmith, as declaring to a Moscow Justice of the Peace in 1894, "Let him give me a passport, then I'll forgive him the beatings."[30] However, as

26. RGIA, fond 1412, op. 250, d. 100, 55 ob.; d. 102, 21; on the fear, see also Ludmer, "Bab'i stony," 449.

27. RGIA, fond 1412, op. 250, d. 103, 5–6. Similarly, in 1887, a Justice of the Peace in the city of Pskov sentenced Aleksei Gomazov, a peasant from Smolensk, to a month in detention for beating his wife, Aleksandra (ibid., d. 101, 45). Peasants resident in urban areas were apparently free of the requirement to resort only to their own institutions.

28. Ibid., op. 223, d. 66 (Mertsalova, A., 1900), 1.

29. Ibid., op. 240, d. 49 (Bokareva, E., 1899), 1–3.

30. Semen Kaftyrev, ed., *Vot ona, nasha matushka Moskva: sbornik dedushki Posiseia* (Moscow: Izdatel'stvo Novogo znakomogo, 1883), 121–23; "Mirovoi sud," *Novosti i birzhevskaia gazeta*, no. 144 (1894): 17.

Iakob Ludmer remarked about comparable agreements that he brokered among the peasantry, men's promises to grant a wife "freedom" were utterly unenforceable in law.[31] And after justices found in their favor, some battered women, the brutally beaten Evdokia Koshkareva among them, simply reconciled to prevent their husbands going to prison, willing to forgive their abuser much as battered women do today.[32]

Thus, as depicted in the files of the chancellery, the recourse offered by Justices of the Peace did little to protect women of the laboring classes from abuse, to say the least, while men's sense of entitlement to "instruct" their wives appears to have remained largely untouched by the more refined elite norms concerning masculine conduct. Given Russia's vast social and cultural divides, not to mention the persistence of domestic violence in most modern societies despite campaigns against it, this is hardly surprising. But as a result, neither the public nature of a Justice of the Peace suit nor the penalty of confinement seems to have served as a deterrent to abusive behavior. It may be that Justice of the Peace courts were more effective in curtailing domestic violence among members of the privileged orders, who had come to regard such behavior as a source of dishonor. The publicity involved alone might have served as a deterrent.[33] Or perhaps privileged women were ashamed to expose their personal relations to the gaze of the public by bringing suit against their husbands in civil court. Whatever the explanation, by contrast with their plebeian counterparts, none of the women of higher status who appealed to the chancellery and included allegations of domestic violence among the charges against their husbands had availed themselves of that recourse, even in cases where the abuse the women suffered was extreme.

ATTITUDES TOWARD DOMESTIC VIOLENCE

Social differences likewise inflected the ways that husbands accused of marital violence responded to their wives' allegations of abuse. Whereas privileged men uniformly denied they had lifted a violent hand, men of the laboring classes often acknowledged that they had struck their wives, while describing, occasionally at length, the behaviors that had provoked them to do so. Their descriptions provide insight into popular attitudes toward masculinity and its prerogatives and ideals of appropriate feminine conduct, matters still relatively new to historians of Russia.

31. Ludmer, "Bab'i stony," 463.

32. RGIA, fond 1412, op. 221, d. 143 (Koshkareva, E., 1893), 1–8, 11, 23, 33. See also op. 212, d. 64 (Akimova, E., 1907), 28.

33. For one case where publicity apparently performed this role, see N. A. Bychkova, "Kak zhili vashi babushki i prababushki," *Rossiiskii arkhiv* 11 (2001): 419.

The views expressed are not unmediated, to be sure.[34] The disparities of power between the chancellery and its agents and the husbands whose wives petitioned for relief were even greater than those between husbands and Justices of the Peace. Justices might only imprison the husband for a few months; officials of the chancellery, by approving a passport, had the power to deprive the husband of authority over his wife entirely. But while husbands were certainly aware of the latent power of officials, as is evident in testimony that is often edgy and defensive in tone, its influence on the content of what they said is less easy to define. On one hand, aware of the sensibilities and preferences of officials, some plebeian husbands accused of abuse denied altogether that they had raised a violent hand, even in the face of overwhelming evidence to the contrary, while most of those who did acknowledge striking their wives claimed to have done so only a few times, again often in the face of considerable contrary evidence. On the other hand, the explanations most men offered for their behavior, it seems to me, reflected the men's genuine convictions: their wives had behaved in ways that seemed to them so self-evidently provocative that officials would understand why they had struck, even "thrashed," their wives.

Men's explanations certainly conform to what others, Christine D. Worobec and Steve A. Smith in particular, have told us about peasant attitudes toward domestic violence and suggest that their urban counterparts shared them. The testimonies of both reflect men's anxieties concerning their authority over their households and financial resources and most commonly of all, over the sexuality of their wives. They also depict the marital relationship as a contest for power in which husbands' authority over potentially unruly wives was fragile and subject to challenges that required a firm and forceful response.

The conflicts over power were sometimes financial. In Russia, a married woman's ability to earn her own wage and right to dispose of it as she chose might be perceived as threatening the husband's position as head of his household, upsetting the conjugal balance of power and eliciting violence in response. Having begun his life in poverty, the townsman Sergei Samodurov, for example, had come to own several houses in Moscow, on the income from which the family had lived well. But in 1883, he had been appointed an elder at the Lazarev Church Cemetery in Moscow, and evidently the honor had gone to his head. He began to drink heavily, would stay away from home for days on end, and, according to witnesses, beat his wife and provided only a pittance at most for support of her and the children, even when he had money to spare. Natalia Samodurova petitioned after all but one of her husband's houses had been sold

34. On the need to be aware of the context within which studies of masculine violence are conducted, see Lois Presser, "Negotiating Power and Narrative in Research: Implications for Feminist Methodology," *Signs: Journal of Women in Culture and Society*, 30, no. 4 (2005): 2067–90.

to pay off debts and the remaining house was mortgaged, and after her husband had thrown her out. In Samodurov's rendering, however, he was the victim, not she: "I've told the police about the improper actions of my wife and children." The most recent of her improprieties, by his telling, was her effort to preserve the remains of the family's assets. "In the summer of 1895, despite all my attempts to dissuade her, she willfully [*samovol'no*] rented a dacha and in my absence transferred all my things to it; when I looked into the shed there, I found two carriages that belonged to me, which I later learned she had sold." Samodurov was also outraged by her efforts to keep the money she earned, which was, by law, hers. "She doesn't give my creditors the money she makes from her boarders but keeps it somewhere unknown to me, so that during this time I myself have had to pay thirty-one thousand rubles to my creditors and various institutions." Although much less money was at stake in the Dobychin case, there, too, quarrels over money the wife had earned provided at least one impetus to violence. In 1898, the townsman Mikhail Dobychin, a stove maker, acknowledged that he beat his wife, Varvara, accusing her of frittering away the money she earned by selling fruit one summer, funds on which he had counted to support the family: "I thrashed my wife for this and then had to go back to Nikolaev to look for work, since we had nothing to live on."[35]

Other challenges men described took the form of wives' efforts to curtail masculine prerogatives, in particular, to drink, spend money, and enjoy their leisure as they chose. In the quarrels over the pay packet that were commonplace in Russia's working-class communities, the homosocial world of work, tavern, and pool hall often competed successfully for a hard-earned ruble against the demands of a wife on behalf of herself and her children.[36] Tensions between a masculine sphere rooted in workplace and tavern and a female sphere of family and kin surface in these contested relationships, too. Ivan Mertsalov, a worker at the Bogorodsk-Glukhovo Textile Mill defended at length his right to do as he pleased: "In my free time I sometimes (not constantly) drink with a circle of friends and come home late. In my opinion, that's no reason to stop living together." Mertsalov blamed his wife's insubordination for their marital problems. Quoting the marriage law verbatim, he reminded the police officer who interviewed him that "the law requires the wife to obey the husband as head of the household; be with him in love, respect, and unconditional obedience, render him every service and affection as mistress of the household, which my wife has certainly not done recently." In consequence, he "occasionally (but not often) quarreled with his wife," to

35. RGIA, fond 1412, op. 228, d. 14 (Samodurova, N., 1895), 11, 30; op. 216, d. 36 (Dobychina, V., 1898), 12.

36. Mark Steinberg, *Moral Communities: The Culture of Class Relations in the Russian Printing Industry, 1867–1907* (Berkeley: University of California Press, 1992), 78–79. See also Engel, *Fields and City*, 232–35; and Smith, "Masculinity in Transition," 98–99.

force her to live in agreement with him. "I swear at her only when I lose patience with her, and especially, if I've been drinking. In that case, my wife has once or twice in our entire life together gone off to the neighbors, coming back when I was asleep." Other men also responded to the power of women's words with their fists. Far less loquacious than Mertsalov, Stepan Vlasov, a painter, blamed his drinking and wife battering on his wife's "nagging." In another case, Ivan Dobrovol'skii attributed his marital conflicts to the "inappropriate" language of his wife.[37]

But the most frequent reason men gave for wife battering was a wife's allegedly provocative sexual behavior. Many abusive men suspected, or claimed to suspect, infidelity behind every act of wifely independence. Such anxieties undoubtedly contributed to the abuses of which wives complained. "I did beat my wife, Anna," acknowledged Aleksei Boldyrev, a fitter, in 1893. She behaved "shamelessly all the time." One day, when he returned early from work, he claimed to have found her in the arms of another man. They fought, and when she refused to cease her licentious behavior he lost his temper and thrashed her. Mikhail Dobychin maintained: "If I beat and insulted my wife, it is because her infidelity forced me to do that." Fedor Pavlov acknowledged beating his wife, Paraskeva, but "only twice," on account of her alleged drinking and infidelity. Yes, Gordei Bakshevnikov acknowledged, he beat his wife, Marfa, but only on account of her infidelity. Aleksei Obraztsov, an assistant machinist on the Transcaucasion railroad, having married Anastasia, a former prostitute, in 1901, would beat her when, he alleged, she reminisced about her former lovers. The Orenburg townsman Fedor Gerasimov, denying that he routinely mistreated his wife, acknowledged that he had hit her twice: once when she allegedly failed to show respect to his father, the second time when she "kissed a Cossack."[38]

Many of these men's narratives underscore the fragility of their own sense of authority and its vulnerability to challenge. They validate R. W. Connell's contention that violence serves as a measure not only of a system of domination but also of its imperfections. "A thoroughly legitimate authority would have less need to intimidate," she observes. While different from Laura Engelstein's observation that violence can be viewed as a "weapon of the weak," Connell's contention points in much the same

37. RGIA, fond 1412, op. 223, d. 66 (Mertsalova), 5; op. 240, d. 78 (Vlasova, E., 1898), 13; op. 216, d. 30 (Dobrovol'skaia, E., 1896), 13.

38. Ibid., op. 213, d. 81 (Boldyreva, A., 1899), 38–39; op. 216, d. 36 (Dobychina, 1898), 11; op. 226, d. 1 (Pavlova, P., 1909), 9; op. 240, d. 24 (Bakshevnikova, M., 1905), 7; op. 225, d. 2 (Obraztsova, A., 1902), 8; op. 250, d. 101, 45. Anna Boldyreva (born Egor'eva), who had met her husband during her first political exile, went on to become a prominent Bolshevik organizer during the revolution of 1905 and to write a brief autobiography that said nothing about her short-lived marriage or the two children it produced. See A. G. Boldyreva, "Minuvshie gody," in *V nachale puti*, ed. E. A. Korol'chuk (Leningrad: Lenizdat, 1975). See also her brief account of her political activities in *Tekstil'shchik*, no. 1–2 (1923).

direction.[39] The following examples illustrate these points with particular clarity. Acknowledging he beat his wife, whose petition introduced this chapter, Fedor Eremeev, a worker at the San Galli plant in St. Petersburg, in 1891 wrote to the chancellery after his stubbornly resistant wife had hit him on the cheek with a samovar chimney during a recent quarrel and then fled their apartment. "I can't live without a wife and so I ask your majesty to have the goodness to summon my wife before the commission [*sic!*] and again instill in her the duties of a good wife: to live peacefully with me and not to go off to live with her mother and to stop meeting with her sister, who will lure her into something bad."[40] In similar fashion, without denying that he sometimes struck his wife, Antonina, and their children, the townsman Fedor Kotliarov, a carpenter, insisted that he had good reason. "When I earned a lot of money, my wife had nothing against me and I didn't beat her." But after he lost his job, he began to beat her "because she made trouble in the family," presumably by urging him to find a job. He acknowledged beating the children, too, because his wife "set the children against me."[41]

In citing "good reason" for raising a hand against their wives, these husbands invoked the widespread understanding that the physical correction of women of the laboring classes might be warranted under certain circumstances. People who spoke on behalf of abusive husbands often justified the husband's violence in much the same way as he had: as a legitimate response to wifely provocations or failure to show the proper deference. According to his fellow villagers—peasants in Bogorodskii district, Moscow province—for example, if Vasilii Gusev and his wife sometimes quarreled, the fault was entirely the wife's: being of a stubborn character, she treated her husband crudely "and didn't show him the proper respect." In the opinion of one of Mertsalov's workmates, his wife, Anastasia, deserved a beating because of her malicious and agitated (*nespokoinyi*) character. According to another, Anastasia Mertsalova had a "difficult character and respected no one," and so "of course" her husband lost his patience. Acknowledging that Fedor Verezhnikov sometimes struck his wife Irina, several witnesses noted in 1910 that his wife shared the blame: "she is obstinate and unyielding," leading to constant discord between them.[42] People were most prone to condone violence when the woman had purportedly misbehaved sexually. Sexual misconduct might be

39. R. W. Connell, *Masculinities* (Berkeley: University of California Press, 1995), 85; Laura Engelstein, "Weapon of the Weak (Apologies to James Scott): Violence in Russian History," *Kritika* 4, no. 3 (2003): 680.

40. RGIA, fond 1412, op. 217, d. 13 (Eremeeva), 9. See also the reconciliation agreement between the Suminovs, in which she promised, among other things, to cease "reproaching her husband" (op. 228, d. 118 [Suminova, N., 1892], 9).

41. Ibid., op. 221, d. 132 (Kotliarova, A., 1895), 25.

42. Further investigation upheld Mertsalova's claims of her husband's drunkenness and severe abuse. The chancellery awarded her a passport. See ibid., op. 150, d. 104, 61 ob.; op. 223, d. 66 (Mertsalova), 8–12; and op. 240, d. 72 (Verezhnikova, I., 1910), 5.

seen to justify not only battering but murder as well. Turn-of-the-century newspapers carried numerous accounts of men who murdered wives they deemed adulterous and of the judges or juries that either acquitted them or let them off lightly.[43]

Still, it was far from the case that members of the laboring classes uniformly considered extreme domestic violence "normal" or that no one condemned it.[44] Relations between husbands and wives were hardly a private matter among the peasantry or townspeople, who lived cheek by jowl. As was the case in other national contexts, neighbors, friends, and family witnessed, condemned, and, more rarely, attempted to curb male violence that they judged to be excessive and/or unwarranted. In the process they contested men's claims that wives provoked them and, by testifying on the woman's behalf, assisted the wife to escape an abusive marriage.[45] The Mertsalovs' former landlady in Moscow, for example, criticized Ivan Mertsalov for excessive drinking and abuse of his wife, which, the landlady testified, maintained Anastasia in a state of fear and abjection. Another landlady described how Stepan Vlasov, in a perpetual state of intoxication, would beat his wife, Ekaterina, ripping out chunks of her hair. The worker Vasilii Ankudinov's landlady, a peasant, had intervened more actively when she witnessed Ankudinov beating his wife. She would try to stop him, only to be rebuffed by Ankudinov. "What business is it of yours?" he would reportedly say. "She's my wife. I'll do as I please with her." The landlady found Ankudinov's behavior so offensive that she eventually evicted the couple from the apartment. "Kind people" in the town of Kologriv, Kostroma, occasionally offered Maria Matveeva refuge from her townsman husband's extreme violence; her father and brothers also tried to protect her, for which Matveev had beaten the brother and broken the father's leg.[46]

Men of the laboring classes as well as women were sometimes willing to criticize violence that was excessive or "unwarranted," although there is no evidence that such men belonged among the "conscious" workers who "valorized self-control, the assertion of reason over emotion...and a more respectful, but not necessarily egalitarian attitude toward women."[47] The dossier of Solomonida Motova, a peasant woman who petitioned for relief in 1891 claiming that her husband "tyrannized her" and tried to get rid of her, contains a statement (*prigovor*) signed by forty-five household heads in her husband's village in Kazan province, upholding her claims. The *prigovor* testified

43. *Novoe vremia*, no. 8110 (1898), 4; *Novosti*, no. 170, 254, 354 (1894); no. 3 (1895). See also Ratov, *Zhenshchina pered sudom*, 1–33.

44. For this claim, see Zorin et al., *Ocherki gorodskogo byta*, 290.

45. See Susan Dwyer Amussen, "'Being Stirred to Much Unquietness': Violence and Domestic Violence in Early Modern England," *Journal of Women's History* 6, no. 2 (1994): 82.

46. RGIA, fond 1412, op. 223, d. 66 (Mertsalova), 25; op. 240, d. 78 (Vlasova, 1898), 4; op. 212, d. 168 (Ankudinova, O., 1902), 20; op. 223, d. 4 (Matveeva, M., 1899), 1.

47. Smith, "Masculinity in Transition," 101.

— Я слышалъ, Дарья, что Ванюха жестоко поколотилъ тебя?
— Ну, и онъ тоже пострадалъ при этомъ.
— Развѣ?
— Да, онъ сломалъ объ мою спину свою палку.

FIGURE II.

"I've heard, Daria, that Vaniukha beat you cruelly."

"Yes, but he also suffered."

"Really?"

"Yes, my spine broke his stick."

Strekoza, no. 49 (1895), M. E. Saltykov-Shchedrin Public Library.

— Ты хорошо живешь съ своимъ мужемъ?
— Да, почитай что очень хорошо: иные дерутся каждный день, а мы — раза три въ недѣлю, — не больше.

FIGURE 12.

"Do you and your husband get along well?"
"Really well, I think. Others knock each other about every day, while we do that maybe three times a week, no more."
Strekoza, *no. 21 (1895), M. E. Saltykov-Shchedrin Public Library.*

to the husband's "tyrannical behavior" and the wife's exemplary conduct.[48] In the case of the townsman Aleksei Bokarev, a shoemaker, his own brother testified in 1899 that Aleksei himself was responsible for the breakdown of his marriage. He drank and beat his wife, Evdokia, "without cause" from the early days of their marriage, which the brother had seen with his own eyes when they shared an apartment. In 1902, one of Vasilii Ankudinov's coworkers in a metalworking plant in Perm claimed that he had tried to convince Vasilii to cease beating his wife, Olga. Although Olga was "quiet and modest," the coworker testified, Ankudinov "grew dissatisfied with her, accusing her of creating disorder in the household."[49] The witness had advised Ankudinov to be more understanding and live more amicably with his wife. Ordinary policemen, usually peasants or townsmen by origin, poorly trained, underpaid, overworked, and themselves prone to resort to the law of the fist, nevertheless occasionally intervened on behalf of an abused wife.[50] At Evdokia Eremeeva's behest in 1891, the Moscow police tried several times to prevent her husband, Petr, from beating her and once exacted a promise from him never to beat her again. Summoned by Anastasia Obraztsova in 1902, the Baku police would try to defend her and urged her husband, an assistant to the engineer on the Transcaucasian railroad, either to treat his wife more humanely or to give her a separate passport.[51] Whether these critical views of domestic violence represented a filtering down of elite attitudes or simply the variety of attitudes that existed among members of the laboring classes themselves is impossible to determine on the basis of my fragmentary evidence, but given the range of times and places in the above examples, I tend toward the latter explanation.

THE CHANCELLERY: MARRIAGE, PATRIARCHY, AND MARITAL DISCIPLINE

Indeed, even chancellery officials rarely expressed critical views toward domestic violence, as such, among the laboring classes in the first decade of the chancellery's existence (1884–94), years coinciding with the reign of Tsar Alexander III. They were far more concerned with maintaining public decorum, which they often defined in terms of female sexual decorum. Their priorities are evident in the outcome of cases that involved wife abuse. By comparison with Justices of the Peace, the chancellery was, indeed, a "giant," enjoying the authority to protect a woman from domestic violence by

---

48. RGIA, fond 1412, op. 223, d. 120 (Motova, S. 1891), 1–3.
49. Ibid., op. 240, d. 49 (Bokareva), 9; op. 212, d. 168 (Ankudinova), 8–9.
50. Neil Weissman, "Regular Police in Tsarist Russia, 1900–1914," *Russian Review* 44, no. 1 (1985): 45–68.
51. RGIA, fond 1412, op. 217, d. 13 (Eremeeva), 1; op. 225, d. 2 (Obraztsova), 1.

approving the separate passport that enabled her to escape it.[52] However, officials did not grant that passport readily. Reflecting the views of the tsars in whose name they acted, they not only held conservative views of marriage but also seemed implicitly to believe in the civilizing affect of marital cohabitation for disreputable laboring men. In this, they were rather like the officials who sought brides for Siberian convicts for the purpose of turning them into productive subjects.[53] Consequently, even when they found in a woman's favor, officials most often exercised their authority in a manner intended to discipline the husband rather than to free his wife permanently from ill treatment. Although over the years a genuine shift occurred in their attitudes toward the conjugal relations of the laboring classes, no doubt in response to the intellectual currents of their time and perhaps the result of turnover in chancellery personnel (see table 1), officials never ceased to use the separate passport to discipline a husband.

As did other members of educated society, chancellery officials viewed domestic violence through the lens of class. They distinguished between "the domestic violence of the poor (expected and ordinary)," and that which occurred "in the homes of the genteel (inconsistent with a wife's legitimate expectations, abusive)," as Hendrik Hartog has put it in reference to such views in the United States.[54] Indeed, rather as members of the laboring classes did, officials tended to view peasant and townswomen as by nature potentially unruly, subversive of the social and sexual order, and therefore of public decorum. Unable to govern the self, such women required a husband's "instruction [uchenie]," by the application of violence if needs be, to keep their anarchic impulses in check, by contrast with genteel and cultivated women against whom violence was always an insult. Officials drew the line precisely at the boundary that separated the privileged from the unprivileged and expressed those differences linguistically. When officials condemned violence against an unprivileged woman (that is, a peasant or townswoman), they almost invariably specified that the violence had occurred "without cause" to a woman who had done nothing to deserve it, implying thereby that under other circumstances, such

52. Internal evidence from dossiers strongly indicates that a woman who possessed a separate passport had far greater claim on protection from the police. The document also had a psychological impact on many a husband, bringing an end, for example, to his violent and drunken appearances at his wife's place of work.

53. Abby M. Schrader, "Unruly Felons and Civilizing Wives: Cultivating Marriage in the Siberian Exile System, 1822–1860," *Slavic Review*, 66, no. 2 (2007): 230–56.

54. Hendrik Hartog, *Man and Wife in America: A History* (Cambridge, MA: Harvard University Press, 2000), 105. "French courts apply very different standards to beatings, according to the class of defendants," writes William Reddy. "For plebeians, it is 'appropriate marital discipline' under some circumstances" (William Reddy, *The Invisible Code: Honor and Sentiment in Postrevolutionary France, 1814–1848* [Berkeley: University of California Press, 1997], 103). In Russia, too, officials were more prone to issue passports to noblewomen and to construe "cruelty" to include psychological as well as physical insults (Veremenko, *Dvorianskaia sem'ia*, 250).

violence might be merited.[55] A husband who struck a privileged woman (merchant wives included), by contrast, invariably had "permitted himself" to do so as officials always put it, indicating both the need for male self-command under all circumstances and the inviolability of privileged women.[56]

That violence against peasant or townswomen might be acceptable under certain circumstances is clear from two early chancellery decisions. The first is particularly revealing, contrasting as it does officials' willingness to condone the very husbandly "instruction" that a Justice of the Peace had found objectionable. In 1888, Maria Gomazova, a peasant woman from Smolensk province, petitioned the chancellery for a passport claiming that her husband beat her. As evidence to support this claim she submitted an 1887 decision by a Pskov Justice of the Peace sentencing her husband, Aleksandr, to a month in prison for striking her. Reviewing the evidence, officials arrived at a different conclusion: Gomazova deserved the treatment she received because of her failure to fulfill her wifely role. "By her frivolous and careless attitude toward her household duties and lack of attentiveness to her husband, [Gomazova] was often herself the cause of family quarrels." On this basis, officials rejected her appeal.[57]

In a second case, a woman's alleged sexual misconduct prompted officials to deny her protection, although witnesses left no doubt that her husband's abuse was severe, perhaps even life-threatening. Anna Glushinskaia, a townswoman also resident in the city of Pskov, petitioned in 1887 requesting a separate passport on the basis of her husband's abusiveness. In her petition, Glushinskaia claimed that her husband, Andrei, had mistreated her cruelly since the earliest days of the marriage, behavior that had forced her to leave him several times. Each time, however, for lack of a passport she was compelled by the police to return. Shortly after the most recent forced return, under police escort, her husband had come to the hotel room where she was staying and attempted to murder her. She shot him with a revolver in self-defense, slightly wounding him in the hand. This convinced a jury to acquit her when she was brought to trial. Officials, however, remained unmoved. Without denying that Glushinskii was a drunkard who often beat his wife and had broken into her room threatening murder, officials declined to grant her a passport because of her own "reprehensible" behavior. Presumably, this was a reference to the sexual liaison that a secret

<hr />

55. This distinction, too, was hardly unique to Russia. See Pleck, *Domestic Tyranny*, 24; and Doggett, *Marriage, Wife-Beating, and the Law*, 31–32. The prerogative of correction belonged only to the husband. Thus the in-laws of the peasant woman Evfrosinia Grundina "even permitted themselves to strike her," reported a local official in 1886 (RGIA, fond 1412, op. 250, d. 103, 97 ob.) Justices of the Peace, insofar as can be determined from newspaper reports and the materials in chancellery files, do not appear to have used such language.

56. In this, officials might be more demanding than the women themselves. While officials referred to merchant men as having "permitted themselves" to beat their wives, those wives might refer to themselves as having been beaten "without cause."

57. RGIA, fond 1412, op. 250, d. 101, 45 ob.

investigation by the Pskov gendarmes, undertaken at the chancellery's behest, had suppos-edly revealed.[58] In their concern with public decorum, defined in this as in other instances as female sexual decorum, in their propensity to regard peasant and townswomen as po-tentially unruly and needing male governance, and in their acceptance of marital violence as an appropriate means to that end, chancellery officials in the reign of Tsar Alexander III appear to have shared the patriarchal attitudes of those whose cases they judged, even as the two might differ over when such violence was warranted and at what point it became "extreme."

Even when they decided that husbands had exceeded or abused their marital au-thority, chancellery officials exercised with restraint their power to curtail it. The legal context affected the character of officials' decisions. Family law, after all, declared il-legal any action that led to the separation of married couples—precisely the outcome of chancellery decisions in women's favor. As a result, chancellery officials most often treated separation as a short-term remedy rather than a permanent solution for marital difficulties and approved a passport only temporarily. Temporary approval required the woman to petition when her passport expired, and sometimes to undergo a new investigation, with all the delays and bureaucratic red tape the procedure might involve for up to five years. At that point she was permitted simply to renew her passport. This was the policy irrespective of the petitioners' social status. In such cases, rather than shielding a woman permanently from neglect and/or abuse, officials used their supra-legal authority to discipline the husband.

The disciplinary purpose is evident in the language not only of decisions approving the passport but also of those in which a woman's request was denied. In the latter, the disciplinary intent might take the form of a warning, a kind of heads-up call to a husband to cease behaviors officials deemed inappropriate. Officials might decline to approve the woman's passport in cases where abuse had occurred, while informing the husband that if he failed to cease the offensive behavior, and if his wife petitioned again, her request for a passport would be satisfied. Such warnings were most common in cases where the couple was newly married and/or officials did not consider the hus-band to be incorrigible. Less often, they sought to discipline the wife as well. To take one example: although the townsman Stepan Vlasov acknowledged beating his wife, Ekaterina, in 1898, officials found this insufficient cause to approve her passport. The couple had been married only two years, Vlasov earned enough to support his wife, and according to Ekaterina's own sister, Ekaterina had a "quarrelsome and stubborn" character. Consequently, officials warned the husband to mend his ways lest his wife's petition be satisfied if she appealed again, but they also warned the wife to provide "no cause for family quarrels."[59]

58. Ibid., op. 250, d. 102, 41–46.
59. Ibid., op. 240, d. 78 (Vlasova), 13.

FIGURE 13. *Working class couple, late nineteenth century. Tsentral'nyi gosudarstvennyi arkhiv Kinofonofotodokumentov.*

In most of the cases retained in the chancellery's archives or summarized in reports, officials treated marital separation not as a solution to marital discord but, particularly in cases involving peasants and townspeople, as a way of disciplining or punishing a miscreant husband. Although it deprived a husband of access to his wife's person, labor, and services in response to his misdeeds, the punishment of approving her passport worked only if it held out the promise of regaining those benefits if he reformed. The short-term (one-year) duration of the passport for which women without privilege were eligible facilitated this punitive function (privileged women were eligible for longer-term passports), but passport duration was not the reason for it. This is evident from a shift in chancellery procedures that occurred in 1889. Until then, officials had followed the practice of the Third Section, approving a one-year passport when they found in a woman's favor and stipulating that the woman could renew the document "whenever she requests it." Therefore, they made separation permanent. The practice changed in 1889. That year, officials began to qualify the possibility of renewal. Initially, the change came in handwritten addenda to reports that had already been composed. To take one of many possible examples, in May 1889, to a report recommending that the townswoman Natalia Gromova be given a one-year passport and the right to renew on request, the qualifying words were added in a different hand: "until the husband is able to support his family and ceases to get drunk."[60] In reports dating from 1890, too, such addenda are often to be found. Thereafter, such stipulations became part of the report itself.

It is likely that these changes came at the behest of Tsar Alexander III, who evidently began to attend more closely to the chancellery's operations. Alexander III presented himself as "the guardian of the sanctity and steadfastness of the family principle" and was well known for his commitment to buttressing the family. According to Sergei Pisarev, the chancellery's only historian and himself a chancellery official, Alexander III also had the habit of writing on chancellery reports such comments as "In my opinion, there is no reason for us to interfere in family matters at present," or "I would have trouble taking responsibility for such a resolution."[61]

It was this change that transformed the granting of a passport into a means to discipline a man unable to discipline himself. Although officials continued to issue renewable passports, often although not invariably to privileged women, and more rarely to unprivileged women whose husbands were guilty of especially egregious behavior over a lengthy period of time, such qualifying phrasing became the norm. For members of the laboring classes, especially, the phrasing often had a distinctively admonitory tone. "He does not recognize his guilt," officials might write of a miscreant husband who

60. Ibid., op. 250, d. 103, 88.
61. S. N. Pisarev, *Uchrezhdenie po priniatiiu i napravleniiu proshenii i zhalob, prinosimykh na Vyso-chaishee imia, 1810–1910 gg. Istoricheskii ocherk* (St. Petersburg: R. Golike i A. Vil'borg, 1909), 163.

denied his own wrongdoing. Reports often emphasized the temporary nature of the passport and enumerated the conditions under which the husband might regain his marital rights. Especially during the reign of Tsar Alexander III, these conditions were set forth in punitive language and phraseology evocative of religiously based morality: the wife would receive a passport "only for one year," during which time, if the husband did not "find himself work that would enable him to support his wife and at the same time free himself from his vicious inclination to alcoholic beverages, which has so fatally affected his family life," she might merit such a mercy again, as one report from 1892 read.[62]

The language of the chancellery's 1892 decision is worth noting for another reason, too—its assumption that abuse of alcohol was to blame for domestic violence. He "permits himself to abuse alcoholic beverages, under the influence of which he ill-treats his wife," as they put it in a different decision.[63] Subsuming domestic violence under the rubric of alcohol abuse, in the first decade of the chancellery's practice officials almost never referred to a husband's ill treatment of his wife as such when she derived from the laboring classes. Instead, their admonitions emphasized public decorum and the husband's fulfillment of his legal obligation to support his wife and family. In one case, for example, in which officials had found that the husband had beaten not only his wife but her mother, they required the husband to "cease his love affair with the maiden Gondarenko, and by his good conduct and industrious lifestyle, expiate [zagladit'] his guilt before his wife." In another, in which the wife had been beaten "without cause," officials required that the husband "unquestionably mend his ways and with his good conduct and sober lifestyle expiate his evil acts."[64]

Whatever the language, to the extent that disciplinary practices succeeded in convincing a husband to mend his ways, his wife may well have welcomed them. But she exercised no control over the process: it was officials, rather than she, who judged whether a husband had reformed. When officials judged that a husband had altered his behavior in the requisite fashion, they rewarded him with renewed access to his wife's self and services, restoring cohabitation whether or not the wife was willing. They did so even in cases where the man had formerly abused his wife quite egregiously. To take one unusually grim example, Vassa Petrova gained a one-year separation from her husband, Ivan, in 1898 on account of his drinking, "cruel treatment," and failure to hold a job. Petrov was warned that, unless his behavior improved, his wife would find protection again. Although Ivan's cruelty consisted of once beating his wife so brutally that she lost consciousness and on other occasions tearing her ear, sticking a fork in her foot, and tearing her mouth, this was not sufficient to win her permanent separation.

62. RGIA, fond 1412, op. 250, d. 101, 83.
63. Ibid., d. 104, 77.
64. Ibid., d. 103, 70; 101, 88 (1891).

In 1901, three years after his wife's successful petition, Petrov, having sobered up and found a job as a guard on the St. Petersburg-Vitebsk railroad with a wage of twenty-five rubles a month, announced to the chancellery that he wanted to live with his wife again. Despite Petrova's understandable insistence that she never wanted to return to her husband, the chancellery denied her petition, "Because he's now mended his ways and earns enough to live with his wife."[65]

The disciplinary element never disappeared, as the Petrov case above clearly shows. However, in the reign of Tsar Nicholas II, concern with public decorum ceased to play such a prominent role in officials' decision making, and their language became less moralistic: "until he fully improves and finds work sufficient to support a wife," "until he improves and stops abusing alcohol," and so on. They also began to express greater solicitude for a woman's person. In the mid-1890s, officials' disciplinary injunctions began to refer to the quality of conjugal relationships among the laboring classes. Not only requiring the cessation of drinking and an end to violence, these references invoked a broader ideal of conjugal harmony as well. To take one example, officials approved a one-year passport for Elena Gosteva in 1896, after investigation revealed that Petr Gostev, a retired soldier, abused alcohol, showed insufficient care for his family, and beat his wife "without cause." If, when her passport had expired and the two renewed cohabitation, Petr did not cease to abuse alcohol and begin to treat his wife "gently and affectionately," then Elena might again find protection should she petition anew. Thereafter, references to the necessity of "gentle and affectionate" treatment became almost standard.[66]

In this period, officials also took steps that enhanced wives' control of the process and greatly increased their bargaining power in relation to their husbands, while leaving the ultimate decision in officials' hands. Awarding a one-year passport, officials might instruct the husband to "take measures to reconcile" with his wife or, during the separation period, to come to an agreement with her about their future. If the husband failed to make overtures to his wife or to take steps to address her complaints, it greatly increased the likelihood that the wife's passport would be renewed. One of the reasons that officials decided in 1900 to renew the passport of Maria Ponomareva, a peasant from Astrakhan province who had left her husband, Fedor, on account of his cruelty, was that he had done nothing to win her back in the three years since they had separated and had instead exercised the coercion that was his right by law. During their cohabitation, Fedor "not only never protected her from oppression [pritesnenie] by his mother but himself treated her coarsely and beat her cruelly," the decision in her favor read. Then, after their separation, "after being informed of the necessity of coming to some kind of agreement with his wife, he never tried to do anything about this himself, but

65. Ibid., op. 226, d. 43 (Petrova, V., 1899), 50. For a similar outcome, see op. 250, d. 100, 108–9.
66. Ibid., op. 250, d. 100, 43–44. For other examples, see ibid., d. 104, ll, 41, 60, 77.

rather turned to the local police with the demand that they install [*vodvorit'*] his wife in his home." In 1903, officials faulted Vladimir Kukin, a peasant from Voronezh who had resettled in the Semireche district, in similar terms. "Since 1898, he has taken no measures to patch up his relations with his wife," officials wrote. Although his parents, with whom he lived, were sufficiently well-off to keep five horses, and Ksenia was their sole daughter-in-law, officials approved her passport. In 1905, they admonished Petr Alekseev, a townsman, on much the same grounds: "he's taken no measures to patch up his family life [*ulazhenie svoei semeinoi s neiu zhizni*] despite being instructed to do so in 1903."[67]

Officials expressed their evolving attitudes toward conjugal relations among the laboring classes in another way as well. In 1902, after decades of referring to women without privilege who had been beaten "without cause," the language of chancellery decisions in domestic violence cases underwent a telling shift. That year, officials ceased almost entirely to criticize townsmen for beating their wife "without cause." Henceforward, such men "permitted themselves" to beat their wives. This linguistic change reflected a shift in officials' understanding of manhood and womanhood as well as of appropriate relations between the sexes. Implying, on one hand, that townsmen were competent to govern the self, such language asserted, on the other, that under no circumstances did townswomen merit violent treatment, however provocative their behavior.[68] In the reports I have read, only once after 1902 did officials refer to a townswoman who had been beaten "without cause"; they remained more prone to use such language about a peasant woman, suggesting that the linguistic change reflected officials' own perceptions, rather than an order from the tsar.

Indeed, there is evidence to suggest that had circumstances permitted, officials would have gladly surrendered altogether their disciplinary role. Toward the close of the nineteenth century, they strongly endorsed the efforts of jurists to reform marital law so as to legalize divorce and marital separation, which would have divested officials entirely of their responsibility.[69] Efforts to reform marital law having failed, they then endeavored to reinforce decisions by the State Senate that, starting in 1888, had permitted abused and neglected peasant women to obtain passports through appeals to their local land captain. Responding to the many problems in the implementation of the Senate decisions, in 1902 the chancellery proposed that the Senate establish consistent

67. Ibid., op. 226, d. 100 (Ponomareva, M., 1896), 116; op. 221, d. 199 (Kukina, K., 1897), 31; op. 212, d. 126 (Alekseeva, T., 1900), 110.

68. As Elizabeth Foyster has noted, once people began to question the legitimacy of physical violence as a form of correction in a marriage, "even a wife who behaved provocatively could be represented as undeserving of violence" (*Marital Violence,* 115).

69. See Barbara Alpern Engel, "In the Name of the Tsar: Competing Legalities and Marital Conflict in Late Imperial Russia," *Journal of Modern History* 77, no. 1 (2005): 70–96.

guidelines to govern local practice and strengthen the legal weight of its decisions by bringing the administrative authority of the Ministry of the Interior to bear. This was, in fact, the solution that the Senate adopted. In December 1902, the powerful Ministry of the Interior, led by Dmitrii Sipiagin, former head of the chancellery, issued a circular aimed at establishing a uniform practice toward abused and/or neglected peasant wives. The circular instructed land captains to examine appeals from such women on their merits, and if their allegations were upheld, to allow them to leave neglectful or abusive husbands.[70] In subsequent years, the Ministry of the Interior further elaborated Senate decisions, between 1902 and 1907 regularly issuing circulars to that affect.

After 1902, the chancellery relinquished almost entirely the responsibility for examining the petitions of peasant wives. Although peasant women continued to appeal to the chancellery for relief in significant numbers, the chancellery instructed virtually all these new petitioners to turn to the local authorities without investigating the case.[71] For peasant women, the results were probably mixed. My own reading of about fifty cases considered by land captains in Moscow and Riazan provinces after 1902 suggests that (1) investigations were less thorough and relied more heavily on the testimony of the husband's fellow villagers than those conducted by the chancellery's representatives; and (2) local officials were rather less inclined than chancellery officials to sympathize with peasant women's plight and rather more inclined to give serious consideration to the economic viability of the husband's household, which was significant for officials, too, but not invariably decisive (see the Kukin case, above).[72] These shortcomings notwithstanding, the reform of 1902 greatly expanded the accessibility of relief for abused and neglected peasant women—indeed, so much so that townswomen and merchant women requested a similar procedure.[73]

• • •

Either by itself or in combination with other abuses, domestic violence was the most common complaint of petitioning wives who derived from the laboring classes. Encouraged, no doubt, by the proliferation of opportunities to earn an independent

70. The chancellery corresponded directly with Sipiagin as well, preparing the ground for the Senate's initiative. See also V. A. Veremenko, "Litso," 214–17.

71. Petitions returned to the woman, with instructions to appeal to local officials, numbered 354 in 1903, 91 in 1904, and 71 in 1905. For the rejected petitions, see RGIA, fond 1412, op. 241, d. 32, 33, and 34.

72. The cases are listed in TsIAM, fond 62, op. 1, t. 1 and 2 and op. 2, and fond 1938–1, op. 1. On the difficulties land captains experienced with the endless directives issued by the Ministry of the Interior, see Christine Gaudin, *Ruling Peasants: Village and State in Late Imperial Russia* (DeKalb: Northern Illinois University Press, 2007), 32, 56.

73. See the letters from the governors of Vladimir and Pskov in RGIA, fond 1412, op. 241, d. 18, ll, 19, 21.

livelihood, as well as the increase in venues to which they might appeal, wives of the laboring classes fled abusive husbands, appealed to the courts for relief, and took their complaints to the tsar himself in an effort to escape from violence or bring it to an end. Their complaints helped keep the issue of domestic violence before the public, providing judicial reformers with examples of the abuses to which arbitrary authority might give rise and which could best be curtailed by granting women the right to legal separation and divorce, preferably in courts over which reformers themselves presided. Domestic violence was thus incorporated into reformers' political agendas.[74]

It played no such role in the deliberations of chancellery officials. Inflected by social differences, officials' views were initially far closer to those of the laboring men whom they judged, for whom wife beating was often an appropriate response to wifely misconduct broadly construed. In the first decade of their operations, officials were thus prepared to condone wife beating when it seemed to them warranted and, even when they condemned it, to regard it as less important than a husband's ability to support his family and maintain public decorum. Social order and stability trumped the individual well-being of wives. Enjoying the authority to grant a separation, officials used it, at least initially in most cases, to discipline husbands rather than to protect their wives.

Yet officials, too, were affected by intellectual currents of their time that were critical of domestic violence and more respectful of women's rights to selfhood. Even as they remained mindful of the strictures of marital law and concerned about social stability and order, their requirements for masculine conduct toward wives grew more exacting. The process culminated in 1902, when officials ceased to refer to virtually all townswomen and many peasant women as potentially meriting violence for misconduct, thereby erasing the distinction that they had hitherto drawn between women of privilege and those without it. In the same year, officials initiated steps more consistently to safeguard the rights of peasant women by administrative means. Even as officials remained unreservedly committed to Russia's absolutist political order, they were prepared to curtail husbands' absolute authority over their wives and to foster greater mutuality (although certainly not equality) between them.

74. Here I echo the argument made by William Wagner but with a slightly different emphasis. See William Wagner, "The Trojan Mare: Women's Rights and Civil Rights in Late Imperial Russia," in *Civil Rights in Imperial Russia,* ed. Olga Crisp and Linda Edmondson (Oxford: Clarendon, 1989), 65–84.

Earning My Own Crust of Bread

In 1897, the townswoman Anastasia Petrova, having completed a dressmaking course in St. Petersburg and obtained her diploma, headed south to the city of Baku, located on the shore of the Caspian Sea in what is now Azerbaijan but was then the thriving center of petroleum production for the entire Russian Empire. There she found work as a dressmaker and seamstress and, "being very literate," as she put it, supplemented her earnings by working as a clerk for several enterprises in the city. Then, in January 1902, she made the "big mistake" of marrying Aleksei Petrov, a man she barely knew, employed as a shop clerk in one of Baku's numerous oil concerns. Something—it is never clear exactly what—went very wrong, very quickly. In the petition she submitted in May 1905, Petrova referred to "endless quarrels," to her husband's abandonment of her after three months of marriage, and to his demands for money in exchange for her passport. She could not possibly continue to live with him, she wrote. The very thought of it repelled her. "Nothing whatever ties me to my husband: we have never had children, there was never any love between us, and our characters are also completely incompatible. Under these circumstances, does it make sense to presume that the exact fulfillment of the civil law requiring cohabitation of spouses can lead to anything but blatant injustice?" Petrova rhetorically inquired.[1]

That her ill-considered marriage had come to threaten her work and the life she had made for herself lent weight to Petrova's rhetorical question: "Two to three times a year," she continued, "Aleksei demands that my passport be taken away ... and that I be sent to him under police escort and the like. As a result of these demands, I must abandon my practice and the position that I acquired exclusively through my own labor." Currently employed full-time as a clerk-typist, she also labored at home in the evening sewing women's dresses. Thanks to all this, she was able to live quite comfortably (*bezbedno*), she informed officials. Re-emphasizing and linking the absence of love and the necessity of work, Petrova expressed her

1. RGIA, fond 1412, op. 226, d. 42 (Petrova, A., 1905), 1, 3.

"categorical" refusal to resume cohabitation with her husband: "I don't want to return to a man I don't love and abandon a difficult position that allows me to live well."[2]

It is virtually axiomatic among historians of marriage, separation, and divorce that the expansion of opportunities for waged labor outside the home was a key contributing factor to the growing numbers of divorces and formal separations that occurred in Europe in the decades before the onset of World War I. Although the availability of work did not cause marriages to break down, according to Roderick Phillips, "it did enable women to survive outside of marriage and thereby enabled them to leave their husbands."[3] Offering an alternative to women's economic dependence on their husbands, the ability to earn an independent wage enabled women to leave intolerable marriages if they chose. But remunerative labor might contribute to marital breakdown in another way as well. By broadening horizons and enhancing wives' sense of self, it could prompt dissatisfaction with a relationship the women might otherwise have accepted. This chapter explores these two, sometimes separate, sometimes inter-related processes in the context of late nineteenth-century Russia, where the significance of extradomestic labor, women's extradomestic labor included, gave it a key role in many women's appeals.

Women's need or desire to work figured prominently in the petitions of the vast majority of unhappy wives from the laboring classes and in about a third of the petitions submitted by their privileged sisters. The need was often expressed in the most down-to-earth terms—"I want to earn my daily bread." It likewise figured in the model letter for petitioners first published in 1895. "I wish to preserve my right to honest labor," the imagined petitioner wrote.[4] In their own appeals and follow-up narratives, petitioning women described the studies they pursued or hoped to pursue in preparation for earning a living or the employment they had found or hoped to obtain, occasionally fallaciously.[5] Because women often required a separate passport to obtain employment or to attend school, emphasizing their need to study and/or work undoubtedly enhanced the appeal of their petitions. But their need to earn a living also offered petitioners a particularly compelling mode of self-presentation, one to which others, officials among

2. Ibid.

3. Roderick Phillips, *Putting Asunder: A History of Divorce in Western Society* (New York: Cambridge University Press, 1988), 377, 592. For Russia, see also William G. Wagner, *Marriage, Property, and Divorce in Late Imperial Russia* (Oxford: Clarendon, 1994), 94; and Barbara Alpern Engel, *Between the Fields and the City: Women, Work, and Family in Russia, 1861–1914* (New York: Cambridge University Press, 1995), 98–99.

4. *Pravila o poriadke priniatiia i napravleniia proshenii i zhalob, na Vysochaishee imia prinosimykh, utverzhdennye 21 marta 1890 g. s dopolnitel'nymi k nim uzakoneniiami. S prilozheniem obraztsov form proshenii i zhalob* (St. Petersburg: D. V. Chichinadze, 1895), 22–23.

5. For one such self-misrepresentation, see RGIA, fond 1412, op. 222, d. 12 (Lazurkina, V., 1908), 1, 41.

them, proved notably receptive. And for a few, labor offered more, as this chapter argues. The ability to earn their own living offered some women a basis for affirming selfhood and subjectivity and for presenting themselves as rights-bearing subjects rather than, or in addition to, supplicants and victims. Women's self-presentations almost invariably elicited a sympathetic response from others, officials among them.

THE WORKING WOMAN: WHO IS SHE?

The final decades of the nineteenth century witnessed a significant expansion of the employment opportunities for women from a range of social backgrounds. Russia's industrialization drive gathered steam in the 1880s; thereafter women's proportion in the burgeoning factory labor force increased steadily, from about one in every five workers to about one in every three by 1914. After 1882, when tariffs were imposed on imported clothing, the needle trades expanded dramatically. By the turn of the century, some 8 percent of the female laboring population in Moscow and St. Petersburg earned a living with the needle. Some women worked in their own homes, but most were employed by workshops in which they also lived. In addition, thousands of women, mainly of humble origin, trained and found employment as nurses, midwives, and medical aides; by 1905, some ten thousand midwives practiced the profession. The expansion of local and state administration created a demand for white-collar workers; shops increasingly hired women as well as men to stand behind the counter. The number of women teaching in village schools grew exponentially, from 4,878 in 1880 to 64,851 in 1911. To be sure, it is important not to overstate either the extent of opportunity or the desirability of the employment on offer: most notably, well into the early twentieth century, the largest proportion of laboring women occupied the humble position of domestic servant. Nevertheless, whatever their level of education or skill, women who sought work in the 1880s and after enjoyed access to a far broader range of employment options than had their own mothers.[6]

For members of Russia's laboring classes, the extradomestic labor of wives, in itself, represented nothing new. The industrialization drive that began to transform Russia's economy in the final decades of the nineteenth century coexisted with, and sometimes drew on, preindustrial and protoindustrial modes of production in which the household served as a unit of production as well as consumption. Thus the overwhelming majority of Russia's married women who labored did so in or near the household and

6. Rose Glickman, *Russian Factory Women: Workplace and Society, 1880–1914* (Berkeley: University of California Press, 1984), 61–62; 80–81; Samuel Ramer, "Childbirth and Culture: Midwifery in the Nineteenth-Century Russian Countryside, in *The Family in Imperial Russia: New Lines of Historical Research*, ed. David Ransel (Urbana: University of Illinois Press, 1978), 220–21; Ben Eklof, *Russian Peasant Schools: Officialdom, Village Culture, and Popular Pedagogy, 1861–1914* (Berkeley: University of California Press, 1986), 189, 195.

for the household economy. In the countryside, peasant women toiled in kitchen garden and barnyard as well as beside their husbands in the fields; peasant women sold eggs and domestic products for extra cash; if the household needed additional income, married women earned it by manufacturing items at home or leaving the village, usually temporarily, to earn money elsewhere.

Similar patterns prevailed among the laboring classes in cities and towns. In the households of craftsmen and artisans, women played an important role in domestic production by participating directly, by boarding apprentices, by seeing to finances, and so on. Even in urban households from which husbands left home to earn their livelihood, wives of the laboring classes often contributed to the household economy in a variety of ways: taking in boarders, doing laundry for others, doing piecework for manufacturers, and the like. Among these groups, at least, the idea that home should provide escape from the world of production remained irrelevant.[7]

The expansion of employment opportunities did not change the expectation that married women would contribute to the household economy if the household required it.[8] Although a division of labor very much stratified by sex figured among the "real life" constraints that structured women's labor choices and women's treatment at the workplace in Russia as everywhere else, the idea that women's "virtue" resided exclusively in motherhood or genteel behavior and precluded work outside the home was absent there.[9] Indeed, work itself was a source of virtue. In peasant villages, marriages customarily brought a worker (*rabotnitsa*) into the household, and the predominant images of femininity were those of mother and the worker.[10]

7. Engel, *Between the Fields and the City;* Glickman, *Russian Factory Women,* chap. 2; Christine Worobec, *Peasant Russia: Family and Community in the Post-Emancipation Period* (Princeton, NJ: Princeton University Press, 1991). Studies of townspeople have far less to say about married women's work, but see A. N. Zorin et al., *Ocherki gorodskogo byta dorevoliutsionnogo Povolzh'ia* (Ul'ianovsk: Izdatel'stvo Srednevolzhskogo nauchnogo tsentra, 2000), esp. 32–44; and Iu. M. Goncharov, *Gorodskaia sem'ia Sibiri vtoroi poloviny XIX–nachala XX v.* (Barnaul: Izdatel'stvo Altaiskogo gosudarstvennogo universiteta, 2002), 181.

8. Much the same expectations prevailed elsewhere in Europe. See Elizabeth A. M. Roberts, "Women's Strategies, 1890–1940," in *Labour and Love: Women's Experience of Home and Family, 1850–1940,* ed. Jane Lewis (Oxford: Basil Blackwell, 1986), 223; and George Alter, *Family and the Female Life Course: The Women of Verviers, Belgium, 1849–1880* (Madison: University of Wisconsin Press, 1988), 99–102.

9. Alice Kessler Harris, *Gendering Labor History* (Urbana: University of Illinois Press, 2007), 117–18. On women's treatment at the workplace, see Engel, *Between the Fields and the City,* 137–39; and Glickman, *Russian Factory Women,* 204–8.

10. T. G. Leont'eva, "Sel'skie zatvornitsy: zhenshchiny i baby v dorevoliutsionnoi derevne," in *Iz arkhiva tverskikh istorikov* 3 (2003): 110.

At the same time, law treated men as the primary breadwinner, obliging a husband to feed and support his wife "according to his station and means."[11] A married woman could not work for someone else without her husband's permission, which may explain why the eighteen-year-old Liubov Aleksandrova, having worked as a telegraph worker for the railroad in the town of Novgorod, was dismissed from the position after she married Platon Aleksandrov, a member of the hairdressers guild, in 1880.[12] When married women did engage in remunerative labor, it was ordinarily part of a "family strategy," aimed at supplementing a husband's earnings and adding to the resources of the household, over which the husband (or in the case of the multigenerational peasant or urban household, his father), presided as head. The goal of women's labor was certainly not to promote women's autonomy or to serve women's personal needs, single women being something of an exception. But especially when work took women away from home for lengthy periods of time, as was the case for a growing minority of women from the laboring classes, work for wages might promote women's autonomy and sense of personal entitlement nevertheless. At the same time, the lengthy separations that employment might require could disrupt traditional family relations and put new strains on a marriage.

Russian intellectuals approached the idea of labor, including women's labor, from a different perspective. By the end of the nineteenth century, argues Bernice Glatzer Rosenthal, Russia's intellectuals had developed a rudimentary work ethic based on the idea that toil was God's commandment. Disregarding personal material gain, this ethic linked work with a higher ideal: "the fulfillment of a divinely ordained task for some; service to the state or to the people for others."[13] When women engaged in it, remunerative labor might serve the individual as well, at least in the view of Russia's progressive thinkers. During the 1860s, women's economic autonomy—their ability to earn their own living—became a major thrust of the "woman question" and was directly linked to that generation's concern for the "emancipation of the person [*raskreposhchenie lichnosti*]." A woman "must toil [*trudit'sia*] just as a man does, and as he does, have her own earnings and be useful to society," as the memoirist Elizaveta Vodovozova recalled the rhetoric of the 1860s. Lelenka, the heroine of Nadezhda Khvoshchinskaia's novella,

---

11. *Svod zakonov Rossiiskoi imperii* (St. Petersburg, 1857), vol. 10, pt. 1, article 106.

12. RGIA, fond 1412, op. 212, d. 103 (Aleksandrova, L., 1882), 42.

13. Bernice Glatzer Rosenthal, "The Search for a Russian Orthodox Work Ethic," in *Between Tsar and People: Educated Society and the Quest for Public Identity in Late Imperial Russia*, ed. Edith W. Clowes, Samuel D. Kassow, and James L. West (Princeton, NJ: Princeton University Press, 1991), 57–58. Liberal Orthodox thinkers in this period had also come to accept work for women, albeit only single women. See William G. Wagner, "'Orthodox Domesticity': Creating a Social Role for Women," in *Sacred Stories: Religion and Spirituality in Modern Russia*, ed. Mark D. Steinberg and Heather J. Coleman (Bloomington: Indiana University Press, 2007), 126–31.

"The Boarding School Girl," published in 1860, made a credo of economic independence: "Liberate yourselves, all of you who have two hands and a strong will! Live alone. Work, knowledge, and freedom—this is what life is all about." In "progressive" circles, to cite Vodovozova again, even married women whose husbands earned enough to support the family felt obliged to add their own earnings to the general family budget. Socialist writers were even more emphatic about the significance of women's labor for women themselves as well as for society as a whole. "I too will live by my labor," Vera Pavlovna, the heroine of Nikolai Chernyshevsky's enormously influential novel, *What Is to Be Done? (1863),* informs her fiancé. "As long as a woman lives at a man's expense, she will be dependent on him." For all their differences, feminists and socialists shared the belief that paid labor was the key to women's emancipation.[14]

Others, far less radical, also embraced the idea that women should labor, although not necessarily the idea that women required emancipation. In 1916, the overwhelming majority of the 574 high-school girls who were queried about their future said they planned to work for a living. Revealingly, even maternal and child welfare movements, which elsewhere in Europe and the United States tended to be dominated by maternalist rhetoric, in Russia emphasized women's participation in the workforce over their role as mothers. Imperial philanthropic agencies, too, based their policies on the belief that "poor women must and should earn their own living."[15] Thus, unlike their middle class contemporaries in Western Europe and the United States, educated Russians might regard with approval the remunerative labor of women, even when the women were married, even when they were mothers.

The mass-circulation magazine *Niva* reflected but also contributed to the acceptance of women's extradomestic labor. An illustrated weekly journal of literature and politics that covered a broad range of topics, with its circulation of a hundred thousand *Niva* was the most popular magazine in Russia. Billed as a "family magazine," each issue carried on the title page a picture of a father reading the magazine, no doubt aloud, with his wife and child by his side. Yet despite the billing, "the family" as such played an increasingly minor role in the visual content of the magazine, while women at work gained steadily in prominence. To obtain a sense of what subscribers to *Niva*

14. Elizaveta Vodovozova, *Na zare zhizni. Memuarnye ocherki i portrety,* 2 vols. (Moscow: Khudozhestvennaia literatura, 1964), 2: 194–95, 198; quoted from "The Boarding School Girl" as cited in Jane Costlow, "Love, Work, and the Woman Question in Mid-Nineteenth-Century Women's Writing," in *Women Writers in Russian Literature,* ed. Toby W. Clyman and Diana Greene (Westport, CT: Praeger, 1994), 65–66; Nikolai Chernyshevsky, *What Is to Be Done,* trans. Benjamin R. Tucker, rev. by Ludmilla B. Turkevich (New York: Vintage, 1961), 108–9.

15. Nikolai A. Rybnikov, *Idealy gimnazistok (Ocherki po psikhologii iunosti* (Moscow: Prakticheskie znaniia, 1916); Adele Lindenmeyr, "Maternalism and Child Welfare in Late Imperial Russia," *Journal of Women's History* 5, no. 2 (1993): 114, 116, 119.

might be seeing, I surveyed the magazine's prints, which were particularly treasured by its readers.[16] I chose ten-year intervals, starting in 1880 and concluding in 1910, categorizing every print in which a woman figured. The results suggest that the acceptance of women's extradomestic labor grew steadily over time: only in 1880 did depictions of women in family scenes or engaging in domestic labor (including fetching water from a well) outnumber depictions of women at work; thereafter, depictions of women engaging in physical labor (peasants in fields), intellectual labor (looking through microscopes, circling the globe, studying agronomy), or artistic endeavors (opera singers, ballerinas, or in the case of Maria Bashkirtseva [1890] painting and diary-keeping) clearly predominated. Women's magazines likewise celebrated the attainments of individual women: the widely read *Vestnik mody*, for example, offered its readers a popularized version of the woman question, challenging notions of women's inferiority and extolling women's achievements in fields such as medicine.[17]

THE NEED TO EARN AN INCOME

"Both my husband and I worked in a factory in Bogorodsk, Moscow province," wrote Agrippina Likhanova, born a townswoman, married to a peasant, in her 1888 petition to the chancellery.

Then he took to playing billiards and gambling and, by failing to do his work, lost his job. After that he simply abandoned me and my child. But he also refused me a passport. As a result, I was fired from my job at the Kuprianov factory, where I worked as a weaver. I'm now living with my parents in Bogorodsk, but they are poor themselves.... Other people's efforts to convince my husband to grant me a passport have led nowhere. As far as he is concerned, I can die of hunger.[18]

Remunerative labor was a necessity rather than a choice for the overwhelming majority of women who petitioned the chancellery, women of the laboring classes in particular. Many already worked for a living at the time of their appeal and required a passport to

16. "I adored *Niva* and impatiently awaited each new issue; I looked at the pictures with joy and read the journal from cover to cover," remembered one merchant daughter (E. A. Andreeva-Balmont, *Vospominaniia* [Moscow: Izdatel'stvo imeni Sabashnikovykh, 1997], 155). Gilt-framed pictures received as supplements to the journal hung in the stuffy drawing room in the lower middle-class Nizhnii Novgorod home where Maxim Gorky served as apprentice (*Autobiography of Maxim Gorky*, trans. Avrahm Yarmolinsky [New York: Collier, 1962], 255).

17. Carolyn Marks, "'Providing Amusement for the Ladies': The Rise of the Russian Women's Magazine in the 1880s," in *An Improper Profession: Women, Gender, and Journalism in Late Imperial Russia*, ed. Barbara T. Norton and Jehanne Gheith (Durham, NC: Duke University Press, 2001), 113.

18. RGIA, fond 1412, op. 240, d. 166 (Likhanova, A., 1888), 1.

keep their jobs; others would need to find a job to provide for themselves and, in some cases, their children. The situations of peasants and townswomen were very similar in this respect. The overwhelming majority of peasant petitioners to the chancellery, roughly 90 percent, no longer lived in their husband's village at the time of petitioning, judging by the cases that figured in summary reports. Only a small proportion of petitioning women enjoyed economic resources sufficient for survival without engaging in remunerative labor or had relatives with the means and willingness to support them and, if necessary, to feed additional mouths.

Indeed, at the time of petitioning a substantial minority of petitioners, and perhaps the majority, already depended entirely on their own labor, married as they were to men who failed to fulfill the most fundamental of masculine roles: providing for their wives according to their means. The catalogue of woes that figured in women's often brief petitions might have been dismissed as formulaic, had not their slender dossiers upheld them in the vast majority of cases.[19] Some of the husbands of petitioning wives existed on the margins of plebeian life. Succumbing to the blandishments of drink or to other lures, unable to adjust to the unfamiliar and demanding routines of factory or workshop life, unwilling to govern themselves yet ungovernable by others, vagrant and without work, even without a roof of their own, such men were incapable of supporting themselves, let alone someone else. Other men who continued to earn a regular income refused to provide for their wives and children, preferring instead to spend the money elsewhere, usually on drink.

A significant minority of female petitioners who labored outside the home endured economic in addition to other abuses. Some husbands laid claim to their wives' income and other possessions. Often using physical violence to overcome their wives' resistance, they carried off chairs and tables, pots and pans, even their wives' dresses, to sell or pawn for drink. The behavior of the townsman Ivan Anisimov offers one extreme but unfortunately by no means unique example. Anisimov had lost his position as a skilled worker (*masterovoi*) on account of drink and, after years of beating his wife, Feodosia, almost murdered her in an effort to get his hands on the money she earned as a seamstress. His violence took place on the streets of St. Petersburg and earned a write-up in the local newspaper *Peterburgskaia gazeta.*[20]

Others sought to take advantage of their wives' need or desire to earn a living by using their power over the passport to extort money in return for approving it. Chan-

19. Folkloric laments, such as those cited by Y. M. Sokolov and recorded in 1872, bemoaning the drunken, abusive husband who spent his earnings on himself surely reflected an unfortunately common female experience, in addition to providing models on which petitioners and others might draw (Y. M. Sokolov, *Russian Folklore,* trans. Catherine Ruth Smith [Hatboro, PA: Folklore Associates, 1966], 30).

20. RGIA, fond 1412, op. 212, d. 66 (Anisimova, F., 1887).

cellery reports indicate that this practice was especially widespread among peasant husbands, some 15 percent of whom forced wives who wished to leave the village or already worked elsewhere and wanted to remain away to pay *obrok* (quitrent), a term deriving from master-serf relations. In some cases, husbands genuinely needed to hire a worker to replace an absent wife, in others, they simply pocketed the money.[21] The practice was surely much more common than the files would indicate, as it left a documentary trail only in cases where the husband became too greedy and or/his wife proved unwilling or unable to provide the payment he required. The case of Tatiana Aborina, one of dozens of possible examples, illustrates the pattern. After eleven years of marriage and the birth of three children, Tatiana Aborina had left her peasant husband in 1877 because he spent every kopeck they had on drink. In St. Petersburg, she found work as a domestic servant and managed to establish all three of her children in the city. Aborina nevertheless sent money regularly home to her husband, in exchange for which he approved her passport. We learn of this arrangement only because she petitioned the chancellery for the first time in 1882, five years after leaving her husband, when, in the hope of extracting more money, he refused to renew her documents.[22]

Materials in chancellery archives make it clear that men of other social backgrounds also engaged in the practice of requiring payment in exchange for the passport, albeit to a slightly lesser extent. In the absence of a farm in the village that required hiring a wife-substitute, such demands for payment constituted an obvious abuse of the husband's administrative and legal authority, even as it might also enable his wife to escape a relationship she could no longer tolerate. Take the case of the townsman Gavriil Grigor'ev and his wife, Agrippina. Agrippina had left Gavriil after only two years of marriage because he treated her "coarsely" and beat her, and she quickly found work in Moscow as a domestic servant. Over the next eight years Gavriil, employed as a factory worker in Moscow and earning nineteen rubles a month, regularly approved Agrippina's short-term passports in exchange for an unspecified fee. Then, in 1906, he demanded twenty-five rubles from her, an amount that far exceeded her monthly earnings, and when she failed to provide it, revoked her passport. Such flagrant abuse of a husband's authority for economic ends was "exploitation," in the opinion of chancellery officials in this case as in others, and almost always prompted them to approve the woman's passport.[23]

Women's economic self-sufficiency, it must be said, did not necessarily translate into self-assertion, either rhetorically or in practice. The willingness to put up with

21. Engel, *Between the Fields and the City,* 92–96.

22. RGIA, fond 1412, op. 240, d. 2 (Aborina, T., 1882), 1, 11. Like almost all petitions submitted in these years of transition, Aborina's languished for several years before the chancellery finally got around to considering it.

23. Ibid., op. 250, d. 103, 30–31.

mistreatment that figures in so many women's petitions was not only an effort to underscore their victimization and to "manipulate the language of female weakness" in pursuit of their own ends, although it certainly was that.[24] It also reflected cultural notions of appropriate feminine behavior embraced by petitioners and officials alike. As a result, women found it difficult to sever ties with a husband even in the intolerable situations in which so many of these petitioners found themselves. To take action often required a measure of resourcefulness and initiative, a willingness to defy the powerful cultural as well as legal forces that reinforced the marital bond and that kept other women in abusive and neglectful marriages even when they earned their own living.[25]

The psychological and emotional obstacles that women might have to overcome before leaving a difficult marriage are evident in the Pavlov case, one of many in which economically self-sufficient wives continued to maintain ties to abusive husbands. The townsman Fedor Pavlov, a beekeeper in Tbilisi, not only failed to provide for his wife, Paraskeva, but also took the money she earned as a laundress to play cards and gamble, then beat her bloody when she protested. Even his priest considered him "coarse and despotic." Nevertheless, the illiterate Paraskeva petitioned only after eighteen years of marriage to him and the birth of three children. Then, having lived on her own for three years on a passport approved by the chancellery, she returned to him out of "pity" for her eighteen-year-old son and in the hopes the son would protect her from his father's violence. On her return, she resumed supporting Fedor on the fourteen rubles a month she earned as a domestic servant.[26] As this case suggests, concern for children might serve as an additional factor that kept women in an intolerable marriage.

ECONOMICALLY DEPENDENT WIVES

Expectations and realities were different for women married to men of the privileged orders. Feminist and socialist rhetoric notwithstanding, women who were married to men of property, profession, or privilege generally did not earn their own livelihood after marriage, nor did others expect them to. But if their marriages turned sour, economics represented a serious obstacle to leaving the marriage and compounded the reasons that women might remain in unsatisfactory unions. If the husband fulfilled his role as provider, a woman who left an unhappy marriage risked not only loss of

---

24. Joanne Bailey, "Voices in Court: Lawyers' or Litigants'," *Historical Research* 74, no. 186 (2001): 405.

25. Elizaveta D'iakonova offers an example. Her family's servant, native to Nerekhta district of Kostroma province, was very unhappily married but "never complained about it, and the possibility of living better never occurred to her: 'There's nothing to be done; it's God's will,'" she would say according to D'iakonova, who paraphrased the servant's view (*Dnevnik Russkoi zhenshchiny* [1912; repr., Moscow: I. V. Zakharov, 2004], 28–29).

26. RGIA, fond 1412, op. 226, d. 1 (Pavlova, P., 1909).

social status but also significant downward economic mobility. Anastasia Verbitskaia's novel *She Was Liberated!* dramatized precisely this situation. "What kind of work can I count on?" the cultivated heroine rhetorically inquires of the student who urges her to leave her adulterous physician husband and miserable marriage. "With a son, no one will hire me as a governess.... A position in an office or on the railroad for some thirty-forty rubles a month, and that's if I'm lucky.... You yourself are surely well aware of the struggle for positions and lessons? Or perhaps the job of a shop clerk in a store for twenty-five rubles?... That's poverty!"[27] So far as can be determined from summary reports, only one of the privileged women who held jobs when they petitioned for the passport had held one before leaving her husband.

How was a separated woman without work experience or prospects, often with children to care for, to survive on her own? Well into the early twentieth century, the difficulty of obtaining alimony or child support compounded the economic obstacles to leaving an unhappy marriage for women across the social spectrum. Initially, the difficulty was due to the law holding marital separation to be illegal, which disinclined the courts and in particular the State Senate, Russia's highest court, to rule in favor of support for separated wives who left abusive husbands. Although courts sometimes ruled in women's favor in the late 1860s and early 1870s, before the mid-1880s the Senate ruled positively on claims for alimony or child support only when separation had occurred for reasons beyond the wife's control—the husband's lack of residence, mental incapacity, or, most commonly, refusal to live with his wife.[28] The Senate first began to alter its stance in 1886, when it extended the grounds for awarding alimony and/or child support to include cases in which the husband expressed a willingness to live with his wife that the court deemed fallacious. In an 1890 decision it took a more serious step, upholding claims for support in cases where the husband was to blame for the separation. In 1906, the Senate went still further, ruling that a wife had the right to leave a husband and demand support in cases where he failed to fulfill his "moral obligations" to her as set forth in the law. That year, for the first time, article 106 of family law, requiring a husband to love his wife as his own body, live with her in agreement, and so on became, if not legally enforceable, then grounds for separation

27. Anastasia Verbitskaia, *Osvobodilas!* 4th ed. (Moscow: Pechatnoe delo, 1912), 125.

28. On the frequency of and comparatively liberal response to such suits in the St. Petersburg circuit court, see Anatolii Koni, *Sobranie sochinenii*, 8 vols. (Moscow: Iuridicheskaia literatura, 1966), 1: 243; see also T. B. Kotlova, *Rossiiskaia zhenshchina v provintsial'nom gorode na rubezhe XIX–XX vekov* (Ivanovo: Ivanovskii gos. universitet, 2003), 48. Justices of the Peace sometimes ordered support as well. See GARF, fond 109, 3-oe otdelenie, 2-aia ekspeditsiia, op. 1872, d. 654, 2–3. For the role of other administrative bodies in determining alimony and/or child support, see V. A. Veremenko, *Dvorianskaia sem'ia i gosudarstvennaia politika Rossii: vtoraia polovina XIX–nachala XX v.* (St. Petersburg: Evropeiskii dom, 2007), 177–78.

with support when egregiously violated.[29] The 1906 decision opened a floodgate for appeals, a proportion of them from poor and laboring women.[30] Eight years later, on March 12, 1914, when the passport law was revised to permit married women to obtain their own passports on request from the authorities, family law was also modified to incorporate these earlier decisions. Thereafter, the law required husbands to support even wives who lived separately, if the separation was the husbands' fault, and notably, *if the wife was in need of it* [*v tom nuzhdaetsia*] (emphasis mine).[31] But until such time as the courts were consistently prepared to provide alimony and child support, and arguably, even after, many of the women who appealed for a passport because they needed to "earn my crust of bread," had little choice but to do so.[32]

Only occasionally do the economic hardships endured by separated women surface in the archival record, and it is worth paying attention when they do, as they surely represent the tip of a much larger iceberg. Sofia Pokrovskaia, for one, did not choose her own situation. Having been abandoned with three children by her well-born husband, a physician's assistant, after he ran off with their servant, she lived with the children in a "pathetic room," wore tattered clothing, and barely supported herself and the children by sewing items for a philanthropic society. Eventually, poverty forced her to place one of her daughters in a shelter for noble children and move in with her daughter and son-in-law, a teacher at a factory school. Varvara Kupriianova took shelter with a relative after she left her adulterous and abusive merchant husband and "experienced dreadful need," as she had no means of her own. Sofia Stefanovskaia, having worked as an assistant in a primary school before her marriage to a teacher, ended up working as a domestic servant after it ended. Whether any of these women succeeded in extracting support from their estranged husbands remains unclear from the record. Anastasia Stsepurzhenskaia, who did receive some support from her estranged husband, a physician, nevertheless barely managed to eke out a living. For a while, she cared for the

29. See Wagner, *Marriage, Property, and Law,* 217–19; for the cases, see *Polnyi svod reshenii Grazhdanskogo kassatsionnogo departamenta Pravitel'stvuiushchogo Senata,* 1886, no. 29; 1890, no. 18; 1906, no. 8.

30. After 1905, advice on alimony and child support suits constituted a substantial proportion of the work of the legal consultations bureaus that catered to those with few economic resources. See William Pomerantz, "Legal Assistance in Tsarist Russia: The St. Petersburg Consultation Bureaus," *Wisconsin International Law Journal* 14, no. 3 (1996): 601, 608.

31. I. V. Gessen, *Razdel'noe zhitel'stvo suprugov. Zakon 12 marta 1914 goda o nekotorykh izmeneniiakh i dopolneniiakh. . .* (St. Petersburg: Pravo, 1914), 79–81.

32. Women often requested that chancellery officials make their husband pay alimony and child support. Until the Senate ruled on this matter, officials sometimes endeavored to comply. For privileged women, at least, Senate decisions did not immediately bring relief. "By no means every woman was prepared to drag her family problems before a court." Many continued to complain to superiors or seek the help of relatives. See Veremenko, *Dvorianskaia sem'ia,* 186.

three small children of a bookkeeper in the factory village of Kokhma; thereafter, she rented rooms to boarders in the city of Kaluga. "The twenty-five rubles a month she receives from her husband is all the means she has," commented an investigator.[33]

CHOOSING A DIFFERENT LIFE

If most of the women who petitioned the chancellery labored out of dire necessity and/or as the only way to escape an intolerable marriage, their stories indicate that in some cases, earning their own livelihood might nevertheless have had an impact on the direction of women's lives and their sense of self. Independence, in the sense of pursuing one's own aims without regard for family constraints, becomes "a more or less powerful pull," for women who engage in waged labor, observes the historian Alice Kessler-Harris.[34] Regenia Gagnier makes a related point about the connection between work and selfhood in her study of autobiographical subjectivities among British working-class women. Working-class women who remained at home caring for their families, she asserts, with their "other regarding subjectivity," were unlikely to become "writing subjects," whereas the women who took up the pen had engaged in work that took them out of the home.[35] These observations are relevant to Russian petitioners. Whereas for some—how many it is impossible to know for sure—work remained simply a means to put bread on the table and keep a roof over their own and in many cases, their children's, heads, for others earning their own livelihood encouraged a more self-oriented and self-reflective subjectivity, framed in and justified by the fact of engaging in remunerative labor. Most but not all derived from the laboring classes. Because their words tell us most about the significance that work might hold, it is to them that this chapter now turns.

This sense of self is evident in both the content and style of petitions. Shaped as they were by the need to appeal to the state, many are in fact a hybrid of two quite different genres. Generally speaking, Sheila Fitzpatrick argues, petitions in Russia fit into one of two frameworks. One type offers the language of submission, requesting the tsar's favor using "the humble terms of the supplicant who trusts in the tsar's benevolence." Such petitions, in which the petitioner figures as victim, reaffirm the existing political hierarchy by offering almost the "archetypal expression of the relation between subject

33. RGIA, fond 1412, op. 226, d. 83 (Pokrovskaia, S., 1892); op. 221, d. 213 (Kupriianova, V., 1901), 85, 99; op. 228, d. 106 (Stefanovskaia, S., 1895), 32, 38; op. 228, d. 126. (Stsepurzhenskaia, A., 1890), 29, 58. Nikolai Kupriianov, for one, had been heard to remark that "he'd rather tear up his last ruble than give his wife a kopeck."

34. Kessler-Harris, *Gendering Labor History*, 118. I have revised her definition of independence to fit the Russian context, where "achievement" as such is less salient than in the United States.

35. Regenia Gagnier, *Subjectivities: A History of Self-Representation in Britain, 1832–1920* (New York: Oxford University Press, 1991), 39.

and ruler in a paternalistic state." The other framework posits a far less hierarchical relationship between petitioner and state, one in which the writer presents herself as an agent, a participant rather than subject, and, invoking rights, employs "the persona of a citizen."[36] But in some of the petitions I have read, the writer, or the person who drew up the petition and spoke in her name, presents herself as both victim *and* agent—that is, as a person with the ability to act in her own world even as she is acted on.[37] Even as petitioners wrap themselves in the mantle of supplicant and victim, detailing the abuses and suffering they have endured at a husband's hands and seeking relief at the feet of the tsar, some also present themselves as agents in the above sense and as persons with rights that are associated with their labor.

The rights that the women assert are entitlements, such as, most notably, the right to enjoy the fruits of their own labor, or "to live well," to return to the words of Anastasia Petrova with which this chapter begins.[38] While such rights may seem modest enough by contemporary Western standards, in the context of the life of the laboring classes they reflected a heightening of individual expectations. Whereas single women workers were permitted to spend some of their wages buying clothing and other goods that would make up their trousseaux, such expenditures for married women were regarded as unnecessary, their earnings intended for the benefit of others or the household as a whole. Controlling their own wages enabled married women to behave more like single women in their consumption practices.

The peasant woman Maria Ponomareva liked to "dress nicely [*chisto odevat'sia*]," for example, in the opinion of the policeman who first reported on her case. Having received a passport in 1897 on the grounds of her husband's cruel treatment, she worked as a servant in the city of Saratov for two years and then petitioned again when her husband renewed his efforts to bring her back to their village. "I lived peacefully and quietly, in service, on the passport you granted me, giving prayers to God for the health of your Imperial Highness, and for the kindness you have shown me," her petition read. Referring to the "miserable life," she would be forced to lead should she have to return

---

36. Sheila Fitzpatrick, "Editor's Introduction," *Russian History* 24, nos. 1–2 (1997): 4, 6. For the role of the state in shaping the content of petitions during the imperial period, see G. B. Lobacheva, "Prosheniia 'Na Vysochaishee imia prinosimye' kak istochnik izucheniia monarkhicheskikh nastroenii Rossii," in *Dom Romanovykh v istorii Rossii* (St. Petersburg: Izdatel'stvo Sankt-Peterburgskogo universiteta, 1995), 245–51, and Madhavan Palat, "Regulating Conflict through the Petition," in *Social Identities in Revolutionary Russia*, ed. Madhavan Palat (New York: Palgrave, 2001), 86–112.

37. I take this definition from Sherry Ortner, *Anthropology and Social Theory: Culture, Power, and the Acting Subject* (Durham, NC: Duke University Press, 2006), 110. Other, more complex but not dissimilar definitions of agency can be found in "Introduction," in *Practicing History: New Directions in Historical Writing after the Linguistic Turn*, ed. Gabrielle Spiegel (New York: Routledge, 2005), 16–17.

38. RGIA, fond 1412, op. 226, d. 42 (Petrova), 1, 3.

to her husband, Ponomareva also emphasized the loss of what she had gained since leaving him. His efforts to bring her back were "an attempt to rob me of the clothes and other things I bought with the fruits of my own labor," Maria wrote.[39]

The far more entrepreneurial Evrosinia Pokrovskaia expressed herself in much the same terms. Born to a peasant household, an orphan according to the account of her husband, Vladimir, she married well above her station to an assistant to the secretary of the Kovrov Justice of the Peace court. According to Vladimir's counternarrative, it was marriage that gave her a chance in life. I "raised her from poverty to a free and comfortable existence and from the very lowest milieu to a decent status [zvanie]," Vladimir wrote. Then, to return to Evrosinia's account, in 1894 he abandoned her and she returned to her native Kovrov, a district of Vladimir province. There she proved so skillful as a dressmaker that she was able to set up a shop that employed eight apprentices, at the same time supporting her elderly peasant aunt and uncle. Her husband's denial of her passport, she wrote in the petition penned in her own hand, was merely his effort "to extort from me everything I've earned with my own labor and to prevent me from earning money with my labor and helping my family." Other separated women expressed their taste for consumer goods in their self-presentation or lifestyle, although not as Ponomareva and Pokrovskaia had, as an entitlement. Evdokia Kulikova, born to an impoverished peasant family and trained as a dressmaker, after her separation dressed like a "wealthy woman," like a "lady" in the eyes of her fellow villagers.[40]

Other laboring women emphasized their own economic self-sufficiency. In referring to their ability to support themselves, some sought to assure officials that all economic ties with the husband had been severed, which might help to convince officials of the merits of their case and the weakness of their husbands'. But such references also conveyed a certain pride in the women's ability to survive on their own. The peasant Evrosinia Kosterina, employed as a domestic servant, asserted: "Full of strength, I labored and with my labor earned a living for myself and my child." The townswoman Tatiana Alekseeva, employed as a cashier in a bakery, averred in 1904: "I earn my own living and am fully independent, getting no material assistance from my husband at all." The Tambov townswoman Aleksandra Sidorova, whose husband had no job and lived a vagrant life, initially sought a passport in 1906 so she could "earn [her] own living." When she renewed her petition three years later (1909), she was in the process of improving her skills by taking lessons in embroidery and sewing in the school of Alek-

39. Ibid., op. 226, d. 100 (Ponomareva, M., 1896), 1–2, 18, 27. A few divorce applicants, too, expressed an "audacious" desire for economic independence. Gregory Freeze, "Profane Narratives about a Holy Sacrament: Marriage and Divorce in Late Imperial Russia," in Sacred Stories, ed. Steinberg and Coleman, 160.

40. RGIA, fond 1412, op. 226, d. 80 (Pokrovskaia, E., 1895), 1–2, 48–9; op. 221, d. 204 (Kulikova, E., 1897), 20, 21.

sandra Strakhovich on the Arbat in Moscow. "I now have the chance to live with my oldest sister in Moscow and earn a living by sewing clothing," she explained to the chancellery. If she passed the examination at the school, she would gain the right to open her own shop.[41]

Literacy or, better still, facility with language as in the case of Anastasia Petrova sometimes enabled more fulsome declarations of the enhanced sense of self that work might engender. Townswomen were more likely than peasants to enjoy that facility and to engage in manual labor that afforded a measure of independence (unlike, for example, domestic service). Townswomen were also more likely than peasants to occupy a social position in the gray area between middle and laboring class. One example is the townswoman Maria Bol'shikh. Her story is worth exploring in some detail, not only because her extensive personal narratives offer considerable information about her marriage, its breakdown, and the course of her life thereafter, but also because she derived from a milieu about which we still know very little. The daughter of an office clerk (*kantseliarist*), Bol'shikh was married in 1873 at age seventeen to a townsman, an accountant in a private trading house in Moscow who earned as much as three thousand rubles a year, more than ten times as much as an ordinary worker might earn. She herself brought to the marriage a dowry worth about two thousand rubles and gold, diamonds, and clothing worth perhaps three thousand more (the amounts were a subject of dispute). Yet, although Vasilii Bol'shikh's earnings were sufficient to hire a nursemaid and at least one additional servant, Maria nevertheless continued to work after her wedding, contributing to the family economy by knitting and sewing at home.

It was Vasilii's conduct that led to the breakdown of the marriage. After years of cohabitation and the birth of two children, Vasilii fell in love with a friend of the family and asked for a divorce. In such despair that she tried to take her own life (the suicide note is in the dossier), Bol'shikh left her husband and their children in 1883 and found work sewing for fashionable Petersburg shops. Then she took her future in hand, as she describes in the letter she sent officials in August 1887.

After I left my husband, I enrolled in the Midwife Institute attached to the Moscow Foundling Home, to attend courses on midwifery. This past May, I completed the courses and received my certificate. After graduation, I remained at the home as assistant to the staff midwife and am there still. I'm living with another midwife, Liudmila Zvozikova, with whom I moved to a new apartment in July, where we have established a shelter for pregnant women, the profits of which we share.... I also

41. Ibid., op. 221, d. 126 (Kosterina, E., 1901), 20; op. 212, d. 26 (Alekseeva, T., 1900), 91; op. 228, d. 51 (Sidorova, N., 1906), 32.

sometimes accompany a district doctor on his rounds to examine factory women for syphilis.[42]

Proud of her work, Bol'shikh nevertheless continued to ask for economic support from her husband, too.

Work, as such, occupied a far less central place in the appeals of women of the privileged classes, many of whom either had property of their own or parents or siblings on whom they could rely. Nor did work appear to render privileged women more self-assertive than their laboring counterparts: in two of the cases below, the women exerted themselves mightily to make marriages work. Aleksandra Noskova repeatedly reconciled with a husband who had no job and took the money she earned from trading together with her mother. Zinaida Smirnova, whose husband was impotent, took chloroform to immobilize herself when he claimed her movement prevented him from performing sexually, then endured a procedure to eradicate her hymen when he declared that that was the real problem. Only when the husband broke into her trunk, read personal letters, and then denounced her to her employer did she finally give up on the marriage.

Nevertheless, when work did figure in their statements, it served as a source of pride. "From childhood, the daughter of a merchant woman... of the city of Boroviki, like all of our family members, I was schooled for trade," wrote Aleksandra Noskova in 1882. In fact, merchant women rarely traded on their own unless they were widows, as was Noskova's mother at the time of her daughter's appeal. Having finally rid herself of her feckless husband, Aleksandra rented land from Prince Putiatin and set up shop in her own house. There, "thank God," she did very well selling groceries, her statement declared. Zinaida Smirnova, daughter of a high official, had also continued to work while married to a defrocked monk who never succeeded in finding a position. "Both before my marriage and during it, I always earned my own livelihood," she asserted in 1892. "Having received a higher education, which my certificates from the Nikolaev Institute and the university with the title Candidate of Pedagogy demonstrate, I can always survive by myself even if in need."[43]

A few women went further, infusing their work with a moral significance that implicitly, and sometimes explicitly, drew on its quasi-sacral character. These women, from a variety of social backgrounds, wrote of waged work not only as a means to eco-

---

42. Ibid., op. 213, d. 84 (Bol'shikh, M., 1886), 1, 10, 19, 39, 69. Training as a midwife was a fairly common recourse for separated women, apparently, and the work must have carried some prestige, at least in certain circles. For a false claim to have trained as a midwife, see ibid., op. 240, d. 264 (Shikhanova, M., 1882), 2, 10.

43. Ibid., op. 224, d. 46 (Noskova, A., 1882), 12–19; op. 228, d. 74 (Smirnova, Z., 1892), 1. See also op. 212, d. 74 (Alad'ina, T., 1894), 24.

nomic independence but also as a form of purification, contrasting it, in two instances, with the sordid character of their married life. Her short-lived marriage to a shop clerk, a drunkard who stole and pawned her things and ended up living in flophouses, had "ruined" her life, the townswoman Natalia Kolkunova wrote in 1899. Now she found comfort "only in honorable toil for the railroad." Employed as a clerk in the accounting department of the Moscow-Brest railroad, for which she earned forty rubles a month, Kolkunova had tried in the course of five years of separation "to earn everyone's respect and trust." The townswoman Melitana Korchuganova invoked the quasi-sacral character of work more directly. Having married a man without wealth, an office worker in Zlatousk, a town in the Ural Mountains, she had nourished "a real desire to help in our need with my own labors," and did so whenever possible. Then, having left the "filthy life" she led with her husband, "full of immoral scenes and drunkenness," she had returned to a "pure and honest" life. Now she earned what she needed with "my own pure, personal toil [*chistyi, lichnyi trud*]."[44]

References to the quasi-sacred character of work blended with surprising ease with the radical vocabulary of the reform era and thereafter. Varvara Ostrovidova, daughter of a priest, who earned less than thirty rubles a month copying papers for various public institutions, wrote of her decision to leave her abusive teacher husband in the following terms. Abandoning her husband, she had "forsaken the creature comforts of my life and resolved to be satisfied with the modest lot of a toiler, because that example of industriousness in itself and the atmosphere it created would be more useful to my son than all the creature comforts and debauched example of his father," she asserted in 1901. "I want no material help from my husband and never asked for it."[45] Another petitioner, the townswoman Varvara Zvereva, whose impoverished widowed mother kept horses for the Arzamas zemstvo, drew attention to the connections among the work that she did, the public good, and her ability to draw close to "the people." "Recovering from the birth of my child, I wanted to support her and myself through honest labor," she wrote in 1911. "So I took the exam for the position of teacher at a parish school, passed, and found a position in the village of Brikov in Nizhnyi Novgorod province." Zvereva described herself as a dedicated teacher, someone who devoted herself not only to the intellectual enlightenment of her pupils but also to the spiritual development of their mothers: "With faith and good cheer, I regarded the parish school as if it were a temple of knowledge and truth." On Saturdays, village women, old and young, would gather at the school and listen as Zvereva read religious texts and prayers aloud. "This seemed to link me closely with the people."[46]

44. Ibid., op. 221, d. 64 (Kolkunova, N., 1899), 1; op. 221, d. 118 (Korchaganova, M., 1895), 53.
45. RGIA, fond 1412, op. 225, d. 21 (Ostrovidova, V., 1897), 72.
46. Ibid., op. 219, d. 37 (Zvereva, V., 1911), 9–10.

Although, as we have seen, women's wage earning by no means invariably translated into women's propensity to assert themselves, women's financial self-sufficiency nevertheless held the potential to unsettle the balance of power in a marriage not only by enhancing women's sense of independence and rights as a person, as I have argued in the preceding section, but also by making them less tolerant of mistreatment by their husbands. This was certainly the case for some women of the laboring classes. The townswoman Olga Ankudinova, who petitioned the chancellery in 1894, offers a revealing example. Born in the city of Kazan, in 1886 she was married at the age of sixteen to Vasilii Ankudinov, a furniture maker and joiner employed in a factory in Perm. Initially, according to the several witnesses who spoke to the investigator, Olga had tolerated ill treatment by her abusive husband, who would demand a portion of the wages she earned as a domestic servant and beat her when she withheld them. A "good and quiet woman," in the words of their neighbor, Olga "patiently bore her husband's blows and tried to please him." Then, four years after the wedding and the birth of a child, the couple having separated and reunited at least once before, she left him, evidently for good. Initially, she supported herself and small daughter by plying her needle; then, paying four rubles a month for her daughter's care, she hired out again as a domestic servant. In 1893, in a letter pleading with her husband to approve her passport, Ankudinova expressed with unusual directness the impact living on her own had had on her sense of self and expectations of marriage:

> You know I'm not alone; I've got to feed and clothe [their daughter], and if you don't help me at least help her. And if you forbid me to get a passport, then you and I will have to live together. But right now, I'm not willing to live with you when you treat me as you did and now, no doubt, it will be worse. Earlier, you felt no jealousy, but now you will undoubtedly be jealous. Then you made my every step and movement unpleasant. Then I had a quiet and subdued character and now I've become completely desperate [otchaianaia] so that I think if we live together something bad will happen [chto nibud' dolzhno u nas vyiti]. Vasia, I beg you to give me a passport, the kind you gave me before. You don't need me at all.

"You don't love me," she added, observing as did other women long separated from their husband, "I've grown completely out of the habit of you [otvykla]."[47]

---

47. Ibid., op. 212, d. 168, (Ankudinova, O., 1902), 10–11. The only good thing said about Ankudinov was that he was a good and conscientious worker; however, even his former lover and workmates thought that he was too hard on his wife.

Women's wage earning might sometimes improve their bargaining position in a marriage, enabling women to renegotiate the terms of a relationship better to suit their own needs and perhaps heightened expectations. Taking advantage of their ability to live independently, women tried to compel their husbands to cease or limit their drinking, find a steady job or hand over more of their wage, and/or provide more affectionate and tender treatment. Even as they illustrate the relationship between women's economic self-sufficiency and women's self-assertion, most such attempts to renegotiate a relationship also highlight the limited nature of women's options and the narrow constraints within which women maneuvered. This was especially true of laboring women. Take the case of Elizaveta Dobrovol'skaia, a townswoman who worked for two years as a servant before marrying a yardman [*dvornik*] at the age of seventeen. She subsequently left her husband, Dmitrii, because of his heavy drinking, which began several years after the marriage and caused him to waste almost all the money the couple had managed to save. When she sought to restrain his drinking or scolded him about the way he spent their money, he would beat her savagely. Once he even followed her to the apartment of her former employer, to whom she had fled and whom the husband insulted, costing Dmitrii his job. Giving two of their children to her husband's parents and the third to her godmother, Elizaveta found work as a cook for the day-care center of the Evangelical church, earning eight rubles a month. No one had anything favorable to say about Dmitrii. The son of a deacon who had dropped out of school during his first year of seminary training, he made a dismal impression on everyone who spoke about him. Still, his wife was prepared to do what she could to restore their cohabitation, no doubt to regain her children. Summoned to the chancellery, Elizaveta endeavored to use the leverage she had obtained to alter the terms of their relationship. If he signed a statement promising to improve the way he treated her and support the family, she expressed her willingness to reconcile and return to him. Dmitrii declined to sign, insisting in the presence of officials on his legal right to cohabitation. However, he subsequently promised his wife that he would mend his ways and treat her "properly," which led her to decline the passport that the chancellery had approved for her. And in fact, for eight years, until a relapse, Dmitrii managed to stay sober and hold a job.[48]

But in a few instances at least, women's waged work could alter more profoundly the power relations in a marriage. The example of the townswoman Appolinaria Ivanova, while very far from typical, illustrates the limits to which a renegotiation might go, stretching the bonds of matrimony to, and indeed beyond, their breaking point. Self-assertive, with a palpable sense of entitlement to the good things in life, Appolinaria left her husband, Nikolai, an electrician at the Nadezhda Steamboat Company in Nizhnii Novgorod, after eight years of marriage and the birth of three children, and found work selling Singer sewing machines, for which she earned the comparatively

48. Ibid., op. 216, d. 30 (Dobrovol'skaia, E., 1896), 1–38.

modest sum of twenty-five rubles a month. In the petition she submitted in 1904 requesting a separate passport, Appolinaria accused her husband of beating and insulting her from the first days of their marriage, of being unable to support her properly, and even of stealing her possessions. The items she listed, which included a dress and a gold watch and gold earrings, bear witness to the couple's comfortable lifestyle as well as Appolinaria's taste for finery, itself a source of considerable contention between the couple. "All I want is to live alone and support my children," she wrote in her appeal. She wanted no financial assistance from her husband: she was perfectly capable of paying her own way and that of all three children.[49]

The investigation, which revealed a husband almost desperate to reconcile with his wife, also indicated the strains that the burgeoning consumer economy had created for this particular couple. Nikolai had just obtained a raise and now earned fifty-five rubles a month instead of the previous forty rubles, far more than the miserable wages his wife alleged. In his opinion, the two quarreled no more than families "normally do," and mainly over his wife's extravagant tastes. Nikolai acknowledged rebuking his wife when she "spent too much money and tried to dress in the latest fashion" and purchased clothing on credit.[50] Given their limited means, he considered such purchases unnecessary and felt responsible for curtailing them. Nevertheless, he was far more generous with his wages than his wife claimed. "I receive my wages twice a month and give all of the money to my wife. So I don't have much with me and once may have given her a mere fifty kopecks some time when she asked." Although he acknowledged taking things from his wife, he explained that the items were acquired with his money and he took them only after his wife threatened to leave him.[51]

Wherever the truth lay, Ivanov was prepared to go to enormous lengths to restore relations with his wife. The officer overseeing the investigation of their case came to serve as a vehicle for their negotiations, in which Appolinaria clearly held the upper hand, if only temporarily. If his wife would return to him, Nikolai initially proposed, he was willing to cohabit "without conjugal relations" for the sake of the children. His wife having rejected that offer, he promised to give her a written agreement entitling her to his entire salary and pledged never to make a fuss over money again. After the second proposal, the crafty Appolinaria tried to play for time. She needed a month or so to consider his offer, she declared. Nikolai was willing to grant her only ten days; thereafter he would summon the police to restore her to his household by force.

49. Ibid., op. 220, d. 3 (Ivanova, A. 1904), 1. She gave the youngest child to her mother to raise; what she did with the other two when she was at work remains unclear. Officials did not inquire.

50. On dress as a signifier of status, see Engel, *Between the Fields and the City*, 153–56; and Christine Ruane, "Clothes Shopping in Imperial Russia: The Development of a Consumer Culture," *Journal of Social History* 28 (Summer 1995): 765–82.

51. RGIA, fond 1412, op. 220, d. 3 (Ivanova), 8.

Wanting more time, she requested that the chancellery continue examining her case, a countermove that entitled her to a three-month passport. After the three months elapsed, the chancellery denied Appolinaria's request for a passport.[52]

WOMEN'S LABOR IN THE EYES OF OTHERS

Whatever their social origins, women petitioners who referred to the necessity of engaging in "honest labor" or "earning my crust of bread" used a vocabulary they shared with, and that evoked a sympathetic response from, men in positions of authority. Those who evaluated women's petitions—among them policemen, gendarme officers, and chancellery officials—treated the remunerative labor of married women not only as nothing exceptional but also sometimes as praiseworthy in itself. This was the case not only in reference to women of the laboring classes, for whom women's labor was the norm in any case, but also in relation to the privileged. To be sure, during the 1860s and 1870s, opponents of the "woman question" had been fiercely critical of the idea of women working outside the home, fulminating about the harm this would bring to both women and their families. It is also true that in the same period the tsarist state acted formally to restrict women's work to appropriately gendered spheres by issuing a law that encouraged women to enter fields deemed compatible with women's nurturing role such as midwifery, nursing, and teaching but explicitly barred them from all civil service and public [*obshchestvennyi*] positions. The relevant decree was issued on January 14, 1871. Thereafter, the Third Section was flooded with denunciations identifying women who continued to occupy such positions, the law notwithstanding, which its officers expended considerable time and energy investigating. If the allegations were upheld, the same officers worked to ensure that women in public positions such as customs officers, postal workers, office clerks, public librarians, railroad ticket agents, and the like were deprived of their positions and replaced with "persons of the male sex." But the fulminations of conservatives otherwise found no echo in official documents or, apparently, official minds: while differentiating between permissible and impermissible employment for women, neither the decree nor the Third Section's correspondence with its agents condemned as such the remunerative labor of women, married or single.[53]

Nor are such condemnations to be found in the documents pertinent to marital breakdown. Although such ideas may have circulated in other venues, absent in the

52. Ibid., 8, 13, 29. Nikolai eventually gave in and approved her passport.

53. On antifeminism in the 1860s and 1870s, see Irina Iukhina, *Russkii feminizm kak vyzov sovremennosti* (St. Petersburg: Aleteiia, 2007), 99–113. The decree and correspondence relating to this revealing and, to my knowledge, untold story, can be found in GARF, fond 109, 3-oe otdelenie, 2-aia ekspeditsiia, op. 1870, d. 685, "Po dopushcheniiu zhenshchin na sluzhbu v obshchestvennye i pravitel'stvennye uchrezhdeniia." Quoted from 59.

reports and testimony about women and work were references to women's delicacy or to the dangers to women's morality, femininity, or sexual honor that women might confront in the workplace—references, that is, to the domestic ideologies that, as Alice Kessler Harris has put it, "legitimize constraints on women's participation...and have a heavy impact on their aspiration with relationship to work-related goals."[54] Men in positions of authority treated the waged work of wives as unexceptionable irrespective of social background, even when the women were mothers. Officials asked every investigator to provide information about the number and age of children in discordant marriages; as for child care, investigators were also asked to ascertain "who cares for the children," a gender-neutral phrasing that suggests the commonality as well as acceptability of caregivers who were other than the mother. Officials also made no assumptions concerning women's economic dependence: they instructed investigators to ascertain the nature of the work women did, and whether they supported themselves or were supported by their husbands.[55]

More important, from the first, officials treated women's wage earning as praiseworthy and adduced it as a factor in their favor. Actually, positive references antedate the work of the chancellery and can be found in the archives of the Third Section, which between 1826 and 1881 was responsible for resolving family disputes. "Bearing in mind the laudable aspirations of Mrs. Briukhova toward having a useful occupation," wrote an officer of the Third Section in 1851, he recommended a passport for Olga Briukhova, the wife of a gendarme officer. Emilia Lapshina, a talented musician and singer as well as the mother of one child, supported her husband, a candidate in law and his sister in the mid-1870s. Finding that he and his family treated her abominably despite her role as the family's breadwinner, the Third Section approved a passport, making no mention of who might care for the children: "He doesn't need a wife, but rather, the significant means she obtains by her exhausting labor.... In return for her work on behalf of him and his family, she has received nothing but unpleasantness. Hence, in light of her high moral qualities, she deserves protection."[56]

Chancellery officials expressed similar views. For them, too, the fact that women supported themselves with their own labor might enhance the strength of their appeal. "Taking into consideration that Aleksandra Nosina [a townswoman and midwife] lives by her own labors...and earns her own living, and that restoring cohabitation with her husband would inevitably deprive the wife of her occupation and still fur-

54. Alice Kessler Harris, "Gender and Work: Possibilities for a Global Historical Overview," in *Women's History in Global Perspective*, ed. Bonnie Smith, 3 vols. (Urbana: University of Illinois Press, 2004), 1: 159. To be sure, husbands sometimes accused their wives of liaisons with men whom they encountered at work, but this seems to me a different matter.

55. TsGIA SPb, fond 569, op. 20, d. 103, "Oprosnyi list," 15.

56. GARF, fond 109, 3-oe otdelenie, 2-aia ekspeditsiia, op. 1851, d. 122, 30; op. 1875, d. 830, 25.

ther antagonize her against her husband," who in any case was far too old for her and insanely jealous, officials approved her passport in 1886. Fridrikh Geints, a townsman and senior telegraph worker, earned 480 rubles a year in 1891 and owned an allotment of land as well. The fact that his estranged wife, Anfia, also a telegraph worker, "not once turned to her husband with a request for financial assistance," was adduced as a factor in her favor, since she supported not only herself but their child on her wages of 360 rubles a year.[57]

On a few occasions, officials became almost fulsome in their praise of women who sought to earn their own living. The gendarme who reported on the case of Anastasia Novokreshchenova, the wife of a merchant in the city of Samara, wrote admiringly of her willingness to sever all economic ties with her dissolute and abusive husband. "She is energetic and her demands and desires are well thought out, logical, and reasonable. Recognizing the impossibility of living with such a husband, she has refused any material assistance from him or her family and wants only the chance to work and support herself with her labor." Matrona Kovalevskaia, whose husband, a hereditary honored citizen, and in-laws had literally prostituted her and then lived on the money she earned, finally left him and resumed her studies in the hope of someday supporting herself. "She is striving firmly and staunchly toward a toiling life, in the words of witnesses," officials reported in their recommendation that she get a passport. Officials carefully recorded the details of the work record of Aleksandra Generopitomtseva, the estranged wife of a retired collegiate secretary who, when he wasn't subsisting on the money extorted from his wife, was employed as a private attorney for the Rogachev circuit court. Not only had Generopitomtseva been employed as a typist for the World Exhibition in Paris and then at a ceramics exhibition, but she had also received awards for her service both times. Everyone familiar with her work, they noted, had given her "most favorable reviews." Officials often praised women for their "industriousness [*trudoliubie*]" or, in a case like that of Geintz, for "supporting herself and her children with her own toil [*trud*], receiving no financial assistance [*posobie*, literally, grant] from her husband." Never did they express curiosity about the child-care arrangements of working mothers, even when those mothers derived from privileged backgrounds.[58]

Although officials never indicated that they expected women to engage in remunerative labor if the women had sufficient means of their own or their husbands were

57. RGIA, fond 1412, op. 224, d. 44 (Nosina, A., 1882), 74; op. 250, d. 100, 19–22.

58. Ibid., op. 224, d. 34 (Novokreshchenova, A., 1896), 66–67; op. 221, d. 51 (Kovalevskaia, M., 1905), 1, 3, 34–35. Her claim of being prostituted was verified by an envelope stuffed with little receipts, signed either by her husband or her in-laws, verifying that they had received the money she sent them; op. 250, d. 100, 22, 67–68. For privileged mothers who worked, see ibid., d. 101, 40 ob.; 55 ob.

willing to provide for them, in the next two examples at least, investigators treated a separated women's lack of employment outside the home as a matter that required explanation, rather than a natural consequence of the women's femininity. One example derives from the period when the Third Section presided over separation cases, the second from the time of the chancellery's tenure. Maria Fedorova, separated from her husband, a townsman from Vitebsk, did not work "because she has a sick child," noted an investigator in 1872. Separated from her husband, a townsman and former shop clerk, the merchant's daughter Aleksandra Razaeva "devotes herself to her children and their education and lives on her parents' means," noted an investigator in provincial Ufa in 1909. The investigator also felt obliged to explain why Razaeva did not herself earn an income: "Because of illness, she is unable herself to work."[59]

At the same time, even as men in positions of authority responded approvingly to wives' waged work, that work alone never provided sufficient reason to approve women's passports. Preserving a marriage remained uppermost in officials' minds, although the circumstances under which they were prepared to consider curtailing men's marital authority broadened considerably in the period under study. Still, if the husband had mended his ways and, especially, become capable of fulfilling his role as primary breadwinner, one of the few enforceable obligations that marital law placed on men, his wife's ability to support herself often became irrelevant to officials, especially if the couple derived from the laboring classes. For every Aleksandra Nosina, the midwife in a relationship beyond repair, whose passport officials approved, there was a Vassa Petrova, forced to abandon her position as a domestic servant to return to her abusive husband.

Petrova, a peasant woman, had appealed to the chancellery in 1899, describing the truly horrific treatment she received from her husband, Ivan, whose abusive behavior was described in the previous chapter. Petrov was prone to show up drunk and disorderly at his wife's workplace—her economic self-sufficiency was evidently a threat to his marital authority—and his unruly behavior cost her every position as domestic servant she managed to obtain although, as Petrova put it in her petition, she "fed and clothed him with the money I earned." Witness after witness confirmed her story. In 1899, the chancellery approved her passport, warning Ivan to mend his ways if he wished to live with his wife again. Three years later, Ivan had found work and declared his desire to restore cohabitation with his wife, then employed as a servant in Nizhnii Novgorod. Despite Vassa's assertion that she never, ever wanted to return to her husband, the chancellery recommended that her passport be revoked, a decision that cost her the job.[60]

59. GARF, fond 109, 3-oe otdelenie, 2-aia ekspeditsiia, op. 1872, d. 654, 8; RGIA, fond 1412, op. 227, d. 6 (Razaeva, M., 1909), 104.

60. RGIA, fond 1412, op. 226, d. 43 (Petrova, V., 1899).

• • •

The ability to earn their own living, however humbly, expanded the limited options of women. To be sure, the work that women found usually provided them with little more than the "crust of bread" that figured in so many petitions. Despite the expansion of employment options in the final decades of the nineteenth century, the occupations employing the largest proportion of laboring petitioners (and of laboring women as a group), were the most humble—domestic service and unskilled day labor—while privileged women fared only slightly better. Women whose husbands had disappeared, ejected them from their home, and/or were unwilling or unable to support them had little choice but to earn their own living. Nevertheless, the ability to support themselves indisputably enabled some women to leave an abusive marriage and, in at least some cases, gave them the leverage to renegotiate a relationship, however modestly, better to suit themselves. For these women, remunerative labor was a choice, albeit a choice made among the most limited of options, a choice that nevertheless enhanced the women's control over themselves and their world.

That choice held meaning both for the women and for others. The positive valence of work in Russian culture is evident in the language of women's petitions and in the response of elite men to them. As this chapter has shown, officials of the chancellery and Third Section, in many respects the very embodiment of the autocratic ethos, regarded women's waged labor not only as unexceptionable but even in some cases as praiseworthy. This was true even of women of the privileged orders, whose remunerative labor was never seen as a violation of women's domestic calling. The positive valence of waged labor provided petitioners with a basis for making claims on the state that rested on the women's own actions and achievements, rather than, or more precisely in addition to, their passive suffering at a husband's hands.[61]

61. Surveying the period 1880–1920, Elaine Tyler May found no evidence that in the United States either men or women believed that a wife should work. See *Great Expectations: Marriage and Divorce in Post-Victorian America* (Chicago: University of Chicago Press, 1980), 28, 125.

Cultivating Domesticity

*Almost from the first moment of my marriage…nineteen years ago,
my husband made my life truly unendurable: he beat me, insulted
me in front of the family and placed me in a position unsuitable for a
wife and mistress of the household [khoziaika] and was unfaithful to
me under our own roof. Despite my husband's substantial means, the
children did not receive proper upbringing or instruction; and as a
result, they did poorly. He beat the children and treated them cruelly,
too, even burning the hands of one of them. I had to turn to my family
even to feed them. Finally, he agreed to give me a separate passport,
but it included only one of our six children, and he provided neither
support nor money to educate the child.…Now my passport has run
out and he doesn't want to renew it.[1]*

Thus read the petition submitted on June 8, 1901, by Varvara Kupriianova, wife of the Moscow merchant Nikolai Kupriianov, a trader
in manufactured goods and hereditary honored citizen. The investigation that followed indicated that, if anything, Kupriianova had
understated her husband's high-handed behavior. Upholding her
allegations and providing telling detail, witness after witness portrayed a man who had abused his marital authority to an extraordinary degree, while reducing his wife to a state of utter abjection. To
take one of the most glaring examples, Kupriianov was in the habit
of coming home at three or four in the morning, waking his wife,
and forcing her to read aloud to him until he fell asleep. If her voice
grew too weak, he would shout at her, even strike her. Even when
Varvara was in the advanced stages of pregnancy, he did not spare
her this ordeal. Nikolai had so thoroughly terrorized his wife that
she did not dare even to leave the house without his permission.[2]

Nikolai had also destroyed her authority over her own domain,
the household. Demeaning her before the servants and the children, he encouraged those who owed her obedience to insult her
by calling her "fool" and even "swine." His flagrant infidelity provided another source of humiliation. He became sexually involved

---

1. RGIA, fond 1412, op. 221, d. 213 (Kupriianova, V., 1901), 1.
2. Ibid., 10, 45, 81–82.

with one of their servants, a liaison he did not trouble to conceal from his wife. When the servant became pregnant at the same time as Varvara, Nikolai showed greater concern with the servant's well-being. Yet Nikolai insisted that he "loved" Varvara, and most witnesses agreed that he did. She had left him once before, five years earlier, and Nikolai had been so distraught he became suicidal.[3]

Most of those who testified in the case belonged to the same merchant milieu as Kupriianov, a milieu that had come to embrace the social and cultural practices of other well-to-do members of Russia's educated and privileged strata, at least in public. Whether they had done so in private remains an open question, however, to which many historians give a negative answer. Alfred Rieber's view that "the patriarchal condition" persisted and "the fate of women" remained terrible well into the 1890s even in merchant families that had achieved a measure of culture has found an echo in more recent studies by others.[4] Indeed, the fate of Varvara Kupriianova at her husband's hands might well be read as a prime example. But it is a less than straightforward example. Even as the witnesses described behavior that was excessive by any criteria, even for a merchant-*samodur* (petty tyrant), in criticizing that behavior, witnesses drew their vocabulary from the wide-ranging critiques of arbitrary authority that circulated in the reform era and after.

To a man, the witnesses condemned Nikolai for his behavior at home. Describing Nikolai's high-handed treatment of his wife and children, a second guild merchant who had known the couple since their marriage called Nikolai "arbitrary and despotic to the highest degree." He had reduced Varvara to a state of "utter subjugation," asserted the townsman who worked for Kupriianov as a shop clerk and visited monthly from Ivanovo. More tellingly, several witnesses noted the contradiction between Nikolai's pretensions to the cultural values of the intelligentsia in public and the ways in which he treated his family. One was Vladimir Zolotarev, a man who retained his merchant status although he did not engage in trade. Married to Nikolai's sister, Zolotarev recalled that when he first met Nikolai in 1884, he took him for a "developed and even humanitarian person, because he was always bragging about this and that contribution to some good cause, and he always tried to have people notice his good deeds...." But close acquaintance changed his mind. Seeing his brother-in-law's behavior at home, Zolotarev realized Nikolai was a "heartless egoist, an extraordinary family despot, with an extremely irritable nature." Varvara's cousin, a military officer, noted the same

3. Ibid., 10, 45, 47, 66, 70, 76.

4. Alfred J. Rieber, *Merchants and Entrepreneurs in Imperial Russia* (Chapel Hill: University of North Carolina Press, 1982), 120. See also Iu. M. Goncharov, *Gorodskaia sem'ia Sibiri vtoroi poloviny XIX–nachala XX v.* (Barnaul: Izdatel'stvo Altaiskogo gosudarstvennogo universiteta, 2002), 284–85. For a contrary view, see Jo Ann Ruckman, *The Moscow Business Elite: A Social and Cultural Portrait of Two Generations, 1840–1905* (DeKalb: Northern Illinois University Press, 1984).

FIGURE 14. *A merchant family, 1890s. Tsentral'nyi gosudarstvennyi arkhiv Kinofonofotodokumentov.*

contrast between Nikolai's conduct in public and his behavior in private: he was "a man who gets on well in society, and who loves to present himself as a cultivated man [*intelligentnyi chelovek*], interested in artistic pursuits," as demonstrated by his practice of collecting the letters and signed portraits of well-known artists. "Yet in the family," the cousin observed, "he is a despot who loves to exercise his power over those weaker than himself."[5]

Such condemnations of "family despotism" provide evidence of new and more exacting norms of marital conduct. By the final decade of the nineteenth century, this chapter argues, these new norms had become familiar not only to the highly educated but also to many literate people further down the social ladder, for whom they had become linked with aspirations to a form of cultivated gentility. They drew on several different but inter-related cultural currents. One was the cult of domesticity, as defined by prescriptive literature, which in the second half of the nineteenth century circulated ever more widely, and which by changing expectations of women's proper role and conduct brought a comparable change in that of men. Another was the ethos of self-restraint that elsewhere accompanied the triumph of the capitalist marketplace.[6] A third was the growing interest in the rights and dignity of the individual, which historians have usually associated with progressive currents of thought, but which my evidence suggests was more pervasive. Although my sources indicate no consensus concerning the appropriate exercise of masculine authority or degree of female submission, the plaints of wives, the self-explanations of husbands, the testimonies of witnesses, and the responses of officials in charge of reporting on and resolving cases all suggest that a redefinition of the proper balance of marital authority was in process toward the close of the nineteenth century, at least among those aspiring to a measure of "culture" and gentility.

THE CULT OF DOMESTICITY

The cult of domesticity contributed to this change by elevating the domestic sphere and the role of wife and mother but, more important, in Russia at least, by redefining the appropriate behavior of men. Those who study women have offered seemingly contradictory accounts of the influence of the cult of domesticity on Russia. On one hand, the work of Catriona Kelly leaves no doubt that a cult of domesticity flourished in postreform Russia in the form of prescriptive literature that propagated separate spheres as never before and to a broad audience. Michelle Marrese also

---

5. RGIA, fond 1412, op. 221, d. 213 (Kupriianova), 22, 66, 76.

6. David Peterson del Mar, *What Trouble I Have Seen: A History of Violence against Wives* (Cambridge, MA: Harvard University Press, 1996), 48. See also Gail Bederman, *Manliness and Civilization: A Cultural History of Gender and Race in the United States, 1880–1917* (Chicago: University of Chicago Press, 1995), 11–12.

notes "a marked shift in gender conventions and family patterns" in the larger discourses of the post-Emancipation period, as reflected in far greater concern than previously with household management and child rearing.[7] This prompted noble commentators to treat noblewomen's economic activity more ambivalently than they had done in the earlier period but by no means brought such activity to an end. On the other hand, Joyce Toomre, Darra Goldstein, and Beth Holmgren, among others, have demonstrated that women's domestic responsibilities were almost never celebrated in Russian poetry and letters, and that nineteenth- and early twentieth-century writers treated women's domestic duties with condescension or distaste.[8] The evidence from disputatious marriages suggests that the contradiction between these interpretations is more apparent than real. As this chapter shows, although people were broadly familiar with the terms of the cult of domesticity, and husbands might fault their wives for their failure to live up to them, domesticity as such carried little cultural weight. In particular, women's role as household manager did not serve as a measure of virtue for women of the middling classes, as it did in Great Britain and the United States.[9] It served this purpose neither for women themselves nor for those who commented on and evaluated their cases, and least of all for the chancellery officials who determined the outcome.

As was the case with so much else, the cult of domesticity—a "transnational, hegemonic discourse," in the words of the historian Judith Walsh—came to Russia from the West and, as Walsh observes, was adapted for its local context just as it was elsewhere.[10] Building on the long-standing idea that women's sphere was "domestic," the cult transformed the definition and significance of domesticity, elaborating on women's responsibilities for house, child, and husband care and reducing but not eradicating the eco-

7. Catriona Kelly, *Refining Russia: Advice Literature, Polite Culture, and Gender from Catherine to Yeltsin* (New York: Oxford University Press, 2001); Michelle Lamarche Marrese, *A Woman's Kingdom: Noblewomen and the Control of Property in Russia* (Ithaca, NY: Cornell University Press, 2002), 200–201.

8. *Classic Russian Cooking: Elena Molokhovets' "A Gift to Young Housewives,"* trans. and intro. Joyce Toomre (Bloomington: Indiana University Press, 1992), 11–12; Darra Goldstein, "Domestic Porkbarreling in Nineteenth-Century Russia, or Who Holds the Key to the Larder," and Beth Holmgren, "Gendering the Icon: Marketing Women Writers in Fin-de-Siècle Russia," in *Russia. Women. Culture,* ed. Helena Goscilo and Beth Holmgren (Bloomington: Indiana University Press, 1996), 128, 321–46.

9. Elizabeth Foyster, *Marital Violence: An English Family History, 1660–1875* (New York: Cambridge University Press, 2005), 89. See also Elaine Tyler May, *Great Expectations: Marriage and Divorce in Post-Victorian America* (Chicago: University of Chicago Press, 1980).

10. Judith E. Walsh, *Domesticity in Colonial India: What Women Learned When Men Gave Them Advice* (Lanham, MD: Rowman and Littlefield, 2004), 2, 25–28.

nomic dimensions of the domestic role.[11] The authority that women had long exercised over their own sphere, as well as the economic dimension of household management, was preserved in the Russian word for mistress of the household, *khoziaika*. It derives from the word *khoziaistvo*, or economy, and as defined by Vladimir Dal'’s dictionary of spoken Russian, is simply the female form of the word *khoziain*, that is "owner [alternatively, proprietor]," or in its second meaning, "responsible manager."[12] Because no English translation of the word *khoziaika*, such as housewife, homemaker, or even the superior but wordier mistress of the household, captures its full authoritative and economic significance, I use the term *khoziaika* in this chapter whenever my sources do.

These dimensions of the role of *khoziaika* are important, as we will see. As historians of domesticity in Western Europe and the United States have noted, in those settings housework acquired cultural significance in almost direct relation to the decline of other income-producing responsibilities that women of the various middling social strata had once performed, in artisans' shops, for example, or keeping the books or standing behind a counter, to name the most obvious. Only after wives and daughters had ceased to contribute to production or earn income were they expected to devote themselves full-time to housekeeping and child rearing, and only then did those roles assume broader cultural meaning. The fact that productive "work" did not occur in the home was essential to its redefinition. As celebrated by the cult of domesticity, one of the most essential functions of the home became providing the husband refuge and relief from worldly cares and strains. As a result, historians of women agree, the cult of domesticity played a key role in the formation of a middle class or bourgeoisie: "domesticity" served to "define and reproduce class structure and identity," as Nancy Reagin has recently put it.[13] Whether it functioned that way in Russia remains a question.

11. On the economic dimensions of women's domestic roles in the earlier period, see especially Kate Pickering Antonova, "'The Importance of the Woman of the House': Gender, Property, and Ideas in a Russian Provincial Gentry Family, 1820–1875" (PhD diss., Columbia University, 2007); Marrese, *A Woman's Kingdom*; and Muriel Joffe and Adele Lindenmeyr, "Daughters, Wives, and Partners: Women of the Moscow Merchant Elite," in *Merchant Moscow: Images of Russia's Vanished Bourgeoisie*, ed. James L. West and Iurii Petrov (Princeton, NJ: Princeton University Press, 1998), 102–4.

12. Vladimir Dal', *Tolkovyi slovar' zhivogo velikorusskogo iazyka*, 4 vols. (1880–82, repr., Moscow: Russkii iazyk, 1978), 4: 557–58. Indeed, a *khoziaika* need not be a married woman. Wives fully commanded their own sphere even in households where the husband's authority was otherwise unquestioned, and the women might exercise their power over subordinates just as strictly as their husbands did. See Iu. M. Goncharov, *Semeinyi byt gorozhan Sibiri vtoroi poloviny XIX–nachala XX veka* (Barnaul: Izdatel'stvo Altaiskogo gosudarstvennogo universiteta, 2004), 230.

13. Nancy Reagin, "The Imagined *Hausfrau*: National Identity, Domesticity, and Colonialism in Imperial Germany," in *Journal of Modern History* 73, no. 1 (2001): 57. Writing of Frenchwomen, Bonnie Smith sums up the transformation succinctly: "Bourgeois women suddenly released from much of the productive activity that had accompanied their reproductive life, began to fashion a home

There can be little doubt that a cult of domesticity flourished in postreform Russia, propagating separate spheres as never before and to a broad range of readers. Evidence for such a cult can be found in the proliferation of prescriptive literature that treated the home as exclusively women's sphere and advised them how to decorate and maintain it, care for and attire themselves, and properly look after their husbands and children. Such literature was aimed at an economically diverse range of imagined readers. In her survey of prescriptive literature, Catriona Kelly rightly emphasizes the degree to which some of these works fostered the kind of boundless consumerism possible only in an age of industrialization, after mass production had made more goods available more cheaply and changed the nature of shopping. Prescriptive literature of this sort encouraged a "vast proliferation of objects" in Kelly's words. Although women had long been expected to "keep house" properly, such literature described housekeeping more elaborate, cooking more refined, and furnishings more elegant and variegated than were to be found in the households where many readers had been raised, or very likely, dwelled.[14]

However, by no means all of the prescriptive literature fostering a cult of domesticity was designed for the well-to-do reader; much of it was far more down-to-earth and intended for a reader accustomed to pinching her kopecks. Thus, for example, the author of *Marital Satisfactions* (1882), having asked "What must a *khoziaika* do?" responded to his own rhetorical question with a list of duties that included keeping house whether or not a woman had a taste for housework and supervising the housekeeping budget. A skillful *khoziaika,* he counseled, must know how to stretch a ruble, and "be aware of prices at the market," articulating a concern with economizing that characterized many publications intended to instruct women as to their duties.[15] The advice offered by the deceptively titled periodical *Sem'ianin* (Family

---

for themselves, their husbands and their children" (*Ladies of the Leisure Class: The Bourgeoises of Northern France in the Nineteenth Century* [Princeton, NJ: Princeton University Press, 1981], 6). See also Leonore Davidoff and Catherine Hall, *Family Fortunes: Men and Women of the English Middle Class, 1780–1850* (Chicago: University of Chicago Press, 1987); Marion Kaplan, *The Making of the Jewish Middle Class: Women, Family, and Identity in Imperial Germany* (New York: Oxford University Press, 1991); and Mary Ryan, *Cradle of the Middle Class: The Family in Oneida Country, New York, 1780–1865* (New York: Cambridge University Press, 1981). For a dissenting voice on the impact of the cult of domesticity, see Amanda Vickery, "Golden Age to Separate Spheres? A Review of the Categories and Chronology of English Women's History," *Historical Journal* 36, no. 2 (1993): 384.

14. On long-standing expectations of housekeeping, see A. N. Zorin et al., *Ocherki gorodskogo byta dorevoliutsionnogo Povolzh'ia* (Ulianovsk: Izdatel'stvo Srednevolzhskogo gosudarstvennogo universiteta, 2000), 134–35. On the literature, see Kelly, *Refining Russia,* 160–66.

15. *Brachnye udovol'stviia. Prakticheskie vrachebnye i nevrachebnye nastavleniia vstupivshim v brak* (Moscow: F. Ioganson, 1882), 16–17, 33. On the widespread concern with economizing in such literature, see V. D. Orlova, "Otrazhenie povsednevnykh zabot zhenshchin v massovykh pechatnykh

FIGURE 15. *Shop clerk and his wife, early twentieth century.*
She has donned fashionable clothing for the occasion and he, an
embroidered peasant blouse. Tsentral'nyi gosudarstvennyi arkhiv
Kinofonofotodokumentov.

Man), published from 1894 to 1897, was also designed for a more humble reader than the purchasers of Kelly's texts. Its self-declared audience was the "middle layer of the population," who sought healthy spiritual nourishment "infused with the Russian spirit." "We address the cultivated [*intelligentnyi*], and especially, not the rich class of people," the editors asserted. In a section titled "Domostroi," the name adopted from the famous sixteenth-century housekeeping manual, the journal purveyed advice to its women readers, "the cornerstone of the family," authored by the prolific Nadezhda Lukhmanova. In her various columns, Lukhmanova stressed the importance of "comfort in all things and coziness" and of an "attractive, elegantly dressed wife" but also dealt with more mundane matters such as how to rid one's home of cockroaches or prepare tasty coffee. A woman's ability to fulfill all her responsibilities well, the journal assured its readers, did not depend on the size of household income but rather on her "taste and skills."[16]

Despite the differences in the imagined audiences' economic status and lifestyle, the prescriptive literature shared several assumptions about the status and role of the *khoziaika* that historians of other places have treated as characteristic of a "bourgeois" or "middle-class" sensibility. Chief among them was the assumption that the *khoziaika* would be assisted by, and have to manage the labor of, at least one servant.[17] So essential was the hiring of such a servant that without one, life became "deficient."[18] The sheer labor required to carry out the daily drudgery of housework, which included tending fires, cleaning, shopping, cooking, and sewing, necessitated the hiring of a servant, but more important still was the role that the servant had come to play as an indicator of status. "Servants not only signified class status in a highly class conscious and newly forming middle class," writes Marion Kaplan of the German Jewish middle class. "They also provided a hierarchy within the home" in which the housewife kept the keys, a sign of her authority, divided the chores, and

izdaniiakh nachala XX v." *Zhenskaia povsednevnost' v Rossii v XVIII–XX vv. Materialy mezhdunarodnoi nauchnoi konferentsii 25 sentiabria 2003 goda*, ed. P. P. Shcherbinin (Tambov: Tambovskii gosudarstvennyi universitet im. G. P. Derzhavina, 2003), 44.

16. *Sem'ianin*, no. 1 (1894): 3, 278, and nos. 5–6 (1894): 250–59. The journal claimed six thousand subscribers; among the first hundred were Fedor Dostoevsky's widow, Anna, the Eliseev brothers' trading house, and three priests. On Lukhmanova, see Charlotte Rosenthal, "Nadezhda Aleksandrovna Lukhmanova," in *Dictionary of Russian Women Writers*, ed. Marina Ledkovsky, Charlotte Rosenthal, and Mary Zirin (Westport, CT: Greenwood, 1994), 389–92. The essay's bibliography of her written work omits Lukhmanova's role as advice purveyor in *Sem'ianin*.

17. *Brachnye udol'stviia*, 33; *Sem'ianin*, no. 1 (1894): 190. See also Kelly, *Refining Russia*, 168.

18. Orlova, "Otrazhenie povsednevnykh zabot," 42, 45. Orlova points to the absence of advertisements for cleaning products as further evidence of the reliance on servants to perform such work.

assigned the work that servants would perform.[19] The role servants played in demonstrating women's status was at least as important in Russia.

The authors of such literature also shared the conviction that the home was women's sphere exclusively. No longer governed by the husband as in the days of the *Domostroi*, it was now to be governed *for* him.[20] The home was to serve as a refuge for the husband from the strains and conflicts of the larger world, a realm of privacy and tranquillity where his psychological needs were met. Over this realm the economically dependent wife presided. "The wife must be the soul of the home," intoned *Good Manners*, employing as other authors did the word "wife" (or woman) instead of *khoziaika* when referring to wifely duty. "The husband is the center around which all of domestic and family life revolves, but that peaceful tinge, that marvelous tranquillity that permits a man to call his home his castle is exclusively the result of the wife's beneficent influence." Other authors elaborated on the responsibilities this placed on a wife. "It would be extremely cruel to force a husband who labors day and night and brings home all his earnings to witness utter disorder in his home," warned the author of *Marital Satisfactions*. "A woman should take care that domestic life appears to her husband as a picture of his favorite pleasures and joys...there he must find peace and rest from his duties." Lukhmanova echoed this view in *Sem'ianin*: "The husband has to deal with the cares of the world; it is the role of his wife to create a hearth and home where he can find true peace and rest." Proper domesticity required psychological skills as well. "A truly devoted, loving wife must study her husband's character, note his habits, and master the skill of starting conversations that will engage him pleasantly and listen to him eagerly, know his favorite authors, and in general be sensitive to all the requirements of his spiritual life." Such "emotional housework," as Marion Kaplan has termed it, might include sharing her husband's cares and concerns in the broader world of business or state service, lending the work of a wife a broader public significance. A man who enjoyed genuine family happiness was better prepared for his responsibilities outside the home, "to serve his fatherland devotedly and with all his strength."[21]

19. Kaplan, *The Making of the Jewish Middle Class*, 36–37. The same could be said of France. See Smith, *Ladies of the Leisure Class*, 74.

20. Kelly, *Refining Russia*, 171. Compare with *Domostroi*, the sixteenth-century advice manual, according to which the male head of household is responsible for what transpires in his domain, the wife his assistant and executor. See *The Domostroi: Rules for Russian Households in the Time of Ivan the Terrible*, ed. and trans. Carolyn Johnston Pouncy (Ithaca, NY: Cornell University Press, 1994), 26–27.

21. *Khoroshii ton: Sbornik pravil i sovetov na vse sluchai zhizni obshchestvennoi i semeinoi* (St. Petersburg: German Goppe, 1881), 31, 35, 44; *Brachnye udovol'stviia*, 16–17; *Sem'ianin*, no. 1 (1894): 278; Kaplan, *The Making of the Jewish Middle Class*, 30. For similar advice, see Kelly, *Refining Russia*, 171–72; V. Silov, *Zhenshchina zamuzhem. Issledovanie o fizicheskikh, dushevnykh i nravstvennykh*

Such views were almost uniformly associated with a more egalitarian conception of marriage than that inscribed in Russian law.[22] By exalting the role of wife and raising the moral and public significance of the everyday work that she performed at home, the prescriptive literature attributed a dignity to the wife as *khoziaika*. It also drew on understandings of women's rights as a person (*lichnost'*) not unlike those propounded by the intelligentsia in the 1860s. Originating in the circles of the educated and privileged, the more expansive understanding of the term *lichnost'* as signifying a sense of personal dignity and worth as a human being achieved broader resonance toward the end of the century, as individuals lower down on the social ladder came to employ the term as well.[23]

Women's rights and dignity as a person were recognized even by the more conservative authors of prescriptive literature, with the important exception of *Sem'ianin*, whose editor was an avowed opponent of women's rights.[24] "Mutual relations between the sexes should always be distinguished by joy, indulgence, deep attachment, and boundless respect," advised *Marital Satisfactions*. Although the wife should do all she could to please her husband, "we don't mean to say that the wife should submit to everything and suppress her own personality for her husband's benefit," the author wrote, affirming women's right to maintain an independent selfhood. A woman should defend her "rights" in marriage and make her husband regard her as a "friend and helper" in all facets of life. V. Silov, writing from an avowedly Christian standpoint, also referred most explicitly to the dignity of the wife and *khoziaika*. Reflecting a "liberal variant" of the Orthodox ideal of domesticity, which regarded women as autonomous beings, Silov insisted on the fundamental equality of men and women in marriage. A woman, like a man, was a "link in the moral world, a person with rights and dignity [*lichnost'*]," Silov wrote in *The Married Woman* (1897). From the Christian point of view, women had "vital personal rights [*lichnye zhiznennye prava*]" that were protected

---

obiazannostiakh i pravilakh zamuzhnykh zhenshchin (Moscow: I. I. Pashkov, 1897), 13–14; V. Debe et al., *Kak vyiti zamuzh i byt' schastlivoi v supruzheskoi zhizni* (Moscow: A. A. Levinson, 1909), 11. Conservative Orthodox writers, for whom the domestic ideal offered an important strategy for "restoring social and sexual order" after 1861, took up many of these themes as well. See William G. Wagner, "'Orthodox Domesticity': Creating a Social Role for Women," in *Sacred Stories: Religion and Spirituality in Modern Russia,* ed. Mark D. Steinberg and Heather J. Coleman (Bloomington: Indiana University Press, 2007), 123, 124.

22. For a comparable contradiction in nineteenth-century Germany, see Lynn Abrams, "Companionship and Conflict: The Negotiation of Marriage Relations in the Nineteenth Century," in *Gender Relations in German History,* ed. Lynn Abrams and Elizabeth Harvey (Durham, NC: Duke University Press, 2007), 101–20.

23. See S. A. Smith, "The Social Meanings of Swearing: Workers and Bad Language in Late Imperial and Early Soviet Russia," *Past and Present* 160 (1998): 178.

24. *Sem'ianin,* no. 2 (1894): 145.

by religion and the state. In her own, women's sphere, she is a "person with equal rights, a free being."[25]

Ideas concerning women's dignity in marriage enriched the vocabulary with which women might speak about and perhaps also conceive the self. They helped expand definitions of marital cruelty to include offenses against women's dignity as well as violations of her physical integrity. They also provided a language with which women might describe their sufferings at another's hands in a manner that rendered them more than mere victims of abuse, enabling the women to discuss their wounded feelings and to judge their husbands at the same time as it affirmed the women's own intrinsic dignity and value. In that sense, the vocabulary of rights served women much the way it served male workers.[26] Almost invariably such women derived from the privileged orders and, unlike workers, spoke as individuals rather than as members of a group (workers). Moreover, the rights and dignity women invoked were associated with private life and, frequently, the values of the new domesticity. At least as important in the reconfiguration of authority relations in marriage was the recasting of masculinity itself.

REFINING MASCULINITY

The exaltation of the domestic sphere and recognition of women's personhood brought with it a redefinition of masculinity and more demanding expectations for men. Like many of the changes traced in this book, it mirrored developments elsewhere in Europe and, like them, required a limitation although not an eradication of men's marital authority. It smoothed the rough edges of patriarchy without rendering men and women equal, even in theory. Invoking the "complementary virtues of benevolent manliness and compliant femininity" as reflected in the literature of advice, the new ideals required from men greater self-discipline and self-restraint, although the extent varied according to the author's own proclivities as well as those of their intended reader.[27]

The more exacting standards were everywhere in evidence. Prescriptive literature urged husbands to control their feelings and their tempers, to treat their wives thoughtfully and be attentive to their needs. "It is a mistake for a man to think that he can permit himself whatever he pleases" at home, cautioned *Good Manners*. To disdain good

---

25. *Brachnye udovol'stviia*, 17; Silov, *Zhenshchina zamuzhem*, 10–11. For the liberal variant, see Wagner, "'Orthodox Domesticity,'" 125–26.

26. On the role that vocabulary played in the rhetoric of male workers, see Mark D. Steinberg, *Moral Communities: The Culture of Class Relations in the Russian Printing Industry, 1867–1907*, (Berkeley: University of California Press, 1992), 114–15. Interestingly, peasant and laboring women did not invoke the concept of *lichnost'* on their own behalf; nor did others invoke it for them.

27. A. James Hammerton, *Cruelty and Companionship: Conflict in Nineteenth-Century Married Life* (New York: Routledge, 1992), 78.

manners at home might bring "ineradicable unhappiness" and completely ruin one's life. "Men should be attentive to their wives and satisfy their reasonable desires; men should not act indifferently, nag, or be unnecessarily capricious or irritable....A man who wants to correct his wife's faults should first correct his own," asserted *Marital Satisfactions*. *The Complete Guide* (1897) advised husbands to observe themselves and try to control their "high-handedness [*krutoi nrav*], anger, and stubbornness." In place of such crude expressions of patriarchal authority, that author advised a kind of genial paternalism: a man required "a solid character, and should be strict but not cruel, tractable, affectionate, although not naively so, and kind. Such a man should condescend to his wife rather than order her around, treating her with caresses, a smile, and joshing." *How to Get Married and Be Happy* (1911) asserted, "no one should give orders in marriage, but if there are disagreements, the wife should give in to the husband, because she has the gentler character and arouses love through obedience and tenderness." Although the wife should defer to the husband when disagreements arose, she should by no means "slavishly fulfill the will of her despot husband." The anonymous author of *A Handbook for Young Spouses*, first published in 1900 and by 1911 in its third edition, was the most exacting of all in the requirements for men. In family disagreements, the author averred, "it is usually the husband who is at fault. Sometimes, he is so carried away by his own authority that he becomes an unbearable despot in the eyes of his wife."[28] The frequent use of the word "despot" to describe men who abused their marital authority, not only by authors of prescriptive literature but also by many others, among them witnesses in the Kupriianov case, suggests how similar the Russian re-evaluation of masculine behavior might have been to developments occurring elsewhere.

But Russian views of masculinity were also shaped by the cultural and political context. Angus McLaren has proposed that the nouns used to characterize misbehaving men indicate the behaviors that are and are not off-limits to them. In Great Britain those negative nouns were cad and bounder; in Russia, despot was by far the most common negative term (egoist was a distant second).[29] In the nineteenth century, Russian writers employed the term "despot" to denote a "person who does not recognize the will or desires of another person or subordinates others to his own, sometimes

28. *Khoroshii ton* (1885), 13; *Brachnye udovol'stviia*, 129; I. K-v, *Polnyi pis'movik i sovety molodym liudiam, kak derzhat' sebia v obshchestve, bezoshibochno delat' vybor zhenikha i nevesty i byt' schastlivym v supruzheskoi zhizni*, (Moscow: Gerbek, 1896), 214; Debe et al., *Kak vyiti*, 43; *Nastol'naia kniga dlia molodykh suprugov s polnym izlozheniem pravil supruzheskoi zhizni* (Moscow: S. A. Zhivareva, 1900), 12.

29. Angus McLaren, *The Trials of Masculinity: Policing Sexual Boundaries, 1870–1930* (Chicago: University of Chicago Press, 1997), 89. In France, the negative term was libertine. I am grateful to Rachel Fuchs for this information.

malicious [*zloi*] will." The word "despot" came into broad usage during the reform era, a time of reaction against the system of serfdom and authoritarian and hierarchical relations of all sorts, when "progressive" individuals struggled to free themselves from the cultural baggage associated with that past, "the moral despotism" that weighed on the private life of the individual, as the radical Sergei Kravchinskii put it. Acknowledging the unlimited authority that rulers (tsars, parents, husbands) enjoyed under the law, the term "despotism" also offered an implicit critique of that authority, much as it had done on the eve of the French Revolution, by condemning its unrestrained or illegitimate exercise and subordination of another's "free will."[30] In the latter decades of the nineteenth century, "narratives of family despotism became a recurring trope."[31]

This more refined masculinity was particularly important to men who aspired to "culture," Nikolai Kupriianov among them. In late nineteenth-century Russia, a period of enormous social flux, a person's cultivation served as a key marker of social status. Russians attributed an exaggerated significance to culture as a means of self-improvement, Joan Neuberger has noted. "Culture" was not a given, she writes, but something to be attained by means of education, moral development, and refinement. "In its pronounced emphasis on education as opposed to, or at least along with, wealth in determining social status," Russia differed from the West, she argues. The salience of culture "as a Russian version of middle-classness," as Stephen Lovell has put it, is evident in the way that *Sem'ianin* defined its readership ("*intelligentnyi*"), and in the labels that ordinary Russians applied to themselves and each other.[32] While English people used the word "gentlemen" as a term of praise, Russians employed the words "cultivated" [*intelligentnyi*] and/or developed [*razvityi*], to refer to men's conduct in their family lives, at home as well as in public. Even Nadezhda Lukhmanova, who favored women's submission to their husbands as the "guarantor

30. Institut russkogo iazyka, *Slovar' sovremennogo russkogo literaturnogo iazyka*, 17 vols. (Moscow-Leningrad: Izdatel'stvo Akademii nauk SSSR, 1954), 3: 739–40. My thanks to Rimgaila Salys for the reference. Stepniak [Sergei M. Kravchinskii], *Underground Russia: Revolutionary Profiles and Sketches from Life*, trans. from the Italian (1883, repr., Westport, CT: Hyperion, 1973), 4. For the political meanings, see Cynthia Whittaker, *Russian Monarchy: Eighteenth-Century Rulers and Writers in Dialogue* (DeKalb: Northern Illinois University Press, 2003). For France, see Jeffrey Merrick, "Sexual Politics and Public Order in Late Eighteenth-Century France: The Mémoires secrets and the Correspondance secrète," *Journal of the History of Sexuality* 1, no. 1 (1990): 68–84.

31. Susan Morrissey, *Suicide and the Body Politic in Imperial Russia* (New York: Cambridge University Press, 2006), 248.

32. Joan Neuberger, *Hooliganism: Crime, Culture, and Power in St. Petersburg, 1900–1914* (Berkeley: University of California Press, 1993), 11–12; Stephen Lovell, "Finding a Mate in Late Tsarist Russia," *Cultural and Social History* 4, no. 1 (2007): 67. See also Vadim Volkov, "The Concept of *Kul'turnost'*: Notes on the Stalinist Civilizing Project," in *Stalinism: New Directions*, ed. Sheila Fitzpatrick (New York: Routledge, 2000), 212.

of family happiness," by contrast with other purveyors of advice, stipulated that "of course," she had in mind a husband who was "kind" and "developed [*razvityi*]."[33]

These more demanding expectations of male behavior shaped the plaints and self-presentations of wives of the propertied and/or privileged orders, the testimonies of witnesses, and the responses of investigators and chancellery officials to the evidence presented in their cases.

THE *KHOZIAIKA* AND HER DIGNITY

The vast majority of petitions deriving from such women described husbands such as Kupriianov, men who abused their marital authority to an extraordinary degree and without regard for the feelings and selfhood of their wives. They alleged that husbands had indulged in a range of objectionable behaviors that included drinking to excess, engaging in domestic violence, failing to support the family adequately, and conducting extramarital affairs, often without any attempt at concealing them and under their wives' very noses, to name just the most common allegations. Although in some respects these plaints are indistinguishable from the complaints of their laboring counterparts, in others they differ substantially. The women's superior social and economic status is evident in the character of many of the offenses they alleged; in the language with which women described those offenses; and in the responses that the women's allegations drew from husbands, witnesses, and officials. The remainder of this chapter focuses on those differences.

Allegations that the husband had offended his wife by demeaning her in her role of *khoziaika* constitute one of the most important differences. Such allegations figured exclusively in conflicts involving the propertied and privileged, not only because the men were most able to afford an economically dependent wife at home but also—and more important—because for their wives, the role offered a primary source of dignity and status. So central was their domain to women's sense of self that, judging by the prescriptive literature, even wives who experienced difficulties fulfilling their domestic duties were supposed nevertheless to guard against the incursions of others into their sphere: "A wife must ensure that her husband's relatives and friends do not exercise dominion [*gospodstvovat'*] over her home, even when she is unable to manage everything herself," *Good Manners* warned.[34] It is the dignity, status, and authority vested in the position of *khoziaika*, rather than homemaking itself, that stands out in women's plaints and self-presentations and in the responses to them of other people. A proper husband trusted his wife's ability to govern the household properly and did

33. *Sem'ianin*, no. 2 (1894): 123.

34. *Khoroshii ton. Sbornik pravil i sovetov na vse sluchai zhizhni obshchestvennoi i semeinoi*, 2d ed. (St. Petersburg: German Goppe, 1885), 160. On women's authority over their sphere, see also Goncharov, *Gorodskaia sem'ia*, 273.

not interfere. He also provided means sufficient to uphold, display, and preserve the family's social standing, which necessitated the hiring of at least one domestic servant. Men's fulfillment of these responsibilities, like wives' fulfillment of theirs, signified a harmonious marriage in which the duties of each complemented those of the other. In conflictual marriages men's failures loomed large. The terms of these conflicts thus offer insight into the cultural significance of housekeeping, one of those "everyday practices" that leave almost no trace in the historical record and about which we know almost nothing.[35]

Criticisms of husbands who interfered in, failed to recognize, or diminished their wives' autonomous authority over their own sphere confirm its centrality to her dignity. Others were at least as likely to describe such insults as were wives themselves, suggesting that to refer to them might have been, for wives, itself a source of shame. The physician Sergei Plotnikov sought to "demean his wife however he could," in the words of a fellow physician. "He countermands everything she tries to do around the house." A Kharkov gendarme faulted the merchant Dmitrii Parmanin in 1887 for intruding so far into his wife's domain that he "even paid the servant himself and made sure that his wife had no influence over her." The report of a Nizhnyi Novgorod gendarme described at length how the merchant Ivan Rukavishnikov had deprived his wife, Elena, of her appropriate role in the household in the early days of the marriage: "When she asked to run the household, he responded crudely that she is 'a boarder' in the house and not the *khoziaika,* and that he wouldn't permit her 'to waste his money and supplies.' Then he gave the responsibility of *khoziaika* to the housekeeper and her husband, the manservant, who had long lived in the house and whom he trusted.... She had neither money nor authority in the household—even the servants talked back to her, which her husband encouraged." Rukavishnikov interfered personally as well. Coming home from work, and taking off his coat, "he'd immediately set off on inspection, and if he found anything wrong, he'd scream at his wife that she and her mother were fools. If there had been guests, he would crawl over the carpet looking for matches and ashes; and if he found some, he would accuse her of spoiling his things, because she had been poor before marriage and wasn't accustomed to fine things. He'd examine the parquet for signs of heels; and if he found them, he'd have them wiped away at once." Varvara Kupriianova, too, "never enjoyed the authority of a wife, mother, or *khoziaika,*" declared her cousin. Less often, chancellery officials also might condemn husbands for failing to respect their wives' appropriate sphere. In 1892, for example, they condemned the well-born lawyer Aleksandr Baranovskii for depriving his wife, Ekaterina, of her

---

35. "Introduction," in *Practicing History: New Directions in Historical Writing after the Linguistic Turn,* ed. Gabrielle Spiegel (New York: Routledge, 2005), 23. See also Francis Martin, "The Domestication of the Male: Recent Research on Nineteenth- and Twentieth-Century Masculinity," *Historical Journal* 45, no. 2 (2002): 639.

role as "*khoziaika,* putting his sister in her place and placing the children in her care" and faulted his brother, Egor, for failing to treat Ekaterina with the appropriate respect, "as a *khoziaika* should be treated, instead treating her like a chambermaid."[36]

Women were most likely to refer to insults to their dignity as *khoziaika* that involved servants and undermined their commanding place in the domestic sphere. As Elizabeth Foyster has noted, to be demeaned in front of servants or treated as one was a form of cruelty "unique to those social classes who could afford to employ them."[37] Ivan Morozov, the scion of a minor branch of the wealthy merchant clan, allegedly threatened to put the family's nanny in the position of *khoziaika,* "so that no one would obey me any longer," asserted his wife, Aleksandra. Such insults sometimes assumed the most extreme and wounding forms. After the physician Ilia Popov became sexually involved with the children's governess, the governess began to act "like the *khoziaika*" and to treat the wife, Sofia, "like a servant," Sofia contended. A similar role reversal occurred in the Sokolov marriage, where, after having become involved with his wife's chambermaid, the merchant Nikolai Sokolov established the maid as *khoziaika.* "There is no way of describing the sufferings that I and my children endured when this simple, illiterate peasant women, who had been our maid, became *khoziaika,*" wrote Tatiana Sokolova. "She did with me as she pleased and if that weren't enough, when my husband came home she would tell tales about me; and he, abusing his rights as a husband, would beat me and do everything she asked."[38]

A husband's withholding of the economic means the *khoziaika* needed properly to maintain and uphold the family's social standing was another affront to her dignity. The townswoman Zinaida Agafonova, married to a trader in ironware, claimed: "My husband gives me only a pittance for necessary expenses in the household and for raising the children." Her husband humiliated her before others and forced her to "beg for money to pay the bills." Vera Molodtsova, married to a merchant, claimed to have been denied money "even for the most minor expenditures." Vera Plaksina held that her physician husband, Sergei, "didn't even trust me with money for expenses," but instead gave the money to the servants. Anastasia Shcherbakova, also married to a merchant, complained that while her husband had "a lot" of money, he kept it all locked up in a cabinet and forbid her to touch it, keeping the keys himself. Allotting her money in very small increments, he always inquired closely as to how she would spend it and

36. RGIA, fond 1412, op. 226, d. 67 (Plotnikova, A., 1912), 10; op. 226, d. 16 (Parmanina, E., 1885), 75; op. 227, d. 54 (Suprugi Rukavishnikovykh, 1889), 104–7; op. 221, d. 213 (Kupriianova), 1, 10; and op. 213, d. 17 (Suprugi Baranovskikh, 1890), 148.

37. Foyster, *Marital Violence*, 75.

38. RGIA, fond 1412, op. 223, d. 114 (Morozova, A., 1885), 7; op. 226, d. 111 (Popova, S., 1901), 15–16; op. 228, d. 83 (Sokolova, T., 1909), 30–31.

then made her account for every kopeck.[39] Elizabeth Foyster has termed such behavior "economic cruelty."[40] This phrase captures the way it undermined a wife's ability to feed, clothe, and care for the dependents in her household in a manner appropriate to the family's status. However, it fails to convey the way it insulted women's selfhood by demonstrating the husband's distrust and disrespect.

The two forms of cruelty, the undermining of a woman's dignity as *khoziaika* and economic cruelty, were combined in a third source of marital discord, the treatment of a wife "as a servant." A complaint that surfaced with some frequency, it bears witness to the extent to which being able to delegate work to and supervise others had become for wives a key marker of social status. Thanks to the overabundance of inexpensive female labor, kept amply stocked by recent peasant migrants from the village, a domestic servant was within reach even of families on a comparatively modest budget in Russia. A servant required merely a roof over her head, a crust of bread for her table, and between three to six rubles a month for her labor. Anyone with aspirations to middle-class comforts hired one, among them 47.9 percent of households in St. Petersburg in 1869 and 39.1 percent in Moscow in 1882. It is likely that in subsequent decades the practice of hiring a servant became even more widespread, because of the rapid expansion in the numbers of peasant women migrating to Russia's towns and cities. At the turn of the century, there were over 92,000 domestic servants in St. Petersburg and 90,199 in Moscow.[41]

The availability of inexpensive domestic labor and its association with rude, untutored peasants made the requirement that women with aspirations to gentility perform it seem a form of cruelty. Performing heavy housework placed them on the same level as peasants, derogating the social standing to which, as several emphasize, they were born and depriving them of the managerial role to which their status entitled them. One of the townswoman Olga Pantiugina's many allegations against her husband linked Pantiugin's high-handedness to his social status. "As a simple townsman," Pantiugina, twice the widow of a merchant, declared, "my husband treated me coarsely...and forced me to do various household labors, which I was unable to carry out since I was not raised to do them." The townswoman Zinaida Agafonova criticized her in-laws for much the same behavior: "They didn't

39. Ibid., op. 212, d. 33 (Agafonova, Z., 1894), 53; op. 223, d. 102 (Molodtsova, V., 1905), 19; op. 226, d. 61 (Plaksina, A., 1890), 1; and op. 236, d. 8 (Shcherbakova, A., 1893), 3–4.

40. Foyster, *Marital Violence*, 75.

41. Barbara Alpern Engel, *Between the Fields and the City: Women, Work and Family in Russia, 1861–1914* (New York: Cambridge University Press, 1994), 140–45, 240; Rose Glickman, *Russian Factory Women: Workplace and Society, 1880–1914* (Berkeley: University of California Press, 1984), 60–61; David Ransel, *Mothers of Misery: Child Abandonment in Russia* (Princeton, NJ: Princeton University Press, 1988), 165.

even want to allow me to hire a nurse after the birth of my first child." Instead, they made Zinaida perform menial labor (*chernaia rabota*), even though in her opinion "they had the means to keep a servant, since they own three houses." Zinaida found this treatment insulting and a derogation of her status: "I wasn't raised to do menial labor in my grandma's house." Olga Kozyreva alleged that her engineer husband, Dmitrii, had put her in the position of "housekeeper [*ekonomka*] and nursemaid," implying his lack of proper respect for her as mistress of the household, but also that these were tasks that hired workers should perform. Varvara Zvereva, married to a bookkeeper working in Arzamas district, Nizhnyi Novgorod province, and living in her widowed mother-in-law's household, complained that the family kept no servants at the mother-in-law's insistence. "I had to wash the floors myself, launder the linens, and do all the menial labor [*chernaia rabota*], which I wasn't taught to do in my mother's house," Varvara maintained in her 1909 petition. "This work was beyond my strength and health. My husband and mother-in-law forced me to do it, humiliating me however they could."[42]

Witnesses sometimes expressed similar views concerning the demeaning nature of ordinary household labor. Among Ilia Petrov's many shortcomings as a husband was that he gave his wife, Iulia, so little money that Iulia had herself to perform "all the housework and take care of the children at night," declared Iulia's old schoolmate, adding an allegation that Iulia herself had not raised. Even members of the laboring classes might recognize these status distinctions. Thus a workshop employee, a peasant from Vladimir province, criticized the townswoman Tatiana Alekseeva's mother-in-law, owner of a gilding workshop, for "treating Tatiana like a cook, crudely, making her carry out all the work of a cook, despite the fact that ... they had means enough to hire a servant."[43] Such allegations point to the symbolic significance of the servant, who served as a confirmation of the managerial role of women who aspired to middle-class status.

EMOTIONAL CRUELTY

The higher expectations held by such petitioners is evident in other ways as well. For some, the essentials—adequate material support, the pleasures of motherhood, the right to preside over a home of their own as *khoziaika,* immunity from physical coercion—were insufficient to ensure conjugal felicity. Some, albeit a minority, had come to embrace the companionate view of marriage propounded by the literature of advice, as reflected in references to disappointed hopes for conjugal happiness, or

42. RGIA, fond 1412, op. 226, d. 8 (Pantiugina, A., 1887), 5; op. 212, d. 33 (Agafonova), 11, 53–54; op. 226, d. 62 (Kozyreva, O., 1900), 2–3; and op. 219, d. 37 (Zvereva, V., 1909), 9.

43. Ibid., op. 226, d. 49 (Petrova, I., 1898), 38–39, and op. 212, d. 126 (Alekseeva, T., 1900), 30.

as one woman put it, the "joys of family life."[44] "I can't present any especially terrible accusations against my husband, except for one, which I'll discuss below," wrote Aleksandra Shcherbakova in 1893. A graduate of the Nikolaevskii Institute, a school for orphaned daughters of ranking civil servants, Aleksandra had married the Moscow merchant Petr Shcherbakov five years earlier, mainly at her older sister's urging. "But life, and especially family life, is made up primarily of trifles, which…made my life with my husband a terrible, unbearable burden for me. Silent, uncommunicative, secretive, and at the same time exceedingly stubborn, he is interested in nothing but money, a money-grubbing petty merchant [*torgash*] in the fullest sense of that word," her petition continued. She portrayed herself as having done everything in her power to draw closer to her husband and to share his interests. "From the first days of our marriage I had to spend days, weeks, and months completely alone, without anyone near me with whom I might exchange a true word. My husband would spend whole days at the shop, coming home only around nine at night. He'd silently drink tea, silently do the accounts, silently count the money collected that day, and then, yawning a few times with his mouth wide open, would turn to me and say 'Well, Shura, it's time to go to bed.'" Thus they lived for five years, except for the evenings (five to six a year at most) when they attended the theater, received guests, or paid visits. "How many times have I said to my husband that such a life is beyond my strength, trying to convince him to share his thoughts with me, his plans, his desires; I asked to be introduced into the circle of his interests, to be familiarized with the course of his trade and the like. But all in vain."[45]

Other petitioners raised similar concerns, although few of them did so at such length. The Novokreshchenovs' "opposite characters" and lack of shared interests—hers for reading and intellectual pleasures, her husband's for drinking and carousing—and the resultant domestic conflicts forced the Samara merchant wife Anastasia Novokreshchenova to "turn inward and completely separate my inner and spiritual world from that of my husband," she wrote in her 1896 petition, invoking her own complex subjectivity. Alevtina Ptitsyna, the daughter of a wealthy Siberian merchant and educated in the Bestuzhev courses, claimed that her future husband, the lawyer Vladimir Ptitsyn, misled her during their courtship. Vladimir had attracted her with his liberal speeches but then, after the wedding, had proved inattentive and often left her alone in the evenings, a major source of her discontent. Although Vladimir and Maria Khlebnikov had married by "mutual inclination," Maria soon realized that Vladimir, nineteen years older than she and an engineer, was utterly egoistic and self-involved, a man who demonstrated no concern whatever for his wife's feelings and needs: "His

44. "My husband, in marrying me, sought neither the joys of family life nor a goal for which to work," Evlampia Parmanina maintained (ibid., op. 226, d. 16 [Parmanina], 1).

45. Ibid., op. 236, d. 8 (Shcherbakova), 2–3.

habits, society, and ways of spending time had only one goal and task," her four-page petition read, "to comfort himself alone, achieve his own advantage without the slightest thought... about me, his wife."[46]

Ironically, perhaps, the clearest articulation of these new expectations is to be found in the personal communication of a woman who had fallen short of them. Acknowledging her primary responsibility for the breakdown of her marriage in a letter to her husband, a musician and conductor, Valentina Avvakumova, the daughter of a wealthy Tomsk merchant, presented her personal failings in the language of the new domesticity. "I did not know how to understand you.... No one ever told me that people should live peacefully and quietly and that it's not always necessary to assert one's ego ["I" with a square around it in the original] in the presence of the man you love." Seeking reconciliation (in vain), she expressed a vision of marital bliss that might have been copied directly from the literature of advice. "You'll do your work and in the evening you'll come home and share your thoughts with your Valia, who loves you very much. My dear, give me that quiet and peaceful life, let me hope that you'll come back to me and that we'll live a life full of happiness together."[47] To be sure, judging by my sample, at least, expectations of companionship were far from widespread, articulated by only a small number of wives in the cases I have read. But the more demanding selfhood such expectations reveal is evident in other cases as well.

Particularly noteworthy in this respect are women's assertions of their own personhood [*lichnost'*], most often associated with their allegations of cruelty of an emotional rather than physical nature. Used in this way, the language of personhood affirmed the dignity of women's insulted self. It provided a vocabulary with which women might discuss their sufferings at another's hands in a manner that rendered them persons with dignity rather than mere victims of abuse, as the following examples show. Vladimir Lazutin, who kept his wife a virtual prisoner in their apartment and "persecuted" her with accusations of infidelity, "mercilessly destroyed my dignity as a person [*lichnost'*], wife, and mother.... In his presence I became the pathetic slave of everyone around me," wrote the nineteen-year-old Vera Lazutina of her husband, Vladimir, a second guild merchant and master weapons maker. The physician Ilia Popov, who brought his lover home and forced his wife to entertain her, acted "openly, rudely, and impudently, with contempt for my feelings and person [*lichnost'*]," asserted his well-born wife Sofia. The Moscow merchant Nikolai Volkov had conducted a clandestine affair for many years before his wife of three decades, Maria, discovered it. Nikolai "paid no attention to my personal desires and allowed me no independence," Maria wrote in her account of her marriage. "He did not recognize me as an individual [*lichnost'*], but considered

46. Ibid.,op.224,d.34(Novokreshchenova,A.,1896),25–26;op.226,d.149(Ptitsyna,A.,1892),1–2; op. 232, d. 9 (Khlebnikova, M., 1899), 1.

47. Ibid., op. 212, d. 4 (Avvakumova, V., 1904), 31–32 ob.

me some sort of nonentity [*nichtozhestvo*], without any rights." Anna Kuzmina, wife of a beekeeper, maintained in 1906: "from the very first days my husband treated me with contempt, considering me some kind of thing that belonged to him [*kakaia-to prinadlezhashchaia emu veshch'*]." The merchant wife Aleksandra Kosul'nikova declared in 1908, "during the entire eleven years of our marriage, my husband engaged in wholesale humiliation and enslavement of me as a person [*lichnost'*]....I did not exist as a person in the eyes of my husband....He demanded my limitless submission before his authority....His feelings and thoughts had to become mine."[48]

Such comparisons of women's position with that of a slave had become a common trope in late nineteenth-century feminist discourse. Like references to despotism, they might carry a political undertone, resembling the appeals of Frenchwomen on the eve of the revolution and similar to them, underscoring "the political implications of marital contestations."[49] This implication is most evident in the petition of Maria Tolkacheva, wife of a hereditary honored citizen, who in 1913 couched her appeal for a passport on the grounds of her husband's sexual incapacity in the language of liberation: "My husband, from the first days of our marriage...tried to turn me into a silent slave....But the demands of life and youth...my difficult position, amounting to complete enslavement [*rabstvo*], to the meek fulfillment of the orders of a master to a silent human animal—all this forced me to tear off the bonds of slavery, and I left my husband without a passport."[50] That such language appeared in petitions to a body that spoke in the name of the tsar is evidence of the extent to which some women had come to expect that others, including chancellery officials, would respect the rights of the person. And in some cases, their expectations were not misplaced.[51]

DEFENDING MASCULINE HONOR

Few men accepted their wives' allegations passively. A wife's appeal to authorities violated a masculine honor that rested at least in part on men's success in keeping their private affairs in order, and it challenged their prerogatives as head of their household. Expressing a sense of outrage that was far from unique to him, the hereditary honored citizen and former teacher Sergei Stefanovskii declared that his wife's petition

48. Ibid., op. 222, d. 13 (Lazutina, V., 1898), 1; op. 226, d. 111 (Popova), 15; op. 214, d. 82 (Volkova, M., 1903), 19; op. 221, d. 195 (Kuz'mina, A., 1906), 18; and op. 221, d. 128 (Kosul'nikova, A., 1908), 1–2.

49. Women's position as "slave" is one of the primary themes of P. B. Bezobrazov, *O sovremennom polozhenie zhenshchin*, 3d ed. (Moscow: A. I. Snegirov, 1892). For France, see Merrick, "Sexual Politics," 76.

50. RGIA, fond 1412, op. 229, d. 53 (Tolkacheva, M., 1913), 1.

51. As the work of Gregory Freeze has shown, women who appealed to the church for divorce sometimes employed comparable language ("Profane Narratives about a Holy Sacrament: Marriage and Divorce in Late Imperial Russia," in *Sacred Stories*, ed. Steinberg and Coleman, 160).

was merely her effort to "insult me, humiliate me, and nail me to the shaming post in front of your majesty, the provincial authorities and the police."[52] To gain the sympathy of officials as well as to correct what they regarded as their wives' misrepresentations, many men, well-educated men especially, crafted extended counternarratives that set forth the history of their marriage from the men's own point of view. Husband's counternarratives are almost always more lengthy and detailed than their wives' initial petitions or subsequent narratives of their marital life. Not only seizing the opportunity to respond to their wives' allegations, as most did, some men went on at exhaustive length, their counternarratives running to thirty or more usually handwritten pages. With appropriate numerical divisions (I, II, III) and/or chapter titles ("How My Marriage Was Destroyed"), they adopted the format of the published memoirs that appeared in "thick" journals. In their lengthy responses, especially, educated men differed from members of the laboring classes, the majority of whom remained silent in the face of their wives' petitions, and from merchants and wealthy townsmen, who with some exceptions (Kupriianov being one) tended to be more sparing of their words, unable to express themselves in "a literary and playful fashion," as one merchant husband put it, and unable or unwilling to purchase the assistance of those who specialized in crafting such narratives for others.[53]

The nature of their self-explanations differed from those of laboring-class men as well. To be sure, some husbands simply denied the allegations against them outright, blaming their marital travails on their wives' failure to adhere to the norms of proper femininity—the women's thirst for "freedom," sexual adventurism, and the like or, more revealingly, their failure to render the requisite domestic services, of which more later. But many educated men and, less consistently, merchants and townsmen described their own behaviors as well, not only at home and in relation to their wives and children but also in the larger world and at work. No doubt addressing the imagined preferences of their well-born readers, when describing their behavior in the domestic sphere, such writers often emphasized their own adherence to norms of masculine conduct and sensibility that in many respects mirrored those presented in the literature of advice. Not only had they married for "love" rather than calculation; according to their

---

52. RGIA, fond 1412, op. 226, d. 106 (Stefanovskaia, S., 1895), 10. For other such reactions, see Barbara Alpern Engel, "Marriage and Masculinity in Late-Imperial Russia: The 'Hard Cases,'" in *Russian Masculinities in History and Culture,* ed. Barbara Evans Clements, Rebecca Friedman, and Dan Healey (New York: Palgrave, 2002), 118–19.

53. RGIA, fond 1412, op. 221, d. 63 (Kokovina, Z., 1899), 64. Chancellery officials might be dismissive of merchants who did employ such writers to compose their responses to the chancellery. "The letter is evidently written by one of those lawyers who specialize in standing up for merchants. It is drawn up with pretensions to eloquence," officials commented on one such, very flowery letter (ibid., op. 224, d. 45 [Nosina, A., 1882], 10).

own self-description, they also recognized the dignity of their wives and exercised or endeavored to exercise the kind of masculine self-discipline and self-restraint that had come to be expected of a man with pretensions to cultivation, even in situations of extreme wifely provocation. At the same time, they spilled considerable ink discussing their role in public life, their success at work or in the widening public sphere. Taken together, these counternarratives suggest norms of masculine conduct that if far from "hegemonic" in the sense that R. W. McConnell has used the term—that is, having become the most honored and desired—were nevertheless widely recognized.[54]

The more refined norms governing masculine behavior in private life are particularly evident in cases where wives alleged domestic violence, as about a third of privileged women did. Domestic violence clearly respected no divisions of class or estate, as the evidence presented by witnesses in many cases makes clear. Nevertheless, engaging in physical cruelty in any form against a woman of the middling classes was now regarded as a violation of her dignity. Aware that a proper husband should treat his wife tenderly and respect a female dignity that there could be no legitimate cause to violate, most respondents emphasized their ability to restrain themselves, even as they described wifely behavior of a most provocative sort. Take the merchant son Ilia Petrov, who had done "absolutely everything" he could for his wife, Iulia, as he put it. Sometimes, angered by her allegedly coquettish behavior with other men and impelled by his "great love for her," unable to contain himself, he did "permit" himself to rebuke her verbally, to which she would respond by stating "I hate you" or "I can't bear you" and the like. "I couldn't be a more tender husband," he maintained, countering his wife's allegations that he struck her. The teacher Mikhail Ostrovidov insisted that he always tried to treat his wife tenderly. "Although sometimes I do get angry, I would never permit myself to beat my wife, as she claims." All he had ever done was to take her by the hands and ask her for God's sake to stop aggravating him "with her woman's scenes [babi stseny]." Only in one instance did he fail to "restrain" himself. And that was when his wife bit his hand, forcing him to defend himself. "I seized her by the hair, so that she'd stop [unclear] and then let go, but I didn't drag her around or shake her by her hair," as she alleged. The engineer Dmitrii Kozyrev, while denying that he had ever struck his wife, acknowledged his difficulty controlling his temper. Due to his struggle to make a career for himself, his character had become "irritable and very unsociable and morose," he confessed in his counternarrative. And his wife "as if on purpose" only aggravated him and made matters worse. Nikolai Molodtsov, a Moscow merchant, rejected the contention of his wife, Varvara, that he hit her so hard that she bruised and bled. "I never did anything wrong except perhaps occasionally to raise my voice," Nikolai declared. Sergei Stefanovskii claimed his wife was the violent one, not he. "Once,

54. R. W. Connell, *The Men and the Boys* (Berkeley: University of California Press, 2000), 10–11.

in the presence of a peasant, she tried to scratch my face with her nails." The physician Ilia Popov actually sought to appropriate the mantle of victim for himself, rejecting the testimony offered by several others that his wife bore such signs of his beatings as black eyes and bruised arms. "My wife is bigger and stronger and healthier than I am, and it is she who mistreats me—she has driven me to tears, deprived me of sleep and appetite." Whenever he pushed her away, she would "cruelly beat me, always trying to do it when we're alone." By falling on purpose, it was she herself who caused the bruises verified by the physician who examined her. The only husband who did not deny striking his wife was Nikolai Kupriianov. Portraying himself as a loving and affectionate husband (his wife had always been "dear and close to me," he wrote in a lengthy deposition, "and I've always loved her and love her now"), he acknowledged the need for self-control even as he held his wife, Varvara, responsible for his loss of it. If he did raise a hand to Varvara, he wrote, it was because of her failures as a *khoziaika:* "as a person who works a lot, I sometimes failed to control myself when faced with her morbid stubbornness or the disorder in our household."[55]

The heightened expectations of masculine self-discipline and self-restraint are also evident in situations where domestic violence did *not* figure among women's allegations, where words rather than deeds were held to offend female dignity, and "cruelty" was economic or psychological rather than physical. In such cases, husbands might emphasize their respect for women's wishes and dignity and their reluctance to exercise the masculine prerogatives to which the law entitled them. When his wife supposedly informed him that due to her political convictions, she no longer wanted to live with him "as a wife" but instead to enjoy "complete freedom," the lawyer Vladimir Ptitsyn claimed that he was "shocked" but nevertheless reluctant to exercise his masculine authority to the full, unwilling to "force her" to fulfill her conjugal duties. The merchant's son Vasilii Lazurkin described how he went out of his way to please his wife, Vera, who had accused him of treating her coarsely and insultingly and of "oppressing" her. "At first, so as not to anger my wife, I rented an apartment in the city of Iuriev, [Kostroma province], where her mother owned a house." Not only was such a life expensive for him, it was unsuitable for his work, he declared, because his job was to oversee his father's estate in the village, where his residence was needed. "But I agreed for the sake of my wife and so traveled back and forth until it became impossible, especially in winter, when I moved to a house on the estate." Witnesses upheld his claims. Even to be accused of psychological, let alone physical, cruelty might offend the dignity of a

55. RGIA, fond 1412, op. 226, d. 49 (Petrova), 11; op. 225, d. 21 (Ostrovidova, V., 1897), 2; op. 221, d. 62 (Kozyreva, O., 1900), 29; op. 223, d. 102 (Molodtsova, V., 1905), 14; op. 228, d. 106 (Stefanovskaia), 13; op. 226, d. 111 (Popova), 31; op. 221, d. 213 (Kupriianova) 20, 23, 27. Officials found Popov's testimony totally unconvincing. It is underlined in the text, with two exclamation points in the margins.

husband. Reacting with understandable outrage to the fallacious charges of his wife, Valentina, that he had married her only for her money and "persecuted" her to obtain it, charges she evidently concocted for the purpose of annulling a financial agreement between them, Stefan Avvakumov, a Ukrainian musician, composer, and pedagogue, took pains to emphasize how far he was from such inappropriate behavior: "I never in any way persecuted my wife, which I never had any right to do, and don't know and cannot imagine how I might have persecuted her, given our mutual love."[56]

Texts composed for a very different audience, the men's estranged wives, indicate that such pleas were not a mere rhetorical device designed to elicit sympathy from chancellery officials. By underscoring how very much their authors had fallen short of them, the two letters that follow reflect the new ideals of masculine conduct. They also demonstrate how those ideals might influence the vocabulary of conjugal negotiations and the balance of conjugal power. In both, the writers acknowledged abusing their authority over wives. In the future, they vowed to control themselves better and to respect their wives' dignity and be more attentive to their feelings and needs. After she left him in 1886, Mikhail Avetchin, an army officer, addressed an apology to his wife: "I am guilty before you and swear before everyone that I'm guilty.... My guilt before you consists of the fact that I cruelly insulted you when I had no right to do so...my conscience torments me for insulting an innocent person and all the more a person that I love." Avetchin blamed his weak character and lack of self-control for his behavior, and he implored his wife to forgive him and come home.[57] Writing in 1910, Ivan Konetskii, co-owner of a steamship fleet in St. Petersburg, developed similar themes at great length. "Not a day has passed when I haven't recalled all the details of our life together," he wrote to his estranged wife, Vera. If she rejoined him, he promised a new life, which she herself would guide. "I understand your moral and spiritual sufferings at my hands.... I can't forgive myself for being so deaf, for failing to understand your torment, for being such an 'egoist' that I even considered it a joke. Only now do I really appreciate your pure and upright soul, and your angelic gentleness and heart, for which I consider myself unworthy.... I've been a thousand times unjust to you and never had the right to treat you so unjustly and egoistically."[58]

THE PUBLIC AND THE PRIVATE

At the same time as they denied any infractions against their wives' dignity and selfhood, many men dwelt at length on aspects of their lives that were less directly connected to the success or failure of their marriage, in particular their ability not only

---

56. Ibid., op. 226, d. 149 (Ptitsyna), 15, 18; op. 222, d. 12 (Lazurkina, V., 1908), 8; op. 212, d. 4 (Avvakumova), 24.

57. Ibid., op. 212, d. 21 (Avetchina, E., 1887), 5–5 ob.

58. Ibid., op. 221, d. 80 (Konetskaia, V., 1910), 31.

to be a successful provider and support a wife and family according to their social station, as marital law required, but also to excel in these roles and earn the recognition of others and in these and other capacities to contribute to the public good.[59] Such statements suggest a conviction that men's standing in public life offered a compelling reason for other men (investigators, officials) to refrain from interfering in the husbands' governance of their homes. To this end, some men emphasized their individual success or social mobility in their counternarratives, sometimes in response to wives' allegations that the men were unable to hold a job, failed to support their family adequately, and/or sought access to their wives' economic resources and sometimes without any such prompting. Indicating the men's pride in their own achievements, narratives of upward mobility also reflect the assumption that others would respect and perhaps even honor a self-made man.

None of the following examples came in response to wives' allegations concerning men's economic failings. "Left a complete orphan at an early age, without any means, I lived a harsh life until at last with God's help and my own arduous labor I finally won for myself a more or less solid position as a worker [*rabotnik*]-engineer," declared Dmitrii Kozyrev in 1900. Ivan Stepanov, removed from school after only four years and set to work under his merchant father's supervision in the family's grain trade, was left with four thousand rubles of capital when the foreign grain markets collapsed in the 1890s. "I could not live on the interest, and because I didn't have the right of a noble to occupy a position in civil service with a salary sufficient to support a decent existence, and because I hadn't received a higher education, which might also provide access to such a position, I had to find some decent labor. Many people, knowing me to be an honest man, trusted me to sell their estate on conditions I found suitable, thanks to which I was able to earn about two to three thousand rubles a year." Ivan Zverev proudly described his modest but hard-won progress up the service ranks: "When as a boy I finished the three-class parish school, I entered service and, not sparing myself, worked without straightening my spine in order to better myself. On May 10, 1905, I began service as a scribe in an office of the Nizhnyi Novgorod state government. My superiors valued my service and on March 1, 1908, I was appointed an accountant and on November 1 of the same year, assistant to the chief accountant. Receiving a salary that was fully adequate, on January 30, 1909, I married...and worked with even greater conscientiousness, in the knowledge that I was no longer alone."[60]

59. Merchant men, who often inherited their status from their father, were something of an exception to this rule.

60. RGIA, fond 1412, op. 221, d. 62 (Kozyreva), 46; op. 228, d. 103 (Stepanova, S., 1900), 40; op. 219, d. 37 (Zvereva), 58.

Теща.—Если только я выиграю хоть 40,000, я сейчасъ-же возьму Сонечку отъ васъ къ себѣ,—извергъ, мучитель!

Зять.—Тогда мы неоцѣненная матушка, оба будемъ въ выигрышѣ.

FIGURE 16.

Mother-in-law: "If I can only win forty thousand rubles, I'll take Sonia back from you, you monster of cruelty! You tormentor!

Son-in-law: "Then, priceless Mama, we will both win."

Strekoza, no. 2 (1885), M. E. Saltykov-Shchedrin Public Library.

In a similar vein, and often without apparent connection to their wives' allegations, husbands in a position to do so highlighted their contributions to the public good, appealing to the service ethos that, having originated with the eighteenth-century nobility, by the late nineteenth century had come to be shared by professionals as well as others. This public contribution and the status it conferred entitled them to respect and special consideration, or so the writers imply.[61] "Merciful monarch! My ancestors are known to almost all of Moscow as honorable factory owners and, equally, as fully moral citizens who have raised more than one generation and have given the fatherland useful and honorable citizens," declared Konstantin Vasil'evich Morozov, a scion of the well-known Morozov clan. The lawyer Vladimir Ptitsyn declared: "After our marriage we lived calmly and well. My wife studied [in the Bestuzhev courses]; I worked as an assistant to a sworn attorney, and in my spare time I wrote and published a book on customary law." Nikolai Kupriianov drew the chancellery's attention to his public accomplishments. A "busy man," in his own words, he had served as elder of the Moscow Peasant Council and then in the Moscow orphan's court; he was currently an elector of the Moscow Merchant Society and a member of the Moscow commercial court, all of them elected posts. The military physician Ilia Popov dwelled at great length on his professional record, relating how he traveled long distances to treat peasants from whom he claimed to have asked no compensation, taking money only from the rich: once, he spent an entire day assisting a peasant woman to give birth and then gave her money, rather than demanding payment for his services. Mikhail Ostrovidov had won "signs of distinction for my excellent work" he declared, during his fourteen years of teaching at a parish school.[62]

Even as they highlighted their own exemplary conduct in public and private, most husbands dwelt at far greater length on the role played by others, wives in particular, in the breakdown of their marriages. The terms in which they did so were both universal and specific to the middling classes. The most common allegation, made by men across the social spectrum, concerned their wives' unchaste behavior before or during the marriage. Two other themes were more specific to the middling classes. The first, that others had violated the sanctity of the domestic sphere, reflected heightened expectations of conjugal privacy and of the need for separation between the nuclear family and everyone else. The second, that wives had failed to fulfill their domestic responsibilities, drew on the new importance of the home as a place of refuge and refreshment for men.

61. Marc Raeff, *Origins of the Russian Intelligentsia: The Eighteenth Century Nobility* (New York: Harcourt, Brace, and World, 1966). On professionals, who took the ethos of service in a very different direction, see "Introduction," in *Russia's Missing Middle Class: The Professions in Russian History*, ed. Harley Balzer (Armonk, NY: M. E. Sharpe, 1996), 9–10.

62. RGIA, fond 1412, op. 223, d. 114 (Morozova), 21; op. 226, d. 149 (Ptitsyna), 15; op. 221, d. 213 (Kupriianova), 20; op. 226, d. 111 (Popova), 30; op. 225, d. 21 (Ostrovidova), 20.

Both were linked to the ideology of separate, gendered spheres and depended on the husband's ability to maintain a home of his own and support a dependent wife.

Among historians of Western Europe and the United States, the celebration of conjugal privacy that accompanied the triumph of the affective, conjugal family is almost universally taken as a sign of marital modernity. Isolated from the influence of kin and community and founded on individual choice, romantic love, and the conviction that the most intimate affections of a husband and wife should be reserved for one another and their offspring, the emergence of the affective family is understood as a key step in the constitution of the autonomous, liberal (male) subject. Charles Taylor puts the matter succinctly: "Rebellion against the patriarchal family involves an assertion of personal autonomy and voluntarily formed ties against the demands of ascriptive authority." By means of such rebellions, individuals "demand and win privacy for the [nuclear] family," while relations with other kin become more attenuated.[63] But even in nineteenth-century Western Europe and the United States, the process—if indeed it is a process—was very far from complete, while whether it had even begun in Russia remains a question. There, even nuclear families were not "fortresses, to which access was forbidden to outsiders," as Boris N. Mironov has put it.[64] Family boundaries remained porous, while relations with other kin continued to be significant in the lives of men and women alike. Indeed, family members were often the first—and last—recourse for help in a troubled marriage.[65] Nevertheless, the allegations in many disputatious marriages indicate that as an ideal, at least, conjugal privacy was salient. It encouraged husbands to police the boundaries of the conjugal household and provided them with a vocabulary with which to discredit the allegations of wives.

Threatening conjugal solidarity and the marital balance of power, the porosity of conjugal boundaries clearly served as a source of anxiety for men. That anxiety is evident, for example, in the stereotype of the "mother-in-law from hell," as Elizabeth

---

63. Charles Taylor, *Sources of the Self: The Making of Modern Identity* (Cambridge, MA: Harvard University Press, 1989), 290–91. See also Jeffrey Watt, *The Making of Modern Marriage: Matrimonial Control and the Rise of Sentiment in Neuchatel, 1550–1800* (Ithaca, NY: Cornell University Press, 1992), 5. For the Indian version of this transformation, see Walsh, *Domesticity in Colonial India*.

64. Boris N. Mironov, *Sotsial'naia istoriia Rossii (XVIII–nachalo XX v.): Genezis lichnosti, demokraticheskoi sem'i, grazhdanskogo obshchestva i pravovogo gosudarstva*, 3d ed., 2 vols. (St. Petersburg: Dmitrii Bulanin, 2003), 1: 256. For Western Europe and the United States, see Steven R. Ruggles, *Prolonged Connections: The Rise of the Extended Family in Nineteenth-Century England* (Madison: University of Wisconsin Press, 1987), 35, 41; Ginger S. Frost, *Promises Broken: Courtship, Class, and Gender in Victorian England* (Charlottesville: University Press of Virginia, 1995), 75–77; and Stephen M. Frank, *Life with Father: Parenthood and Masculinity in the Nineteenth-Century American North* (Baltimore: Johns Hopkins University Press, 1998), 19.

65. V. A. Veremenko, *Dvorianskaia sem'ia i gosudarstvennaia politika Rossii: vtoraia polovina XIX–nachale XX v.* (St. Petersburg: Evropeiskii dom, 2007), 186.

— Отчего вы не танцуете?
— Холостой, знаете, танцовалъ, а теперь уже пляшу подъ женину дудку...

FIGURE 17.
"Why aren't you dancing?"
"When I was a bachelor, you know, I used to go dancing. But now I dance to my wife's tune."
Strekoza, *no. 2 (1895), M. E. Saltykov-Shchedrin Public Library.*

— Michel, что ты будешь дѣлать, когда я съ тобою разведусь?
— Усиленно совѣтовать всѣмъ прочимъ мужьямъ, имѣющимъ такихъ женъ-мегеръ какъ ты, тоже поскорѣе развестись съ ними.

FIGURE 18.

"Michel, what will you do when we get a divorce?"
"I'll urge all other husbands who have shrewish wives like you also to divorce them as soon as possible."

Strekoza, *no. 45 (1900), M. E. Saltykov-Shchedrin Public Library.*

Foyster has titled her, which circulated widely in Russia as elsewhere.[66] "Whoever wants peace in his family first makes it his business to keep his mother-in-law at a respectable distance," warned *Marital Satisfactions.* "Nothing could be more dreadful than the tribe of mothers of married daughters. In the eyes of the mother-in-law, the daughter is always a sufferer, the husband a beast and a tyrant. No one is more successful than a mother-in-law in sowing discord between spouses."[67] Cartoons cast a baleful eye on the negative role of the mother-in-law in her daughter's marriage, as did satirical stories.[68]

The interfering mother-in-law was a common trope in disputatious marriages, too. During their marriage, Varvara Ostrovidova visited her mother "often, too often," and at her mother's would have assignations with her alleged lover, asserted her husband, Mikhail, a teacher. Subsequently, Varvara "found support from her mother, leaving her legal husband and going off with a student," although Mikhail claimed to have done nothing to deserve such treatment. Vasilii Korobkov, employed as an official on the railroad and an army officer until he was cashiered for excessive drinking, card playing, and assaulting a fellow officer, held his mother-in-law to blame for his problems: "Many times my mother-in-law dragged my wife away from me, filling her with hostility toward me and influencing her, a weak woman who lacks character." The "constant interference" of Olga Kozyreva's mother in the couple's "intimate life" had an unfortunate affect on that life, claimed her husband, Dmitrii, so that finally, he forced his wife to sever relations with her mother.[69] One such case even came before the State Senate in 1892. Aleksandra Dudenko had left her husband, the titular councilor Pankratii Dudenko, after he forbade her to see her mother and threatened violence if she disobeyed him. When Dudenko brought suit to restore cohabitation, the Senate ruled in his favor. "Hostile relations of a husband to his mother-in-law and the demand that his wife cease all relations with her mother, even threats to her, are insufficient grounds for the wife to refuse her legal obligation to cohabit with her husband," the Senate ruled in that case.[70]

66. Elizabeth Foyster, "Parenting Was for Life, Not Just for Childhood," *History* 86 (July 2001): 319.

67. *Brachnye udovol'stviia,* 68. See also *Kak vyiti zamuzh,* 58.

68. V. Likhachev, "Rodstvennyi sovet," in *Semeinye idilii. Iumoristicheskii al'manakh* (St. Petersburg: A. A. Kaspari, 1911), n. p., related the tale of a mother who eagerly welcomed her newly wed daughter who had fled her husband and encouraged her to seek a divorce. The story ends with the couple reconciling, sending the mother-in-law into a fit of hysterical disappointment.

69. RGIA, fond 1412, op. 225, d. 21 (Ostrovidova), 22, 29; op. 221, d. 104 (Korobkova, A., 1894), 24; op. 221, d. 62 (Kozyreva, O., 1900), 28–29.

70. G. V. Bertgol'dt, ed. *Razdel'noe zhitel'stvo suprugov. Sbornik reshenii grazhdanskogo kassatsionnogo Departamenta Pravitel'stvuiushchego Senata* (Moscow: Pravovedenie, 1910), 88–89.

Although satire and prescriptive literature invariably portrayed the problematic figure as female, husbands were just as likely to identify other family members as a threat to marital solidarity. The St. Petersburg merchant Nikolai Olzhgikhin attributed the petition of his wife, Olga, exclusively to his father-in-law's initiative, for example. "My father-in-law, feeling bitterness toward me…permitted himself to forcibly remove from me my beloved wife and only son." "You must ignore my wife's claims that she no longer wants to live with me," Olzhgikhin informed the chancellery in a letter. "It is clear that it is not she who is speaking.…Her father is responsible for everything." The merchant Petr Sergunin declared in response to his wife's petition: "It's all the fault of her youth and her family, who instructed her to leave me and demand a passport." Nikolai Kupriianov maintained that his wife's relatives hated him. Their attempts "to convince my wife to restructure our family life" had had "a fatal effect" on his marriage, prompting him to forbid them access to his home. In the opinion of the Tiumen bank clerk Sergei Skachkov, the wealthy family of his wife, Zinaida, was to blame for her petition. "They have never liked me," he declared." The well-born Petr Koriakin, a lawyer, blamed his sister-in-law, Ekaterina Trubnikova, for his marital problems. Trubnikova had purportedly declared in Petr's presence that he was a "despot" and that her sister, Elizaveta, "should abandon at once a husband like me."[71] Emphasizing the degree to which the family "fortress" had been breached, such allegations drew their rhetorical weight from the ideal of conjugal privacy, however far reality may have fallen short.

Complaints that wives had failed to fulfill their domestic responsibilities drew on a related expectation, that the home was a place of refuge and refreshment for a husband, over which his wife was duty-bound to preside. According to the physician Sergei Plaksin, his wife, Anna, denied him the most fundamental of wifely attentions: "Returning home hungry and cold, I wouldn't find my wife at home, and I would find neither something to eat nor a boiling samovar." Although he was far more likely to be home than his wife, Sergei Pakhitonov, an artist, nevertheless expected her to perform her duties. While she was at school, his medical student wife Matilda was gone from seven in the morning until seven at night, as a result of which "the household matters that usually fall to a *khoziaika* fell to me." Although Sergei accepted his wife's work as a physician, to his way of thinking that work did not free her from responsibility for the home. Pakhitonov looked forward "like manna from heaven" to the day when his wife completed her classes and defended her dissertation, when, he anticipated, she would spend only a few hours of the day at the hospital, looking after the sick, "and the rest of the time occupy herself with the household and life would improve." After the couple

71. RGIA, fond 1412, op. 225, d. 7 (Olzhgikhina, O., 1900), 13, 51; op. 228, d. 42 (Sergunina, O., 1890), 24; op. 221, d. 213 (Kupriianova), 22; op. 228, d. 59 (Skachkova, Z., 1901), 21; op. 221, d. 121 (Koriakina, E., 1888), 21. The wife's attachment to her family of birth was a central issue of contention in the Khlebnikov marriage as well. See ibid., op. 232, d. 9 (Khlebnikova).

fell to quarreling, Varvara Ostrovidova became "hostile to running the household," forcing her husband, Mikhail, a teacher in a parish school in Iaroslavl, to assume that role, too, or so he claimed in 1897. Nikolai Kupriianov, as we have seen, blamed his own propensity for violence on the "disorder" in his home. Invoking the new ideals of womanly attentiveness, Aleksei Kotov, a *gimnazia* teacher in Vilno, faulted his wife, Liubov, for failing to fulfill them: "When I come home exhausted from work, needing a warm and affectionate welcome, I find my wife silent and gloomy, mercilessly stubbing out her cigarettes. . . . She's not interested in anything but looking after herself, rolling cigarettes and smoking." Sergei Stefanovskii, a village teacher in Viatka province, presented the purported failings of his wife, Sofia, as a housewife as part of a more general pattern of wifely resistance to his appropriate authority and expectations. "Considering herself something of a heroine-advocate of free love, she conducted herself with me like an eye for an eye and a tooth for a tooth. She fulfilled none of my orders around the house as I needed her to, but instead either didn't do as I asked or did the opposite of what I wanted." In the Koriakin marriage, interfering relatives and wifely failures were linked: "re-educating" his wife, Elizaveta, her sister had given her "various French novels" to read, including those of Emile Zola, as a result of which Elizaveta ceased to care for her family and children.[72]

Witnesses who supported a husband's case touched on similar issues. According to her sister-in-law, Aleksandra Boiarina, wed to a townsman, a clerk in a Moscow railroad office, was ignorant and unwilling to assume her proper domestic responsibilities. "My brother's wife didn't know how to run a household and didn't like to. She had no inclination to work," the sister-in-law maintained in 1893. "My sister and I tried to teach her how to do things, but without success." The townswoman Melatina Korchaganova, wife of a former teacher in Ufa, "wants her husband to be her slave, to carry out all her whims, and even to clean up her garbage and filth, while she herself does nothing or plays the piano that she forced her husband to buy for her," claimed Melatina's sister-in-law in 1895. According to the German-born wife of a fellow physician in the city of Kharkov, the physician's wife Antonina Plotnikova showed no interest at all in keeping house for her husband, Stepan. "I've often had the occasion to see him do the shopping at the marketplace. The wife was completely incapable of maintaining decent order in the home. Sometimes the husband had to sew on his own buttons. He couldn't entertain friends at home, because she refused to receive them or take any part in entertaining."[73]

72. Ibid., op. 226, d. 61 (Plaksina), 32; op. 226, d. 19 (Pakhitonova, M., 1892), 23–24; op. 225, d. 21 (Ostrovidova), 27; op. 221, d. 134 (Kotova, L., 1907), 23; op. 228, d. 106 (Stefanovskaia), 13; op. 221, d. 121 (Koriakina), 21.

73. Ibid., op. 213, d. 95 (Boiarina, A., 1893), 32; op. 221, d. 118 (Korchaganova, M., 1895), 15; op. 226, d. 27 (Plotnikova, A., 1912), 25.

The gendarmes and other well-born men in positions of authority who reported on the reasons for marital breakdown were often exacting in the standards they applied to men of the middling classes. While judging women almost exclusively on the basis of their sexual conduct, these well-born men might fault husbands for a range of marital transgressions that included not only egregious offenses such as infidelity, extortion, and domestic violence but also far more subtle misdemeanors, such as using insulting language or failing to respect their wives' dignity or demonstrate the requisite tenderness and attentiveness, as the following examples illustrate. After Vasilii and Evlampia Parmanin moved into their own apartment and away from her father's protection, the head of the Kharkov district gendarmes reported in 1887, Vasilii began treating Evlampia like a "slave." "He made horrible scenes over the smallest trifles. He refused when she asked him to accompany her to some social gathering in the evenings or to go for a walk, but if she went out with another friend he would insult her." As did others, the officer carefully distinguished between Parmanin's self-presentation in public and his character flaws in private: "moving, because of his material well-being, in a circle of cultivated people, he has acquired an outward polish (in the provincial sense, of course) and a decent appearance; he doesn't get drunk, doesn't gamble, hasn't descended into debauchery; but he's insufferable in family life." In 1893, the St. Petersburg city governor held Vladimir Ptitsyn to an even higher standard. Blaming him for the breakdown of his marriage, the governor's report highlighted the husband's lack of concern for his wife's feelings and needs. Having married her lawyer husband Vladimir on the basis of his speeches in the Irkutsk city duma celebrating civil courage and liberal values, Alevtina Ptitsyna was soon disillusioned, the account began, narrating the history of the marriage almost entirely from the wife's perspective:

Even on the road to St. Petersburg he was inattentive to her, driving her to tears. In St. Petersburg, he was rarely home and even more inattentive. She felt alone and abandoned and became terribly nervous. Her husband ignored her distress....He shared neither his thoughts nor his interests with her. He spoke only of the most ordinary things. She decided he regarded her only as a wife, not as a friend or comrade, only as a female of the species [*samka*], and not as a person worthy of respect and love. She was insulted and humiliated.[74]

Men in official positions rarely assumed that a good worker must necessarily be a good man.[75] Contrasting public behavior with private conduct, as the investigator did

74. Ibid., op. 226, d. 16 (Parmanina), 62; op. 226, d. 149 (Ptitsyna), 92.
75. On the importance of men's public life in shaping responses to their private behavior elsewhere, see McLaren, *Masculinity on Trial,* 121.

in the Parmanin case, they might dismiss as irrelevant the very achievements in the world of work or public life that husbands had highlighted in their self-presentation. Dmitrii Kozyrev was "a man of impeccable morality who gives his entire salary to his family and lives for it," reported a gendarme officer from Kaluga. "However, the difficult circumstances of his childhood...left a stamp on his character, making him irritable, nervous and proud, unable to restrain himself...while the habit of relying only on his own strength left him difficult and despotic." The achievements of the engineer Vladimir Khlebnikov were likewise dismissed by chancellery officials: "Deriving from a poor family, achieving his well-paid and comparatively comfortable position only thanks to his own labor...Khlebnikov turned out to be a petty man, if not limited and dried up [sukhoi], with an egoistical character, very easily offended personally and unable to get used to the proclivities and feelings of his young wife." Ilia Popov was "a fine doctor but a poor family man," a gendarme officer asserted, summarizing his investigation of the case. The bookkeeper Sergei Zverev did not drink and was well regarded by his superiors, reported another investigator in 1910. Nevertheless, because he "has no real friends and lives a self-contained and secretive lifestyle, he seems completely incapable of family life," he wrote in a report supporting the claims of the wife.[76]

Especially in cases involving men of the commercial classes, these judgments about male behavior were sometimes inflected by social prejudice and by a dislike and suspicion of commerce and moneymaking that had long characterized noble culture. The negative images of merchant life that continued to circulate in art, in literature, and on the stage provided a template through which well-born men perceived merchant men, sometimes prompting a critical stance toward the qualities needed for the very commercial endeavors that underpinned such men's success.[77] "Having neither education nor firm moral principles, involved in purely material affairs, [Vasilii Parmanin] grew coarse; and his one aim in life became wealth, the attainment of which became his single goal," reported the gendarme captain investigating his case. Parmanin's efforts to compensate for these lacks only aroused the officer's disapprobation, in part because of the political tendencies of his reading but also because of Parmanin's purported inability to understand what he read: "Sometimes at home he reads books but evidently

76. RGIA, fond 1412, op. 221, d. 62 (Kozyreva), 46; op. 232, d. 9 (Khlebnikova), 130–31; op. 226, d. 111 (Popova), 80; op. 219, d. 37 (Zvereva), 15.

77. The literature on negative stereotyping of merchants is enormous. For an overview, see Beth Holmgren, *Rewriting Capitalism: Literature and the Market in Late Tsarist Russia and the Kingdom of Poland* (Pittsburgh: University of Pittsburgh Press, 1998), 19–21, 25–26; Catriona Kelly, "Teacups and Coffins: The Culture of Russian Merchant Women, *Women in Russia and Ukraine,* ed. Rosalind Marsh (New York: Cambridge University Press, 1996), 58–59; and M. N. Baryshnikov and A. I. Osmanov, *Peterburgskie predprinimateli vo vtoroi polovine XIX–nachale XX v.* (St. Petersburg: Nestor, 2002), 40–41.

without any use and, more likely, harming himself. Having received no education, he reads, for example, Proudhon and Spenser; and the scope of his comprehension remains narrow as before and even then, he makes his way with difficulty." A Nizhnii Novgorod land captain, attributing the marital misunderstandings of Ivan Rukavishnikov and his well-born wife, Elena, to their different backgrounds and the different expectations to which they gave rise, clearly found the wife's cultural preferences more appealing. "He gets up early, drinks tea, goes off to work, comes home, eats, retires to his study, goes out to visit relatives, comes home, and goes to sleep. She, being developed [*razvita*], wants more out of life: a conversation and social life." However, "as a merchant," Rukavishnikov disliked it when she mixed in society. A second gendarme officer who reported on this case at a different juncture was likewise dismissive of Rukavishnikov's commercial achievements: "Among the merchants he [Rukavishnikov] enjoys a reputation as a businesslike and honorable man. People who don't belong to that estate say he's a great materialist and stingy, with a very difficult character." After a lengthy disquisition on the shortcomings of the merchantry, in the process of which he quoted lines from an Ostrovskii play, the gendarme reporting on yet another case, that of the Kokovins, summarized his argument in a single critical sentence: "It isn't the man who possesses the millions and spends them according to his own wishes; rather, he himself is the slave of his capital."[78]

Whether or not merchant family culture truly differed from that of other estates, a question impossible to address on the basis of the sources I use for this book, gendarme officers in particular were convinced that such distinctions were real, perhaps because of status anxieties connected to their position on the lowest rung of the nobility. Family cultures helped explain, for example, why Ivan Rukavishnikov had difficulty handling his wife: "On one hand, he didn't want to treat his noble wife in the merchant fashion [*po kupecheski*]; and on the other, he had no idea how people of higher estates behaved in these circumstances." Although Anastasia Novokreshchenova was born, like her husband, into the merchant milieu, in the opinion of the gendarme officer reporting on her case, she "began to find that life burdensome, since by her cast of mind and character, she required more respectability [*poriadochnost'*] and the appearance of propriety [*naruzhnoe prilichie*]," than the merchant milieu could provide. "The notions of family life that exist in that milieu continue to the present to be exceedingly coarse, lacking the kind of humane relations that exist in the more cultivated [*intelligentnye*] classes of society." Thus the source of the Novokreshchenovs' dissension was "on one hand, the husband's attachment to the existing order of merchant life, with its coarse practices

78. RGIA, fond 1412, op. 226, d. 16 (Parmanina), 71, 82; op. 227, d. 54 (Suprugi Rukavishnik-ovykh, 1889), 99. The mother-in-law was "proud, power-loving, and stubborn. This is a type to be found in a comedy written by the late A. N. Ostrovskii" (ibid., op. 221, d. 64 [Kokovina, Z., 1899], 28 ob., 29).

and, on the other, his wife's utter hostility to that order." If Vera and Nikolai Molodtsov held different views, in the opinion of the officer reporting on his secret investigation in 1905, "it is only because he is a man without any education and devoted entirely to his business," where as she, "having obtained some education, is an intellectually curious woman and a reader."[79]

When they evaluated the behavior of men and women of the middling classes, chancellery officials employed standards similar to those of the men who reported to them, although their language was usually more restrained and their judgments more measured and, unlike others, officials avoided entirely negative references to the merchant order. As was the case with disputes involving men of the laboring classes, their practice grew more exacting over time. To be sure, officials remained hesitant to approve a passport, eager to promote a couple's reconciliation, and, especially in the first decade of their operation, inclined to deny a wife's petition when they had become convinced of her sexual infidelity, whatever her husband's ill-treatment. Nevertheless, when officials did decide in women's favor, they drew on much the same vocabulary as investigators. In cases involving women of the middling classes, officials, too, expressed concern about women's "human dignity" and invoked images of slavery and despotism in cases of gross abuse of husbandly authority, divesting those images, or so I assume, of the political associations that those terms might harbor in other contexts.

The decision in the Kupriianov case with which this chapter begins serves as one example: "As time passed, the petitioner increasingly lost her will and finally became a toy in the hands of her despot husband, who crushed in her all that is human and turned her into a silent slave," officials wrote in their report recommending a passport. The Khlebnikov case, much less typical and involving emotional cruelty alone, is another and more telling example. "The petitioner was first to recognize how little she really had in common with her husband," officials wrote in their 1899 decision in the wife's favor. Commending her for defending her person [*lichnost'*] against her husband's "moral violence [*nasilie*]," they were highly critical of the husband: "egoistic and arid, he was completely unable to understand the idealistic strivings of his still-young wife...crudely rejected her feelings, presented formal demands to her concerning their family life, and, noticing that she cooled to him over time, began persecuting her every step."[80]

By contrast, women's satisfactory performance of their domestic duties, such as keeping an orderly home or providing for a husband's emotional needs (motherhood is a significant exception), appears to have mattered little to officials, at least when they evaluated cases deriving from the middling classes. Their reaction here is very unlike their response to women of the peasantry who failed to fulfill their housekeeping

79. Ibid., op. 227, d. 54 (Suprugi Rukavishnikovykh), 8; op. 224, d. 34 (Novokreshchenova), 5; and op. 223, d. 102 (Molodtsova), 33.

80. Ibid., op. 221, d. 213 (Kupriianova), 94; op. 232, d. 9 (Khlebnikova), 132, 133–34.

responsibilities and whom they judged quite harshly. Despite the frequency with which husbands and those who spoke on their behalf accused wives of the middling classes of shortcomings in the domestic realm, no chancellery report that I have read takes up the charge either to affirm or deny it. When reports do mention women's role as *khoziaika*, it is almost invariably to condemn a husband's infringement of a woman's sphere. In the one exception to this rule, the case of the Shcherbakovs, officials referred to the wife's household responsibilities only to criticize the husband for regarding her duties so narrowly.

This 1893 case, in which the wife alleged that her husband had forced her into anal intercourse during and after her pregnancy in addition to neglecting her emotional needs, demonstrates officials' hesitancy as well as their standards. Initially, officials pressed hard for reconciliation; their decision in Shcherbakova's favor came a year after her initial petition, and only after her husband had rejected her efforts to return to his home at the chancellery's insistence. But when they did decide in her favor, officials explained their decision in terms that reflected their own sentimentalized and spiritualized view of marriage and is thus worth quoting at length:

> As a undeveloped man who grew up in a family where there reigned an opinion that the solidity of family relations depended on a wife's complete subordination to her husband's will, where the need for a spiritual union of spouses was absent, and where it was a crime for a wife to leave a young husband without caresses for two nights, he assumed that a wife's sphere of activity should consist exclusively of household concerns and pleasing her husband. Limiting his obligations to his family to the purely external—that is, care of their material needs—he allowed himself to put in first place the satisfaction of his sensual inclinations in his relations with his wife, and, not understanding any other kind of union with her, regarded with suspicion her attempts to help him in his affairs.... There is no direct evidence that he treated his wife badly, but there is that he was far from affectionate with her, even though they were young and newly married; and he was coarse and easy to anger by nature. Everyone agrees that he is stingy.... As for her sexual allegations, while they cannot be proved, they seem entirely plausible.[81]

COMPETING LEGALITIES

As the evidence in this chapter demonstrates, by the late nineteenth century, educated elites and some members of the middling classes had come to embrace new and more modern norms concerning marital behavior based on a companionate ideal of marriage and respect for women's rights as individuals. These ideals were far from universal, to be sure. Testimonies by husbands and by others on their behalf sometimes

81. Ibid., op. 236, d. 8 (Shcherbakova), 94.

demonstrate a marked propensity to regard marital relations as a kind of battle between the sexes.[82] Nevertheless, others who bore witness in separation cases were critical of men who exercised their authority arbitrarily over their wives and children. They expected men to exercise self-control in their conduct, be more attentive to women's emotional needs, and refrain from behaviors that in today's courts might be characterized as "mental cruelty." Most critical of all tended to be well-born gendarme officers, whose reports on marital conflict influenced the outcome of appeals.

As time went on, chancellery officials increasingly expressed similar modern values. They applied them, however, in a setting that was entirely anachronistic, not only separate from but sometimes in conflict with the postreform legal order that in other respects was at the leading edge of Russia's modernization and of the defense of individual rights. Acting on the basis of their supralegal authority, when they rendered decisions favorable to women, officials restricted the rights that belonged to men according to law and brought the power of the state to bear in a realm hitherto outside the state's purview. One consequence of the extralegal character of their authority was that by contrast with court cases, chancellery decisions in particular cases remained just that—particular decisions, seemingly arbitrary, and lacking broader social significance or the potential to change prevailing social norms.

This characteristic influenced the ways in which many husbands from the middling classes responded to decisions in a wife's favor. Attributing decisions against them to personal rather than to widely shared or universalistic values, husbands portrayed themselves as victims of arbitrary state authority or the prejudice of particular officials. Sergei Stefanovskii professed outrage at the way his case was handled. It was conducted by "some kind of gendarme officer, as they say." In Stefanovskii's opinion, the officer was under the thumb of his wife's lover, who himself was connected to the higher circles of Viatka society. (Stefanovskii was eventually accused of trying to murder his wife.) Mikhail Iartsev, a townsman who traded in fish products, alleged of an investigation that found in favor of his wife: "There is clearly prejudice and favoritism [*kumovstvo*] at work here," in which the police themselves were involved. When a police investigation upheld his wife's charges of his drunken and cruel behavior, the townsman and former teacher Ilia Korchuganov insisted that this was because "the local authorities regard the matter one-sidedly and with prejudice, preferring women to men." The townsman Ilia Razaev, married to the daughter of a wealthy merchant, claimed authorities were complicit with his wife. "The police officer tried so hard to please the rich merchant Kalinin [the father-in-law] that he didn't even propose that my wife and I reconcile, as the chancellery requires; and in his turn, the district police officer gave my wife a temporary passport without my permission." In 1902, Nikolai Olzhgikhin, a St. Petersburg merchant, wrote to the head of the chancellery expressing outrage at the efforts

82. See, for example, ibid., op. 223, d. 102 (Molodtsova), 16.

of Nikolai Lodyshinskii, a senior chancellery official, to convince him to approach his estranged wife lovingly and to refrain from resorting to the courts to bring her home. "Mr. Ladyshinskii [*sic*!] said to me, how can there be peace between you when you take your wife to court. But I've never brought my wife to court, except to circuit court to get my beloved wife back." Olzhgikhin wondered why his wife's wishes were honored but not his: "How come she can ask for a separate passport, but I'm not permitted to ask for anything? I thought that rights were equal or even that the husband had greater rights if the wife conducted herself improperly." Nikolai Lobanov, a scribe, told chancellery officials in 1902 that he was prepared to issue his wife a separate passport if the notation on his passport that he was married were removed. Informed that what he wanted was impossible, Lobanov responded that in that case, he had "no desire to continue the conversation" and walked out of the chancellery. In 1904, the well-born engineer Georgii Azancheev tried to appeal over the head of Baron Aleksandr Budberg, head of the chancellery, writing a letter directly to the tsar to complain of Budberg's high-handed behavior. In an effort to force Azancheev to accept a custody arrangement that Azancheev found objectionable, Baron Budberg had supposedly declared "in a raised voice," and "with a sneer, ironically," that Azancheev "was only the physiological father." He also, in the presence of Azancheev's estranged wife, expressed distrust of Azancheev's words ("I don't believe you, all the same," Budberg purportedly declared). Azancheev refused to have further contact with Budberg.[83]

More ironic still, men might invoke the law and their own legal rights to resist the validity of chancellery decisions in favor of their wives. As had Vladimir Khlebnikov, several took their case to court. Ilia Korchaganov wrote to the chancellery, complaining of the conduct of the investigating official: "I consider the actions of Mr. Shatov a violation of justice, leading to the destruction of my life and my household." Because of the intervention of the chancellery, the lawyer Vladimir Ptitsyn felt himself "deprived of the protection of our laws." In 1901, the hereditary honored citizen Nikolai Kupriianov chided the chancellery for the secrecy in which it maintained the testimony of witnesses: he wanted to confront his wife's witnesses, many of whom, he insisted, could not possibly know the details of their family life. Referring to the appropriate article of the criminal code, he reminded chancellery officials that "the evidence of the accusing side cannot and should not be kept secret from the accused; if it is, the investigation will be conducted incorrectly"—all the more important because of the seriousness of the matter: false testimony could "destroy the family." He demanded, in vain, that his legal rights be restored. The chancellery's 1902 decision in his wife's favor enraged Nikolai Olzhgikhin. "I ask that I be shown the tsar's decree, requiring the issuing of

83. Ibid., op. 228, d. 106 (Stefanovskaia), 48, 51; op. 239, d. 11 (Iartseva, A., 1899), 54; op. 221, d. 118 (Korchaganova), 58; op. 227, d. 6 (Razaeva, M., 1909), 17; op. 225, d. 7 (Olzhgikhina), 44; op. 222, d. 68 (Lobanova, M., 1900), 51; op. 212, d. 51 (Azancheeva, T., 1900), 127.

separate passports to wives, as the chancellery does, by force," he demanded in a letter, declaring: ""You can get no sense from His Majesty's chancellery." The tradesman Iartsev accused the chancellery of interfering with his moral and legal authority as a husband. Instead of preserving his marriage, as the law required, the chancellery helped destroy it by releasing his wife from her husband's lawful authority and guidance and encouraging her insubordination. If the chancellery had not granted his wife "freedom" from the very start, he maintained, then "she would have made her peace with her lawful husband and would have lived with me in complete happiness." Summoned to the chancellery, he cast aspersions on his wife's morality, refused to sign the protocol of his statement, and then left the office, muttering invectives against the chancellery.[84]

• • •

Based as they were on the testimony of witnesses and reports of gendarmes that established the "truth" of a case, chancellery decisions on behalf of abused wives often reflected a broader consensus concerning appropriate masculine behavior that had emerged among educated members of the middling classes, and that is evident as well in the literature of advice. The frequently used term "despot," in particular, underscored the importance of a husband's self-discipline, self-restraint, and recognition of the rights of others in the private realm of the family. At the same time, the language of rights and the dignity and worth of the individual, which offered women a vocabulary with which to speak of the suffering self, also contributed to the redefinition of masculinity.

Still, if these unhappy marriages suggest that a kind of consensus had emerged among a sector of the middling classes about the need for masculine self-command, they also suggest that there was no agreement whatsoever on where the line should be drawn, except in cases of domestic violence. Many of the husbands whose wives appealed to the chancellery were guilty of the most egregious of marital offenses, among them brutal beatings, extramarital affairs under the conjugal roof, and concerted efforts to gain control of women's resources. Some men abused their authority to an extraordinary degree, as had Kupriianov. In other cases, the Khlebnikov case being among the more notable, the husband had failed merely to be sufficiently attentive, loving, and concerned with his wife's feelings and needs.

The documents in chancellery archives indicate even less agreement on the proper role of the wife, the keystone of bourgeois family ideals as they developed in Western Europe and the United States. Even as domesticity and motherhood remained women's primary social calling and advice literature celebrated women's sphere to an unprecedented degree, domestic duties such as presiding over a clean and well-ordered

84. Ibid., op. 221, d. 118 (Korchaganova), 77; op. 226, d. 149 (Ptitsyna), 42; op. 221, d. 213 (Kupriianova), 4; op. 225, d. 7 (Olzhgikhina), 52; op. 239, d. 11 (Iartseva), 163.

home and tending to a husband's needs figure in these dossiers mainly as tropes in husbands' counterarguments, not as criteria according to which men in authority evaluated a wife's conduct. Apart from motherhood, positive references to women's domesticity are strikingly absent from testimonies in women's favor, as they are in chancellery decisions. Indeed, we learn about women's proper sphere primarily from a husband's transgression of it.[85] As articulated by unhappy wives, reported by gendarmes, and enforced by officials, heightened expectations of marriage, it would seem, applied primarily to men.

85. Compare with the language of reforming jurists, who were quite concerned with a woman's fulfillment of "the obligations of a wife, mother, and mistress of the household" (Wagner, *Marriage, Property, and Law,* 163).

The Right to Love

On October 2, 1882, the twenty-year-old Liubov Aleksandrova, former telegraph worker, appealed for separation from her husband of two years, Platon. A widower forty-four years her senior, retired soldier, and member of the hairdressers' guild in the city of Novgorod, Platon had been chosen by Liubov's widowed mother in a marriage arranged by the widow, a townswoman who earned her living by renting rooms to boarders. After the marriage, Platon beat and mistreated his wife and insulted her in public, Liubov alleged in her petition. Once he even declared in the presence of others that she led "an adulterous life." So offensive to her was this statement that Liubov had sued Platon in Justice of the Peace court for public insult, an actionable offense in Russia, where a person's public standing depended on her reputation.[1]

However true the allegations against Platon—and the evidence remains unclear on that score—it was the alleged misconduct of Liubov herself that proved decisive to the outcome of her appeal. In her case, as in others during the 1880s and into the early 1890s, a woman who transgressed the boundaries of sexual propriety could expect neither sympathy nor mercy, whatever she may have suffered at her husband's hands. And the evidence that emerged in the course of investigation suggested strongly that Liubov had indeed transgressed those boundaries. A doctor who had treated Liubov for syphilis confirmed Platon's contention that his wife had taken a cure for venereal disease. Platon also produced two letters written by Liubov's own mother, in which she chastised Liubov for her late-night drinking bouts and pursuit of pleasure in the company of men who were not her husband and for bringing shame not only on herself and her husband but on her own mother, too:

> Liuba, can it be that you don't value your reputation, letting people say such nasty things about you? Don't you know that the whole neighborhood condemns you for your spree [*kutezh*] at the circus?...It's shameful and base that you forget yourself

1. RGIA, fond 1412, op. 212, d. 103 (Aleksandrova, L., 1882), 1.

in that way, and then drag yourself home at 3 a.m.... The very men who invite you for drinks at the buffet laugh at you behind your back. You should be considerate of your old mother and not stain the name of your husband.[2]

The chancellery's investigator cast still more damaging aspersions on Liubov's sexual conduct. He held that Liubov was a "secret prostitute," that is, a woman who sold her favors without registering for the special passport that after 1843 required such women to submit to regular venereal examinations. Providing no evidence that she obtained money in exchange for her favors or had sex with more than two men, at most, he reported to the chancellery that after Liubov left her husband, she had invited one Solov'ev to spend time with her at a hotel and after that, lived with and was supported by a telegraph worker named Osipov. All this was more than sufficient to convince officials that Liubov was unworthy of the emperor's mercy. "Although some of the evidence showed that she lived honorably in St. Petersburg, investigation revealed that she engaged in 'secret prostitution' and besides, cohabits with Osipov, on whose means she lives.... On account of her immoral behavior, she does not deserve sympathy," the report dated 28 October 1886 concluded, instructing the authorities to revoke Liubov's temporary passport and deny her one thereafter.[3]

Once a wayward woman, always a wayward woman, insofar as officials were concerned. After Liubov's initial, unsuccessful appeal, officials refused to consider evidence that her behavior might have changed. Having twice tried and failed to reopen her case, in mid-March 1887 Liubov convinced the chancellery to grant her another hearing. She was now resident in St. Petersburg, unemployed, and living with her stepfather. This time, Liubov accused Platon of denying her food when she returned to him after the negative chancellery decision and of demanding three hundred rubles in exchange for a passport. Composed by Liubov and rewritten by a scribe, the petition declared her to be so desperate that she was prepared to take her own life. Since leaving Platon, Liubov claimed, she had reformed completely and had not taken a drink for nearly six years, as her former employer, a Mr. Fall in Novgorod, could attest. The investigation unequivocally upheld her story. Various St. Petersburg authorities confirmed that Liubov now conducted herself properly and was known to have done

---

2. Ibid., 34–35, 44.

3. Ibid., 22, 42, 45. On regulated prostitution, see Laurie Bernstein, "Yellow Tickets and State-Licensed Brothels: The Tsarist Government and the Regulation of Urban Prostitution," in *Health and Society in Revolutionary Russia*, ed. Susan Gross Solomon and John F. Hutchinson (Bloomington: Indiana University Press, 1990), 45–65; and Barbara Alpern Engel, *Between the Fields and the City: Women, Work, and Family in Russia, 1881–1914* (New York: Cambridge University Press, 1995), chap. 6. Alleged "secret prostitutes" were often pressured to register as professionals. No one seems to have pressured Liubov.

nothing "disreputable [*predosuditel'nyi*]." Nevertheless, having become convinced of her immoral character, officials denied her petition. "The petitioner cried bitterly," reported the policeman who conveyed the bad news to Liubov. He endeavored in vain to convince her to acknowledge her "frivolous [*legkoe*]" behavior and return to her husband. And there the file ends.[4]

Such a negative outcome was typical of early cases in which the petitioner was found to have become sexually involved with a man other than her husband, even if circumstances were far less flagrant than they appear to have been in Liubov's case, even if the spouses had separated years before. During the reign of Tsar Alexander III chancellery officials demonstrated an almost obsessive concern with the sexual behavior of wives, a key dimension of the concern with public decorum discussed earlier. This concern is evident even in the questions that chancellery officials initially asked investigators to address: "What is the behavior, character, and lifestyle of the petitioner?" reads the very first question. "Has she been observed in any disreputable actions? Is she involved with anyone in an illicit relationship?"[5] Although officials were exceedingly cautious in their judgments, weighing evidence carefully before affixing negative labels, once they decided that a woman was sexually "immoral," they treated her as irredeemable.[6]

Although this concern extended to all women, women of the laboring classes were the primary targets, as they were deemed more prone to unruliness than their better-bred and privileged sisters. In the reign of Tsar Alexander III, this overriding concern with female sexual conduct determined the outcome of every one of their cases, far outweighing a husband's "insults" of word and deed. If such a wife was found to have engaged in extramarital sexual relations, it served as sufficient grounds to deny her requests for separation even when every allegation against the husband proved true, or when, as in Aleksandrova's case, there was compelling evidence that the conduct officials viewed as immoral had ceased.

Take the case of Anna Gurova, a peasant woman originally from Olonets province, who petitioned for separation in 1886. The chancellery found that while living in St. Petersburg her husband had engaged in "very poor behavior, constantly beat his wife, drank heavily, and in several instances committed theft." Officials nevertheless refused

---

4. Ibid., 51, 54, 56.

5. TsGIA SPb, fond 569, op. 20, d. 103, "Voprosnye punkty," 1885, 15. By the mid-1890s, questions had become far more general and gender neutral, requesting information about the lifestyle, etc., of both spouses.

6. For an example of their caution, see the case of Aleksandra Andreeva, wife of an artisan. "No one can confirm beyond all doubt [*dostoverno*]" that she was involved with other men, they noted, although not only the husband but also several witnesses claimed precisely that. Rejecting the rumors and gossip, officials approved her passport time after time. See RGIA, fond 1412, op. 212, d. 138 (Andreeva, A., 1890), 28, 44, 64, 71–72, 90, 93, 107, 121, 131.

Anna's petition in view of her (unspecified) "immoral [*beznravstvennoe*] lifestyle." That same year, they reached a similar decision in the suit of Paraskeva Gorlova, married to a retired noncommissioned officer. Having become sexually involved with a worker in a steel foundry after leaving her husband eight years earlier, she remained in the relationship with her lover at the time of her petition, or so the investigator reported. Therefore, despite officials' acknowledgment that the husband, Vasilii Gorlov, was violent, drank to excess, lacked an occupation, and had treated his wife "extremely cruelly, without any cause whatsoever," when they lived together, the chancellery declined to approve her passport on the basis of her "immoral conduct."[7]

During this period, a formula depicting chancellery decision making would look something like this:

Husbandly adultery + wifely sexual virtue = passport (until he reformed);

Wifely adultery + husbandly sexual virtue (irrespective of his other transgressions) = passport denied;

Husbandly adultery + wifely adultery (a much less common equation) = passport denied.

Until 1914, when passports became available to wives who requested them, women's morality, defined in sexual terms, never ceased to preoccupy chancellery officials. However, as this chapter shows, toward the end of the nineteenth century, officials' stringent definition of "immorality" underwent a perceptible if subtle shift. Expanding the parameters of acceptable female sexual conduct, the shift reflected changes in popular and elite attitudes toward women's sexuality and a growing acceptance of women's capacity for self-governance and agency in the sexual sphere as in others.

ADULTERY IN CONTEXT

Russians' attitudes toward adultery both resembled and differed from those of continental Europe. Unlike English, French, and German law, Russian law judged adultery according to a single sexual standard, defining it in identical terms for men and women.[8] The law treated adultery as both a criminal and religious offense, a violation of public order as well as of the sacrament of marriage. If the betrayed party sued

7. Ibid., op. 250, d. 104; 38–39, d. 101, 90–91. For other examples of the decisive role of women's sexual conduct, see Elizaveta Gendler, ibid., op. 250, d. 100, 29; Maria Griazkova, d. 104, 35–37 ob; op. 212, d. 125 (Alekseeva, T., 1882), 49–50, op. 223, d. 42 (Matrosova, N., 1882), 23.

8. On law and adultery in England, France, and Germany, see Ursula Vogel, "'Whose Property?' The Double Standard of Adultery in Nineteenth Century Law," in *Regulating Womanhood: Historical Essays on Marriage, Motherhood, and Sexuality*, ed. Carol Smart (London: Routledge, 1992) 148, 150. Swedish and Saxon law employed a single standard, and its presence in Russian law may be due to their influence. See Laura Engelstein, *The Keys to Happiness: Sex and the Search for Modernity in Fin-de-Siècle Russia* (Ithaca, NY: Cornell University Press, 1992), 51.

successfully in civil court, adultery was punishable by incarceration in a monastery or a prison; if in an ecclesiastical court, adultery served as grounds for divorce. In religious law, the single sexual standard reflected the sacramental view of marriage held by the Russian Orthodox Church. "Infidelity is the deadly foe of the marital union—a denial of man's most sacred obligations," declared the archpriest N. Favorov in 1880. "According to the laws of Christianity, the duties of husband and wife are absolutely identical; and identical, too, is their responsibility for transgressing the vow of fidelity."[9]

Nevertheless, the double standard was just as prevalent as elsewhere. Female chastity played a crucial role in maintaining family and community honor, which rested on the opinion of others.[10] Female chastity was particularly important to peasants and townspeople. Single women who violated the norms of sexual propriety might be publicly humiliated. For example, public shaming rituals penalized a peasant woman known to be engaging in sexual intercourse prior to marriage by tarring her gates or baring her torso and parading her through the village. Well into the twentieth century, public display of the bloody sheets, evidence of a bride's virginity, usually followed the wedding night of peasants and townspeople alike. The sexual conduct of married women was scrutinized as well, but communities usually left the punishment of women who conducted themselves improperly to the husband whose honor they had besmirched.[11] Gossip provided an important element in the maintenance of community norms, acting as a kind of backup system for the authority of husbands and fathers. By delivering opinions to correct behavior *before* it became necessary to punish the offender, as well as by penalizing her afterwards, communities ensured that norms of sexual conduct were upheld.[12] The politics of reputation were particularly effective in peasant villages, where no clear boundary separated private from public life, and it was virtually impossible to avoid others' prying eyes.

They worked less well in cities. Urban life increased the opportunities to earn one's own living and broadened the range of temptations, while reducing the ability of communities to discipline errant members. To be sure, the degree to which cities did so

9. Protoierei N. Favorov, "O khristianskoi nravstvennosti," *Trudy Kievskoi dukhovnoi akademii,* no. 1 (1880): 107.

10. See Nancy Shields Kollmann, *By Honor Bound: State and Society in Early Modern Russia* (Ithaca, NY: Cornell University Press, 1999).

11. Christine Worobec, *Peasant Russia: Family and Community in the Post-Emancipation Period* (Princeton, NJ: Princeton University Press, 1991), 139–43, 146–50, 171–72, 201–4; A. N. Zorin et al., *Ocherki gorodskogo byta srednego Povolzh'ia* (Ulianovsk: Izdatel'stvo Srednevolzhskogo nauchnogo tsentra, 2000), 134–35; Iu. M. Goncharov, *Gorodskaia sem'ia Sibiri vtoroi poloviny XIX–nachala XX v.* (Barnaul: Izdatel'stvo Altaiskogo gosudarstvennogo universiteta, 2002), 275.

12. Sandra Cavallo and Simona Cerutti, "Female Honor and the Social Control of Reproduction in Piedmont between 1600 and 1800," in *Sex and Gender in Historical Perspective,* ed. Edward Muir and Guido Ruggiero, trans. Mary M. Galluci (Baltimore: Johns Hopkins University Press, 1990), 87.

varied according to size, level of economic development, and levels of in- and out-migration, among other factors, with the larger and more economically developed cities, Moscow and St. Petersburg, at the forefront. But the loosening of controls over women's (and men's) sexual conduct occurred in smaller cities as well, albeit to a lesser degree. This is evident in illegitimacy rates, which were far higher in cities than in villages in the second half of the nineteenth century. Highest in Moscow and St. Petersburg, even in relatively small and medium-size cities illegitimacy rates might be four to five times those reported in the countryside, where illegitimate births remained under 2 percent of overall fertility according to the census of 1897.[13]

But if efforts to enforce sexual norms proved less effective in urban areas than in peasant villages, and perhaps less urgent because the economic well-being of the community did not rest on them, it does not mean that those norms became less stringent or that people ceased to apply them, especially in towns and cities where women had lived all their lives in settled communities. The letters that Liubov Aleksandrova's mother sent to her wayward daughter, which, as quoted above, refer to the condemnation of "the whole neighborhood," bear eloquent witness to one such effort. The community's condemnation prompted the townswoman Anna Ponomareva to flee her town. Having abandoned her husband, Aleksei, for another man, in 1891 she wrote to her husband begging for the passport that would enable her to leave the naval town of Kronshtadt where she had lived her entire life. "I can't live this way, not able even to show myself on the street or meet people without their pointing their fingers at me." As had Liubov Aleksandrova, Ponomareva claimed to have been "dishonored and shamed" by her husband's allegations of her sexual misconduct—a rhetorical device to be sure, but one based on the assumption that officials would appreciate the dire consequences of such an accusation for a woman's public reputation. To protect her honor against aspersions, another wife, the townswoman Akulina Verigina, proprietor of a small shop in a rural area, in 1898 sued in *volost* court the peasant woman who had declared in the presence of witnesses that Verigina was conducting a liaison with a teacher. Even a relatively large city such as Samara, located along the lower Volga and boasting a population of over ninety thousand at the turn of the twentieth century, might be apprised of the private affairs of its citizens, or so suggests the ringing condemnation of Anastasia Novokreshchenova, a merchant's wife, by the Samara clerical court in 1897. "I know, as does the entire city [of Samara], that the petitioner...abandoned her husband and children and went off somewhere with some officer, with whom she exchanged love

13. See the graphs provided by David Ransel, "Problems in Measuring Illegitimacy in Prerevolutionary Russia," *Journal of Social History* 16, no. 2 (1982): 111–27. See also Barbara Engel, "Peasant Morality and Pre-Marital Sexual Relations in Late Nineteenth-Century Russia," *Journal of Social History* 23, no. 4 (1990): 695–714.

letters."[14] As Iu. M. Goncharov has observed in relation to the citizens of Siberian cities of the late nineteenth century, in cities as in villages "sexual relations remained under the rigid control of public opinion, especially for women."[15]

Even newcomers could not be sure of anonymity, although the opinion of others may have mattered to them considerably less. Privacy remained a rare commodity in Russia's cities. The laboring classes and even the privileged resided in overcrowded apartments, living cheek by jowl with strangers from whom it was hard to conceal one's actions, and for whom the sexual transgressions of others provided grist for the mill of conversation.[16] A railroad worker, for example, spoke with assurance concerning the misconduct of Varvara Dobychina. For several months, he had shared a room with Varvara and her husband, Mikhail, a stove maker, in the port town of Poti in what is now Georgia. In a room divided only by a wooden screen, he had had many opportunities to witness Varvara engaging in misconduct, "drinking vodka by the glass, and fooling around [guliaiushchaia] with young bachelors." He and all the neighbors had observed her improper behavior with the man alleged to be her lover. Evidently having discussed these matters among themselves, they were convinced the allegations against her were correct, he testified. Another case reveals a similar dynamic. Everyone who lived in their apartment house in Nizhnii Novgorod believed that Anna Kuz'minskaia, married to a scribe, was involved in an adulterous affair with Gusev, a boarder in their apartment, because "in the evening Gusev would enter the apartment, and Anna would go off with him by herself." Gossip figured in the Agafonov case as well. A peasant woman who for two years lived in the same apartment in Moscow as the Agafonovs, both townspeople, reported that the couple's marital difficulties began when they moved to a dacha and, as rumor had it, "Agafonov's wife began to drink and conduct herself in a manner inappropriate to a married woman."[17]

Gossip might even follow a woman who had left the village behind. Tatiana Mosgova, who had left her husband's village to work in the Mikhailov Factory in Moscow "showed her worst side when she lived in the village," carrying on with other men, peasants in his village claimed. "She lives the same way now in Moscow, having lovers and in general not leading the life of a proper married woman." The fellow villagers of

14. RGIA, fond 1412, op. 226, d. 98 (Ponomareva, A., 1891), 11; op. 214, d. 46 (Verigina, A., 1900), 5; op. 224, d. 34 (Novokreshchenova, A., 1896), 44. See also *Moskovskie prelesty: stseny u mirovykh sudei, ugolovnye protsessy, ocherki obshchestvennoi zhizni, rasskazy i prochie* (Moscow: T. Ris, 1869), 97–105.

15. Goncharov, *Gorodskaia sem'ia*, 275–76.

16. I take this point from Sarah C. Chambers, *From Subjects to Citizens: Honor, Gender, and Politics in Arequipa, Peru 1780–1854.* (Baltimore: Johns Hopkins University Press, 1999), 109.

17. RGIA, fond 1412, op. 216, d. 36 (Dobychina, V., 1898), 56; op. 221, d. 192 (Kuz'minskaia, A., 1891), 27; op. 212, d. 33 (Agafonova, Z., 1894), 25.

Evdokia Kulikova's husband claimed to know a lot about Evdokia, too, although she had left the village years before and currently lived in St. Petersburg. "She is being kept by someone," one villager assured the investigator. "She has her own apartment, and bore a child who lives with her and for whom she has hired a wet nurse."[18]

Anonymous letters found in dossiers likewise bear witness to the intrusive gaze of others as well as the ubiquitous lack of privacy. For example, in 1899 an anonymous letter deriving from a resident of the alleged lover's apartment house warned the St. Petersburg physician Sergei Preobrazhenskii of his wife's improper conduct: "Mr. doctor, I am very sorry to upset you, but I must write to you so that others don't make fun of you. Your wife abandoned you... for a lover. She visits him practically every day at four. If he hasn't gotten back yet, she waits for him, pacing the corridor outside his door; if he's home, she goes in, they lock the door and remove the key so that everyone will think he's not at home. She leaves at six but everyone in the building knows about their relations," the writer concluded, alluding to the collective judgments characteristic of other testimonies, too.[19] Even those who could afford to live in their own apartments or houses and shut the doors were scarcely safe from others' scrutiny, that of servants in particular. Servants' testimony in separation cases provides evidence of the most intimate knowledge of their employers' lives.

MALE HONOR

A wife's sexual impropriety had public consequences for her husband, as the anonymous author's warning to the physician (so that others don't "make fun" of you) attests. An adulterous wife damaged her husband's honor, providing evidence of his failure to fulfill a key responsibility of manhood: to maintain order in his home. Doubts about a husband's ability to manage his wife harmed his public standing in a variety of ways. Not only might it subject him to malicious gossip, but it might also undermine his ability to obtain respect from his peers and/or deference from his underlings. Although the outraged (and misspelled) letter that Ilia Shibanov, a peasant from Kaluga and proprietor of a painting workshop, addressed to his wife, Natalia, in 1896 came in response to her allegations of his "unnatural" sexual practices rather than to her own sexual transgressions, it so clearly captures the importance of the maintenance of domestic order to a man's public standing that it is worth quoting at some length:

I'm a man, and even I was ashamed of your testimony, and you're a nineteen-year-old woman, and already you know backwards and forwards how women of the street [bul'varnye] behave... and you are the legal wife of a husband... but as it turns out you are fouler and more worthless than all those women who stroll about the

18. Ibid., op. 223, d. 98 (Mosgova, T., 1897), 10; op. 221, d. 204 (Kulikova, E., 1897), 26.
19. Ibid., op. 226, d. 133 (Preobrazhenskaia, E., 1899), 12.

streets, so it must be true that you know how they are used [*ikhnee upotreblenie*] and that must be because you yourself have experience. You call yourself my wife but you've stained my name and reputation, which no one has done before.... You shameless thing!

The fact that investigators had queried his apprentices about the way he treated his wife only intensified Shibanov's sense of outrage: "As I see, you want to stain my reputation," he complained to the investigating officer who had questioned several former apprentices after they had returned to their home villages. "The testimony of residents of Moscow isn't enough; you've begun to turn to provincial cities as well." In another case, so humiliated was Vasilii Vozdvizhinskii, the foreman of a print shop in Ekaterinoslav province, by the behavior of his wife, Elena, that he tried to take his own life. When Elena left for Moscow and refused to come back, the husband "was ashamed to look his friends in the eye.... Then he began to avoid people and finally tried to shoot himself with a revolver, without success," according to one of his workers.[20]

Other examples indicate that the connection between a wife's sexual propriety and her husband's public standing transcended Russia's social divides. Anguish about his lost public honor shaped the plea of the Nizhnii Novgorod merchant Ivan Rukavishnikov, one of the few men to petition the chancellery. His wife's sexual misconduct had become the talk of the town. "I request that you free me and the city from my wife's further residence," he implored officials in 1897, revealing in the process his own inability to ensure her proper behavior. Her removal "will enable me once again to walk without shame in the streets of the city in which I was born, and receive everyone's respect.... For God's sake, help me as one Christian to another." The reputation even of a well-known professional might be vulnerable to such a stain. In 1903, Olga Romanova, a friend, informed the musician and composer Stefan Avvakumov about his wife's unseemly conduct while Stepan was away from Tomsk, Siberia, on business.

Your wife lives, as they say, "in full..." I ran into her strolling about last night, surrounded by the engineers Ivanov [and] Kondakov, the contractor Tumikhin, and Uncle Iakso-Kviatkovskii-Zlotukhin—you know, that well-known Don Juan. He says that Valentina Evgrafovna [the wife] often invites him over for tea. Doctor Kreisman says that she invited him to a celebratory dinner that she's having for her birthday or the birth of her son.... Everyone is talking about her, even at the bazaar.... So she's become the possession of everyone. But they say she can't find anyone to her taste, which is why she's gathered so many admirers.

20. Ibid., op 220, d. 15, (Ilin, M., 1893, filed on behalf of his daughter, Natalia Shibanova), 69, 112; op. 214, d. 71 (Vozdvizhenskaia, E., 1904), 26–27.

It would be preferable if the wayward wife conducted her flirtations "somewhere else and not in Tomsk, where everyone knows you," Rozanova wrote.[21] As one advice book warned, with reason, men might be held accountable for the conduct even of women who no longer lived with them. "A separated husband is responsible for his wife's actions," advised *Marital Satisfactions* in 1882.[22] In 1908, another anonymous letter, addressed to Ivan Lazurkin, a merchant's son and manager of his father's estate in the countryside, blamed Lazurkin for the behavior of his estranged wife, Ekaterina. Ekaterina had left him to live in the town of Iuriev, Kostroma province, in the home of her widowed and well-to-do mother. The letter faulted Lazurkin for his failure to exercise the requisite control: "Why do you leave your wife to live with her mother, when she debauches herself on every side....It's senseless [*netolkovatovo*] to let your wife behave as she does...everyone who wasn't lazy felt her [*shchupali*] all over on New Year's Eve."[23]

The importance of women's sexual propriety to masculine honor and reputation helps explain the public sympathy, or more precisely, male sympathy, for husbands who murdered or attempted to murder wayward wives. Murdering an adulterous wife was "a man's crime, par excellence," in Russia as elsewhere.[24] A man who committed such an act of violence was regarded as not fully responsible for his behavior, acting in an "impaired psychic state," rather like a woman who murdered an illegitimate infant, although the man supposedly acted from outraged honor rather than shame.[25] Thus the protagonist of Leo Tolstoy's "The Kreutzer Sonata" is free to tell the story of how he came to murder his wife, having been acquitted of his crime. "At the trial it was decided that I was a wronged husband and that I had killed her while defending my outraged honor (that is the phrase they employ, you know).'"[26] Such decisions in

21. Ibid., op. 227, d. 54 (Suprugi Rukavishnikovykh, 1889), 97; op. 212, d. 4 (Avvakumova, V., 1904), 34–35.

22. *Brachnye udovol'stvie. Prakticheskie vrachebnye i ne vrachebnye nastavleniia vstupivshim v brak* (Moscow: F. Ioganson, 1882), 77. Men sometimes explained their unwillingness to approve a wife's passport in precisely these terms.

23. RGIA, op., 222, d. 12 (Lazurkina, 1908), 10. See also op. 225, d. 21 (Ostrovidova, V., 1897), 63. Anonymous letters denouncing women's sexual conduct were by no means a uniquely Russian phenomenon. Frenchwomen were similarly denounced during World War I—but to the authorities, not their husbands. See Jean-Yves Le Naour, *Misères et tourments de la chair durant la Grande Guerre: les moueurs sexuelles des Français 1914–1918* (Paris: Aubier, 2002), 232. My thanks to Martha Hanna for this reference.

24. Martin Wiener, *Men of Blood: Violence, Manliness, and Criminal Justice in Victorian England* (Cambridge: Cambridge University Press, 2004), 201.

25. See the discussion in Engelstein, *Keys to Happiness*, 108–14.

26. Leo Tolstoy, "The Kreutzer Sonata," in *Great Short Works of Leo Tolstoy*, trans. Louise and Aylmer Maude (New York: Harper and Row, 1967), 398.

favor of wife murderers were commonplace, especially when members of the laboring classes were involved. If a man's reputation was otherwise untarnished and his wife was believed to have misbehaved sexually, juries either acquitted or gave light sentences to a defendant who murdered his wife, while punishing harshly the wife who murdered her husband. "How cheap women's lives are in the eyes of jurors," observed Mikhail Ratov in 1899, commenting on such decisions.[27]

The link between women's sexual propriety and men's masculine honor made women's sexual impropriety the most common rhetorical device in men's counternarratives. In an appeal to a presumptively shared masculine culture that transcended social divisions, almost all such men accused petitioning wives of engaging in sexual misconduct before marriage, after marriage, or both, and many referred to the stain on masculine honor to which such behavior led. "Your Excellency! Perhaps you too are a husband and father as I am," wrote the former teacher Sergei Stefanovskii in 1896 in an unusually explicit example of such an appeal. "You will understand my suffering, suffering not so much for myself, but for the children and for their peace and good name!...My wife has soiled my family hearth...lives now like a prostitute, kept by a man....Will her slander of me succeed?" he rhetorically inquired.[28] Sometimes, men's allegations of womanly impropriety were clearly just instrumental, an effort to challenge the integrity of their wives in the eyes of others, officials in particular, and to undermine the women's case. But often claims about wifely impropriety also reflected genuine anxieties about female insubordination, as well as the risk posed by a child born of her illicit relationship to the inheritance rights of legitimate heirs.[29]

Female sexual impropriety tested the limits of conjugal authority as nothing else did.[30] Although there is no evidence to suggest that the suffering engendered in women by a husband's sexual betrayal was any less acute than that endured by betrayed husbands, the double standard, buttressed by men's superior economic position, is evident in the grounds women gave for seeking separation. While it was a rare husband who

27. M. Ratov, *Zhenshchina pered sudom prisiazhnykh (Mysli i fakty)* (Moscow: A. I. Mamontov, 1899), 33. See, for example, *Sudebnaia gazeta*, no. 30 (1892): 10; *Novosti dnia i birzhevaia gazeta*, no. 254 (1894) and no. 106 (1895), as well as the accounts in Ratov. Despite Ratov and others' castigation of peasant jurors for being inordinately forgiving of murderous husbands, the peasants' decisions differed little from those offered by British jurors just a few decades earlier, in similar cases (Wiener, *Men of Blood*, 202, 204, 205, 218).

28. RGIA, fond 1412, op. 228, d. 106 (Stefanovskaia, S., 1895), 50.

29. Konstantin Kuz'min, for one, expressed understandable concern about the "property rights of my legitimate heirs," when his wife left him and took up with another man. Ibid., op. 221, d. 195 (Kuz'mina, A., 1906), 60.

30. Robert L. Griswold, *Family and Divorce in California, 1850–1890: Victorian Illusions and Everyday Realities* (Albany: State University of New York Press, 1982), 74.

refrained from accusing his petitioning wife of adultery, men's adultery, in the absence of other transgressions, played very little role in the plaints of petitioning wives.

The double standard is also evident in the comparatively public way in which many married men conducted their sexual liaisons, evidently from a feeling of impunity rarely to be seen in wives. By contrast with women, indeed, some men appeared to flaunt their sexual misconduct. The physician Ilia Popov, parading his familiarity with the most recent scientific findings concerning the necessity of sexual activity for human health, actually had the audacity to blame his wife for his liaisons with other women. This was an accusation that, as marginal notes attest, failed entirely to impress the officials to whom it was addressed: "Eight years ago, after the birth of our last daughter, my wife announced to me that she would no longer live as a wife with me, because I hate her, and she can 'always find herself someone better, for example, doctor Rozov,'" a physician with whom he alleged his wife to be involved.

> Knowing as a physician that complete abstinence from women is as harmful for the organism as extreme abuse, I nevertheless lived for four to five years a fully ascetic mode of life [an official underlined this last clause in pencil, and wrote "!?" in the margin] and in that time didn't betray my wife. But in 1898, in connection with my work, I got to know a patient, a former seamstress, and in fact secretly became engaged in debauchery…about this I honestly told my wife.[31]

While Popov's arrogance was unique, his behavior was not. Like Tolstoy's fictional Stiva Oblonsky, the "handsome amorous" thirty-four-year old husband of a wife already faded by childbearing and housekeeping, some men felt entitled to such adventures and repented only when caught.[32] Although men enjoyed far more opportunities than women to elude the prying eyes of others while working away from home or traveling elsewhere on business, a significant minority of adulterous husbands never even tried to conceal their behavior, taking up with their servants, wards, workers, governesses, and other women close to hand, and sometimes flaunting those liaisons in the face of their aggrieved spouses.[33]

The foregoing discussion has emphasized the pervasiveness of the double standard and the intensive scrutiny of others, especially scrutiny of women, to which the documents in chancellery dossiers abundantly attest. Nevertheless it is also important to note that from the first, by no means everyone in a position to give testimony was ready

---

31. RGIA, fond 1412, op. 226, d. 111 (Popova, S., 1901), 27.

32. Leo Tolstoy, *Anna Karenina. The Maude Translation. Background and Sources. Essays in Criticism*, ed. George Gibian (New York: W. W. Norton, 1970), 2–3.

33. See, for example, RGIA, fond 1412, op. 213, d. 84 (Bol'shikh, M., 1886); op. 221, d. 213 (Kuprianova, V., 1901); op. 221, d. 9 (Kurushina, F., 1902), among others.

to corroborate allegations of women's misbehavior or to point an accusatory finger, even in cases where the evidence strongly suggested that the alleged sexual transgression had occurred. For example, the governor of the city of Novgorod, alone among the respondents, concluded that the responsibility for the Aleksandrovs' marital difficulties belonged exclusively to Platon, not to Liubov. Calling their marriage an "unequal union," alluding to Liubov's attractiveness and implying the jealousy of Platon, more than twice as old as his young wife, the governor's report to the chancellery completely omitted mention of sexual improprieties on her part.[34] Caution about besmirching a woman's sexual reputation might be displayed even by the ubiquitous *dvornik,* usually a peasant in origin, who was posted at the gates of apartment buildings in big cities and charged with registering everyone who entered and left. Sexual misconduct was difficult to conceal from him. As students of Russian radical movements know, the *dvornik* operated as the lowest rung in Russia's police hierarchy. Enjoined to carry out the commands of the police and to "watch everyone who enters and leaves their building and if a stranger appears, to find out whom they are visiting and why," *dvorniki* were required to bear witness to the conduct of their tenants whenever the police requested it.[35] The testimony of the St. Petersburg *dvornik* who detailed the conduct of Aleksandra Andreeva, wife of an artisan whom numerous witnesses reported to be involved in an extramarital liaison, to take one of dozens of possible examples, demonstrates both his close knowledge of her behavior and his unwillingness to allege misconduct of which he had his doubts. Queried by officials, he reported in 1891 that Andreeva was a senior embroiderer at a store on Nevskii Prospekt, for which she left every morning at 9 a.m., returning around 8 p.m. "Nothing bad is said about her," he reported. "No men visit her and she doesn't walk out with men."[36] Chancellery officials tended to place enormous weight on the testimony of *dvorniki,* making their account often decisive in a case, as it proved to be in the case of Andreeva.

The reasons for this reluctance to point an accusatory finger surely depended on the individual witness. Some refrained from discussing sexual improprieties because they believed that someone else's conduct was nobody's business but their own; others because they depended on or liked the woman involved and/or had nothing to gain by denouncing her behavior (hints of bribery in exchange for testimony occasionally surface in dossiers); still others because they were uncertain about the truth of allegations

34. Ibid., op. 212, d. 103 (Aleksandrova), 22. Or, to take another case: "Yes, there were rumors that Kuz'minskaia was Gusev's lover, but I myself can say nothing definite about it," declared the landlady of the apartment in which the couple and the alleged lover had lived for three months (ibid., op. 221, d. 193 [Kuz'minskaia], 28).

35. *Instruktsiia dlia dezhurnykh dvornikov* (St. Petersburg: Tip. Sanktpeterburgskogo gradonachal'nika, 1901).

36. RGIA, fond 1412, op. 212, d. 183 (Andreeva, A., 1890), 54.

and refused to say what they did not believe, or, as appears likely in the case of the governor of Novgorod, did not regard such allegations as of primary importance. But in many cases, the unwillingness of witnesses to voice an opinion one way or the other seems to be more than a reluctance to besmirch a woman's sexual reputation, given the seriousness of a charge of sexual misconduct; it also reflected the respondent's conviction that a person's sexual behavior might be a private, not a public, matter. Although there is no evidence that the view of sexual conduct as a private matter became predominant, it either became more prevalent toward the turn of the century, or people became more disposed to express it in words rather than by silence—or, most likely, both. This development was the product both of far-reaching social and economic changes that fostered women's mobility and of cultural trends that undermined longstanding notions of sexual propriety.

DIVORCE: A DIGRESSION

But what about divorce? The reader may recall that adultery was one of the few grounds on which a divorce might be obtained, albeit only with considerable difficulty and expense that included not only the nominal fees but also the hiring of lawyers and, in many cases, the bribing of witnesses.[37] Separations were much cheaper, the expense of investigations being born by the chancellery, and women often found them easier to obtain because the grounds were so much broader than for divorce and included ill-treatment, failure to support the family, and the like.[38] Still, divorce does figure in a significant minority of separation cases. Sometimes, separation appeals served as a kind of way station to divorce, a stage in the bargaining process between husbands and wives. At least as often, separation suits reveal either failed or abortive efforts to dissolve the marriage. These divorces manqué are particularly interesting, illuminating as some do the complex negotiations that might lurk beneath the smooth façade of a successfully crafted divorce suit; they also show how gender expectations might influence the outcome of a couple's negotiations.

37. One historian estimates the costs in thousands of rubles, inflated by market forces and growing demand for a quick outcome. See V. A. Veremenko, *Dvorianskaia sem'ia i gosudarstvennaia politika Rossii: vtoraia polovina XIX–nachala XX v.* (St. Petersburg: Evropeiskii dom, 2007), 356–57, 371–73. On the cost, see also G. Trokhina, "'Pikantnye situatsii': Nekotorye razmyshleniia o razvode v Rossii v kontsa XIX v.," in *Sem'ia v rakurse sotsial'nogo znaniia. Sbornik nauchnikh statei*, ed. Iu. M. Goncharov (Barnaul: Azbuka, 2001).

38. Women of the laboring classes who sought divorces, unaware of the legal grounds, often included in their pleas allegations of cruelty, etc., very similar to those discussed in preceding chapters, but in the case of divorce, to no avail. See Gregory L. Freeze, "Profane Narratives about a Holy Sacrament: Marriage and Divorce in Late Imperial Russia," in *Sacred Stories: Religion and Spirituality in Modern Russia*, ed. Mark D. Steinberg and Heather J. Coleman (Bloomington: Indiana University Press, 2007), 146–78.

The number of applications for divorce on the grounds of adultery increased steadily in the final decades of the nineteenth century and even more rapidly in the early twentieth, and members of the laboring classes constituted a substantial minority of applicants.[39] Obtaining a divorce was most straightforward if both parties agreed to it and had the wherewithal sufficient to hire a lawyer to steer them through the process and bribe at least two witnesses to testify that they had seen the "guilty" party having sex with someone other than the spouse. The lawyer whom the fictional Alexei Karenin consulted in the mid-1870s held out little hope of obtaining a divorce without the collusion of both spouses. Divorce on the basis of adultery, he informed his client, might be achieved in two ways: "adultery of husband or wife and the detection of the guilty party by mutual consent, or involuntary detection without such consent," adding that "the latter case [i.e., divorce without collusion] is seldom met with in practice."[40] But one of the parties almost inevitably paid a heavy price for colluding. Until 1904, the "guilty" party was condemned to seven years of penance and deprivation of the right to remarry; thereafter the guilty party could remarry only after seven years, which might be reduced to two on the petition of the party's spiritual adviser. The guilty party would also lose her children if custody were disputed; courts invariably granted custody to the "innocent" party, except in cases where the chancellery intervened.[41] Thus collusion might come at a hefty personal cost for the party held to be guilty.

For women, guilt in a divorce suit brought an additional burden, damage to the sexual reputation on which their social standing rested. In a short story published in 1879, the writer Kapitolina Nazar'eva depicted the price paid by the "guilty" woman. Her heroine, utterly miserable in her marriage, was prepared to do anything to escape it and so assumed full responsibility for obtaining a divorce except for the cost of three thousand rubles, which her husband paid. Forced to bribe church officials as well as witnesses, and to confess before the court an illicit sexual act that never occurred, the

39. Ibid., 146, 149. See also William G. Wagner, *Marriage, Property, and the Law in Late Imperial Russia* (Oxford: Clarendon, 1994), 99.

40. Tolstoy, *Anna Karenina*, 335. "Divorce *was* easy only if both partners desired it, for they could easily collude, manufacture the requisite evidence, and arrange a prompt dissolution of their union." See Gregory L. Freeze, "*Krylov vs. Krylova:* 'Sexual Incapacity' and Divorce in Tsarist Russia," in *The Human Tradition in Modern Russia*, ed. William B. Husband (Wilmington, DE: Scholarly Resources, 2000), 8; and Freeze, "Profane Narratives," 154–55.

41. On the "high price," see, for example, V. N. Kulik, "Zhenshchiny dinastii Riabushinskikh," in *Rod i sem'ia v kontekste Tverskoi istorii* (Tver: Tverskoi gosudarstvennyi universitet, 2005), 184. Of course, colluding couples could settle such matters between themselves, as did, for example, the physician Sergei Plaksin and his adulterous wife, Anna, whose 1890 divorce on the grounds of his infidelity rather than hers was clearly the product of collusion and involved her written promise to surrender custody of the children. But whether such agreements were enforceable in courts of law remains a question. See RGIA, fond 1412, op. 226, d. 61 (Plaksina, A., 1890), 3.

heroine became thereafter a "debauched woman" in the eyes of other residents of her large provincial town.[42] Although the stigma attached to "guilty" women declined over time among the social and intellectual elites of major towns and cities, as divorce grew increasingly common, it remained a powerful deterrent for others, especially among those whose Orthodox faith was strong.[43]

This prompted a few men to acts of considerable gallantry. The greater burden of shame that women bore and the "ruination" that they faced—their reputation tainted, their husband's economic support and protection lost—sometimes prompted even a betrayed husband to sacrifice his own interests not only to rid himself of a spouse in name only but also, very likely, to safeguard the reputation and ensure the future of his wife for one last time. Needless to say, such actions cast considerable doubt on the veracity of their wives' allegations to the chancellery against them. "I bear witness that Mr. Lazurkin slandered himself by assuming the guilt in this affair, behaved with the utmost decency, and having agreed to divorce, told me directly that the hardest thing for him was that he couldn't marry again for seven more years," a gendarme commented in 1911, for example.[44]

Not surprisingly, however, given the nature of my sources, when divorce figures in separation cases, most often it is to showcase men at their worst, not their best. While the following examples may not be typical, they make it clear that the difficulties associated with divorce made it rife for abuses of power. Husbands (or wives, for that matter) could stymie a partner willing to assume guilt by bringing a case in civil rather than religious court, for example, which precluded divorce but subjected the guilty woman to public shame. This is how Nikolai Semenov, a townsman and representative for the Maltsev commercial empire, revenged himself on his adulterous wife, Lidia. In 1906, she sent a letter to her estranged husband, imploring him to change his mind, evidently to no avail:

> I decided to write to you personally, and to make a great request. Knowing you as a kind person, I appeal to your heart, Nikolai Alekseevich, for the sake of those happy moments that perhaps I gave you during the six years of our family life. And we did have happy moments—you can't deny that. We haven't always been such bitter enemies.... I can't return to you, to endure again the hell [*ad*] that arose in our life together, especially toward the end.... Don't take your revenge on me, don't do me evil, that won't do you one bit of good. Give me my freedom, since we can no longer

42. K. Nikulina (Kapitolina Nazar'eva), "Spetsialist: Stranitsa iz zhenskoi zhizni," *Vestnik Evropy*, no. 1 (1879): 63–95.

43. On growing tolerance, see Veremenko, *Dvorianskaia sem'ia*, 367, 372–73.

44. RGIA, fond 1412, op. 222, d. 12 (Lazurkina), 58. For another husband who assumed the guilt in place of his adulterous wife, see op. 226, d. 61 (Plaksina).

live together, give me a divorce, don't take this case to court and to shameful publicity, it won't make you any happier. Why should you cause me extra trouble, extra expenses—there is already a lot of grief and tears in this world. For the last time, I ask you not to oppose a divorce, and return my freedom to me.[45]

Other husbands exacted a heavy price for assuming the burden of divorce, or used their authority to force their wives to assume it.[46] If a wife wanted her freedom so badly, let her pay for it, some husbands clearly believed. Men's ability to withhold the passport their wives required to live apart and/or earn their own living, or to command their wives' presence, gave them considerable leverage over wives desperate to live a life of their own. The well-known comic actor I. I. Monakhov, for example, had long ago abandoned his wife, Anastasia, also an actress, to live with another woman. Until she agreed to assume the guilt in a divorce suit, however, Monakhov refused to approve a separate passport for her. The well-born engineer Iurii Azancheev likewise demanded that his innocent wife, Sofia, become the guilty party in a divorce suit, although there was considerable evidence to indicate that he, not she, had been involved in an adulterous liaison (and with the prolific author of marital advice Nadezhda Lukhmanova, of all people!). If she refused to accept the guilt, he threatened to require her to live with him and then to make her life unbearable. He held the authority to do this because, as he expressed it in a letter to her, "the man is the head of the household and can create for a wife whatever kind of home life he pleases."[47]

Such behavior, while high-handed, is also understandable. For men, divorce, especially divorce with the wife as the "guilty" party, was far preferable to a wife living on a separate passport. Unable to remarry but bereft of the various domestic services that their wives normally provided, men sought to use such leverage as they had to obtain a more favorable outcome. The former Ufa teacher Ilia Korchuganov declared: "I can't consent to give [my wife] a passport and destroy entirely my family life and leave myself in a very difficult and undefined position. But I have nothing against her instituting a suit for divorce, taking the guilt on herself, and in that way resolving the matter." Declining to approve his wife's passport, the townsman and former shop clerk Sergei Petrov said much the same in 1905: "If my wife doesn't want to live with me, let her get a divorce so I can remarry," he asserted. In 1909, the accountant Dmitrii Zverev likewise refused his wife's request for her documents: "If she wants her freedom so badly let her

45. RGIA, fond 1412, op. 228, d. 35 (Semenova, L., 1906), 25. Four years later, the couple remained married.

46. For examples, see ibid., op. 228, d. 39 (Sergeeva, S., 1892), 28; op. 227, d. 6 (Razaeva, 1909), 87; op. 212, d. 74 (Alad'ina, T., 1894), 13.

47. Ibid., op. 223, d. 107 (Monakhova, A., 1911), 8; op. 212, d. 51 (Azancheeva, S., 1900), 10.

give me the right to sue for divorce—then she'll get complete freedom," he declared.[48] Until a wife could obtain her own passport simply by requesting it, men held an advantage in negotiations over divorce suits.

NEW TEMPTATIONS, NEW POSSIBILITIES

Although the double standard in judging women's extramarital sexual conduct remained in force through the early twentieth century, the economic, social, and cultural developments of the second half of the nineteenth century brought a change in sexual behavior. Industrialization and urbanization, which drew tens of thousands of women as well as men away from their home and family, reduced spousal and community control over the sexual conduct of unprecedented numbers of people. The growth of primary education brought many more people, young people especially, into contact with print culture, while girls' high schools (*gimnazii*) and institutions of higher education for women, one of the achievements of the early women's movement, broadened women's horizons and introduced them to new ideas. Urban life, with its expanding civic culture and opportunities for entertainment, offered married women of the middling classes far broader opportunities than their mothers had enjoyed for social contacts outside the home. Married women participated in voluntary societies, took cures at spas (where Anton Chekhov's married "Lady with the Pet Dog" [1899] fell in love with another man), attended balls, the theater, restaurants, and other public entertainments, even held jobs of their own. The growing significance of money and what money could buy raised the social profile of the middling classes and challenged hierarchies based on birth and ascribed social status, while reducing although by no means eliminating the importance of sexual honor to their maintenance.[49] Although it would be a mistake to exaggerate the degree of personal freedom enjoyed by married or single women or the extent to which public scrutiny of women's behavior had eased, the changes were nevertheless real and paralleled developments elsewhere in the industrializing world.

The new consumer culture both reflected and amplified these changes. The final decades of the nineteenth century witnessed a mass culture that celebrated sexuality or, more precisely, heterosexuality to an unprecedented degree and in a wide range of media. Urban mass entertainments portrayed love that was passionate and romantic, and explored questions of individual choice and sexual freedom "with an exuberance

48. Ibid., op. 221, d. 118 (Korchuganova, M., 1895), 77; op. 226, d. 42 (Petrova, A., 1905), 17; op. 219, d. 37, (Zvereva, V., 1911), 26.

49. On the changes, see Barbara Alpern Engel, *Women in Russia, 1700–2000* (New York: Cambridge University Press, 2004), chaps. 5–6. On the relationship of women's sexual propriety to the emergent middle class after 1905, see Roshanna Sylvester, "Cultural Transgressions, Bourgeois Fears: Violent Crime in Odessa's Central Entertainment District," *Jahrbücher für Geschichte Osteuropas* 44, 4 (1996): 503–22.

that was historically unprecedented," in the words of S. A. Smith.[50] The increasing emphasis on the self and its pleasures encouraged the modern idea that romantic love was something immensely valuable, so essential a component of what made life worth living that it overshadowed all else, including duty to others, even one's spouse. Such a view was articulated privately in letters that a few wives addressed to the husbands they had abandoned.[51] In 1891, after five "peaceful" years in an arranged marriage, having decided to run off with her lover, Anna Ponomareva referred to love in that all-encompassing, romantic sense in a letter she addressed to her husband, a scribe employed by a private firm in Kronshtadt. "Had I not met a man who loved me I would have lived with you forever," she wrote.

> But what is to be done when my fate is such that I could not marry the man whom I wanted to marry, because evil people prevented it. Now fate has brought the two of us together again and we cannot live without one another. Forgive me for offending you in this way.... It's better for you to repudiate me, because we cannot be happy together.... I didn't want to do it but couldn't do anything with myself.... A person cannot live without love; that's the main thing for a person.[52]

Sofia Zakharova—the daughter of an impoverished aristocrat (she was born Baroness Girt) and a graduate of the Bestuzhev courses who had married a man of her choice, a physician, in 1894—declared in the tradition of the 1860s that love required a meeting of minds as well as bodies. In her rendering, unlike Ponomareva's, and befitting perhaps her higher education and quasi-professional status (she was employed as a researcher at an astronomical observatory), romantic feelings are tempered by reason:

> You must believe me when I say to you that I'm in love with someone else.... I don't know what will come of this love, but in any case I ask you to believe that even if it hadn't happened, I would nevertheless have left you. This love happened after I had decided to leave you, and on a purely ideological [ideinyi] basis, only because this

50. S. A. Smith, "Masculinity in Transition," in *Russian Masculinities in History and Culture*, ed. Barbara Evans Clements, Rebecca Friedman, and Dan Healey (Houndsmill, UK: Palgrave, 2002), 105.

51. I borrow this language from Charles Taylor, *Sources of the Self: The Making of Modern Identity* (Cambridge, MA: Harvard University Press, 1989), 292. In her diary entries for 1895, Elizaveta D'iakonova, the cloistered daughter of a provincial merchant family, describes a heated debate with a family friend about the rights bestowed by "love," in which she emerges as a fierce proponent of duty. These issues were clearly on people's minds. See Elizaveta D'iakonova, *Dnevnik russkoi zhenshchiny* (1912, repr., Moscow: Zakharov, 2004), 129–31.

52. RGIA, fond 1412, op. 226, d. 98 (Ponomareva), 10–11.

man embodies my ideas and helps me to realize them in life. If I join my life to his, our lives will proceed along the same lines. I'll not return to you.

Taking with her the third volume of Karl Marx's *Capital* and some clothing, Zakharova moved in with her lover, Vladimir Obukh, a Social Democrat since 1892 who had already suffered banishment from St. Petersburg and had a pregnant wife and a child.[53]

In this period, too, female sensuality was paraded on the stages of dance halls and the popular *café-chantants,* where brazen women singers might trill, "Come up, come up, and sweep my chimney." Despite censorship that forbade them, pornographic postcards that graphically depicted a range of sexual postures appear to have been easily available, at least in major cities. *Chastushki,* the couplets that were popular among the laboring classes in both cities and villages, were sometimes frankly erotic in their content and referred to the adulterous desires of the married as well as the marriageable. In the early twentieth century, folklorists recording tales in northern Russia heard many more tales about wives who betrayed their husbands sexually than about wives who were faithful and true.[54]

Popular ideas had their counterpart in scientific and elite discourse. Toward the end of the century, scientific writings came increasingly to emphasize the physiological aspects of sexuality and the necessity of sexual activity for "full womanhood." Reflecting the broader shift in popular attitudes, the tenor of the published debates over Tolstoy's "Kreutzer Sonata" began to shift around the mid-1890s away from the previous emphasis on continence and repression toward the rehabilitation of the flesh and its pleasures. The novella itself contributed to the change, according to Peter Ulf Møller, "For many people, this delicate subject, which had hitherto languished in silence, became a theme for discussion by virtue of Tolstoy's authority." Seeing the subject of sexuality mentioned so directly, readers of the "Kreutzer Sonata," female as well as male, experienced a kind of "liberation" and felt free to speak of sex themselves.[55]

These cultural changes, which offered the means to conceive of and speak about sex in new and less judgmental ways, coexisted with more restrictive views of sexuality.

53. Ibid., op. 219, d. 33 (Zakharova, S., 1898), 12, 15. On Obukh, see *The Modern Encyclopedia of Russian and Soviet History* (Gulf Breeze, FL: Academic International Press, 1976-).

54. Catriona Kelly, *A History of Russian Women's Writing, 1820–1992* (New York: Oxford University Press, 1994), 132. For pornographic postcards, see RGIA fond 1412, op. 213, d. 95 (Boiarina, A., 1893), 1–2; and op. 228, d. 35 (Semenova), 27. On censorship and its shortcomings, see Paul W. Goldschmidt, "Article 242: Past, Present, and Future," in *Eros and Pornography in Russian Culture,* ed. Marcus C. Levitt and Andrei L. Toporkov (Moscow: Ladomir, 1999), 469, 504. For the *chastushki,* see A. V. Kulagina, "Russkaia eroticheskaia chastushka," ibid., 94–120. For the folk tales, see N. E. Onchukova, ed., *Severnye skazki,* 2 vols. (1908; repr., St. Petersburg: Tropa Troianova, 1998), 1: 44–45.

55. Peter Ulf Møller, *Postlude to the "Kreutzer Sonata." Tolstoj and the Debate on Sexual Morality in Russian Literature in the 1890s,* trans. John Kendal (Leiden, Brill, 1988), xii, xiv, 117.

Although the domination that the Russian Orthodox Church had once exercised over sexual discourse had long since ended, its influence could still be discerned. In consequence, for all the discussion of sexuality and its pleasures, writers, even those on the left, including most socialists, continued into the early twentieth century to articulate "doctrines of sexual continence" that emphasized the importance of control, not indulgence. In the aftermath of the revolution of 1905, such views gained new authority from scientific and quasi-scientific writings that stressed the necessity of sexual restraint and self-mastery for men and women alike, now in the service of sexual hygiene and individual self-command rather than spiritual salvation.[56] Still, a more relaxed view of sexual conduct is evident in my sources. Although they cannot yield a comprehensive picture, the appeals of wives, the testimonies of witnesses and investigators, even the reports of chancellery officials suggest how individuals from a variety of social backgrounds might have come to think about women's sexuality, including extramarital sexuality, differently as a result of new cultural developments.

THE RIGHT TO LOVE?

"In 1885, I was married off at the age of fifteen and a half by my father... and have borne three children," began the petition of Anastasia Novokreshchenova, submitted to the chancellery in December 1896, not long after she left her husband to go off with another man. Her petition, designed to explain what had led her to take such a drastic step, was written in her own hand. In it, Novokreshchenova portrayed her marriage as a struggle for her very selfhood. Raised in a traditional merchant household in the provincial city of Samara, she was married to the twenty-one-year-old Petr Novokreshchenov, a merchant like her father and a man whom she barely knew. Their characters, she quickly learned, were "entirely opposite." Crude and violent, with a propensity to drink, he repeatedly pressured the household help for sexual favors. Six years earlier, during one of his frequent visits to brothels, he had contracted a venereal disease that he then transmitted to his wife.[57]

But it was the incompatibility of their habits and tastes and their conflicts, "often over trifles," on which Anastasia's petition and subsequent narrative dwelled. Petr emerges from his wife's accounts as a merchant of the old school, hostile to the education and cultural interests that increasingly attracted a sector of his estate, his wife included. The result was clashes over a range of matters. Whether Anastasia could engage in the pleasure of reading, so conducive to the development of an inner life, potentially so threatening to others, provided one source of conflict.[58] Anastasia described

56. Kelly, *History of Russian Women's Writing*, 127; Engelstein, *Keys to Happiness*, 221–25.

57. RGIA, fond 1412, op. 224, d. 34 (Novokreshchenova), 1.

58. The fears that female reading elicited in France are treated in Martine Lyons, *Readers and Society in Nineteenth-Century France: Workers, Women, Peasants* (New York: Palgrave, 2001). Some

in detail the subterfuge she would employ to indulge her taste for books: picking up a book and some handiwork, in her husband's presence she would work, but when he left the room, she would set aside the handiwork to read. "If he caught me reading, he'd either put out the candle or tear the book from my hands and make cruel and insulting comments." Their arguments grew more frequent as the years passed and his drinking increased; sometimes, they culminated in angry and violent scenes. Her own family offered neither sympathy nor support. These unhappy circumstances forced Anastasia to depend on her own resources and to develop an interior world at odds with the life she lived: "I turned inward and completely separated my inner and spiritual world from my husband and family, since not one of them was able to sympathize with me or share my oppressed moral state."[59]

The companionship that Petr could not provide and the understanding denied by her merchant father and siblings Anastasia described finding in a different milieu, which was also, and not incidentally, the milieu where she first encountered her lover. Three years before she petitioned, she met and was drawn to a Mrs. Smosh, the teacher of her brother-in-law's children. At the Smosh home, she made the acquaintance of other people whose views and convictions fully coincided with hers. Validating her own view of things, her new acquaintances provided a kind of moral support. Their ideas, "completely opposite to those of the milieu in which I had always lived, were so similar to mine that the time I spent with them offered me enormous moral relief," she wrote in her self-explanation. These people soon became another source of conflict. Irritated and perhaps jealous of the conversations she struck up with members of the circle when the couple encountered them on the street or at the theater, Petr picked quarrels with his wife when the two returned home and finally forbade her to continue her visits to the Smosh home. At some point, Anastasia began a secret correspondence with one of her new friends, a Captain Bodzenko-Beliatskii, an army officer. One evening when she was visiting her sister, Petr broke into Anastasia's trunk, read her diary and the captain's letters, evidently love letters, and on her return demanded an explanation. At that point, Anastasia had had enough. "I told my husband that I was leaving him and the children," she acknowledged in her petition. On November 14 she walked out, removing her jewelry and valuables and handing them over to her husband. "Blessing the children, I left Samara with Captain Bodzenko-Beliatskii, taking none of my things and no money with me," she wrote.[60]

It was by no means unusual for a petitioner to acknowledge an extramarital liaison, if not in her petition than in testimony to police or other officials. To one or another

---

linked solitary sex and reading. See Thomas Laqueur, *Solitary Sex: A Cultural History of Masturbation* (New York: Zone Books, 2003).

59. RGIA, fond 1412, op. 224, d. 34 (Novokreshchenova), 25–26.

60. Ibid., 27–28.

representative of authority, petitioner after petitioner "announced that…she was in an illicit connection," "acknowledged betraying" her vow of fidelity, "testified that they had begun an illicit connection," and so forth, according to the chancellery's terse and unrevealing summary rendition of their words.[61] The women's readiness to acknowledge their transgression is surely related to the habit of confession and bears signs of its influence, including acceptance of guilt and the probability of penance. Representatives of the state—be they gendarmes, policemen, or officials—were agents of the tsar, God's anointed on earth, and presumably shared God's capacity (and right) to know and see everything.[62] Thus, to take one example, Anna Andreeva acknowledged to chancellery officials in 1896 that after having left her peasant husband and supported herself and her daughter for over a decade doing laundry, she had become sexually involved with another man just as her husband alleged. One day her husband's bachelor friend, whose laundry she had washed for six years, forced her to have sex with him [ona vynuzhdena byla voiti s nim v sviaz]. The sexual relationship, sustained by her presumably voluntary weekly visits to him, had ceased after two months, Andreeva reported, then said no more.[63]

Around the mid-1890s, however, the language of some petitioners underwent a subtle but perceptible change. Some of them, and Novokreshchenova is clearly one, began to present petitions and narratives that bore none of the marks of confession. Instead, even as they spoke of their extramarital liaison, the women implicitly or even explicitly denied its transgressive character by explaining their sexual behavior in terms of their own subjectivity. Indeed, a handful of women had become so convinced of their right to emotional fulfillment that they even declared it in their petitions. Vera Lazutina, a merchant's wife, wrote in her petition of 1898: "I have the right to exist, the right to love and to raise my son." Lidia Alekseeva, after describing her husband's crude treatment and the dashing of her hopes for marital happiness, acknowledged in 1905: "What I wanted to find in my husband I found in another man, who understood at once that while I was married, essentially I was alone. His constant attention, warm sympathy, and support in difficult moments had their effect. I became intimate [soshlas'] with him."[64] In representing themselves in this fashion, petitioners resembled the female divorce applicants whom Gregory Freeze has studied, who insisted on the

---

61. Ibid., op. 250, d. 103, 24, 47, 92 ob.; d. 104, 17; op. 212, d. 125 (Alekseeva, 1882), 44–45.

62. This confessional element may also have influenced the readiness of a surprising number of women petitioners to detail intimate sexual behavior between themselves and their husbands. On confession, see Nadieszda Kizenko, "Written Confessions and the Construction of Sacred Narrative," in Sacred Stories, ed. Steinberg and Coleman, 93–118.

63. Ibid., op. 212, d. 199 (Andreeva, A., 1886), 22, 26.

64. Ibid., op. 222, d. 13 (Lazutina, 1898), 1; op. 212, d. 117 (Alekseeva, L., 1905), 7.

importance of affection in marriage or, more radically, asserted the sacrality of love.[65] Imagining a reader who would understand and be moved by the power of such appeals, petitioners to the chancellery, at least, may also have helped bring such readers into being.

VALUES IN FLUX

The testimonies of spouses, witnesses, and investigators strongly suggest that toward the turn of the century, benchmarks for evaluating women's "improper" conduct had begun to shift, for some people at least. The increasing visibility of women in public space, the attention devoted to unhappy marriages on stage and in fiction, and the unprecedented exploration of sexuality in a range of public venues combined to erode many of the guidelines according to which earlier generations had separated right from wrong. As a result, the criteria for judging women's sexual behavior grew notably less stringent. Concern with public decorum lessened while people became more likely to regard sexual behavior as a private rather than public matter. To be sure, a woman's sexual misconduct might still offend or stain her husband's reputation. But it no longer represented a real threat to society. The change was reflected in the way that people used the word "debauchery" [razvrat]. Conveying the height of moral opprobrium throughout this period, the word was employed by early twentieth-century respondents, especially but not exclusively well-educated respondents, primarily to reject its applicability to a particular case.

The treatment of Anastasia Novokreshchenova's appeal provides evidence of such shifting attitudes, while highlighting the contrast between religious and secular views of women's adulterous behavior. The gendarme officers who reported on the case over an eighteen-month period offered the secular perspective. Although Novokreshchenova never denied leaving her husband for her lover, the officers were manifestly hesitant to condemn her conduct. Summarizing his initial investigation three months after Novokreshchenova initially petitioned, the first gendarme to report placed the primary blame for the couple's discord on the husband, Petr. His behavior really was "very bad," the officer wrote. Petr liked to drink in the company of other men and, when drunk, to "spend time gaily in the company of public women." A violent drunk, he was inclined to beat his wife or whomever else fell to hand. The couple's fundamental differences, the gendarme concluded, meant that a reconciliation between them would likely end in "catastrophe." If the couple tried living together again, "the fact of her infidelity would always serve as an obstacle." Besides, he wrote, "she intensely dislikes both his family circumstances and the husband himself." He thus recommended that the chancellery satisfy her request for a passport.[66]

65. Freeze, "Profane Narratives," 160–61.
66. RGIA, fond 1412, op. 224, d. 34 (Novokreshchenova), 6–7.

A second gendarme officer, writing after the chancellery had rejected Novokresh-chenova's original appeal and after she had tried and failed to reconcile with her husband, saw even more merit in the wife's claims. Praising Anastasia for displaying the character and self-command that her husband so obviously lacked, he made no negative reference at all to her relationship with her lover: "As became clear from the investigation and my own impressions, Petr Novokreshchenov is a man without character, petty, and under the influence of relatives and friends." In contrast, the officer wrote admiringly of Anastasia as a woman of character, determined to choose her own path. "She's energetic and her demands and desires are well thought out, logical, and reasonable.... Her testimony is just and frank."[67]

The opinion of the Samara ecclesiastical court, to which Novokreshchenova brought suit on the basis of her husband's adulterous relations with prostitutes, offers a marked contrast to such views, reminding the reader that the more relaxed attitudes toward women's sexual misconduct and selfhood that are emphasized not only in this chapter but also in this book were not the only ones in circulation. Rejecting Anastasia's divorce petition, on August 8, 1897, the court condemned her behavior in the strongest of terms and admonished her to reconcile with her husband and accept her lot in life. She should abandon her "venture [zateia]" and "with a feeling of gratitude toward her husband, for Christ's sake, as a wife and mother of small children, return to him for a peaceful conjugal life in full satisfaction and happiness and cease to drag herself from place to place." Continuing her present behavior would not only bring misery to everyone else, it would also condemn Anastasia herself to the life of a fallen woman. She would end up "being passed from hand to hand and then abandoned as a useless thing.... That is the fate that awaits Anastasia Novokreshchenova if she doesn't return to the husband given to her by God! [Bogom ei dannomy!]" Nothing justified a woman's decision to leave her husband in the opinion of the ecclesiastical court: almost as objectionable as Novokreshchenova's adultery was her failure to show "a single sign of repentance" for the "crime" of fleeing her husband's home, for which Anastasia was verbally chastised in her father's presence.[68]

People were most likely to hesitate before condemning a woman who had become sexually involved with another man after separating from her husband. Commenting on the frequency with which wives living apart from their husbands entered "civil unions" with unmarried men, the historian Tatiana Kotlova observes: "Evidently, it was easier for a 'straw widow' than for an unmarried woman to enter an illicit relationship. She had a different social status and greater self-reliance and independence from

67. Ibid., 66.
68. Ibid., 43–45.

her parents."[69] Evidence in separation dossiers bears out this observation and suggests that the changes discussed earlier in this chapter contributed to the tolerance. By the late 1890s, policemen and others who testified in separation cases, at least those set in major cities, had become less likely to judge wives' stable extramarital liaisons as evidence of their immorality or debauchery, especially when the marriage had been troubled, and/or husband and wife had long lived apart, although most were not so forgiving of women who enjoyed more than one lover or those who became involved with another man while cohabiting with their husbands. This was very much an urban phenomenon; residents from rural areas and some recent peasant migrants to the city remained far more prone to condemn women who transgressed the boundaries of sexual propriety.

Although the evidence of necessity is impressionistic, it is sufficient to suggest the change was real and that it occurred within a very short period of time. Whereas in the 1880s and early 1890s, hesitant respondents might simply have said "I don't know" when asked about sexual behavior they knew to be transgressive, such respondents became more prone to excuse, even to defend women's transgressive sexual conduct. One unusually vivid example of the more relaxed views dates to 1898, when two of the jurists who had taken the peasant migrant Evdokia Kulikova under their wing put considerable effort into convincing the chancellery of her reputability, despite the evidence of the child that she had borne long after leaving her husband. In one of the letters written for this purpose, Lev L'vovich Breitfus, a judge in the St. Petersburg circuit court, endeavored to demonstrate that Kulikova was not immoral. He was "profoundly and sincerely" convinced, he wrote to the chancellery, that Evdokia Ivanovna fully merited his kindness. A "decent woman in all respects," she earned her daily bread with her own honest labor. Anatolii Alekseevich Khodnev, a judge in the St. Petersburg court of appeals, likewise attested to Kulikova's excellent character and impeccable conduct: Evdokia Ivanovna is "industrious to the highest degree, honorable and indisputably moral," he wrote. A trained seamstress, Kulikova worked in these men's homes and interacted with their wives and children, despite her previous "fall." (By contrast, the senior *dvornik* of the building where Kulikova had previously lived declared that she "led an immoral life, coming together for debauchery [*nepotrebstvo*] with the junior *dvornik* and, at the same time, being lovers with a carter.") The jurists were not unique. Testifying about the behavior of his domestic servant Natalia Terekhova in 1898, the collegiate secretary Pavel Shcheglov reported: "She was visited by a man, with whom

69. T. B. Kotlova, *Rossiiskaia zhenshchina v provintsial'nom gorode na rubezhe XIX–XX vekov* (Ivanovo: Ivanovskii gosudarstvennyi universitet, 2003), 47.

Везд‸ не везетъ.

М у ж ъ (заставъ жену въ манежѣ цѣлующей ло-
шадь).—Чертъ возьми, и тутъ у меня соперникъ!

FIGURE 19.

*The husband (finding his wife in the stable, kissing a horse): "The devil
take it! Even here I have a rival!" Semeinye illiuzii (1908), M. E.
Saltykov-Shchedrin Public Library.*

he supposes she had some kind of intimate relations." Nevertheless, Shcheglov declared he "found nothing amiss in her behavior."[70]

People of more humble background showed a similar tolerance. Because of her employer's age and ill health, the Moscow police officer who reported in 1899 on the conduct of the peasant migrant Agrippina Abusova doubted she was sexually involved with the employer, as her husband alleged. "But even if she has cohabited with him," the officer added, acknowledging Abusova's sexual needs, "having lived apart from her husband for fifteen years, then it was with him and him alone and at present, while not yet an old woman, she has had no other." Anna Boldyreva, the former political exile and future Bolshevik organizer, separated from her husband and lived with and was partially supported by her lover, a turner, after her return to St. Petersburg. "She lives modestly and does nothing at all reprehensible," testified her *dvornik* in 1903, having mentioned the sexual tie. Letters submitted by her husband left no doubt that Lidia Semenova, wife of a townsman from Riga and residing in St. Petersburg, who petitioned in 1906, was conducting an affair with another man. "I kiss you in the place that only I can kiss and press you to my breast," reads one of the letters preserved in her dossier. Their relationship did not, however, compromise her in the eyes of some who testified about the case. One witness, a retired major general, declared categorically that, having had neither emotional attachments nor a lover before the break with her husband, "if such appeared afterwards, then that is completely normal, as the natural result of that coarse and vulgar behavior of her husband." Reporting on their secret investigation of the case, the police affirmed that Lidia Semenova "has a good character and lives on the support of the Moscow townsman NMK, whose lover she is."[71]

This easing of attitudes toward women's extramarital sexual transgressions and greater willingness to recognize women's emotional needs as a factor in marital breakdown was also reflected in the deliberations of chancellery officials. These are especially revealing, because officials' language in the post-1895 period can be compared with that of the previous decade. And it clearly underwent a change. While they never, ever ceased to inquire into wives' sexual conduct and to condemn liaisons that began while the couple cohabited, again beginning around the mid-1890s, officials became more inclined to discount a woman's postmarital sexual liaison as a reason for denying a passport if the liaison was monogamous or had subsequently ended. Officials also became more prone to avoid moralizing language and, albeit only rarely, to link women's marital suffering with their transgressive sexual behavior. One example is officials' decision in 1901 to approve Anastasia Novokreshchenova's petition, having ini-

70. RGIA, fond 1412, op. 221, d. 204 (Kulikova, 1897), 37, 39, 41; op. 229, d. 35 (Terekhova, N., 1898), 22.

71. Ibid., op. 212, d. 17 (Abusova, A., 1899), 17; op. 213, d. 81 (Boldyreva, A., 1899), 34; op. 228, d. 35 (Semenova, L., 1906), 20, 27.

tially rejected it three years earlier. In doing so in this case, as in many others, officials invoked the morally loaded word "debauchery" only to deny its applicability in this particular instance.

> Taking into consideration that although the petitioner was unfaithful to her husband, however her illegal attachment did not have the character of debauchery, in that in the course of several years she lived with only one man and, in addition, that attachment has evidently ceased. Moreover, as became clear in the first deposition in this case, her infidelity had some justification in the genuinely difficult circumstances of her life with her husband and the influence on her of outsiders, forcing her to feel burdened by her circumstances and the character of her family. Also, her husband's coarse treatment and drinking provided cause for her action as well.[72]

In other decisions, too, officials showed greater reluctance to employ the language of moral opprobrium or to treat a woman who had transgressed sexually as an ongoing threat to public decorum. In explaining why Agrippina Grigor'eva, a peasant woman from Vitebsk, merited a passport in 1897, officials noted that her husband, Osip, was responsible for the breakdown of the marriage and that "although the petitioner permitted herself to betray her vow of conjugal fidelity and to drink to excess, currently she was known to have done nothing blameworthy." Although Natalia Gur'ianova, the wife of a peasant from Tver who drank excessively and was unable to support his wife, had entered an "illicit relationship" with another man after leaving her husband, "besides that relationship she has done nothing else that is blameworthy," wrote officials, recommending in 1898 that her passport be approved. Evdokia Bakova's relationship with a man other than her husband "doesn't have the character of adultery," officials concluded, again in 1898, because the relationship had continued for years. In the same year, Anastasia Golovina, a migrant peasant then living in the town of Stavropol, obtained a passport, because "although she is in an illicit cohabitation, she leads a modest and industrious life." Officials were influenced as well by the governor's belief that although it was Anastasia's "reprehensible" conduct that had led to the couple's disputes in the first place, her husband, Mikhail, might seriously harm or even murder her if she were forced to return to him. In the case of the ill-used Matrona Kovalevskaia, whose husband literally prostituted her for his own material gain until she left to live with one of her lovers and to pursue her studies of music, officials likewise invoked the language of moral opprobrium only to reject its relevance to the case in question. In the 1905 report on the case, officials concluded: "Aside from her illicit tie, Matrona Kovalevskaia has done nothing disreputable. She currently lives with her lover and on his means, studies music and drama.... The husband himself forced her into the life she

72. Ibid., op. 224, d. 34 (Novokreshchenova), 85.

leads, which, besides, does not have the character of debauchery." Anna Gromnitskaia, they reported in 1909, was in an illicit relationship, but apart from that relationship, no one had seen her doing anything wrong. Vera Alekseeva, whose husband had left her for another woman, "lives in St. Petersburg with the hereditary honored citizen Anosov, and besides that, has been seen doing nothing disreputable," they wrote in yet another case in 1912.[73]

Thus, although women's sexual morality as such never ceased to preoccupy officials or to figure as a factor in their reports, the ways that morality was construed underwent a subtle but perceptible shift. In particular, officials became less ready to condemn a married woman for becoming involved with another man, especially if that relationship began after the wife had left a husband responsible for the marital breakdown; nor did they invariably associate a woman's sexual misconduct with public disorder. Eschewing in such cases the language of moral opprobrium (but in so doing implying its relevance in other cases), they also drew a rhetorical distinction between a woman's illicit conduct, which involved betraying her marital vows, and the far more damning and socially dangerous "debauchery," which connoted a moral flaw and a public threat. These changed attitudes were reflected in their willingness to free some adulterous wives from the husband's tutelage rather than condemning them as unworthy of the emperor's mercy, which had been the practice during the reign of Tsar Alexander III.[74]

. . .

Adultery, historians of women have argued, can be read as an assertion of female autonomy and selfhood, privileging as it does a woman's own desire over the stability of her marriage. "For a woman to choose a man other than her husband has a principled element, for it signifies the awakening in her of the individual [*lichnoe nachalo*], and a striving for independence and originality," writes Maria Litovskaia.[75] Such an assertion must surely be qualified, as other factors, economic need foremost among them, might also prompt a wife who was miserable in her marriage to take up with another man. Nevertheless, the assertion also contains a grain of truth. The far-reaching social, economic, and cultural changes that occurred in the final decades of the nineteenth

---

73. Ibid., op. 250, d. 86, 67; d. 101, 14; 103, 30 ob.; d. 104, 49–49 ob., 91 ob.; op. 221, d. 51 (Kovalevskaia, M., 1905), 34–35; op. 212, d. 108 (Alekseeva, V., 1909), 43.

74. Another kind of evidence for these more tolerant attitudes is the chancellery's suggestion in 1900 that peasant women merited a passport in cases where their husbands refused to take their illegitimate children into the household, if those children had played no role in the woman's departure—that is, if she bore the children while working away from home or after having left her husband. See RGIA, fond 1412, op. 241, d. 18, 4.

75. Maria Litovskaia, "Ot 'semeinogo kovchaga' k 'krasnomy treugol'niku': adiul'ter v russkoi literature," in *Semeinye uzy: modeli dlia sborki. Sbornik statei*, ed. Sergei Ushakin, 2 vols. (Moscow: Novoe literaturnoe obozrenie, 2004), 1: 266.

century made it easier for women to defy the strictures on sexual conduct, even when the strictures themselves did not ease, even as the language of "love" encouraged some women to act on their feelings, to privilege their own desire over marital stability, and to "choose their own fate," whatever others may have thought of them.[76]

That such women flouted prevailing norms in doing so is undeniable. The cartoons that graced the pages of satirical journals bear witness to the unsettling impact of feminine sexual transgression and the anxieties it provoked, especially when misconduct involved women who were demonstrably middle-class. The sexual freedom celebrated, for example, in Anastasia Verbitskaia's trailblazing *Keys To Happiness* (1910–13) found no echo whatsoever in the testimonies of witnesses or respondents or in the deliberations of officials. Women's sexual conduct remained the object of scrutiny. Women who enjoyed more than one lover, behaved too freely in public, or violated other norms of sexual propriety continued to risk condemnation by others in their community (remember the anonymous letters), as well as by tsarist officials. Although the definition of "immorality" had shifted, expanding the range of acceptable female behaviors, the idea that extramarital liaisons were immoral remained alive and well. Chancellery officials still drew the line more strictly than most. Even the explosion of sexual imagery after the revolution of 1905 failed to eradicate their sense of responsibility for the sexual conduct of women who lived apart from their husbands. But however limited, the change was palpably real.

76. I borrow the language from V. N. Kulik, "Zhenshchiny dinastii Riabushinskikh," 185, 195.

The Best Interests of the Child

Late in the spring of 1914, the wife of a well-to-do Moscow businessman appeared in the office of Vasilii I. Mamantov, director of the Imperial Chancellery for Receipt of Petitions. Relating a heartbreaking story of abuse at her husband's hands, the woman pleaded for assistance. Her marriage had become a nightmare. Her husband had taken to drinking and carousing and running around with other women, all the while "tyrannizing" his wife. Most recently, he had become involved with a well-known operetta singer, with whom he set up housekeeping in St. Petersburg, using up the remains of his once-substantial fortune. To supplement his diminished resources, he demanded that his wife transfer to him her own wealth, some 150,000 rubles, threatening to take custody of their ten-year-old son if she refused. When she nevertheless resisted, he carried out his threat, kidnapping their son. He then settled the child in the apartment he shared with the singer, forcing the child to be an involuntary witness to the orgies he conducted there, or so his wife alleged, to force her to surrender her assets. In utter despair, the unhappy mother resolved to seek the tsar's protection.[1]

But Mamantov confessed himself unable to help her. However sympathetic he felt—and his heart went out to her—it was his duty to tell her that the chancellery was no longer in a position to involve itself in custody arrangements. On March 12, 1914, the passport law had been revised so as to grant a wife the right to obtain her own passport simply by requesting the document from the appropriate authorities. The revision was accompanied by the deceptively titled "certain changes in the Laws concerning the personal and property rights of married women and the relations between husbands and wives and parents and children," which constituted a substantial revision of marital and family law. Incorporating previous decisions by the State Senate, portions of the draft code governing marital separation that had been drawn up by the Editorial Commission of the Civil Cassation Department of the Senate over a decade earlier but never promulgated,

1. V. I. Mamantov, *Na gosudarevoi sluzhbe. Vospominaniia* (Tallin: Tallina Eesti Kirjastus, 1926), 194–95.

and other piecemeal revisions of marital law devised by other administrative bodies over the years, it set forth principles for resolving the legal issues arising from marital separation—child custody, child support, alimony, and so on.[2]

These changes brought an end to the chancellery's role. Thereafter, all legal questions arising from marital breakdown belonged in the jurisdiction of the courts, including the custody of her child that had brought the distraught mother to Mamantov. Pursuing the case in court, Mamantov informed her, was the only means for her to regain her "maternal rights." She had already explored this option, she told him, and learned to her dismay that child custody suits might drag on for years. By the time a court resolved the case, even if in her favor, her son would have become "utterly debauched" as a result of living with his father. "Touched by the petitioner's genuine grief," as Mamantov remembered it later, he met with the chief justice of the St. Petersburg circuit court to ascertain whether the court had the authority to remove the child from his father's custody while the case was still pending. The answer was no.

Yet how could he fail to act in such compelling circumstances? Mamantov declared himself torn between respect for the law and his own higher sense of justice: "The new law...deprived me of the right to become involved in the petitioner's affairs, but simple humanity kept me from reconciling myself to that situation." His higher sense of justice prevailed. First, Mamantov dispatched members of the special corps of gendarmes, who conducted a secret investigation that confirmed her story. Then, having assured himself that the mother was telling the truth, he took action. Mamantov summoned a staff officer of the special corps of gendarmes and instructed him to assist the petitioner in kidnapping her own son, "of course, without using any force," and to ensure that no one learned of the chancellery's role. The kidnapping took place within a matter of days. Once she had regained custody of her child, the chancellery was able to satisfy the mother's appeal for protection while her custody suit made its way through the courts.[3] This episode, illustrating with unusual clarity both the chancellery's capacity for arbitrary, supralegal action and its self-declared mission to secure the moral and physical well-being of a child, concluded a history of administrative action in matters of child custody that had lasted almost eighty years.

THE THIRD SECTION AND CHILD CUSTODY

The right to claim child custody is a key element of married women's rights: when that right belongs by law to the father, mothers are far more likely to remain in

---

2. I. V. Gessen, *Razdelnoe zhitel'stvo suprugov. Zakon 12 marta 1914 goda o nekotorykh izmeneniiakh i dopolneniiakh...* (St. Petersburg: Pravo, 1914), 15–166. For the political maneuvering that led to these changes, see William G. Wagner, *Marriage, Property, and Law in Late Imperial Russia* (Oxford: Clarendon, 1994), 188–95.

3. Mamantov, *Na gosudarevoi sluzhbe*, 195–98.

FIGURE 20. *Vasilii I. Mamantov. S. N. Pisarev,* Uchrezhdenie
po priniatiiu i napravleniiu proshenii i zhalob, prinosimykh na
Vysochaishee imia, 1810–1910 gg. Istoricheskii ocherk.

abusive or unhappy marriages for fear of losing their children. Laws that ensured paternal custody "promoted the maintenance of strong patriarchal hierarchies," as Danaya C. Wright has put it. They permitted men who insisted on their wife's compliance to hold the children "hostage" or use them to punish a wife who failed to obey.[4]

From this perspective, especially, the practices of the chancellery and its predecessor, the Third Section, appear surprisingly progressive when compared to those of law courts in Great Britain or the United States or, for that matter, to the postreform courts in Russia in the early decades. "Presumptive paternal custody rights" were the norm in Anglo-American law in the first half of the nineteenth century. In Great Britain, between 1804 and the passage of the first Infant Custody Act in 1839, courts awarded custody to the father in virtually every contested custody case, in the conviction that the rights of the father of a legitimate child were superior to those of the mother. Although in the years that followed, maternalist arguments and a growing concern for the "best interests of the child" sometimes inclined the courts to favor the mother, paternal custody remained the default mode at least until the passage of the third Infant Custody Act in 1886 (there was a second in 1873), and not until 1925 did "the best interests of the child" become the rule for determining custody. After 1840, U.S. courts adjudicating custody disputes also became increasingly likely to favor the mother; nevertheless, practices varied considerably from state to state. Courts in the slaveholding antebellum South, in particular, almost invariably regarded paternal rights as superior in cases of marital breakdown.[5]

In the few child custody disputes the Third Section resolved during the first half of the nineteenth century, it appears at least as prepared as Anglo-American courts to award custody to the mother.[6] Like the chancellery's, the Third Section's authority derived directly from that of the tsar, and its decisions were at least as particularistic. If any principles guided the Third Section, it was the tsarist government's overriding interest in the proper moral education of the young, reflected in the language of

4. Danaya C. Wright, "De Manneville v. De Manneville: Rethinking the Birth of Custody Law under Patriarchy," *Law and History Review* 17, no. 2 (1999): 301.

5. Michael Grossberg, *A Judgment for Solomon: the d'Hauteville Case and Legal Experience in Antebellum America* (New York: Cambridge University Press, 1996), 52–54; Wright, "De Manneville v. De Manneville," 287; and Mary Lyndon Shanley, *Feminism, Marriage, and the Law in Victorian England* (Princeton, NJ: Princeton University Press, 1989), 131–55. See also Mary Ann Mason, *From Father's Property to Children's Rights: The History of Child Custody in the United States* (New York, Columbia University Press, 1994). Practices in the South varied from state to state; South Carolina was the most resistant to maternal custody. See Peter Bardaglio, *Reconstructing the Household: Families, Sex, and the Law in the Nineteenth-Century South* (Chapel Hill: University of North Carolina Press, 1995): 80–88.

6. The numbers complicate comparisons. Custody was at issue in only a fraction of Russian women's appeals, which in any case numbered no more than four a year, and often less, until the reform era. See GARF, fond 109, 3-oe otdelenie, 2-aia ekspeditsiia, op. 1826–55.

the law. The law held both parents responsible. "Parents must give all their attention to the moral education of their children and strive by means of domestic upbringing [*vospitanie*] to school their morals and further the goals [*sodeistvovat' vidam*] of the state," reads article 173 of the law governing parent/child relations, its gender-neutral language explicitly linking parents' fulfillment of their duties to the concerns of the state.[7] Still, even after the publication of Russia's first *Digest of Laws* in 1832, decisions of the Third Section never alluded explicitly to the law when assessing parents' ability to fulfill their duties.

Nor, for that matter, did decisions refer explicitly to conceptions of moral motherhood that were first introduced from abroad into Russia in the late eighteenth century. But doubtless, both the values reflected in the law and those associated with the new conceptions of motherhood exerted an influence on officials' decision making. The two coincided neatly. In this period, prescriptive literature encouraged a shift away from the down-to-earth and practical understanding of motherhood that had previously prevailed among the nobility. Celebrating motherhood's sanctity, the literature instructed mothers to be the moral and spiritual guides of their children. During the reign of Tsar Nicholas I (1825–1855), the empress herself personified this ideal. Thereafter, expectations of appropriate parenting grew ever more exacting, especially of the mother. Limitlessly self-sacrificing, able to "endure much" for the sake of her children's tranquillity, as depicted in the literature of advice the ideal mother was loving and patient, tireless in her efforts on behalf of her offspring.[8] Autobiographies and biographical fiction, too, promoted a "cult of the perfect mother," saintly and self-abnegating.[9] This emphasis on self-abnegation and willingness to suffer, evident in Russian women's self-presentations as well, suggests that the cult of motherhood, like the cult of domesticity, mutated when it crossed Russia's borders by incorporating elements of the Russian Orthodox cult of the Virgin Mary. As Valerie Kivelson has recently argued, elaborating a point originally raised by George Fedotov, the Russian Orthodox veneration of the Virgin Mary differed from that of the West, focusing on Mary's physical pain and emotional suffering, not on her virginity.[10] In their more Westernized form

7. *Polnyi svod zakonov* (St. Petersburg, 1857), vol. 10.

8. Catriona Kelly, *Refining Russia: Advice Literature, Polite Culture, and Gender from Catherine to Yeltsin* (New York: Oxford University Press, 2001), 28. Quoted from Maria Korsini, "The Ideal Family (1846)," in *Russian Women, 1698–1917: Experience and Expression*, ed. Robin Bisha et al. (Bloomington: Indiana University Press, 2002), 26–27. On the empress, see Richard Wortman, "The Russian Empress as Mother," in *The Family in Imperial Russia: New Lines of Historical Research*, ed. David Ransel (Urbana: University of Illinois Press, 1978), 63–65.

9. On the cult of the perfect mother, see Andrew Baruch Wachtel, *The Battle for Childhood: Creation of a Russian Myth* (Stanford, CA: Stanford University Press, 1990), 96–97, 99.

10. Valerie Kivelson, "Sexuality and Gender in Early Modern Russian Orthodoxy," in *Letters from Heaven: Popular Religion in Russia and Ukraine*, ed. John-Paul Himka and Andriy Zayarnyuk

or in the original Orthodox version, ideals of moral motherhood provided models for women's behavior as well as a vocabulary with which women might challenge the paternal rights of fathers. They also prepared officials to respond favorably to women's appeals when they deemed it appropriate.

Two early examples from Third Section archives demonstrate officials' overriding concern for proper moral rearing, and the role that moral motherhood might play in decisions that favored the mother. The first, the case of the Kushevs, unfolded in 1828, when the wife appealed for protection from a husband who had married her for her money six years earlier and subsequently employed physical violence to force her to sign over a significant portion of her assets. Relevant here, however, is what happened after Major Kushev kidnapped all three of their children, the eldest aged six, and carried them off to his own estate, about fifty miles away from their mother's, very likely to compel his wife to resume cohabitation. The authorities roundly condemned Kushev's behavior: "The children are without the necessary moral oversight," wrote the Nizhnyi Novgorod civil governor in 1829 to the Third Section, referring to the fact that the children were with their father, not their mother. Terming Major Kushev's kidnapping of his children "arbitrary and self-willed," and omitting any mention of Kushev's authority as head of household, "for the sake of justice" the governor insisted that the children be restored to their mother. They were.[11]

The second case involved the forceful removal of children from their father. In 1836, the estranged wife of Staff Captain Kazakov appealed for custody of her two sons, warning of the "harmful moral impact" on the children if they continued to live with their father. Five years earlier, the father had become sexually intimate with a Gypsy woman, with whom he continued to live on his estate, dispatching the children she bore to a foundling home. The gendarme reporting on the Kazakov marriage favored the mother's appeal: "It would be well to remove the children from the presence of this [the father's] bad example," he wrote. When several attempts to convince the father voluntarily to surrender the children failed, the Third Section ordered a gendarme to remove them from the father's custody and to deliver them to their mother.[12]

Even after the number of women's appeals for a passport grew dramatically in subsequent decades, and the social background of petitioners became considerably more diverse, concern with the moral circumstances of the child continued to determine the

(Toronto: University of Toronto Press, 2006), 103–4; G. P. Fedotov, *The Russian Religious Mind*, 2 vols. (Cambridge, MA: Harvard University Press, 1946–66), 2: 103.

11. How, exactly, is unclear from the records. Subsequently, the couple reconciled, but at the mother's insistence, "to keep the children morally untainted," the three daughters were placed in a closed school in St. Petersburg, near which she settled (GARF, fond 109, 3-oe otdelenie, 2-aia ekspeditsiia, op. 1828, d. 119, 32, 71, 95).

12. Ibid., op. 1836, d. 229, 14.

outcome of custody disputes. Judging by the documents in the dossiers I have read, a father's presumptive legal rights played no role in officials' decision making; instead, which parent gained custody depended on officials' evaluation of the particulars of a case, especially, which of the parents was responsible for the breakdown of the marriage. The chancellery's summary history of its predecessor's practices confirms this impression: "When children were involved, the Third Section always left them with the innocent party, and if the other spouse resisted this, with His Majesty's permission the children were removed from him by the police," the summary reads, in appropriately gender-neutral language.[13] The Third Section continued to resolve child custody disputes even after 1864, when such disputes also began to come before the newly reformed courts. Its successor, the chancellery, did the same. Both remained more likely than the courts to favor the mother.

THE COURTS AND CUSTODY

It is one of the many ironies of the history of late imperial Russia that its courts, which liberal reformers aspired to make the basis for the rule of law, in their willingness to protect women's rights in the family for many years lagged behind both the Third Section and its successor, the chancellery, the quintessential expressions of absolutism. This ironic situation, a theme of this book, was partly a consequence of chancellery officials' relative freedom to respond flexibly to the particular requirements of particular cases as well as of the limitations of the law that jurists were bound to uphold. But it also derived from the predispositions of Russia's progressive jurists, influenced as they were by Western conceptions of appropriately gendered spheres. While perhaps less consistently than liberals elsewhere in the West, Russian liberals, like their Western counterparts, tended to give priority to male authority in the family and to emphasize the husband's role in the wider world while consigning the wife to domesticity. And perhaps more than their Anglo-American counterparts, with a few exceptions, Russian liberals demonstrated a preference for the father in disputes over child custody.[14]

---

13. RGIA, fond 1412, op. 241, d. 21, 4 ob. On the Third Section's role in child custody, see also V. Bogucharskii, "Tret'e otdelenie Sobstvennoi ego imperatorskogo velichestva kantseliarii o sebe samom," *Vestnik Evropy*, no. 3 (1917): 117. Cases in which the mother was determined to be the superior custodian include GARF, fond 109, 3-oe otdelenie, 2-aia ekspeditsiia, op. 1837, d. 480; 1874, d. 301; op. 1879, d. 167 and 999.

14. Wagner, *Marriage, Property, and Law*, 122–23. The jurist Aleksandr Borovikovskii was a notable exception to this preference for the father, arguing that the best interests of children should govern custody decisions. His views are discussed in William G. Wagner, "Family Law, the Rule of Law, and Liberalism in Late Imperial Russia," *Jahrbücher für Geschichte Osteuropas* 43, no. 4 (1995): 519–35. The idiosyncratic Vasilii V. Rozanov adopted much the same position. See V. V. Rozanov, *Semeinyi vopros v Rossii*, 2 vols. (St. Petersburg: M. Merkushev, 1903), 2: 26.

As a result, child custody disputes set into high relief the differences between chancellery practices and those of the courts. Although chancellery officials, too, gave priority to male authority, including authority over children, they made no assumptions as to which parent had the greater legal right to children in cases of marital breakdown; indeed, they were mindful of the legal rights of *both* parents, even as they proved willing to circumscribe or even terminate them when the particular circumstances appeared to warrant it. By the 1890s, their decisions in custody disputes were often couched in terms of the well-being of the child, considerably expanding the narrowly moral language of the Third Section. This evolution surely reflected the increasingly psychologized and medicalized views of a small child's needs, which had become familiar to a broad reading public in the final decades of the century. Such views also influenced liberal jurists, who after 1890 became more inclined to recognize the needs of children under particular circumstances, much as the chancellery had long been doing.[15] But until that time, and arguably even thereafter, nowhere was the ironic contrast between the practices of autocratic institutions and those of the law-governed courts more in evidence than in the question of child custody.

On that issue, especially, Russian law offered ambiguous guidance. On one hand, reflecting long-standing customary practices, Russian family law made no distinction between the role of fathers and mothers in the lives of their children. The law consistently referred to parental rather than paternal authority (*vlast' roditel'skaia*), and parental rather than paternal responsibility. According to Russian law, *parents (roditeli)* had a responsibility to feed, clothe, and provide a good and honorable moral education for their children according to their station. Russian law thus recognized no "vested right" of a father to his children, which as Peter Bardaglio has noted, in Anglo-American law derived from the father's duty to support, protect, and educate his children.[16]

15. Elizaveta Vodovozova's book intended for people who reared small children (its title notably gender-neutral) first appeared in 1871 and went through seven editions by 1914. By that date, the physician Vladimir Zhuk's *Mother and Child*, devoted to the health and physical welfare of infants and small children, had appeared in its tenth edition. See Elizaveta N. Vodovozova, *Umstvennoe razvitie detei ot pervogo proiavleniia soznaniia do vos'miletnego vozrasta: kniga dlia vospitatelei* (St. Petersburg: A. M. Kotomin, 1871); and Vladimir N. Zhuk, *Mat' i ditia. Gigiena v obshchedostupnoe izlozhenie* (St. Petersburg: V. F. Demakov, 1881). See also the citations in Andy Byford, "Turning Pedagogy into a Science: Teachers and Psychologists in Late Imperial Russia, (1897–1917)," *Osiris* 23, no. 1 (2008): 52.

16. *Polnyi svod zakonov* (1857), vol. 10, art. 172–73. The term "vested right" is borrowed from Michael Grossberg, "Who Gets the Child? Custody, Guardianship, and the Rise of a Judicial Patriarchy in Nineteenth-Century America," *Feminist Studies* 9, no. 2 (1983): 235–60; and Bardaglio, *Reconstructing the Household*, 80. On customary practices, see M. F. Vladimirskii-Budanov, *Obzor istorii russkogo prava*, 6th ed. (1910; repr., The Hague: Russian Reprint Series, 1966), 458–59; Natal'ia V. Kozlova, " 'Na cei opeke…dolzhny byt' vospitany…' Opeka, popechitel'stvo v srede moskovskikh

On the other hand, Russian family law was unquestionably patriarchal, making the husband and father head of his household and requiring from his wife unconditional obedience to his will.

It was the father's superior authority to which the courts initially gave preference. To be sure, confronted with these ambiguities, the postreform courts initially arrived at contradictory decisions—sometimes favoring the mother, sometimes the father, sometimes refusing to hear a case altogether.[17] But when the Senate finally ruled on the matter, as it did in 1890 in the precedent-setting case of Grinevich v. Grinevich, it made paternal custody the default mode. Reflecting both the Civil Cassation Department's growing concern for the rights of women in marriage and the increasingly elaborate understanding of a child's needs, the decision did open the door to maternal custody. It noted that the law "makes no distinction between the rights of fathers and mothers" and "provides no guidance" as to which of the two separated parents enjoys greater right to child custody. When the couple cohabited, the father's right took precedence over the mother's, based on the husband's legal position as head of the household. However, when wife and husband lived apart, the father's right to raise the children, while remaining the more compelling, ceased to be automatic if it conflicted with the welfare of the child. It was up to the courts to decide. As the decision put it: "The primary right to raise the children belongs to the father as head of the family unless a court determines that under *special circumstances* [my emphasis], the welfare of the children require that they be raised by the mother."[18]

In the context of earlier decisions, Grinevich represented a significant advance. For the first time, it provided grounds for women to pursue custody suits in the courts, and it opened the door to arguments concerning the impact on the child of a father's moral or other failings and the superior virtues of the mother. However, the enthusiastic celebration of the decision by *Sudebnaia gazeta* was certainly unwarranted. Echoing arguments concerning mothers' "natural rights" to their children that had been heard in

kuptsov v XVIII veke," in *Ot Drevnei Rusi k Rossii Novogo Vremeni. Sbornik statei k 70-letiiu Anny Leonidovny Khoroshkevich* (Moscow: Nauka, 2003), 344.

17. On the overall pattern, Anatolii F. Koni, *Sobranie sochineniia*, 8 vols. (Moscow: Iuridicheskaia literatura, 1966–69), 1: 244–45. For decisions favoring the mother, see *Sudebnyi vestnik*, no. 22 (January 23, 1870), 2–3; no. 83 (March 27, 1870), 2–3; and no. 267 (October 5, 1870), 1. For decisions favoring the father, see *Sudebnyi vestnik*, no. 65 (March 23, 1869), 1–2; no. 114 (May 28, 1869); no. 160 (July 24, 1869); and no. 330 (December 7, 1870). Even in cases where the courts granted custody to the mother, in principle they recognized the father's authority as superior. See V. A. Veremenko, *Dvorianskaia sem'ia i gosudarstvennaia politika Rossii (vtoraia polovina XIX–nachalo XX v.)* (St. Petersburg: Evropeiskii dom, 2007), 485.

18. *Resheniia Grazhdanskago Kassatsionnago Departamenta pravitel'stvuiushchago Senata* (1890), no. 18; reproduced in G. V. Bertgol'dt, *Razdel'noe zhitel'stvo suprugov. Sbornik reshenii Grazhdanskago Kassatsionnago Departamenta pravitel'stvuiushchago Senata* (Moscow: Pravovedenie, 1910), 77–94.

the lower courts for years, the editors expressed the hope that Grinevich would ensure the protection of "the sacred rights of the mother."[19] In fact, the "right" emphasized in the language of the decision was the "primary right" of the father, qualified not by the mother's "right" (recognized nowhere at this time), but by the welfare of the child. The preference for paternal custody was reiterated in a decision of 1908.[20] The revised family law that accompanied the new passport rules of 1914 appears more evenhanded. It awarded underage children to the "innocent party" when separated parents failed to agree on child custody, and when exceptions had to be made, left it to the courts to decide how the well-being of the child might best be served.[21]

THE CHANCELLERY AND CHILD CUSTODY

These were precisely the practices that officials of the imperial chancellery had long followed. It is true that officials had recourse to them only in a very small minority of the cases that came to their attention. Unable to support themselves and dependent children or fearful of losing them to their husband, many mothers of underage children simply chose to stay in a miserable marriage. Anastasia Verbitskaia's novel *She Was Liberated!* dramatized their dilemma: her well-educated heroine fears losing her beloved child if she leaves her despised husband to join the man she loves.[22] Although in real life, women who faced such romantic dilemmas were considerably less common than women who faced a choice between enduring neglect and/or abuse and losing their children, the choice remained a real one. One reflection of the restraining influence of underage children is that the majority of women who petitioned the chancellery were not mothers of them, although most had been married for years. Even when petitioners were mothers of underage children, officials often had no need to decide between contending custody claims. In the overwhelming majority of such cases, the women had left with their children and custody was determined de facto.

19. "Prava roditelei zhivushchikh razdel'no na detei," *Sudebnaia gazeta*, July 7, 1891, 1–2. For earlier arguments based on a mother's "natural rights," see *Sudebnyi vestnik*, no. 65 (March 23, 1869), 1–2; and no. 83 (March 27, 1870), 2–3.

20. "A mother who lives separately from her husband through no fault of his and retains a child against his will arbitrarily limits the paternal authority of the father," according to the Senate in the case of Grigorii Z. See *Resheniia Grazhdanskago Kassatsionnago Departamenta pravitel'stvuiushchago Senata* (1908), no. 48; reproduced in Bertgol'dt, *Razdel'noe zhitel'stvo*, 106–9. The preference for paternal authority was also expressed in the draft code revising family law prepared by the Editing Commission of the Civil Cassation Department of the State Senate. See Veremenko, *Dvorianskaia sem'ia*, 486; and Wagner, *Marriage, Property, and Law*, 162–64.

21. Gessen, *Razdel'noe zhitel'stvo*, 87–92. In a decision of 1915, the Senate reaffirmed and clarified this stance. Courts could decide against the innocent party in a custody suit, leaving the child with the other parent if the child's well-being necessitated it. Cited in TsGIA SPb, fond 356, d. 17044, 45.

22. Anastasia Verbitskaia, *Osvobodilas!* 4th ed. (Moscow: Pechatnoe delo, 1912).

The women simply requested from the chancellery that their separate passport include the children as well as themselves. If officials found the women's case meritorious, they almost invariably acceded to the request to include the children, thereby deciding the issue of child custody at the same time as they approved the passport.

Fathers rarely contested such de facto decisions. The drunken, brutal, and improvident men who constituted a substantial proportion of husbands in separation suits appear to have had little interest in supporting, let alone caring for, their offspring without the help of a wife. But social status mattered a lot, too. Even if they wished to retain custody of their children, as some men clearly did, working-class men who labored long hours, earning barely enough to support themselves and a dependent or two, and who relied on the unpaid labor of a wife to provide housekeeping and child care were in no position to hire a replacement. His departing wife had "left on my hands our five-year-old son, Petr, which interferes with my work for the merchant Tsyngali [*sic*] as a turner," wrote the townsman Petr Eremeev to the chancellery in 1892, misspelling the name of his employer, the merchant R. K. San-Galli. "I have no one with whom to leave the child." Eremeev asked officials to talk some sense into his wife and make her return home from her mother's. "To tell you the truth, I can't live without a wife." Mikhail Dobychin, a stove maker, was perfectly willing to give his adulterous wife a passport, but only if she gave him custody of their child.[23] But there was no way he himself could care for his daughter; instead, he intended to ask his sister to raise her.

For all these reasons, only in a minority of cases was child custody actually contested. Some disputes arose when mothers sought to regain children who had been left with their father, either because the woman had initially gone off without them, or because their husbands had taken advantage of a "voluntary" agreement to issue their unhappy wives a passport, requiring in return that the wife surrender the children as Dobychin had tried to do—voluntary in quotes because such agreements inevitably reflected the husband's superior negotiating position. The chancellery also became involved in custody decisions when fathers sought custody from their estranged wives; and when couples, planning to separate, sought out officials' assistance in working out a custody arrangement. Most of the disputing parents derived from the propertied and/or educated classes, in which fathers had the means to hire a mother-substitute as well as the desire to shape the character of their offspring.

Chancellery officials devoted considerable bureaucratic energy to resolving such disputes. Mindful of legal rights, including the "parental rights" of both parties, as they sometimes put it, they were reluctant to violate them, and often worked hard to convince disputing parents to arrive at a voluntary agreement. Assuming the role of mediator, officials might assist the contending parties to arrive at written custody agreements

23. RGIA, fond 1412, op. 217, d. 13 (Eremeeva, E., 1891), 9; op. 216, ed. 36 (Dobychina, V., 1898), 20. See also op. 212, d. 168 (Ankudinova, O., 1902), 6.

in which the rights of both were honored and the welfare of the child protected; where such agreements already existed, officials ensured that parents abided by them. Such negotiated agreements might be exceedingly labor-intensive, often involving extensive consultations with the disputing spouses and multiple drafts. Officials played a role in elaborating details and dealt repeatedly with the complaints of one or both parties about alleged violations of the terms, sometimes for many years.[24] And when mediation failed, and officials made the judgment themselves, they did so only after carefully sifting through information on the quality of the children's supervision, education and overall care.[25] This information, like all the information adduced in the chancellery's cases, was obtained through an administrative and police apparatus and might involve undercover investigation, as happened in the case that introduced this chapter. Judging by the dossiers retained in the archive, although not by the chancellery's own self-reporting, they were at least as likely to decide in favor of the mother as the father.[26]

Even after 1890, when the Grinevich decision brought child custody arrangements into the purview of the courts, child custody remained important to officials, and they continued to involve themselves in such disputes, albeit to a more limited extent. If, as officials put it in one case, they found "the personal qualities of the spouses to be such that neither deserved to have their parental rights circumscribed," they became increasingly likely to refer disputing parties to the courts; they did the same when wives had left children behind and sought to regain them or had signed "voluntary" agreements.[27] But when parents appealed for their mediation, officials continued to provide it. And when women's appeals for a passport involved disputed custody, and officials found what they deemed to be serious moral failings in one of the parents, they preempted the courts and preserved the authority to choose the custodian themselves.

PATERNAL AUTHORITY AND MORAL MOTHERHOOD

Morality mattered a lot to officials. Considering the rights of father and mother to be the same, they decided custody cases on the basis of the "moral qualities"

24. For examples of these negotiated agreements, see ibid., op. 226, d. 16 (Parmanina, E., 1885); op. 227, d. 54 (Suprugi Rukavishnikovykh, 1889); op. 213, d. 17, 18, 19, 20, 21 (Suprugi Baranovskikh, 1890); and op. 212, d. 51 (Azancheeva, S., 1900).

25. See, for example, ibid., op. 212. d. 33 (Agafonova, Z., 1894), 45.

26. In 1893, officials reportedly satisfied only 311 of the 797 requests by women for custody of their children. See Wagner, *Marriage, Property, and Law*, 97 n. 102. The circumstances are not discussed. I suspect that most of the unsatisfied requests involved wives who left husbands without taking their children, then sought to reclaim them at a time when the courts were beginning to rule on these matters. Under these circumstances, officials were often reluctant to intervene unless it could be demonstrated conclusively that the children were in moral or physical danger; instead, they preferred to refer women to the courts.

27. RGIA, fond 1412, op. 232, d. 9 (Khlebnikova, M., 1899) 135.

of both parents, as officials construed them, and the parents' ability to fulfill the requirement, as set forth in law, of providing moral education for their children. In Great Britain and the United States, this understanding of parental rights would have given mothers a significant rhetorical advantage. There, greater concern for child welfare and belief in what Michael Grossberg calls women's "innate childrearing instincts" strengthened women's claim for custody of their children, especially if the women could present themselves as "moral." Eventually, claims based on a child's need for her mother came far to outweigh the father's "vested right." By the end of the nineteenth century, the maternal presumption had become so widespread in Anglo-American courts that it was rare for a mother to lose custody.[28]

The same evolution did not occur in Russia, despite the growing concern with child welfare expressed both by the courts and by administrative institutions.[29] In the courts, at least until 1914, the father's right remained the default mode unless the court found the father responsible for the breakdown of the marriage. Although the chancellery became increasingly prone to interpret "moral rearing" as involving the welfare of the child and remained more inclined than the courts to give weight to mothers' claims, a maternal presumption never became the norm. One reason is the very gender neutrality of Russia's law, which assigned fathers as well as mothers responsibility for "moral rearing." This, as we shall see, shaped the terms of most child custody disputes. Another reason is, ironically, the increasing propensity of chancellery officials to refer such disputes to the courts.

What did it mean to be a "moral mother" in late nineteenth-century Russia? It meant, first and foremost, self-abnegation in one's devotion to one's children and willingness to suffer on their behalf. These qualities, which echo the "maternal love and suffering that identify [Mary] in the Russian tradition," not only appealed to officials' sensibilities; they also reflected cultural norms that appear to have transcended social divides and shaped many women's conduct.[30] They certainly shaped women's rhetoric, creating new opportunities to challenge their husband's conduct but at the same time limiting the terms by which women might defend their own interests.[31] Thus, in their petitions, women commonly referred to their own suffering on their children's behalf (language that is absent from the model petitions published in this period): "I endured

---

28. Michael Grossberg, "Who Gets the Child?" 237; Wright, "De Manneville v. De Manneville," 249.

29. For the growing attention to the welfare of mother and child, see Abby Schrader, *Languages of the Lash: Corporal Punishment and Identity in Imperial Russia* (DeKalb: Northern Illinois University Press, 2002), 128–30.

30. Kivelson, "Sexuality and Gender," 103–4.

31. On the positive role of maternalism in Great Britain, see Elizabeth Foyster, *Marital Violence: An English Family History, 1660–1857* (New York: Cambridge University Press, 2005), 131.

everything when the children were small and sacrificed everything for the sake of preserving if only the ghost of the family world," asserted Evlampia Parmanina, using language virtually identical to that of countless other petitioners. But such rhetoric, foregrounding as it did female passivity, made it difficult for women to say much more about the care they actually provided. Rather like housekeeping, mothers treated the practice of mothering as self-evident. Thus, with a few exceptions—here, Parmanina again comes to mind—mothers' references to their maternal role were brief, limited to expressions of maternal love and concern for their children's moral and physical welfare and to statements about the children's need for protection from their father's ill-treatment, sexual misconduct, propensity to quarrel in the children's presence, and the like. Maria Bol'shikh, for example, who elaborated at length on the work she did after leaving her husband, explained her appeal for custody of the children she left with him, aged ten and twelve, in a simple phrase: "I fear for their morality." Women left it to others, the witnesses whom they named in their appeals, to elaborate on their maternal virtues.[32]

Fathers emerge as far more articulate and self-confident. A few were indeed so confident of their legal advantage in child custody disputes on the basis of their authority as head of the household that they did not even bother to defend their paternal rights. "I'll never willingly give my wife the children," declared Vasilii Parmanin to the chancellery in 1885, assuming he held the right to "give." "I refuse to surrender the children," avowed the physician Stepan Stsepurzhenskii after the chancellery ordered him to do precisely that when his wife petitioned in 1890. The physician Ilia Popov asserted in 1900, "I can't give my wife the children—it would be a crime." Vladimir Khlebnikov, an engineer, invariably referred to the couple's child as if he were exclusively the father's ("my son"), language to which his wife took heated exception. In 1910, Andrei Pykhanov, an agronomist, declared that his wife's decision to leave him was no reason to "deprive me of my children, whom no one can force me to give to her." So outraged was the well-born engineer Georgii Azancheev at the timing of the chancellery's custody decision in favor of his wife, which preempted the custody suit he had already initiated in court and was convinced he would win, that he eventually refused to have anything further to do with his son.[33] Most men, however, did not take their custodial right for granted, but rather felt compelled to defend it rhetorically.

They did so in language that was shaped by the legal responsibility for moral rearing and by heightened expectations of child care. Thus moral mothers played at least as prominent a role in husbands' counternarratives as they did in the self-presentations of

32. RGIA, fond 1412, op. 226, d. 16 (Parmanina), 1, 233–34; op. 213, d. 84 (Bol'shikh, M., 1886), 2.

33. Ibid., op. 226, d. 16 (Parmanina), 9; op. 148, d. 228 (Stsepurzhinskaia, A., 1890), 14 ob.; op. 226, d. 111 (Popova, S., 1901), 38; op. 232, d. 9 (Khlebnikova), 4, 5–6; op. 226, d. 163 (Pykhanova, A., 1910), 12, 27; op. 212, d. 51 (Azancheeva, S., 1900), 95–135.

— Софья Ивановна, я ничего не могу подѣлать съ Анютою: она шалитъ и меня не хочетъ слушаться.

— Въ такомъ случаѣ справьтесь въ книгѣ «*Совѣты матерямъ*» и поступите съ нею какъ тамъ сказано.

FIGURE 21.

"*Sofia Ivanovna, I can't do anything with Aniuta. She's being naughty and won't listen to me.*"

"*In that case, check* Advice to Mothers *and do whatever the book tells you to do.*"

Strekoza, *no. 40 (1895), M. E. Saltykov-Shchedrin Public Library.*

wives, but in this case as a standard from which the wife fell woefully short. Aspersions on a woman's sexual morality were particularly potent in child custody disputes in Russia as elsewhere, and it was a rare husband and father who failed to level them when children were at issue. If the allegation of illicit sexual conduct was upheld, it deprived the woman of "innocence" in the marital breakdown and by itself provided sufficient reason to deny the mother custody.[34] Hoping for just this outcome, Aleksandr Baranovskii bribed a witness to testify that his wife was involved in a sexual liaison, a ruse that the investigating gendarme uncovered. The gendarme officer who sympathized with Anastasia Novokreshchenova, merchant wife, and supported her desire for a passport in 1896, nevertheless rejected her request for child custody in terms that are notable not only for their concern with sexual morality but also their attentiveness to child psychology: "As for her desire for the children, that can hardly be satisfied, because her social position, as someone who has left her husband and gotten involved with another man, will negatively affect the children in every possible way, and all the more so because her older daughter is ten and is entering the stage where external impressions strongly affect a child and cannot help but have a painful effect on the moral rearing of the children." The chancellery dismissed the claims of Elena Rukavishnikova, merchant wife, for similar reasons. "In light of her not entirely reputable [*nebezuprechnyi*] morality, she cannot be seen as a suitable guide for her son," officials agreed in 1897. In 1899, rejecting the townswoman Varvara Dobychina's petition, the chancellery endorsed the need "to protect the child from the harmful influence of a mother who is in an illicit cohabitation with another man."[35]

Officials judged paternal sexual transgressions less harshly. Petr Novokreshchenov, who gained custody of the couple's children, for example, had been known to consort with prostitutes; and officials were well aware that he had become involved with another woman, although his involvement was not quite so public as his wife's. This outcome was far from unique. Acknowledging in the decision that the merchant Mikhail Shcherbakov was sexually involved with his son's nurse, three pages later an official wrote: "there is insufficient basis to take the boy away from his father and to deprive the latter of his parental rights."[36]

But fathers, in particular highly educated fathers, also drew on the new, more demanding expectations of parenting, both to fault their wives for their failure to live up to them and to extol their own virtues as parents. Their accounts of their wives'

---

34. This was the case elsewhere, too. See Mason, *From Father's Rights,* 63.

35. RGIA, fond 1412, op. 213, d. 19 (Suprugi Baranovskikh), 160; op. 224, d. 34 (Novokreshchenova, A., 1896), 7; op. 227, d. 54 (Suprugi Rukavishnikovykh), 176; op. 216, d. 36 (Dobychina), 66.

36. Ibid., op. 236, d. 8 (Shcherbakova, A., 1893), 112–13. The physician Stepan Stsepurzhenskii, also involved in an extramarital liaison, was eventually granted custody in preference to his wife, too (ibid., op. 148, op. 228 [Stsepurzhinskaia]).

failures to be a good mother are noteworthy for their assumption that a mother must be *personally* involved and herself care for children—noteworthy because the memoirs of merchants as well as nobles tell us that hands-on care by mothers, especially of small children, was still comparatively rare among those who could afford to hire a mother-substitute.[37] By the end of the nineteenth century, it had evidently become unacceptable to regard children as a "burden" which "one hastened to hand over to various uncles and nurses of the common people to raise," in the words of one respondent in a custody case, although no one saw anything objectionable about hiring governesses, tutors, or even nannies if mothers properly supervised such hired help and the mother continued to spend considerable amounts of what we would now call "quality time" with her children.[38]

Selfish and neglectful mothers who disdained such motherly duties loom large in their husbands' accounts. Requesting that the couple's daughter be transferred from the mother to him, for example, the nobleman Mikhail Koriakin, a lawyer living on his own estate in Tver province, claimed that his wife, Elizaveta, "ceased to bother with the family and children, whom she left to governesses, thinking only of her own pleasure and spending only a rare night at home."[39] His wife, Alevtina, handed their son over to wet nurses, barely taking an interest in him, the lawyer Vladimir Ptitsyn maintained in 1893, invoking, as did others, the importance of breast-feeding to the idealized image of maternity.[40] Due to her careless oversight, their only son had broken his arm not once but twice. The teacher Mikhail Ostrovidov complained in 1897 that his wife, Varvara, had little interest in child care. Once when he scolded her for neglectfulness, she purportedly cursed him and asserted that she was not "a nursemaid" and did not want to nurse the child. "I spit on your child," Varvara supposedly declared, adding, "I don't want to sacrifice my feelings and my freedom for the sake of my son." The townsman Mikhail Agafonov, a trader in ironwares, asserted that his wife neglected their two children once she became an heiress, leaving them to the care of others and preferring to spend her time pursuing pleasure. The teacher Zakhar Sabbashev contended that after

37. On mothering, see Kniagina Mariia Tenisheva, *Vpechatleniia moei zhizni. Vospominaniia* (Moscow: Zakharov, 2002), 1–28; and Vera N. Kharuzina, *Proshloe: Vospominaniia detskikh i otrocheskikh let* (Moscow: Novoe literaturnoe obozrenie, 1999). Merchant parents "did not bother much" with their children. (M. V. Briantsev, *Kul'tura russkogo kupechestva. Vospitanie i obrazovanie* [Briansk: Kursiv, 1999], 72).

38. Quoted from RGIA, fond 1412, op. 226, d. 16 (Parmanina), 58–59.

39. Ibid., op. 221, d. 121 (Koriakina, E., 1888), 22.

40. Ibid., op. 226, d. 149 (Ptitsyna, A., 1892), 15, 17. Sofia Tolstoy and her husband, the novelist Leo Tolstoy, fought bitterly over this issue, Sofia begging to be freed from nursing in consequence of her cracked and painful breasts, her husband insisting that she endure the pain and discomfort for the sake of proper mothering. See Anne Edwards, *Sonya: The Life of Countess Tolstoy* (New York: Simon and Schuster, 1981), 118–22.

his wife, Maria, abandoned him, taking along the children, she often left them alone in the evening while she went out on the town. The moral consequences were dreadful. "The older girl, seeing her mother's bad example, allowed herself to be seduced and deceived and became an unhappy woman, and my son fell into the company of fallen people and tramps and engaged in vicious actions, for which he was placed in a house of correction, where he remains to this day."[41]

Many well-educated fathers went further, not only casting aspersions on their wives' mothering practices but also donning the mantle of moral parent themselves. What did it mean to be a moral father? These men, usually highly educated professionals, projected a vision of active manhood that included their own direct and, in some cases, self-sacrificing involvement in the care and education of their children. Their tendency to dwell on their own virtues as fathers may reflect the gender-neutral nature of a portion of late nineteenth-century advice literature, despite the growing emphasis on mothering, in addition to the legal requirement that *parents* provide moral rearing. But their statements also suggest that among Russia's educated elites, at least, the division between gendered spheres was less than clear-cut. Some Russian fathers, or at least educated Russian fathers, expected to be involved in the everyday tasks of child care in ways comparable to, or perhaps even greater than, those that historians have begun to uncover in the United States and Great Britain. "Education and moral training were central to a father's concerns, especially in relation to sons, who embody his future," John Tosh writes of Victorian Britain. Fathers participated actively in child rearing, both when children were young and as they grew older, asserts Steven Frank concerning the nineteenth-century United States.[42] In Russia, where men's role in public life was far more circumscribed, fatherhood may have held an additional satisfaction—the promise of contributing to a better future for the nation. Some reform-minded intellectuals regarded the rearing of a self-respecting, autonomous individual as one means to transform Russia's authoritarian and hierarchical social and political order.[43]

Thus some fathers offered detailed accounts of their own attentive parenting. The physician Stepan Stsepurzhenskii contrasted his own careful nurturance to his wife's

41. RGIA, fond 1412, op. 225, d. 21 (Ostrovidova, V., 1897), 23; op. 212, d. 33 (Agafonova), 6; op. 228, d. 2 (Sabbasheva, M., 1905), 14.

42. John Tosh, "Authority and Nurture in Middle-Class Fatherhood," *Gender and History* 8, no. 1 (1996): 50; Stephen M. Frank, *Life with Father: Parenthood and Masculinity in the Nineteenth-Century North* (Baltimore: Johns Hopkins University Press, 1998), 2. See also Shawn Johansen, *Family Men: Middle-Class Fatherhood in Early Industrializing America* (New York: Routledge, 2001).

43. On parenting and social reform, see Julia Lise Kinnear, "Childhood, Family, and Civil Society in Late Imperial Russia: P. F. Kapterev, the St. Petersburg Parents' Circle, and Family Education, 1884–1914" (PhD diss., University of Toronto, 2003).

purported neglect. Under his supervision, his daughters had been taught to play music and to converse in foreign languages. For their sake, he subscribed to a number of the new journals intended for children, including *A Sincere Word, Readings for Children*, and more recently, *Spring*. Having taken such care with his children's education, he refused to hand them over to his wife, a woman who did not derive, as he did, from a "cultivated family"; who, as he put it, had neither studied in an educational institution nor been educated at home; and who lacked a proper understanding of morality. The engineer Vladimir Khlebnikov wrote: "I often had the child on my hands. I spent time with him and gave him toys to play with, at the same time teaching him to put everything in its place." Ivan Sabbashev, a teacher, declared in 1900, "It was I and not my wife who instructed the children.... I prepared them for the second or third class of middle school, saving the fee for the first one or two classes. Only thanks to my efforts did the three eldest finish middle school."[44]

Suggesting a still greater blurring of gendered boundaries, a few men even declared themselves to be mother-substitutes, usurping, at least rhetorically, the role of wife and mother. While his wife was in medical school in the 1880s, Ivan Pakhitonov, an artist, claimed to have assumed the duties of housewife and mother. He "bathed the children, bought what was needed for the kitchen, even cut out dresses." Pakhitonov found this role reversal very trying: "Having to do work uncharacteristic [*nesvoistvennyi*] of us men drove me to a state of almost sickly irritability and nervousness." But other men apparently took pride in their nurturing role. "I was everything to my children," wrote the physician Pogozhev to the Third Section in 1879, "father and mother, breadwinner, nanny and nurse, governor and educator." The physician Sergei Plaksin claimed to have provided the most essential care after the birth of his children. The daughter, born in 1881, "grew up entirely under my supervision; her mother only nursed her, whereas I alone looked after her until her death in 1884. I spent all my free time with her," he wrote in 1890. When his wife bore a second child, a son, it was Plaksin who was responsible for the infant's proper nourishment. Initially, he reported, his wife, Anna, "refused to breast-feed him and wanted to hire a wet nurse, because breast-feeding would spoil her figure and make her fat, but I said I'd never allow another woman to feed my child and would sooner feed him with cow's milk. Only because of this did she nurse him." The teacher Mikhail Ostrovidov boasted that his nurturing abilities were such that he could dispense with a woman altogether. "My love for my son is so great that my tender care is better than that of any nurse or mother, as everyone will tell you.... I'm the one who has cared for the child—fed him, put him to sleep, taken him for walks and so forth, all with love.... I live only for my son, I cannot breathe without him, I love him more than life, he is my only

44. RGIA, fond 1412, op. 148, op. 228 (Stsepurzhinskaia), 56–57; op. 232, d. 9 (Khlebnikova), 28–29; op. 228, d. 2 (Sabbasheva), 10.

treasure now.... And my son loves me so much that voluntarily, he'd never go to his mother."[45]

MORAL PARENTING AND THE STATE

In some cases, contending parents also framed their claims more broadly, attempting to align their own interests explicitly with those of the state. Taking advantage of the political and cultural/religious preoccupations of Russia's last two rulers, they accused the other party of political or national disloyalty and/or religious apostasy. When such expansive definitions of "moral rearing" involved religious faith, they might prove effective. Accusing the other spouse of seeking to convert or raise the children in a "non-Russian" fashion and/or outside the Orthodox faith as Old Believers, Catholics, Shtundists, Judaizers, or, in one late case, atheists, to name the allegations that surfaced in the cases I have read, parents implicitly referred to the law that required the children of an Orthodox parent to be raised in the Orthodox faith.[46] Officials not only took those charges seriously; in some cases, they permitted them to outweigh the welfare of the child, as they did, for example, in the case of the severely abused Aleksandra Shniavina, a teacher from the Pskov peasantry, whose alleged membership in the Judaizer sect cost her custody of the couple's two children and eventually cost one of the children her life as a consequence of paternal neglect.[47]

Officials appear to have been far less concerned about political apostasy, or the radical movements that attracted substantial segments of educated society, than they were about religious affiliation. In their efforts to win officials to their side, women and men alike invoked the threat of "nihilism," the phrase by which the radical movement of the 1860s and 1870s was popularly known.[48] Only in one case I have read did such allegations influence the decision in a custody dispute. This was the case of the lawyer Vladimir Ptitsyn and his wife, Alevtina, the daughter of a wealthy Siberian merchant. Accusing his wife of involvement with "Marxist" and "nihilist" circles, Vladimir repeatedly warned the chancellery of the threats to his son's future should the child remain with

---

45. Ibid., op. 226. d. 19 (Pakhitonova, M., 1892), 23; GARF, fond 109, 3-oe otdelenie, 2-aia ekspeditsiia, op. 1874, d. 536, 83; RGIA, fond 1412, op. 226, d. 61 (Plaksina, V., 1890), 31, 34; op. 225, d. 21 (Ostrovidova, V., 1897), 21, 24.

46. Paul Werth, "Empire, Religious Freedom, and the Legal Regulation of 'Mixed' Marriages in Russia," *Journal of Modern History* 80 (June 2008): 296–331.

47. RGIA, fond 1412, op. 235, d. 27 (Shniavina, A., 1892). For other allegations involving religious apostasy in custody disputes, see op. 223, d. 114 (Morozova, A., 1885); op. 216, d. 36, (Dobychina); op. 219, d. 37 (Zvereva, V., 1911). Interestingly, Zinaida Agafonova's claim that, although raised as an Old Believer, she wanted to convert herself and her children to Orthodoxy gained her neither the passport nor child custody. See ibid., op. 212, d. 33 (Agafonova).

48. Cases where political allegations appear include RGIA, fond 1412, op. 228, d. 19 (Pakhitonova), 1; op. 221, d. 118 (Korchuganova, M., 1895), 15; op. 228, d. 59 (Skachkova, Z., 1901), 21, 23.

his errant mother. She would turn the child into "a moral monster and enemy...of the motherland," Vladimir contended. The Ministry of the Interior confirmed Alevtina's association with known radicals, in particular one Aleksandr Krutovskii, once exiled to his hometown of Krasnoiarsk for possession of populist publications. This determined the outcome of the case, the welfare of the child notwithstanding. Reporting to the chancellery in early February 1893, the governor of St. Petersburg had nothing favorable to say about the husband's character and conduct: Vladimir had done everything he could to get his hands on his wife's substantial capital and had "never demonstrated parental feeling for the child, whom he used mainly as a means to torment his wife." Nevertheless, it was clear to the governor that sole custody should go to Vladimir, about whom no politically compromising information had been unearthed: "To leave the child with the mother, attracted to Krutovskii's ideas, will inevitably lead to an incorrect and harmful moral upbringing," the governor asserted. Before the chancellery could render a decision, however, Alevtina, aware that she was likely to lose her case, reconciled with her husband under terms that preserved the shell of the marriage while allowing both parties to live their own lives. Two months later, Alevtina kidnapped their son and fled abroad with the help of Krutovskii and his radical connections. Mother and son remained in England until 1904, despite Vladimir's furious but futile efforts to convince the secret police to locate them and bring them home.[49]

Political accusations became less rather than more salient to the outcome of disputes during the reign of Nicholas II, perhaps because the attitudes of officials had changed, perhaps because the new tsar in whose name they served paid less attention to these matters. In 1899, officials rejected the plea of the physician Petr Zakharov, whose wife, Sofia, had run off with a radical activist, asking that they inform the St. Petersburg gendarme administration of his wife's political unreliability: Zakharov "should turn to them himself," they wrote, "if he has the evidence for doing so." Two years later, in 1901, officials simply ignored allegations leveled by the physician Ilia Popov that his wife, Sofia, was associated with political radicals. Instead they found her maternal virtues and his paternal failings sufficient grounds for a decision. Ilia alleged that his wife's older sister had introduced Sofia to a circle of suspicious people, mainly Polish students, before their marriage, and that her apartment had twice been searched and she had spent time in the house of preliminary detention, where political prisoners were held. Recently, he claimed, she had become sexually involved with a student radical. Telling a story that might have been lifted from the pages of Anastasia Verbitskaia's *She Was Liberated!* published two years before, Popov declared that the student tutor Sofia had hired for their son had become her lover and that the two "carried on in the most shameless fashion" and together became involved in politics. "When the student demonstrations began in February 1899, the student was gone for days on end, and

49. Ibid., op. 228, d. 149 (Ptitsyna).

my wife looked for him all over the city." To give the children to her would thus be a "crime." Except for the sexual allegation, however, officials demonstrated no interest in these charges and requested no investigation of them. Having become convinced that the sexual allegation was false, they dismissed the rest as "having nothing to do with his family affairs." In this case as in others, the mother's ability to provide better care for her children determined the outcome of the dispute. Popov, they concluded in 1901, was a "poor family man" [*plokhoi sem'ianin*], who treated his wife crudely and impudently and paid little attention to the children. It was the mother who merited custody, as the person who "ran the household and cared for their children, educated and looked after them."[50]

THE CHANCELLERY AND THE COURTS

While the chancellery was prone to award custody to the mother in cases where they found her the more "morally worthy," over time officials became increasingly less likely to make custody decisions at all. This development was a direct response to the precedent-setting Grinevich decision of 1890, and to the growing assertiveness of the postreform courts, which sometimes brought the courts into conflict with the chancellery. One of the consequences of the new willingness of the courts to rule on family disputes after Grinevich, at least initially, was the propensity of some courts to challenge chancellery decisions in women's favor, including decisions over custody.[51] And because the chancellery's authority to resolve marital disputes rested on neither statutory nor administrative law, some judges not only treated its decisions as lacking legal substance but also took the opportunity to strike a blow on behalf of the law. The result was rulings that conflicted with those of the chancellery.

Two custody disputes that husbands brought to court illustrate the problem. The first involved Nikolai Andreev, a Moscow merchant, and his wife, Olga. In 1891, Olga left him and went to live with her parents in St. Petersburg, taking along two of the children and leaving the third, a seven-year-old son, with Nikolai and his parents in Moscow, with the understanding that the child would be allowed to visit her regularly. The chancellery would eventually find no difficulty approving a separate passport for Andreeva that included the two children. The investigator found that Nikolai Andreev was physically abusive and sought to extort money from his wife; he had also been condemned to four months in debtor's prison for swindling his own customers. However, while the case was still pending before the chancellery, Nikolai Andreev sued successfully in St. Petersburg circuit court for restitution of his conjugal rights and custody of his children. The circuit court ruled in his favor despite a letter from

---

50. Ibid., op. 219, d. 33 (Zakharova, S., 1898), 80; op. 226, d. 111 (Popova), 4, 28, 29, 86.

51. On the propensity of the courts to raise challenges to chancellery decisions, see ibid., op. 241, d. 21, 54 ob.; and Veremenko, *Dvorianskaia sem'ia*, 245.

the chancellery that Olga presented, which stated that she had a case pending before the chancellery and, until its resolution, the right to live separately from her husband. The court's decision of January 17, 1892, ordered Olga and the children to return to her husband's home in Moscow. The husband's witnesses had convinced the court that Olga had no grounds for departure: their priest testified to the "complete agreement" between the spouses, while their *dvornik* reported that his wife wept when Nikolai was sent to prison. The decision made no mention of the letter from the chancellery. Instead, it concluded that the evidence showed that couple's life was "friendly and happy" before Nikolai's imprisonment, and that he gave her no reason to leave.[52]

The chancellery's authority eventually overrode that of the court, but only after Tsar Alexander III himself became involved. Initially, officials sought merely to re-open the court case. But a letter from Otto Rikhter, head of the chancellery, to Nikolai Manasein, minister of justice, asking for assistance and setting forth in general terms the reasons for the chancellery's approval of Andreeva's passport, elicited a negative response. As his answer, Manasein merely appended the court decision and listed the various witnesses and their relation to the parties involved, the implication being that the witnesses knew whereof they spoke.[53] Case closed. A new investigation by the St. Petersburg police not only upheld Andreeva's version of her marriage, however, but also uncovered additional, quite damning evidence concerning the husband's parents, a brother and sister, and the husband himself, the product of their incestuous union. Reporting on the investigation, the gendarme recommended that the court's ruling be ignored: it "deserves no attention because when the court examined this case, it was misled by the testimony of witnesses," who with one exception knew nothing about the couple's relations. The gendarme judged that on the basis of Olga Andreeva's "exemplary moral qualities" she merited a passport and custody of all three of her children, including the son currently living with his father and grandparents. Because the decision involved forcibly removing the son from his father, it required the tsar's consent. Provided with a report that dwelled on Olga's sterling qualities and Nikolai's numerous vices, Tsar Alexander III gave his approval on September 22, 1892. Eight days after the tsar's decision, a detective in the employ of the Ministry of the Interior removed the child from his grandparents' home and delivered him to his mother.[54]

In the case of Khlebnikov v. Khlebnikova the tensions between the law-governed courts and the extralegal authority of the chancellery assumed an explicitly political form. At the end of 1899, Vladimir Khlebnikov brought suit against his wife, Maria, in a St. Petersburg circuit court, seeking custody of their nine-year-old son. A month

---

52. RGIA, fond 1412, op. 212, d. 148 (Andreeva, O., 1891), 48–49.
53. Ibid., 46, 50.
54. Ibid., 70, 72, 75, 77.

earlier, the chancellery had approved a one-year passport for Maria Khlebnikova and the child, referring the couple to the courts for the final custody decision, because, as officials put it, "the personal qualities" of the spouses were such that neither wife nor husband deserved to have "their parental rights circumscribed." Initially, when Khlebnikov sued for custody, the court refused to act, however; instead, it ruled that the case could not be considered until the wife's one-year passport had expired. The passport, awarded on the basis of the tsar's supralegal authority, constituted "an exception to the general laws."[55] Khlebnikov appealed the decision to the St. Petersburg court of appeals, which agreed to hear the case.

During the court's proceedings, the chancellery's authority became the primary issue. Challenging the decision of the lower court, and arguing that civil law codes outweighed the chancellery's administrative authority, Khlebnikov's lawyer attacked the legal standing of the chancellery's original decision to award a passport. Such decisions, the lawyer contended, were mere bureaucratic dispositions or instructions, and not imperial commands that carried the force of law. In the absence of the words "His Majesty Orders," chancellery decisions lacked the authority to abrogate the law that forbade marital separation. The lawyer based his case for paternal custody on Grinevich, noting that the decision of 1890 awarded the husband the primary right to the children when the couple lived apart, and arguing that Khlebnikova had failed to establish a compelling reason for leaving her husband. Because the language of the chancellery's decision in favor of Khlebnikova was key to the case, Khlebnikov's lawyer requested that the chancellery provide the court with documentary evidence of the decision on Khlebnikova's behalf. The chancellery complied, but as it always did, in a manner designed to preserve the strict secrecy of its proceedings. Thus the judges but not the husband or his lawyer were granted the opportunity to review the document. Khlebnikov's lawyer made much of the secrecy: "A document labeled secret cannot serve as evidence in a court." Not only had her lawyer failed to establish the chancellery's legal authority, he maintained; in his view, "the existence of secret papers" raised serious doubts about whether such authority even existed, doubts confirmed by the laws establishing the chancellery, which made no mention of its authority to separate married couples.[56]

His argument convinced the court. Addressing explicitly the question of whether the chancellery enjoyed the legal authority to separate a married couple, on November 24, 1900, the St. Petersburg Court of Appeals answered in the negative. Because

55. RGIA, fond 1412, op. 232, d. 9 (Khlebnikova), 72, 135.

56. TsGIA SPb, fond 356, op. 1, d. 11126, 54–55, 80–81. The documents are not included in the archive of the court proceedings. The chancellery also refused a request from Khlebnikov to view the evidence on which the decision against him was based. In fact, the primary evidence against Khlebnikov, atypically, was his own counternarrative.

Khlebnikova had neither established to the court's satisfaction the legal grounds for her separation, nor asked the court for the right to live apart from her husband—a right she already enjoyed thanks to the chancellery—the court found her separation "willful and unauthorized [*samovol'no*]," and in violation of the law forbidding marital separation. Therefore, as a woman still subject by law to the will of her husband, she lacked the right to custody of her child if her husband opposed it. The court took the opportunity explicitly to reject the chancellery's authority. The chancellery's decision awarding her child custody "could serve as no basis for rejecting the [husband's] suit because the grace granted her by permission of His Majesty...constituted only a grace and not the recognition of a [legal] right."[57]

On November 1, 1901, the State Senate, to which Khlebnikova appealed, overturned the appeals court's decision and, returning the case to the St. Petersburg court of appeals, instructed the court to base its decision on "the best interests of the child in the given situation." After almost two years of deliberations, the court decided in Khlebnikova's favor. Reserving judgment about custody after the eight-year-old child reached the age of twelve, when, as the decision put it, "the authority and influence of the father become especially important for the development of his character," the court ruled that until then the child should remain with his mother, whose care he still needed, who loved him ardently, and who provided the requisite moral and spiritual upbringing.[58]

The growing readiness of the courts to rule in child custody and other matters relating to marital breakdown affected the chancellery's practice in two ways. First, it prompted officials increasingly to refer custody disputes to the courts.[59] Second, it led the heads of the chancellery to propose a series of initiatives aimed at formalizing the chancellery's procedures and giving them the force of law in order to fend off further legal challenges. These efforts culminated in 1902, when Baron Budberg formulated a document entitled "His Majesty's Secret Instructions," which established the chancellery's legal authority to resolve marital disputes and, at the same time, clarified the jurisdictions of the chancellery and those of the courts. The "Secret Instructions" granted to the chancellery's director the authority to receive petitions from wives

57. "Because she is not asking the court to establish her right to separation, there is no reason for the court to determine which of the parties is at fault for the breakdown of the marriage nor to query witnesses about which parent is the more suitable for child rearing" (ibid., 37, 40, 87–88).

58. RGIA, fond 1412, op. 232, d. 9 (Khlebnikova), 246–47.

59. For example, having initially decided that Varvara Ostrovidova merited custody as the party who was "fully cultivated and educated," and who could provide the child with a lot better upbringing and would be able to place him in "more beneficial circumstances than those he finds at his father's," two years later, in 1899, when she appealed again, chancellery officials found it "unnecessary to resolve the question," because "according to the law, the conflict belongs in the courts" (ibid., op. 225, d. 21 [Ostrovidova], 129, 151).

involved in marital disputes and, if circumstances warranted, to permit wives to live apart from their husbands with the hope that the couple would eventually reconcile. Treating separation as a temporary measure, the instructions eliminated the open-ended renewals that had remained part of the chancellery's practice; instead, it limited the duration of the woman's passport to a year (article 11); she might obtain a longer-term separation only after a subsequent petition and if her circumstances had not changed. With the tsar's approval, chancellery decisions would attain the status of a decree—that is, of law. Budberg requested that the tsar approve the "Secret Instructions" in order to give chancellery decisions a "firm legal basis," as he put it, and to facilitate the work of the courts, which would no longer have to request from the chancellery clarification of whether a particular decision derived from His Majesty's orders.[60]

The "Secret Instructions," which went through several drafts, had much to say about the issue of child custody, essentially formalizing some of the practices discussed in this chapter while ceding others entirely to the courts. Of the sixteen articles, custody figured directly or indirectly in five. The chancellery explicitly reserved for itself the authority to award custody to a mother who already had custody de facto, and who requested custody at the same time as she requested a passport; it also reiterated its authority to confirm custody agreements at both parents' request. Nevertheless, officials were now to refer to the courts all custody disputes that arose *after* separation had been established through the chancellery's authority—that is, after a woman's passport had been approved. Having created this general rule, the "Secret Instructions" nevertheless permitted exceptions. The instructions reserved for the head of the chancellery the right to act on his own authority in "exceptional circumstances" where the petitioners might experience "extreme difficulty in realizing their rights under the law" or when "extraordinary circumstances" required immediate action "to prevent criminal acts by one of the spouses or to remove circumstances of their family life that were clearly intolerable," informing the tsar as soon as possible thereafter. That this general language was intended to apply primarily to child custody disputes is evident from earlier redactions of the instructions and their rationale, which made the connection explicitly.[61] The tsar approved the instructions; thereafter, all chancellery decisions in favor of the wife bore the statement,

60. Ibid., op. 241, d. 21, 21–23; 38 ob.–39; for the instructions themselves, see 102–4. Earlier redactions of the instructions set forth specific grounds for separation; these do not appear in the final version.

61. "Spouses already living separately...who petition for child custody or in general for the solution of all quarrels about the further fate of the children...will be referred to the relevant judicial instance, with exceptions to this rule permitted only in exceptional cases," read an earlier draft (25). For the reasoning behind these exceptions, see ibid., 18–24.

"in accordance with his Majesty's Secret Instructions." So far as can be ascertained from cases involving women's efforts to regain custody after 1902, both Budberg and his successor proved notably hesitant to exercise the authority they had reserved for themselves, referring mothers to the courts even in cases where paternal care was demonstrably cruel or neglectful.[62]

• • •

As the nineteenth century drew to an end, the maternalist discourses of the late nineteenth century and the intensified concern for child welfare came increasingly to influence the thinking of tsarist officials, as they did that of other members of Russia's educated elites, among them reforming jurists and gendarmes. In consequence, officials' understanding of "moral rearing" grew more expansive over time and came to involve not only the welfare of the state but that of the child as well. Indeed, in deciding on the proper custodian, officials sometimes employed "modern" touchstones for evaluating child custody disputes—that is, they took into account not only the "moral" qualities but also the "psychological assets and liabilities of each parent, and the quality of their interactions with the child."[63] That concern emerges with particular clarity in the Gushchin case, an unusual case in which the children's father lost custody to their aunt. In 1896, the chancellery had approved the separation of Nadezhda Guzheva from her husband, Fedor, a townsman, and awarded the mother custody of their two children. Two years later, the mother died, leaving a will that gave the children to her sister to rear and excluded Fedor from guardianship. Fedor appealed to the chancellery for restoration of custody: the children, after all, were his. The chancellery, however, rejected his appeal in 1898 on the grounds that Fedor, unemployed and remarried, with another child currently in a shelter, lacked the means to support his children and had shown neither love nor interest in them before they inherited their mother's property.

---

62. Judging by cases preserved in the archives of the St. Petersburg courts, custody suits remained relatively few in number by comparison with appeals for alimony and child support. When they resolved such conflicts—and sometimes judges failed to rule on questions of custody for a variety of reasons—unless the mother had left the father for reasons the courts deemed "frivolous," courts were more likely to favor the mother than the father and to base decisions on the well-being of the child, or so indicate the handful of cases involving small children that I have surveyed. See TsGIA SPb, fond 356, op. 1, d. 8692 (1895), d. 22010 (1910), d. 22264 (1912), and d. 17044 (1915). For cases in which mother's custody claim was rejected because she failed to provide a compelling reason for leaving her husband, see d. 16716 (1915) and d. 18681 (1914).

63. Jacob Goldstein and C. Abraham Fenster, "Anglo-American Criteria for Resolving Child Custody Disputes from the Eighteenth Century to the Present: Reflections on the Role of Socio-Culture Change," *Journal of Family History* 19, no. 1 (1994): 42–43. U.S. courts began to use such criteria comparatively recently. See Andre P. Derdeyn, "Child Custody Contests in Historical Perspective," *American Journal of Psychiatry* 133 (1976): 1369–76.

The aunt, in contrast, "loved the children as if they were her own," and was bringing them up as well as anyone might wish [*deti... nakhodiatsia v nailuchshikh usloviiakh vospitaniia, kakikh mozhno zhelat' detiam*].[64] Officials' concern with the welfare of the children had prompted them to play an active and often very time-consuming role in helping separating parents negotiate satisfactory custody arrangements, agreements that officials subsequently helped enforce.

Officials' demonstrated concern with the best interests of the child seems at odds with the patriarchal relations that continued to provide the model for the Russian polity, according to which hierarchical relations of authority and subordination remained the norm. In officials' eyes, good fathers were certainly not absolute monarchs.[65] Indeed, for officials (and for gendarmes, governors, and other men highly placed in state service), the affective and sentimental family long beloved of legal reformers might comfortably coexist with the autocratic political system to which they remained devoted.[66] At the same time, officials' practice was comparatively free of the paternal presumption implicit in legal thinking, prompting them to award custody to mothers in disputes where the courts were likely to have found in favor of fathers, at least until 1902. Officials' flexibility in custody disputes, like their approach to marital disputes in general, was a product of the very paternalism, particularism, and absence of abstract legal principles that governed their overall practice. In ceding custody disputes to the courts after 1902, officials accepted the rule of law, at least in matters of child custody. It is no small irony that their recognition of the growing reach of the courts put an end to the even-handed approach to child custody that had characterized administrative practice for almost eighty years.

64. RGIA, fond 1412, op. 250, d. 104, 90–91.

65. I take these points from Jeffrey Merrick, "Sexual Politics and Public Order in Late Eighteenth-Century France: The Mémoires secrets and the Correspondance secrète," *Journal of the History of Sexuality* 1, no. 1 (1990): 68–69; and Leslie Tuttle, "Celebrating the Père de Famille: Pronatalism and Fatherhood in Eighteenth-Century France," *Journal of Family History* 29, no. 4 (2004): 372.

66. In their attitudes toward parent-child relations, officials differed substantially from members of the urban middle classes of Siberia, at least, where children remained in "complete subjection" to their parents. See Iu. M. Goncharov, *Gorodskaia sem'ia Sibiri vtoroi poloviny XIX–nachala XX v.* (Barnaul: Izdatel'stvo Altaiskogo gosudarstvennogo universiteta, 2002), 245.

Conclusion

THE POLITICS OF MARITAL STRIFE

The change in the passport law of March 12, 1914, ended the chancellery's role in resolving marital disputes. The revised law granted married women the right to obtain a passport without a husband's permission, and if living apart from the husband (although not if cohabiting), to take a job or enroll in school, also without requiring permission. These changes, which made marital separation possible de facto but not de jure, brought additional adjustments to the law. It was modified to incorporate earlier decisions concerning such related matters as alimony, child support, and child custody and to specify the grounds on which a spouse's request for the restoration of cohabitation might be denied. One of these grounds was "obvious abuses" of marital rights by the spouse of the party seeking separation; another, the perception by the separated party that cohabitation had become intolerable (*nevynosimo*). The revised law nevertheless continued to require spouses to cohabit.[1]

The modifications of family law were an effort to accommodate the profound social and cultural changes that accompanied Russia's rapid industrialization and urbanization, and that transformed attitudes toward personal life at least among the more modern sectors of the population. By the early twentieth century, individuals across the social spectrum had grown more assertive not only of civil and political rights but also of personal prerogatives such as the right to autonomy and self-fulfillment. Nevertheless, and the modifications to family law notwithstanding, key components of it remained in place until the revolutions of 1917. Until then, the law continued to bestow on fathers and husbands near absolute authority over other household members. The law now extended to the consequences of separation, but separation itself remained outside the law. Divorce continued to be adjudicated in religious rather than civil courts. While access broadened over time, the

---

1. For the revised laws, see I. V. Gessen, *Razdel'noe zhitel'stvo suprugov. Zakon 12 marta 1914 goda o nekotorykh izmeneniiakh i dopolneniiakh*... (St. Petersburg: Pravo, 1914).

process remained not only arduous but also out of reach for the vast majority of people who wanted to terminate their marriages in order to remarry. When divorce became a civil process in 1918, under Bolshevik rule, state registry offices were deluged by divorce applications.[2] The persistence of the more restrictive aspects of the law was primarily due to the ultraconservative role of the Russian Orthodox Church, which in the face of considerable popular discontent staunchly resisted more fundamental revisions, among them the legalization of separation and reform of the laws governing divorce. The church's inability to respond more flexibly to popular pressure for change undermined its own support even among the faithful. Its stance contributed, or so argues Gregory Freeze, to a growing perception that family crisis and political crisis were one and the same.[3]

The very embodiment of Russia's absolutist, supralegal political order, the imperial chancellery had proved considerably more flexible than the church, although the remedy at its disposal, approving separate passports, was no substitute for divorce, and those who benefited were almost exclusively female. Traditionally inclined by their paternalism to regard women as the weaker and more vulnerable sex, chancellery officials began around the mid-1890s to demonstrate increasing responsiveness to female aspirations and greater respect for the female person. At the same time, they became more demanding of men. These processes continued into the twentieth century, in part as a result of turnover in personnel, for younger cohorts were more likely to have received a university and/or legal education with a humanistic bent. But the changes were also the product of officials' own experience, as well as of profound shifts in Russian culture and values, vividly expressed in the self-presentations of wives and the testimonies of witnesses who spoke in their favor.

As a result, officials became willing to relinquish their own paternalistic role and to endorse limited but meaningful systemic change. They had concluded that the problems women confronted could not be dealt with by focusing only on the acts of individual male deviants, leaving the patriarchal family order intact. They understood that the problems facing women were also—and more significantly—a function of the patriarchal system itself, as embodied in the passport law and the law forbidding spousal separation. In short, they realized the need for structural change.[4] This realization is

---

2. Wendy Z. Goldman, *Women, the State, and Revolution: Soviet Family Policy and Social Life, 1917–1936* (New York: Cambridge University Press, 1993), 104–5.

3. Gregory L. Freeze, "Profane Narratives about a Holy Sacrament: Marriage and Divorce in Late Imperial Russia," in *Sacred Stories: Religion and Spirituality in Modern Russia*, ed. Mark D. Steinberg and Heather J. Coleman (Bloomington: Indiana University Press, 2007), 168–69.

4. This analysis has been influenced by Peter W. Bardaglio's discussion of state paternalism in the nineteenth-century U.S. South, wherein the state intervened only when the male head of the household "abused his rights and neglected his obligations in such an obvious and undeniable way

Поневолѣ придется.

— Господи, какая масса бѣлья и платьевъ у меня!
Да тутъ никогда не уложишься. Положительно придется
помириться съ мужемъ и не уѣзжать отъ него!

FIGURE 22. *"Lord, what a lot of dresses and underwear I own! I can't
possibly pack them all. I'll have to reconcile and stay with my husband
after all."*
Strekoza, *no. 37 (1905), M. E. Saltykov-Shchedrin Public Library.*

evident in a memorandum to Tsar Nicholas II composed in 1902 by Baron Aleksandr A. Budberg, who had succeeded Dmitrii Sipiagin as head of the chancellery. Expressing himself bluntly concerning the negative impact of the passport law, Budberg explained why, despite Senate decisions establishing legal precedents for awarding custody, alimony, and child support, the chancellery's work remained as necessary as ever. Russian law, he wrote, weighed most heavily on women: "occupying a subordinate position in the family, made completely dependent on the husband, women incomparably more than men experience all the burdensome affects of marital discord." Because the Senate decisions left the passport law unchanged, it remained exceedingly difficult for women to escape an unhappy marriage.[5]

The chancellery officials' critique of the patriarchal legal system was articulated explicitly and, so far as I know, uniquely in 1898, in response to the draft code revising family law that the Editing Commission of the Civil Cassation Department of the Senate had produced after years of work. The draft was a compromise, aimed (unsuccessfully) at overcoming ultraconservative opposition to legal reform. It relied primarily on marital separation instead of divorce to protect wives and to resolve marital discord. As grounds for separation, it proposed cruelty, grave insult, the syphilitic illness of a spouse, drunkenness, abandonment and neglect, shameful or dissolute behavior, and extreme extravagance. The chancellery responded positively to the prospect of legal reform, which would have ended its role in resolving marital disputes and transferred such disputes entirely to the courts. Dmitrii Sipiagin composed the response. Then head of the chancellery, from 1899 Sipiagin served as minister of the interior, and because of his repressive response to political dissent was the bane of the left, at whose hands he would die in 1902. Despite serious reservations about some of the draft code's provisions, he appears to have regarded the draft neither as the outcome of complex negotiations nor as reflecting jurists' efforts to circumscribe absolute authority but rather as the institutionalization and legalization of many of the chancellery's own long-standing practices.[6] According to Sipiagin, if approved, the draft code would serve to

---

that he posed a threat to the legitimacy of patriarchy as a social system." Such interventions, Bardaglio emphasizes, particularized the man's behavior by treating him as a deviant, thus laying the blame for abuses on the individual, rather than the larger structures of power. See Peter W. Bardaglio, *Reconstructing the Household: Families, Sex, and the Law in the Nineteenth-Century South* (Chapel Hill: University of North Carolina Press, 1995), 27–28. On a different, and colonial, context, see Elizabeth Thompson, *Colonial Citizens: Republican Rights, Paternal Privilege, and Gender in French Syria and Lebanon* (New York: Columbia University Press, 2000), 67.

5. RGIA, fond 1412, op. 241, d. 21, 110–11.

6. On the complex negotiations and the aspirations of the reforming jurists who devised the draft code, see William G. Wagner, *Marriage, Property, and Law in Late Imperial Russia* (Oxford: Clarendon, 1994). The terms of the draft code are discussed on 165–69. The code itself can be found in RGIA, fond 797, op. 91, d. 53, 31–33.

"legalize existing practices in these kinds of cases and at the same time, establish legal guidelines for the process of resolving marital disputes."[7]

At the same time, however, Sipiagin found the draft code both too formalistic and too limited. His critique of the abstractions offered by legal experts derived explicitly from the chancellery's lengthy experience in resolving marital conflicts, the lessons of which Sipiagin attempted to incorporate into the proposed code. But his critique also expressed the values chancellery officials espoused in their practice, including a respect for individual autonomy and individuals' ability to control their person that was far greater than that reflected in the draft code itself. Sipiagin noted the vulnerable status of peasant wives left alone in the household of their in-laws while their husbands served in the army, for which the draft code seemed to make no provision. The women's "refusal to carry out the most insignificant demand from the husband's kin, or the often immoral demands of the father-in-law (*snokhachestvo*) [word and parentheses in original], leads to extremely poor treatment, forcing her to leave the family and support herself. Sometimes, her in-laws take advantage of her labor in the summer and then, when summer ends, force her out of the house so as to avoid having to feed her," the report read, identifying a practice with which Soviet jurists would grapple, too.[8] The report recommended, without success, that the code be amended to recognize such situations.

Other suggested changes were more substantive. Acknowledging the dignity of the individual and her right to self-fulfillment, they demonstrate that Sipiagin had come to embrace an "affective ideal" of marriage, albeit one inflected by his hierarchical view of society and sacramental concept of marriage. Thus, the draft code was criticized for offering too limited a definition of marital breakdown, one incorporating "only the material, physical aspect of marital relations, and envisaging only the most crude destruction of the rights of one spouse by the other." Such a view of the marital union, the critique observed, "can hardly be said to correspond to the exalted notion of marriage as a sacrament." Such exalted notions, the critique continued, were most likely to be held by the cultivated elites: "Concepts of marriage and its purpose differ according to the level of social development. On the lower level, they consist of the satisfaction of animal instinct; while on the higher, of the satisfaction of man's rational nature, of his need for the association [*obshchenie*] of all the capacities with which he is endowed for his development and enjoyment of life." When such association becomes impossible, incompatibility (*polnoe neskhodstvo kharakterov*) results. The critique observed that none of the grounds provided by the draft code applied to incompatible couples, whose relations are characterized "neither by violence nor cruelty nor disreputable behavior." Such people are "fully moral, cultivated [*intelligentnyi*], educated, and well

7. RGIA, fond 1412, op. 241, d. 15, 25.
8. Ibid., 14 ob.–15.

bred," but nevertheless find cohabitation impossible due to the "moral burden [*nravst-vennyi gnet*]" arising from the particulars of their character—from incompatible habits, upbringing [*vospitanie*], and education. And they seek to put their marital relations in order only because other circumstances (usually, children) prevent them from arriving at an agreement on their own." Incompatibility rendered it impossible for couples, "especially cultivated people," to sustain a "moral union."[9]

But even peasant couples might become incompatible as a result of the personal growth that followed, rather than preceded, their marriage. Here, especially, one can detect the impact of the narratives of the chancellery's overwhelmingly peasant clientele, most of whom had left the village years before to live in Moscow, St. Petersburg, or other major cities. Sipiagin noted that peasant women who had gone off to work elsewhere, usually with the husband's consent, often found themselves in a difficult situation when, after long years of living independently, their husbands for one reason or another demanded renewed cohabitation. By then, the woman had changed so much that she could no longer return to her former life: "After a while, the woman becomes so alienated [*otvykla*] from peasant labor and the conditions of village life that it is exceedingly burdensome for her to think about returning to the village and to her husband, who has likewise become alien to her, and with whom she has had no contact for many years. Indeed, for her to return is out of the question." Although neither physical nor psychological abuse was involved, Sipiagin recommended that such situations be included among the grounds for legal separation.[10] Here he implicitly acknowledged that in such cases, peasant women, too, had a right to self-development and self-fulfillment, even in the absence of abuse and even when women's rights threatened marital stability and patriarchal authority. Interestingly, in Sipiagin's response to the draft code we find no mention of the threats to public decorum that women on their own might represent. Nor are there references to the narrowly domestic role of the wife that most reforming jurists embraced, suggesting that Russia's illiberal order offered women advantages as well as disabilities.[11]

9. Ibid, 10–11. Chancellery officials left without comment those aspects of the draft code that critiqued the chancellery's own procedures. Included in that critique were the concentration of all cases in just one venue, making the recourse less accessible to parties in far-flung places; and the fact that proceedings took place in the absence of the parties involved, and all evidence from witnesses was presented in written form. For the critique, see RGIA, fond 797, op. 91, d. 53, 32.

10. RGIA, fond 1412, op. 241, d. 15, 11 ob. In making this point, Sipiagin referred to the many appeals from peasant women that the chancellery had resolved on precisely these grounds.

11. On the link between the emergence of the liberal state and women's loss of rights and relegation to a private life over which men are empowered to preside without interference, see Carole Pateman, *The Sexual Contract* (Stanford, CA: Stanford University Press, 1988). On jurists and domesticity, see Wagner, *Marriage, Property, and Law*, 122.

The recognition of an individual's right to self-determination, implicit in many of the statements noted above, became explicit in Sipiagin's response to article 5 of the draft code. Declaring that "the separate residency of spouses cannot be resolved solely on the basis of their agreement," this provision arrogated to the courts sole power to grant a separation.[12] To article 5, Sipiagin took vociferous and lengthy exception. In his opinion, men and women had the right to determine their own personal arrangements, if they could manage to arrive at an agreement on their own. Here, too, the chancellery's practice provided the model. Officials had registered separation and custody agreements and assisted in their crafting from the first, as we have seen, and from the mid-1890s they also encouraged disputing couples to negotiate their own agreement during their year of separation. If such agreements could be reached, what was to be gained by interposing the courts, Sipiagin wondered? While fully concurring with the Editing Commission's opinion that "all possible caution" should be observed when permitting spouses to live apart, he questioned whether such a prohibition would serve that purpose. Even if couples "on their own initiative [*svoevol'no*]" separated because of the "most trifling incompatibility," resorting to separation "in the first heat of conflict" (a concern expressed by the Editing Commission in its introduction to its draft), the article still served no purpose. Such couples were perfectly free to restore cohabitation by mutual agreement—indeed, such agreements were actually anticipated in a subsequent article, no. 15. Sipiagin reasoned that sanctioning separation agreements reached by spouses "can lead to no undesirable consequences."[13]

Indeed, Sipiagin continued, the courts' recognition of such agreements would play a positive role, protecting the privacy of individuals by freeing quarreling couples from having to air their dirty linen in public, before a court: "Couples, for one reason or another, find it impossible to continue their married life, but at the same time find it extremely unpleasant to bring their disagreements to the attention of others without any need.... It is hardly desirable or just to force the couple to be present at a discussion of the substance of the disagreements that led them voluntarily to separate." Court proceedings might serve to revive and deepen disagreements. Why, then, insist on such proceedings, "When all that could be avoided simply by the courts' sanctioning

12. RGIA, fond 797, op. 91, d. 53, 31 ob. (p. 4 of draft code). This provision would have imposed on marriage a "judicial patriarchy," of the sort that Michael Grossberg has described for the nineteenth-century United States, whereby courts usurped the role previously held by husbands and fathers to govern the movement of dependents. See Michael Grossberg, "Who Gets the Child? Custody, Guardianship, and the Rise of a Judicial Patriarchy in Nineteenth-Century America," *Feminist Studies* 9, no. 2 (1983): 235–60.

13. RGIA, fond 1412, op. 241, d. 15, 14–16, 25.

their agreement"?[14] The chancellery proposed, again unsuccessfully, that the draft be amended to permit courts to recognize separation agreements between spouses.[15]

Although Sipiagin's views went considerably further than did those of the draft code in terms of their respect for individual autonomy and the right to self-determination, they could and did coexist with unyielding support for the absolutist political order. In his capacity as head of the Ministry of the Interior, Sipiagin employed repressive measures against all forms of political dissent and blocked all efforts by women to organize themselves, except in organizations that could be subsumed into the category of philanthropy.[16] Baron Budberg, who succeeded Sipiagin in 1899, went further, endorsing the system of social estates on which autocracy rested. Advocating a passport of her own for each wife who requested one, Budberg embraced a view of the social world in which family culture varied with social estate. Whereas Sipiagin was prepared to transfer marital disputes to civil courts, Budberg preferred estate-based justice. Budberg expressed grave doubts as to whether the "average member of the district court" was capable of treating the family affairs of peasants, nobles, merchants, and state servitors with "identical equity." Budberg remained convinced that cultural differences continued to exist between *sosloviia,* at a time when such differences, while still in evidence, were growing increasingly less salient. He recommended that estate-based institutions rather than regular courts resolve marital disputes. "Only someone who is deeply familiar with the life circumstances, views, traditions, and...prejudices of the milieu to which the quarreling couple belong" would be capable of such judgments, he averred.[17]

---

14. Ibid., 17–18. After legal reform failed, the chancellery continued to sanction separation agreements already reached by spouses until it ceased to involve itself in marital disputes in 1914. In his concern about the dangers of "airing dirty linen" Sipiagin echoes that of the archconservative Konstantin Pobedonostsev, who raised that issue among other objections to transferring separation cases from the chancellery to the courts (RGIA, fond 797, op. 91, d. 53, 110).

15. The revised law of 1914 also did not contain this provision. Compare Sipiagin's view with that of Pobedonostsev, who played a key role in blocking reform, and who expressed concern about the draft law easing the way for those who sought to live a life "free from control [*vol'naia zhizn'*]," or who sought "freedom." Pobedonostsev was particularly concerned about the prospect of women "taking advantage of that freedom to the detriment of their own morality" (ibid., 20–22, 104 ob.). Pobedonostsev's views of women and the family are discussed in A. Yu. Polenov, *K. P. Pobedonostsev v obshchestvenno-politicheskoi i dukhovnoi zhizni Rossii* (PhD diss., Moscow State University, 1910), 139–41. Sipiagin also took exception to the code's provision that proposed awarding child custody to the parent of the same sex. This hardly served the "welfare of the child," as Sipiagin put it. See RGIA, fond 1412, op. 241, d. 15, 19.

16. On state resistance to women's self-organization, see Irina Iukhina, *Russkii feminizm kak vyzov sovremennosti* (St. Petersburg: Aleteiia, 2007).

17. RGIA, fond 1412, op. 241, d. 21, 111–12. Communication dated March 12, 1902.

The chancellery officials' willingness to relinquish responsibility for adjudicating marital disputes suggests that they had ceased to regard it as enhancing the aura of autocratic power. In a monarchy, the act of bestowing mercy on petitioners, like granting pardons to offenders, ideally serves to exalt the authority of the ruler. As Natalie Zemon Davis observes in her study of pardon petitions in early modern France, the king in the act of granting a pardon displayed his capacity for mercy and reminded subjects of his power.[18] A. V. Remnev makes a similar point about the chancellery. The chancellery, he writes, helped "preserve monarchical feelings in the masses and created the image of the tsar as the embodiment of a higher court and justice."[19] But at least in the case of marital disputes, the effect was never straightforward. Unlike the French kings who entertained pleas for pardon, whenever the chancellery resolved a marital dispute it had to weigh the merits and moral claims of two stories, not just one. Charged with protecting the weak and unfortunate, chancellery officials who responded sympathetically to compelling, sometimes quite harrowing, narratives of men's marital abuses were impelled to violate the legal rights of husbands. Whether such decisions enhanced the tsar's authority in the eyes of the wife, and perhaps her friends and relatives, is impossible to ascertain. But as men's irate responses to decisions in their wives' favor make abundantly clear, such decisions unquestionably alienated husbands and underscored the fragility of legal rights in an absolutist system.

The significance of the chancellery's work had diminished in other ways as well. By the early twentieth century, the chancellery's purview had considerably narrowed, as responsibility for entertaining petitions from peasant women reverted to local authorities, and the increasingly assertive courts claimed jurisdiction over many of the chancellery's original functions, such as determining alimony and child support and resolving child custody disputes. Divested of its larger political significance, limited to approving passports primarily for deserving urban and privileged women, the chancellery played an almost purely administrative role. As Baron Budberg put it in 1902, "except for a few rare cases, [the chancellery] has become a passport office [*pasportnaia ekspeditsiia*] with special powers."[20] Nevertheless, in the absence of other venues to which such wives might appeal for relief, the chancellery continued to provide a kind of safety valve, performing that function until March 12, 1914, when all wives gained the right to claim a passport of their own.

But the chancellery officials' embrace of legal reform also signified something new and important. Staunch adherents of the absolutist political order they continued to

18. Natalie Zemon Davis, *Fiction in the Archives: Pardon Tales and Their Tellers in Sixteenth-Century France.* (Stanford, CA: Stanford University Press, 1987), 52–58.

19. A.V. Remnev, "Kantseliariia proshenii v samoderzhavnoi sisteme pravleniia kontsa XIX stoletiia," *Istoricheskii ezhegodnik* (1997): 18.

20. RGIA, fond 1412, op. 241, d. 21, 111.

defend to the end, these officials nevertheless proved willing to circumscribe—even to curtail entirely—men's absolute authority in private and for an increasingly broad range of reasons. The evolution of their practice was prompted not by abstract principles but by women's effectively crafted narratives, by what officials learned in the course of their practice, and by the resonance of both with their own values. While chancellery officials, like the legal reformers whose draft code they had endorsed, sought to circumscribe rather than abolish altogether husbands' authority over their wives, the two parties' methods and goals differed fundamentally. Whereas Russia's legal reformers aimed more broadly to limit the arbitrary authority of the tsar by extending the rule of law and expanding the realms where their own expertise might be applied, the chancellery officials' primary goal remained better protection of women's personal dignity and selfhood. The result was a surprisingly flexible approach to family breakdown, especially noteworthy in the context of its time, even as the chancellery remained embedded in, and in its supralegal character epitomized the character of, Russia's absolutist political order.

This flexibility was evident in the officials' decisions and their suggested revisions of the draft code. Easing constraints on female mobility, recognizing a greater right to self-determination for both sexes in personal if not in public life, the changes officials endorsed suggest their reconsideration not only of long-standing gender norms but also of the relationship between the personal and the political. If these officials had once believed that Russia's absolutist political order depended on its patriarchal family order as a guarantee of social stability and public decorum, by the close of the nineteenth century they believed it no longer. In their eyes if not in the eyes of the church, absolutism might accommodate a considerably less authoritarian family than that which imperial law upheld to the end.

APPENDIX A *Archival Sources*

Gosudarstvennyi arkhiv Rossiiskoi Federatsii (GARF)
    Fond 109 Tret'e otdelenie sobstvennoi ego imperatorskogo velichestva
    kantseliarii

Rossiiskii gosudarstvennyi istoricheskii arkhiv (RGIA)
    Fond 797 Kantseliariia ober-prokurora Sviateishego Sinoda
    Fond 1412 Kantseliariia po priniatiiu proshenii, na "Vysochaishee" imia
    prinosimykh

Tsentral'nyi gosudarstvennyi istoricheskii arkhiv gorod Sankt-Peterburga
    (TsGIA SPb)
    Fond 356 Sankt-Peterburgskaia sudebnaia palata
    Fond 569 Sankt-Peterburgskii gradonachal'nik

Tsentral'nyi istoricheskii arkhiv Moskvy (TsIAM)
    Fond 62 Moskovskaia gubernskaia uprava
    Fond 1938 Zemskii nachal'nik. Zaraiskii uezd, Riazanskoi gubernii

Index

adultery: double standard and, 205, 211–212, 218, 247; as grounds for divorce, 4, 15, 205, 214, 215; by husbands, 95, 211–212, 247; law and, 204–205; male honor and, 45, 208–211, 224; passport denial for, 195, 203–204; popular responses to, 212–214, 225–226, 228; tolerance of, 224–226, 228–230, 231; wife murder and, 210–211; women's acknowledgement of, 222–224; women's subjectivity and, 223–224, 230–231
Alexander II (tsar of Russia), 1, 29
Alexander III (tsar of Russia), 1, 27, 31, 120, 125, 126, 203, 254
alimony, 141–142, 233, 258n62, 260
Andreeva, Elizaveta, 64–65
Arsen'ev, K. K., 28

Bakhrushin, Aleksei and Vera, 68
Bashkirtseva, Maria, 137
Bekhterev, Vladimir, 96
Borovikovskii, Aleksandr, 97, 238n14
Budberg, Aleksandr, 21, 27, 256–257, 258, 263, 267, 268
Bychkova, Natalia, 52, 60

chancellery. See Imperial Chancellery for Receipt of Petitions
Charcot, Doctor Jean Martin, 65n50
Charter of the Nobility (1785), 103
Chekhov, Anton, writings of, 62, 218
Chernyshevskii, Nikolai, *What Is To Be Done?*, 56, 136
child custody, 95; the chancellery and, 198, 233, 239, 241–244, 251–259; civil courts and, 233, 238–239, 240–243, 247, 253–259, 268; divorce and, 215; in exchange for passport, 242; in Great Britain, 235, 239, 244; laboring classes and, 242; law of March 12, 1914 and, 233, 241, 260; maternal rights and, 233, 235, 240–241, 244, 259; moral motherhood and, 236–237, 243–244, 247, 258; paternal rights and, 235, 239, 240–241, 244, 245; political radicalism and, 251–253; religious

affiliation and, 251; State Senate decisions and, 233, 256; Third Section and, 235–238; in the United States, 235, 239, 244; welfare of child and, 239, 240–241, 244, 256, 258–259; women's sexual misconduct and, 247. *See also* child support; children
child support, 95, 141–142, 233, 258n62, 260, 268
children: and marital breakdown, 140, 241; parental responsibilities and rights towards, 236, 239–240, 259n66
civil courts: alimony and, 141–142, 268; chancellery rulings and, 29, 198–199, 253–256; child custody and, 233, 238–239, 240–241, 243, 253–259, 268; child support and, 141–142, 268; expense of, 38; marital separation and, 239, 254, 255; women's property and, 97–99. *See also* Justice of the Peace courts
Complete Guide, 169
consumerism: culture of, 4, 163, 218–219; women and, 96–97, 144–145, 151, 163
courts of equity, 28–29
courtship, 53, 65–66, 69
culture, as marker of status, 170–171

despotism: familial, 57–58, 73, 79, 158, 160, 170; marital, 169–170, 199; political, 103, 170, 177
D'iakonova, Elizaveta, 34, 219n51
divorce: child custody and, 215; consequences of, 15, 215, 216; difficulty of, 4, 15, 215, 260–261; expense of, 38; gendered power and, 214–218; grounds for, 4, 15, 205, 214, 215; male gallantry and, 216
Dobroliubov, Nikolai, 29–30, 56, 70, 72
domestic servants, 174; as marker of status, 165–166, 174–175
domestic violence: alcohol abuse and, 126; chancellery officials and, 120–123, 125–128, 130; elite ideas about, 102–104, 121–122; Justice of the Peace courts and, 105–112; laboring classes and, 101–102, 104, 112–120, 129–130; legal system and,

domestic violence *(continued)*
105–106, 108–109; in men's counternarratives, 113–117, 120, 181–182; middling classes and, 102, 181–182, 199; nobles and, 103–104; peasants and, 101–102, 106–108, 121–122, 128; popular critiques of, 117, 120; privileged women and, 112, 122; Russian backwardness and, 104–105; sexual anxiety and, 113, 115, 116–117; townspeople and, 102, 121–122, 128; and women's property, 91–92, 95–96, 113–114

domesticity: absence of, 152–153, 161; chancellery officials and, 195–196, 199–200, 265; characteristics of, 44, 46, 161–162, 166; cult of, 99, 160–163, 166, 199–200; influence of, 82, 84, 99, 161, 168, 199–200; role of servants in, 165–166, 174–175; and social status, 7–8, 162, 165–166, 174–175; women's purported neglect of, 185–186, 190–191, 196. *See also* motherhood; separate spheres

Domostroi, 165, 166

dowry, 58–60, 71, 76; control over, 81, 82, 87–89, 90–92, 99; ideas about, 63, 83–84, 87, 99; legal status of, 81, 82; prescriptive literature and, 84–87. *See also* property rights of women

dvorniki, 213

Enlightenment ideas, 50, 54, 103

fashion. *See* consumerism
fatherhood, 249
fathers: assumption of paternal rights, 245; political denunciations and, 251–252; self-presentations of, 249–251

feminists, 18, 178, 218. *See also* Russian Society to Protect Women; woman question

First Woman's Calendar (Praskovia Ariian), 37

gendarmes: adultery and, 224–225; background of, 40–41; marital ideals of, 74, 197, 199–200, 259; middling classes and, 191–195, 197, 199–200; role of, 10, 28, 40, 223; stereotypes of merchants, 193–195; women's work and, 152

Good Manners, 62, 66n52, 87, 166, 168–169, 171

governors and governors-general, 41, 43–44, 74, 192, 259

Great Reforms, 1, 29–30, 105

Handbook for Young Spouses, 63, 169

honor: divorce and, 215–216; female sexuality and, 205–208, 224; masculine, 178–179, 208–211; private sphere and, 208; public status and, 201–202, 208–211, 218; violence and, 103–104

housekeeping, significance of, 171–174, 199–200. *See also* domesticity; *khoziaika*

How to Get Married and Be Happy, 63, 169

husbands: adultery and, 95, 211–212, 247; child custody appeals and, 245, 247–249; disciplining of, 125, 126–128, 130; divorce and, 216–218; emotional cruelty and, 177–178, 181–182; expectations of, 168–175, 181–182, 191–196, 197, 199, 200, 210; exploitation by, 138–139; honor of, 178–179, 208–211; legal authority of, 3, 82; legal responsibilities of, 135, 141–142; public life and, 182–183, 185, 192–193; response to loss of rights, 197–199, 217, 245, 268; vulnerability of, 115–116. *See also* domestic violence; fathers; masculinity

ideology of separate spheres. *See* separate spheres

illegitimacy rates, 205–206

Imperial Chancellery for Receipt of Petitions (the chancellery), 6; autocratic authority and, 21, 223, 268, 269; child custody and, 198, 233, 239, 241–244, 247, 251–259; and civil courts, 29, 198–199, 253–259, 268; compared to courts of equity, 28–29; critiques of, 28, 37; decisions by, 46–47, 50, 195–196, 197, 199, 204; domestic violence and, 120–123, 126–128, 130; domesticity and, 195–196, 200, 265; expectations of husbands, 125–128, 130, 155, 193, 195, 197, 200, 261; and female decorum, 46, 121, 126, 265; functions and practices of, 10, 20, 28–29, 36–41, 125, 198, 243, 255; individual rights and, 265–266, 269; legal reform and, 128, 261, 263–269; legal system and, 197, 242–243, 255–259, 269; marital choice and, 50, 77–78; marital ideals of, 27, 121–122; 195–197, 259, 264–265; mediating role of, 242–243, 259; men's rights and, 197, 242, 268; middling classes and, 195–196; model letters to, 37, 132; moral motherhood and, 247; officials of, 21, 25–27, 29, 261; paternalism of, 26–27, 259, 261; peasant women and, 129, 130, 195–196, 264,

265, 268; political radicalism and, 252–253; religious affiliation and, 27n30, 251; "Secret Instructions," 256–258; social biases of, 121–123, 130, 155, 203–204; welfare of child and, 244, 258–259; women's personal rights and, 130, 195–196, 242, 261, 269; women's property rights and, 97; women's sexuality and, 46–47, 202–204, 228–230, 247; women's work and, 152–155

Iuridicheskii vestnik, 107, 108n19

Justice of the Peace courts, 18, 120; domestic violence and, 105–112; 113, 122; female petitioners and, 110; honor and, 201; outcome of decisions of, 110–112; peasants and, 107–108, 111; townswomen and, 111–112. *See also* civil courts; legal system

khoziaika: role of, 162, 163, 165; as source of women's dignity, 167–168, 171–175, 196. *See also* domesticity; housekeeping

Khvoshchinskaia, Nadezhda, "The Boarding School Girl," 135–136

Kravchinskii, Sergei, 170

Krestovskaia, Maria, "The Howl", 34–35

laboring classes: child custody and, 242; definition of, 8; disciplining of, 125–128, 130; divorce and, 215; domestic violence and, 101–102, 104, 109, 112–120, 129–130; gender norms of, 109, 110–120; stereotypes of, 101, 121, 203; women's work and, 133–134, 149–152

land captains, 129

legal professionals: aspirations of, 3, 18–19, 107–108, 238, 269; child custody and, 238–239; domestic violence and, 107–108, 130

legal system: adultery and, 204–205; alimony and, 141–142, 260; chancellery critique of, 263–267; chancellery decisions and, 197–199, 253–258; child custody and, 238–241, 244, 260; child support and, 141–143, 260; children of mixed marriages and, 251; comparative, 3–4, 16, 18, 81–83, 204, 235, 239–240; domestic violence and, 105–106, 108–109; efforts to reform, 19, 128, 232–233, 263–267; family law, 3, 49–50, 82, 232–233, 239–241, 260–261; and marriage, 3, 15, 18, 49–50, 135, 232–233; and parents, 49–50,

236, 239–240; passports and, 3, 16–18, 82, 108, 132, 142, 232, 260, 263; patriarchal authority in, 49–50, 240, 260–261; property law, 3, 80–81. *See also* civil courts; Justice of the Peace Courts

lichnost', 30, 56, 167, 177, 199

Ludmer, Iakob, 107, 112, 167

Lukhmanova, Nadezhda, 165, 166, 170–171, 217

Mamantov, Vasilii, 25, 232–233, 234

Manasein, Nikolai, 254

marital choice: chancellery officials and, 50, 77–78; female initiative and, 65–66; ideas about, 50–51, 54–58, 60, 64, 74, 78, 186; and marital failure, 57, 72–75, 78–79, 89; in Ostrovskii's plays, 55, 56, 62; women's self-realization and, 56–57, 64–65, 78–79. *See also* romantic love

marital ideals: of the 1860s, 30, 56–57; autocracy and, 27; of chancellery officials, 27, 121–122, 195–197, 259, 264–265; companionate, 19, 176, 177, 196; conjugal privacy and, 185–186, 189–191; cult of domesticity and, 160–163, 167–168; Enlightenment and, 50, 54, 103; of middling classes, 160–163, 171–172, 176–178, 180–182, 196–197, 199–200

Marital Satisfactions, 63, 163, 166, 167, 169, 189, 210

marital separation, 3–4; children as restraining factor in, 233, 235, 241; as disciplinary device, 123–128, 130, 257; divorce and, 214–218; expense of, 214; family law and, 3–4, 16, 18, 19, 123, 141–143, 260–261, 255; grounds for, 141–142, 214, 260, 263–266; passport law and, 16–18, 19, 260, 263; State Senate project to legalize, 263–267; the Third Section and, 19–20, 125; women's wage earning and, 132, 149–152, 155

marriage: age of, 52, 53, 66, 67, 89, 90n23; arrangement of, 48–49, 51–54, 70–72, 84, 88–89; law and, 3, 15, 18, 49–50, 135, 232–233; money and, 52, 58, 60, 62–64, 69, 76–77, 83–84; the Russian Orthodox Church and, 4, 15, 161. *See also* romantic love

Married Woman, 167–168

masculinity: cult of domesticity and, 168–171; nuclear family and, 185–186; self-command

masculinity *(continued)*
    and, 104, 168–171, 180–182, 197, 199, 221;
    self-made men, 182–183; service ethos and,
    185; social aspirations and, 170. *See also*
    husbands
matchmakers, 52
men. *See* fathers; husbands; masculinity
merchant women, 66
merchants: childcare and, 248; domesticity
    and, 82, 84; dowry and, 58, 60, 62; lifestyle
    of, 9, 64, 70, 158, 221–222; marriage and,
    52–53, 67, 68–71, 88; passports and, 17, 129;
    property and, 82–84; status of, 2, 8–9, 53;
    stereotypes of, 55, 193–195
middling classes: conjugal privacy and,
    185–186, 190; controversies concerning,
    7–8; definition of, 7–9; domestic violence
    and, 102, 180–182, 199; domesticity and,
    7–8, 160, 161; marital norms of, 158, 160–
    163, 171–172, 176–178, 180–182, 196–197,
    199–200; social status of, 218; urban life
    and, 218
midwifery, 99, 146–147
Ministry of the Interior, 129, 252, 254, 263, 267
Moscow, 206
motherhood, 199; idealization of, 236–238,
    244–245, 258; in men's counternarratives,
    247–249; morality and, 243–245, 247, 253;
    Russian Orthodox influence on, 236–237; in
    women's self-presentations, 244–245, 247;
    women's work and, 153

Nazar'ev, Valerian, 107
Nazar'eva, Kapitolina, 215–216
Nicholas I (tsar of Russia), 27, 236
Nicholas II (tsar of Russia), 1, 25, 27, 127,
    252, 263
Niva, 136–137
nobles, 58; childcare and, 247; domestic
    violence and, 103–104; domesticity and, 161;
    women's property and, 80–81, 83
Novobrachnaia Gazeta, 63–64
nuclear family, 185–186, 188–189, 190, 191

Obukh, Vladimir, 220
Old Believers, 68, 89, 90n22, 96
Ostrovskii, Aleksandr, plays of, 54, 55, 62,
    194

passports, internal: chancellery critique of,
    263; child custody and, 242; disciplinary
    function of, 121, 123–127; divorce and,
    217–218; and extortion, 42–43, 94, 131,
    139–140; history of, 16–17; in fiction, 35,
    36; legal system and, 3, 16–18, 82, 132, 142,
    232, 260, 263; passports and, 17, 19, 108,
    125, 128–129, 230n74, 268; peasant women
    and, 17, 19, 108, 125, 128–129; marriage and,
    51–52, 70, 134; townswomen and, 17, 19, 125,
    129; women's work and, 132, 135, 137–138, 155
peasant men, images of, 106–107
peasant women: chancellery and, 128–129,
    130, 195–196, 264, 265, 268; domestic vio-
    lence and, 101–102, 106–107, 121–122, 128;
    images of, 106–108, 121–122, 134; Justices of
    the Peace and, 111; labor of, 134; literacy of,
    146; marriage and, 51–52, 70, 134; passports
    and, 17, 19, 108, 125, 128–129, 230n74, 268;
    personal rights of, 265; as petitioners, 6, 36,
    129, 265; property rights of, 81; sexuality
    of, 205, 220, 230n74; State Senate and, 17,
    108, 128–129
Peter the Great (tsar of Russia), 27, 80–81
petitioners: Justice of the Peace Courts and,
    110–112; necessity of wage earning, 132,
    137–138; profile of, 6–7, 11, 37–38, 138, 265;
    religion of, 6–7
petitioning, conventions of: 38–39, 143–144
Pobedonostsev, Konstantin, 267nn14–15
policemen: background of, 40; domestic vio-
    lence and, 120; role of, 10, 40, 223; women's
    adultery and, 226; women's work and, 152
pornography, 220
prescriptive literature, 4; cult of domesticity
    and, 81, 160, 163, 165, 167, 171; dowry and,
    84–87; marital choice and, 62–63; mascu-
    linity and, 168–171; motherhood and, 236.
    See also titles of individual publications
privileged women: domestic violence and, 112,
    122; economic dependence of, 140–141, 171;
    impoverishment of, 142–143; remunerative
    work and, 140, 147, 148, 156
property rights of women, 3, 80–81; chancel-
    lery decisions and, 97; civil courts and,
    97–99; female autonomy and, 99; female
    deference and, 90–93, 94–96, 100; legal
    basis of, 80–83; male violence and, 91–92,

95–96, 113–114, 149; marital law and, 81–82, 91; men's legal authority and, 93–96, 97, 100; merchants and, 82–84; nobility and, 80, 81–83; passport and, 81, 94, 100; peasant custom and, 81; separate spheres and, 82; State Senate decisions and, 80; townspeople and, 82–84. *See also* dowry

prostitution, 202

Rakhmanova, Serafima, 68–71, 72
Revolution of 1905, 221
Rikhter, Otto, 21, 27, 264
romantic love, 4; marital breakdown and, 219–220, 231; marriage and, 50–51, 54–55, 62–63, 67–72, 74–78; modernity and, 50–51, 65, 186, 218–219; popular culture and, 74, 218–219; self-realization and, 51, 78–79
Runova, Olga, "How I Fell in Love," 34
Russian Orthodox Church: adultery and, 205; divorce and, 4, 15, 261; domesticity and, 167–168; and idealization of motherhood, 236–237; marital reform and, 19, 261; marriage and, 4, 15, 261; sexuality and, 221, 225
Russian Society to Protect Women, 37, 95–96, 100

Sand, George, 55
Sem'ianin, 163, 165, 166, 167, 170
separate spheres, 82, 83, 90, 160, 163, 186. *See also* domesticity
sexual freedom, 218, 231
sexual incapacity, 15, 90, 147
sexual relations: control of, 205–208, 218; deviant, 196, 209; double standard and, 205, 211–212, 218, 231, 247; popular culture and, 218–219, 220; scientific ideas about, 220. *See also* adultery; sexuality, female; sexuality, male
sexuality, female: anonymous letters and, 208, 210, 231; anxieties concerning, 113, 115, 211, 231; chancellery officials and, 46–47, 202–204, 228–230, 247; domestic violence and, 113, 115, 116–117, 201; gossip and, 205, 206, 207–208, 231; honor and, 205, 208–211, 215–216, 224; *Kreutzer Sonata* and, 31, 34, 220; in men's counternarratives, 115, 211; motherhood and, 247; peasants and, 205, 220, 230n74; popular entertainment

and, 220; as private matter, 213–214, 224, 226, 228–230; public order and, 45, 203, 224; Russian Orthodox Church and, 221, 225; self-assertion and, 223–224, 230–231; townspeople and, 205; urban life and, 205–208, 226. *See also* adultery
sexuality, male, 42, 212, 221, 246. *See also* adultery; husbands
Sipiagin, Dmitrii, 21, 25, 27, 129, 263–267
Skabichevskii, Aleksandr, 56–57
sosloviia (singular, *soslovie*), 1–2, 267
St. Petersburg, 206
State Senate, Civil Cassation Department of, 96; alimony and, 141–142, 233; chancellery and, 128–129; child custody and, 233, 240–241, 243, 255, 256; child support and, 141–142, 233; conjugal privacy and, 189; domestic violence and, 105–106; marital reform project of, 108n19, 232–233, 263–267; peasant women and, 17, 108, 128–129; women's property rights and, 80, 81. *See also* legal system
Strekoza, 12, 63
Sudebnaia Gazeta, 240–241
suicide, 57–58

Tenisheva, Maria, 17
Third Section, 104; and child custody, 235–238; and marital separation, 19–20, 28, 125; and women's work, 152, 153
Tolstoy, Leo, 248n40; *Anna Karenina*, 1, 212, 215; *The Kreutzer Sonata*, 31, 34, 210, 220
townspeople (*meshchane*), 2; domesticity and, 82; Justice of the Peace courts and, 110–112; marriage and, 51–52, 53, 146–147; passports and, 17, 129; property and, 83–84. *See also* laboring classes
townswomen: domestic violence and, 102, 110–112, 121–122, 128; images of, 121–122; literacy of, 146; as petitioners, 6; sexuality of, 205
Tret'iakova, Vera, 64–65

Valuev, Petr, 104–105
Verbitskaia, Anastasia, *Keys to Happiness*, 231; *She Was Liberated!*, 35, 141, 241, 252
Vestnik mody, 137

Virgin Mary, 236, 244
Vodovozova, Elizaveta, *Umstvennoe razvitie detei,* 239n15

wifebeating. *See* domestic violence
woman question, 27, 30, 31, 34, 35, 135, 137; opponents of, 152. *See also* feminists
women: access to education, 30–31, 218; as consumers, 96–97, 144–145, 151, 163; entrepreneurial activity of, 30, 92, 100; equal rights of, 30, 31, 34; gendered expectations of, 82, 84, 99, 139–140, 153–154, 190–191, 199–200; legal rights of, 3, 19, 80–82, 97–99; leisure activity of, 218; marital rights of, 167–168, 171–178, 192–196, 199–200, 269; occupations of, 133, 134, 146–147, 152, 156, 174. *See also* property rights of women; sexuality, female; women's waged work
women's waged work: chancellery officials and, 152–155, 156; ideas about, 135–137, 152–155, 156; laboring classes and, 133–134, 135; and marital breakdown, 132, 150–152; motherhood and, 153; peasants and, 134, 174; privileged women and, 147, 148, 156; as reason for petitioning, 132, 137–138, 142; representations of, 136–137; significance for women, 135, 139, 143–152, 156; state effort to restrict, 152; Third Section and, 152, 153, 156. *See also* women: occupations of

Zagorodskii, Aleksandr, 87, 98
Zhuk, Vladimir, *Mat' i ditia,* 239n15

CPSIA information can be obtained
at www.ICGtesting.com
Printed in the USA
FSOW02n2211160517
34350FS